HOUSEHOLD INTERESTS

HOUSEHOLD INTERESTS

PROPERTY, MARRIAGE STRATEGIES,
AND FAMILY DYNAMICS
IN ANCIENT ATHENS

Cheryl Anne Cox

PRINCETON UNIVERSITY PRESS   PRINCETON, NEW JERSEY

Library of Congress Cataloging-in-Publication Data
Cox, Cheryl Anne, 1953–
Household interests : property, marriage strategies, and
family dynamics in ancient Athens / Cheryl Anne Cox.
p.   cm.
Includes bibliographical references and index.
ISBN 0-691-01572-4 (cl : alk. paper)
1. Family—Greece—Athens—History.   2. Athens (Greece)—
Social conditions.   3. Greece—Social
conditions—To 146 B.C.   I. Title.
HQ662.5.A15   1998
306.85′09385—dc21   97-11775

To Elbert and Benjamin

WHO ALWAYS ADD TO MY HOUSEHOLD INTERESTS

Contents

Figures and Tables

Figures

Tables

Preface

THIS BOOK ends with a question. This is as it should be, for there are no definite answers to the problem of defining the family and household in ancient Athens. The student can only appreciate the complexities and contradictions that made up family and household interests, some of which are looked at in this book. And so I offer this work as a contribution to understanding the ancient domestic unit and hope it will be a stimulus for further discussion at a time when social history in general is a strong and popular discipline.

Most of this book was written during a Professional Development Assignment granted me by the College of Arts and Sciences at The University of Memphis for the academic year 1991–92, and the work was supported in part by a grant from The University of Memphis Faculty Research Grant Fund. This support does not necessarily imply endorsement by the university of my research conclusions. Funding was also granted by the National Endowment for the Humanities Travel to Collections Grant for the summer of 1992. I am grateful to these institutions for their encouragement and support.

I have also been fortunate in the help I have received from individuals. First and foremost I would like to thank my former professor and mentor, Virginia Hunter, for reading the entire manuscript and offering a great deal of advice and encouragement. I would also like to acknowledge Bob Develin, Mark Golden, John Oates, Josiah Ober, Kent Rigsby, Richard Saller, Barry Strauss and John Traill, who read the manuscript in part or offered me assistance. Further, I would like to thank Celeste Newbrough for indexing this work. The indexing was funded by the Offices of the Dean of the College of Arts and Sciences and of the Vice Provost for Research and Dean of the Graduate School at the University of Memphis. Chapter 4 is a revised version of an article that originally appeared in the *Journal of Family History* (1988), published by JAI Press. Furthermore, because I work at a university whose library has a small collection in classics, the assistance of the interlibrary loan staff at The University of Memphis was invaluable. Finally, I would like to thank my husband Elbert Wall, whose computer expertise made this whole project possible.

Introduction

WE ARE witnessing a renaissance in social history, the goals of which have been provisionally, at least, defined by Charles Tilly. For Tilly, the historian necessarily reconstitutes the experience of life as a particular group saw it; by so doing, the historian begins to focus on the ordinary person. However, the study of a particular group would be nonsensical if the historian did not connect this smaller entity with larger social structures and processes. How this connection is interpreted, however, is a matter for debate.[1]

The present work is about the family and household in ancient Athens, but because of the nature of the sources it will necessarily focus on the elite. The main thrust of the present work will be to describe the instability of the basic domestic unit in ancient Athens, the *oikos*. Just as scholars of Roman society have shown that the major domestic unit, the *domus*, goes beyond the nuclear family,[2] so now studies of Athens need to recognize the complexity of the *oikos*. By presenting the smaller scale of an individual's motivations within the larger-scale context of family and household dynamics, the present book will examine the difference between law and practice.

Until recently family history in Athenian studies was dominated by legal history. Historians were interested in compiling catalogues of Athenian family law, and reduced succession law to a series of rules of what was permitted and what was not. They were not concerned with the fact that the law was frequently defied and circumvented[3]—in particular as regards agnation, that is, descent through the patriline, the father's side of the extended kin group. Athenian succession law first provided for transmission first of all among males, from father to son, and then, in the absence of sons, to daughters. In the absence of both

---

[1] C. Tilly, "Family History, Social History, and Social Change," in *Family History at the Crossroads,* ed. T. Hareven and A. Plakans (Princeton, N.J.: Princeton University Press, 1987), 319–30.

[2] R. Saller, *Patriarchy, Property and Death in the Roman Family* (Cambridge: Cambridge University Press, 1994), 80 ff.; K. Bradley, *Discovering the Roman Family* (Oxford: Oxford University Press, 1991).

[3] L. Beauchet, *Histoire du droit privé dans la république athénienne,* 4 vols. (Paris: Chevalier Marescq, 1897); J. H. Lipsius, *Das Attische Recht und Rechtsverfahren,* 3 vols. (Leipzig: O. R. Reisland, 1905–15); A. R. W. Harrison, *The Law of Athens,* vol. 1 (Oxford: Clarendon Press, 1968); D. M. MacDowell, *The Law in Classical Athens* (Ithaca, N.Y.: Cornell University Press, 1978); G. E. M. de Ste Croix, "Some Observations on the Property Rights of Women," *CR* 20 (1970): 273–78; D. M. Schaps, *Economic Rights of Women in Ancient Greece* (Edinburgh: University of Edinburgh Press, 1979). Most recently the series of essays edited by Cartledge, Todd, and Millett argue that Athenian law cannot be severed from its social context, that the ancient Athenian was concerned with procedure rather than substantive law: S. Todd and P. Millett, "Law, Society and Athens," in *Nomos: Essays in Athenian Law, Politics and Society,* ed. P. Cartledge, P. Millett, and S. Todd (Cambridge: Cambridge University Press, 1990), 1–18. In her work on adoption Lene Rubinstein also argues for a focus on procedure: *Adoption in IV. Century Athens* (Copenhagen: Museum Tusculanum Press, 1993).

male and female children, male agnates were the preferred heirs, and then female agnates; only then was the matriline, the mother's side, admitted to succession. In examining how these rules could be circumvented, this book will study attitudes and practices that went beyond the legal and social norms,[4] and which in fact determined how interests in and arrangements for transferring property affected family relations. For this purpose, it will depend heavily on anthropology and as such it will be part of a recent trend in classics to apply anthropology to social history.[5]

The first two chapters examine marriage patterns: why people married and whom they married. Chapter 1 examines the rather narrow topic of agnatic relations, exploring how even though kinship endogamy, or marriage within the kinship group, reflected the agnatic bias in succession law, inheritance strategies, or the ways in which property was transferred to individuals, could nevertheless

---

[4] Some works recently have applied anthropology to classics in order to study social attitudes and ideologies. For instance, D. Cohen, *Law, Sexuality and Society* (Cambridge: Cambridge University Press, 1991), and *Law, Violence, and Community in Classical Athens* (Cambridge: Cambridge University Press, 1995); V. Hunter, *Policing Athens: Social Control in the Attic Lawsuits 420–320 B.C.* (Princeton, N.J.: Princeton University Press, 1994); J. Ober, *Mass and Elite in Democratic Athens* (Princeton, N.J.: Princeton University Press, 1989); J. Ober and B. Strauss, "Drama, Political Rhetoric, and the Discourse of Athenian Democracy," in *Nothing to Do With Dionysos? Athenian Drama in Its Social Context,* ed. J. Winkler and F. Zeitlin (Princeton, N.J.: Princeton University Press, 1990), 237–70; B. Strauss, *Fathers and Sons in Athens* (Princeton, N.J.: Princeton University Press, 1993). For the growing interest in the use of anthropology for historians in other fields: D. Kertzer, "Anthropology and Family History," *Journal of Family History* 9 (1984): 201–16.

[5] Not until recently (see above, note 4) has classical scholarship embraced anthropology, though there were earlier efforts to use an interdisciplinary approach. Two of the leading names in this context are Louis Gernet and Moses Finley. An extensive list of Gernet's work is to be found in S. C. Humphreys, *Anthropology and the Greeks* (London: Routledge and Kegan Paul, 1978), 322–24. Gernet studied succession law to demonstrate that the family was severing itself from the extended kin. Fundamental to the discussions of family relations in chapters 3 and 4 of this book are two of Gernet's studies: "La création du testament," *REG* 33 (1920): 123–68, 249–90 = "La loi de Solon sur le 'testament,'" *Droit et société dans la Grèce ancienne* (Paris: Sirey, 1955), 121–49; "Sur l'épiclérat," *REG* 34 (1921): 337–79. For bibliography on Finley's writings: B. Shaw and R. Saller, "Bibliography of M. I. Finley," in M. I. Finley, *Economy and Society in Ancient Greece,* ed. and introd. B. Shaw and R. Saller (Harmondsworth: Penguin, 1981), 312–18. For the influences on Finley's writings see ibid., ix–xxvi. Finley did discuss the influence of anthropology on classics in "Anthropology and Classics," in *The Use and Abuse of History,* rev. ed. (New York: Penguin, 1987), 102–19. Finley did not write extensively on the family and household for ancient Athens but did study these institutions in Homeric society, which is not relevant to our present study. See: "Marriage Sale and Gift in the Homeric World," *RIDA* 2 (1955): 167–94; *The World of Odysseus,* 2d ed. (London: Chatto and Windus, 1977). For an early overview of anthropology and classics see C. Kluckhohn, *Anthropology and the Classics* (Providence, R.I.: Brown University Press, 1961). For a more recent overview: Humphreys, *Anthropology,* 31–75. Humphreys has writen extensively on kinship structures in ancient Athens. See for example, *The Family, Women and Death* (London: Routledge and Kegan Paul, 1983); "Social Relations on Stage: Witnesses in Classical Athens," *History and Anthropology* 1 (1985): 313–69; "Kinship Patterns in the Athenian Courts," *GRBS* 27 (1986): 57–91.

defy that agnatic bias.[6] Chapter 1 will also study specific marriage patterns, in particular how kinship endogamy could balance exogamy (marriage outside the group) and how women followed kinswomen into the same geographical area and at times the same kin group.[7] As the study focuses on marriage patterns it will show the important role of the neighbor. Although the role of the neighbor has been downplayed in recent scholarship on Athens,[8] the study will show in chapter 2 through the use of funerary inscriptions how rural marriages demonstrated a strong tendency toward local endogamy, marriage within the

[6] This study of agnatic relations runs counter to the tendency for some historians, such as Humphreys (see note 5 above), to see the Athenian inheritance structure as bilateral, a system that allowed the individual to inherit from both sides of the family. The emphasis on agnation is an emphasis on what side of the extended kin group a male individual had a right to inherit from. The male individual in Athens had an automatic right to inherit from his father and father's side of the kin group. As for kinship endogamy, it is an acknowledged practice for classical Athens. Though traditionally seen by structural materialists in the social sciences as a means for consolidation of property, endogamy is now seen as a result of a combination of variables which may include material considerations, but may also include political or even symbolic interests. For the variability of motivations see: P. Bourdieu, *Outline of a Theory of Practice*, trans. R. Nice (Cambridge: Cambridge University Press, 1977), esp. 64 ff.; L. Holy, *Kinship, Honour and Solidarity* (Manchester: Manchester University Press, 1989); D. Eickelman, *The Middle East*, 2d ed. (Englewood Cliffs, N.J.: Prentice Hall, 1989), 175–77; for political consolidation: J. Goody, *The Development of the Family and Marriage in Europe* (Cambridge: Cambridge University Press, 1983), 31–33. Agnatic endogamy may be practiced when the choices for partners are limited: H. Rosenfeld, "Social and Economic Factors in Explanation of the Increased Rate of Endogamy in the Arab Village in Israel," in *Mediterranean Family Structures*, ed. J. G. Peristiany (Cambridge: Cambridge University Press, 1976), 115–36. Or agnatic endogamy may be practiced when village exogamy is on the rise: M. Herzfeld, *The Politics of Manhood* (Princeton, N.J.: Princeton University Press, 1985), 58. Other societies have only a vague patriliny: E. L. Peters, "Aspects of Affinity in a Lebanese Maronite Village," in *Mediterranean Family Structures*, 27–79. Though Bourdieu criticizes the distinctions made between bilateral and agnatic systems he nevertheless emphasizes the force of agnatic biases in succession laws. For his criticism: "Marriage Strategies as Strategies of Social Reproduction," in *Family and Society*, ed. R. Forster and O. Ranum, trans. E. Forster and P. Ranum (Baltimore and London: Johns Hopkins University Press, 1976), 119; for his use of the agnatic bias: *Outline*, esp. 62.

[7] The study of marriage patterns is inevitably based on works of prosopography. Some of the chief works used in this book are Davies, *APF;* Kirchner, *PA;* P. J. Bicknell, *Studies in Athenian Politics and Genealogy*, Historia Einzelschriften, vol. 19 (Wiesbaden: F. Steiner, 1972). Works on the Bouselidae also proved invaluable: M. Broadbent, *Studies in Greek Genealogy* (Leiden: Brill, 1968); W. E. Thompson, *De Hagniae Hereditate: An Athenian Inheritance Case*, Mnemosyne Supplement, no. 44 (Leiden: Brill, 1976). The examination of marriage patterns per se in Athenian studies has not been popular. Broadbent has pointed up the balancing of kinship exogamy and endogamy. For other short studies: W. E. Thompson, "The Marriage of First Cousins in Athenian Society," *Phoenix* 21 (1967): 273–82, and "Athenian Marriage Patterns: Remarriage," *CSCA* 5 (1972): 211–26; S. Isager, "The Marriage Pattern in Classical Athens: Men and Women in Isaios," *ClMed* 33 (1981–82): 81–96.

[8] R. Osborne, *Demos: The Discovery of Classical Attika* (Cambridge: Cambridge University Press, 1985). Another work on the demes but which is less anthropologically oriented is D. Whitehead, *The Demes of Attica 508/7–ca. 250 B.C.* (Princeton, N.J.: Princeton University Press, 1986).

deme or rural neighborhood.[9] Urban marriages, on the other hand, were not as concerned with the deme and therefore were more heterogamous. Therefore there was a difference in behavior between town and country.

From marriage strategies the book will turn to family relations, showing how the agnatic bias in succession law actually encouraged friction among agnates. Chapter 3 will study the relations between generations, and chapter 4 will discuss sibling relationships, showing how conflicts between fathers and sons,[10] and between brothers, led individuals to seek help and support through female agnates such as sisters, or through the matriline. This view of the influence of women will contrast with studies up until now which have emphasized the woman's legal inferiority.[11] In other words, though women were denied access to the political arena, they gained power at the private level through their role in inheritance processes and marriage practices.[12]

At the same time, it will be stressed that women could enhance agnation practices but they could also defy them. Claims of descent through women specifically through the institutions of adoption and remarriage could challenge the

[9] For the use of funerary inscriptions to describe burial practice and marriage connections: Osborne, *Demos,* 127–53; Humphreys, *Family,* 79–130; R. Garland, "A First Catalogue of Attic Peribolos Tombs," *ABSA* 77 (1982): 125–76.

[10] On agnatic tensions: Bourdieu, *Outline,* 62. The present study's emphasis on the influence of material interests on emotions has depended upon the essays of Medick and Sabean. See H. Medick and D. W. Sabean, "Introduction," and "Interest and Emotion in Family and Kinship Studies: A Critique of Social History and Anthropology," in *Interest and Emotion,* ed. H. Medick and D. W. Sabean (Cambridge: Cambridge University Press, 1988), 1–27. On relationships between fathers and sons in Athens: Strauss, *Fathers;* see also M. Golden, *Children and Childhood in Classical Athens* (Baltimore: Johns Hopkins University Press, 1990).

[11] W. K. Lacey, *The Family in Classical Greece* (Ithaca, N.Y.: Cornell University Press, 1968); S. Pomeroy, *Goddesses, Whores, Wives, and Slaves* (New York: Schocken, 1975). Pomeroy's book was shaped by the anger of the rebirth of the women's movement in the 1970s. It would be an injustice to Pomeroy's work not to mention her recent shift away from legal strictures on women. See, for instance, her review, "Mark Golden: *Children and Childhood in Classical Athens,*" *EMC* 36 (1992): 73–76. For an insistence on women's inferior position, see also J. Gould, "Law, Custom and Myth: Aspects of the Social Position of Women in Classical Athens," *JHS* 100 (1980): 38–59. More recent works include R. Just, *Women in Athenian Law and Life* (London: Routledge, 1989); R. Sealey, *Women and Law in Classical Greece* (Chapel Hill: University of North Carolina Press, 1990).

[12] The early studies of Hans Julius Wolff on the Athenian family are exceptional in their attempt to go beyond legal restrictions. Wolff argued that the woman's dowry legally belonged to her original family and therefore gave her some influence in her marital household: "Marriage Law and Family Organization in Ancient Athens," *Traditio* 2 (1944): 43–95; for his views on the dowry, see also *RE* 23, 134–70, s.v. Προίξ. The dependence on the matriline may be a manifestation of agnation, not an obstruction to it: I. M. Lewis, "Problems in the Comparative Study of Unilineal Descent," in *The Relevance of Models for Social Anthropology,* ed. M. Banton (London: Tavistock, 1965), 105, referring to agnatic systems in general. For recent views on the woman's strength in the private sphere: Hunter, *Policing Athens;* Hunter's views are also evident in her earlier works: "Women's Authority in Classical Athens," *EMC* 33 (1989): 39–48; "The Athenian Widow and Her Kin," *Journal of Family History* 14 (1989): 291–311.

standard practice of claims of descent through men. This needs to be emphasized for Athenian society.

For Roman society Saller has discussed how individuals circumvented the strict agnation of Roman succession law. The trust, for instance, was devised so as to encourage flexibility in transferring property.[13] In Athenian society wills and adoptions could offset the agnation of succession law but these in turn led to protracted squabbling among the members of extended kin groups so that wills could be overturned or adoptions contested.[14] In other words, the book will not focus on just the event of property transmission, the who-gets-what, but the interest in how property is bequeathed and used over a period of time.

The focus on property use and transmission requires an examination of the nature of the entity that used and transmitted it, namely the household or *oikos*. Until recently historians of ancient society concentrated on the nuclear family, but now they are noticing the complexities of the ancient household. Just as in Roman society the *domus* meant much more than the nuclear triad, mother, father, and child,[15] so too in the Athenian sources the nuclear family is rarely so prominent as the *oikos*.[16] Hence chapter 5 examines the structure of the *oikos*, how wealth and property shaped it. At the same time, property concerns mingled with the institutions of guardianship, adoption, and remarriage to make household boundaries fluid, as guardians held control of their wards' estates while remarriage and adoption allowed members of different households to share in property. Moreover, because individuals, and especially men, were away from home for extended periods of time, their membership in an *oikos* could be illusory. Hence, the chapter also focuses on the mobility of the elite Athenian—how war and exile could change the configuration of an *oikos*.

Continuing the discussion of the complexity of *oikos* membership, chapter 6 considers the influence in the *oikos* of the nonkinsman.[17] Members of an *oikos*

---

[13] Saller, *Patriarchy*, 162–72.

[14] For inheritance and bequest as process see L. Bonfield, "Normative Rules and Property Transmission: Reflections on the Link between Marriage and Inheritance in Early Modern England," in *The World We Have Gained: Histories of Population and Social Structure*, ed. L. Bonfield, R. M. Smith, and K. Wrightson (Oxford: Basil Blackwell, 1986), 155–76.

[15] Saller, *Patriarchy*, 80–88.

[16] As Richard Smith has pointed out, the procreative cycle may well go on before, during, and after marriage: R. M. Smith, "Marriage Process in the English Past: Some Continuities," in Bonfield, Smith, Wrightson, *The World We Have Gained*, 43–99. Other social scientists and historians have studied the life cycle of the family and household. For instance, J. Goody, ed., *The Developmental Cycle in Domestic Groups* (Cambridge: Cambridge University Press, 1962); P. Laslett and R. Wall, eds., *Household and Family in Past Time* (Cambridge: Cambridge University Press, 1972). For the variability of the household in ancient Athens: T. W. Gallant, *Risk and Survival in Ancient Greece* (Stanford, Calif.: Stanford University Press, 1991); L. Foxhall, "Household, Gender and Property in Classical Athens," *CQ* 39 (1989): 22–44.

[17] For discussions of households not necessarily based on descent or blood lines, see the essays in R. McC. Netting, R. R. Wilk, and E. Arnould, eds., *Households: Comparative and Historical Studies of*

who were not kinsmen could have a great deal of influence over the use of wealth. The legal marginality of the prostitute (*hetaira*) and concubine (*pallakē*) was emphasized by the inability of their children to inherit.[18] Nevertheless, the concubine or prostitute could share extensively in her lover's wealth,[19] and there were even attempts to pass off illegitimate children as legitimate, especially when a man was at odds with his kinsmen. Another legally marginal figure who could be influential was the slave. For Rome Keith Bradley has shown the complexity of the household resulting from the fact that children were reared by and formed emotional attachments to slaves.[20] Likewise in Athens the slave had a great deal of say over the use of wealth and could even be absorbed into the kinship structure.

A man's friends, whether Athenian or foreign, were not in line to inherit his property, but they could have a good deal of influence over the wealth of an *oikos* as they performed services for its members and became involved in machinations over the use and transmission of property.[21] Male friendship in Athens could

---

the Domestic Group (Berkeley, Calif.: University of California Press, 1984). The series of essays in R. Wall, J. Robin, and P. Laslett, eds., *Family Forms in Historic Europe* (Cambridge: Cambridge University Press, 1983) includes discussions on the nonkinsman, specifically the laborer and servant. For example, P. Schmidtbauer, "The changing household: Austrian household structure from the seventeenth to the early twentieth century," ibid., 347–78. At times poorer relatives were servants: A. Carter, "Household Histories," in Netting, Wilk, Arnould, *Households,* 44–83.

[18] Because of its focus on law classical scholarship has been obsessed with whether an Athenian man could have legitimate children by an Athenian concubine. For instance, Buermann's argument that Athens permitted a man to have legitimate children by an Athenian concubine, "legitimate" or "legal concubinage" as it has been called, was discussed, criticized, and dismissed by the German scholars, but the notion of legitimate concubinage has recently resurfaced in the writings of both British and American scholars. H. Buermann, "Drei Studien auf dem Gebiet des attischen Rechts," *Jahrbücher für classische Philologie,* suppl., vol. 9 (1877–78): 569–91, 619–46; O. Müller, "Untersuchungen zur Geschichte des attischen Bürger- und Eherechts" *Jahrbücher für classische Philologie* 25 (1899): 661–866 ; A. Ledl, "Das attische Bürgerrecht und die Frauen," *WS* 29 (1907): 173–227; 30 (1908): 1–46, 173–230. The theory of legitimate concubinage has been resuscitated by D. M. MacDowell, "Bastards as Athenian Citizens," *CQ* 26 (1976): 88–91, and R. Sealey, "On Lawful Concubinage in Athens," *ClAnt* 3 (1984): 111–33; MacDowell was answered by P. J. Rhodes, "Bastards as Athenian Citizens," *CQ* 28 (1978): 89–92; most recently C. Patterson, "Those Athenian Bastards," *ClAnt* 9 (1990): 40–73, has reviewed the scholarship in a skeptical study of the whole question of legitimate concubinage.

[19] For discussions of prostitution in medieval society on which chapter 6 of this book will depend: J. Rossiaud, *Medieval Prostitution,* trans. L. G. Cochrane (Oxford: Basil Blackwell, 1988); L. Otis, *Prostitution in Medieval Society: The History of an Urban Institution in Languedoc* (Chicago: University of Chicago Press, 1987).

[20] Bradley, *Discovering the Roman Family.* For another discussion of the compexity of the Roman household see S. Dixon, *The Roman Family* (Baltimore: Johns Hopkins University Press, 1992).

[21] On friendship in Athens: G. M. Calhoun, *Athenian Clubs in Politics and Litigation* (New York: Burt Franklin, 1970, reprint); W. R. Connor, *The New Politicians of Fifth-Century Athens* (Princeton, N.J.: Princeton University Press, 1970); Gallant, *Risk;* G. Herman, *Ritualised Friendship and the Greek City* (Cambridge: Cambridge University Press, 1987); P. Millett, *Lending and Borrowing in Ancient Athens* (Cambridge: Cambridge University Press, 1991).

often be sexual,[22] and as with the *hetaira,* kinsmen could fear that an individual was devoting too much of his wealth to a male lover. Chapter 6 therefore considers the effect both of nonkinsmen in general, and also of homosexuality on the *oikos.*

A brief appendix discusses the marriage strategies of the elite political families of the fifth century. While the book as a whole relies mainly on the orations, the appendix will consider a variety of sources, many of which were not contemporary with the fifth century. Nevertheless these sources are valuable in demonstrating how marriage patterns reveal concerns about political and material consolidation.

In any study of classical Athens the historian must depend on three types of sources: inscriptions, political biographies of prominent Athenians, and the orations. Inscriptions often refer only to a single event, and in particular the grave stelae, though extensively used in chapter 2, tell us little beyond the names of individuals who married and died. The political biographies are late in date, having been mostly composed in imperial Roman times. The orations, however, are fairly contemporary with the events they describe, and give us a wealth of information on motivation and behavior. Because the orations are the major source of our discussion, it is essential to discuss their advantages and disadvantages.

The private orations–the speeches of Andocides, Antiphon, Demosthenes, Isaeus, Lysias, and the minor orators–date from the last third of the fifth century B.C. through the end of the fourth century B.C.[23] Generally inaccuracies do plague the speeches. Chronological and historical gaps, both unintentional and deliberate, abound. Moreover, the orations are notorious for their use of rhetoric, exaggeration, and lies, because their purpose was simply to win the case for the speaker. In the past thirty years or so, classicists have become increasingly aware of the many topoi shared by both Attic comedy and the orations: slander, at times obscene, was resorted to for the sake of humor, and if one's opponent was shamed and undermined in the process—all the better.[24] Furthermore, because the private orations were meant to deal with property disputes, inheritance conflicts,

---

[22] On homosexuality in Athens, see for instance: Cohen, *Law, Sexuality,* 171–202; K. J. Dover, *Greek Homosexuality,* 2d ed. (Cambridge, Mass.: Harvard University Press, 1989); D. M. Halperin, "The Democratic Body: Prostitution and Citizenship in Classical Athens," in D. M. Halperin, *One Hundred Years of Homosexuality* (London: Routledge, 1990), 88–112, 180–90.

[23] G. Kennedy, *The Art of Persuasion in Greece* (Princeton, N.J.: Princeton University Press, 1963), 125–263, for an overview of these orators and their works. For early works on the orators: C. Savage, *The Athenian Family: A Sociological and Legal Study Based Chiefly on the Works of the Attic Orators* (Baltimore: Lord Baltimore Press, 1907), which was not an interdisiciplinary approach to the orators; W. Wyse, *The Speeches of Isaeus* (Cambridge: Cambridge University Press; New York: Arno, 1979), which was a very skeptical treatment of Isaeus's orations.

[24] For the famous political slandering between Demosthenes and Aeschines and the comic elements entailed see P. Harding, "Rhetoric and Politics in Fourth-Century Athens," *Phoenix* 41 (1987):

and feuds over transmission of wealth, the texts were necessarily biased toward the affluent. Consequently, these speeches were vehicles for competition and aggression, as conflicts and power struggles were frequently aired in the courts. As David Cohen has argued, in an agonistic society the lawcourt was an important part of the process of feud, in which individuals pursued ongoing conflict without necessarily finding resolution.[25]

With that stated, there are several advantages to these sources as historical documents. Their emphasis on matters involving the succession to property makes them essential for the historian studying the property interests of the elite. Second, many of the sources for the marital alliances of the politically prominent families of the late fifth century are late Hellenistic or Roman in date, whereas the orations date to the classical era and are contemporary with the marriages and conflicts they discuss. Furthermore, although the orations, like any legal speech, depend on the point of view or selectivity of the speaker or witness, there are many instances of behavior or attitudes, often presented unintentionally, that find their parallels in the "anthropological experience" of European societies.[26] In addition, the practices evidenced in the orations can be seen in other sources, whether literary or inscriptional. On balance, therefore, the orations are reliable enough evidence, both for the practices they describe and for the values underlying these practices, to make them indispensable as evidence for the social history of classical Athens.

25–39. On the symbolic links between drama and rumor see Ober and Strauss, "Drama, Political Rhetoric" in Winkler and Zeitlin, *Nothing to Do With Dionysos?* 237–70. On rumor and gossip in the orations: Ober, *Mass,* 148–50; V. Hunter, "Gossip and the Politics of Reputation in Classical Athens," *Phoenix* 44 (1990): 299–325 = *Policing Athens,* 96–119.

[25] D. Cohen, *Law, Violence,* esp. 66 ff. See also G. Herman, "Tribal and Civic Code of Behaviour in Lyisias I," *CQ* 43 (1993): 406–419, and "Honour, Revenge and the State in Fourth-Century Athens," in *Die athenische Demokratie in 4 Jahrhundert v. Chr.,* ed. W. Eder (Stuttgart: Franz Steiner, 1995), 43–60, who argues that violent, personal revenge was suppressed by the state; revenge, rather, was channeled through the court system. R. Garner, *Law and Society in Classical Athens* (New York: St. Martin's, 1987), 3, on the aristocratic ideal of competition; 68–71, on personal feuds; 75, on the quantity of lies producing victory in the orations; see also S. C. Humphreys, "Social Relations," 317 ff.

[26] Hunter, "Athenian Widow," 292; A. Plakans, *Kinship in the Past: An Anthropology of European Family Life 1500–1900* (Oxford: Basil Blackwell, 1984), 258–59; the quote is from Plakans.

HOUSEHOLD INTERESTS

CHAPTER 1

The Families of the
Private Orations

DESPITE the difficulties inherent in the orations, the chronological gaps, the telescoping of events and the falsification of fact, they are valuable sources for the study of how individuals, families, and extended kin manipulated blood and marriage ties and wealth. Within this process of manipulation, patterns emerge which suggest how interests in property could be sustained for several generations. The focus here will be on how such patterns or strategies could reflect an individual's interests in his or her patriline, that is, the line of descent through males from a male ancestor. We will then assess the role and importance of locale in the formation of marital alliances; "locale" here refers to marriages within the deme and the local interests motivating these unions, which have been studied by Osborne in his work on the deme.[1] In addition, the discussion will focus on the effects of kinship exogamy, or out-marriage, and endogamy, or in-marriage, in a family's marriage strategies. "Locale" can also refer to the location of property holdings and of residence, and the discussion here will consider how they motivated families to ally. To what extent, then, did families and kinship groups focus on a particular deme or region when forming marital alliances? To what extent was the neighbor used both in marriage and the larger political network? Any discusion of the neighbor must consider proximity; in the following discussion proximity will not entail just those individuals living close to each other in the city but those rural "neighbors" who lived up to eight kilometers from each other.

Case studies will be provided of those families in the orations for whom we have the most information: by way of illustration, the practices of other families will be mentioned, for whom our information is not as complete. We begin with two kin groups, domiciled in the city, whose marriage alliances suggest interests in various parts of Attica and whose family trees can be traced back to the early and mid fifth century.

THE BOUSELIDAE

No discussion of the Bouselidae is ever uncomplicated. Although the disputes which resulted from the death of Hagnias II have been discussed in great detail

[1] R. Osborne, *Demos: The Discovery of Classical Attika* (Cambridge: Cambridge University Press, 1985), 127 ff.

by others, it is nevertheless possible, even by going down some well-worn paths, to reassess the role of the location of landed holdings in the selection of marriage partners and to indicate how kinship endogamy and adoption could be interconnected.

Bouselus of Oeum Ceramicum, whose floruit is dated to the early fifth century, sired five sons, each of whom produced his own descent group ([Dem.] 43.19).[2] One of these sons, Hagnias I, sired Polemon and, perhaps, Phylomache I, although her paternity was in doubt.[3] Their descendants and extended kin would carry on their squabbling throughout the first three quarters of the fourth century over the estate of Hagnias II, son of Polemon. From a series of trials dating to the mid-fourth century, marriage patterns emerge for the Bouselidae, such as the alternation of exogamy with endogamy combined with marriage and adoption. These maneuvers set one *oikos* of the kin group against another and allowed the encroachment of nonagnates onto Bouselid property (figure 1).

The Bouselidae were notorious, by Athenian standards, for their in-marrying and infighting over the estate of one individual, Hagnias II, son of Polemon. Polemon's sister, Phylomache I, whose paternity and legitimacy were in question, contended for the estate of her brother's son, Hagnias II, against the claims of Hagnias's half-brothers through his mother, Glaucus and Glaucon. Phylomache I had married her first cousin, her father's brother's son, Philagrus: this marriage produced Euboulides II who continued Phylomache I's claim to Hagnias's estate after her death. There is no information as to whom Euboulides married, but he in turn sired an only child, a girl, Phylomache II, who continued the claim for her descent group, the offspring of her endogamous marriage to a second cousin, Sositheus.[4] Sositheus ultimately descended from the Bouselidae on his mother's side: his maternal grandfather was Callistratus, a Bouselid, and the full brother of Philagrus, Phylomache I's husband.

The alternation of exogamy with endogamy is quite evident for Callistratus's side of the family. Callistratus had married a kinswoman (father's brother's daughter's daughter). Callistratus's daughter, on the other hand, was married outside her kin group to one Sosias. This marriage then produced Sositheus, who in turn married a kinswoman, his second cousin Phylomache II (mother's father's brother's son's daughter). Phylomache II's son, Euboulides III, was then adopted into the estate of her father Euboulides II, the son of Phylomache I.[5]

The propensity for endogamy within the Bouselidae is obvious: indeed the group is known to have contracted five such unions, and possibly several more.[6]

---

[2] See also Davies, *APF,* 79 ff.

[3] W. E. Thompson, *De Hagniae Hereditate: An Athenian Inheritance Case, Mnemosyne,* suppl. 44 (Leiden: Brill, 1976), 5; M. Broadbent, *Studies in Greek Genealogy* (Leiden: Brill, 1968), 82.

[4] Phylomache was mother's father's brother's son's daughter to Sositheus: Davies, *APF,* 80–81.

[5] Ibid., 80.

[6] Ibid., 77 ff.; the marriages of Polemon's widow (ibid., 83) and Oinanthe (ibid., 87) to fellow demesmen might have been marriages to kinsmen, although this is not certain. Also, Thompson's re-

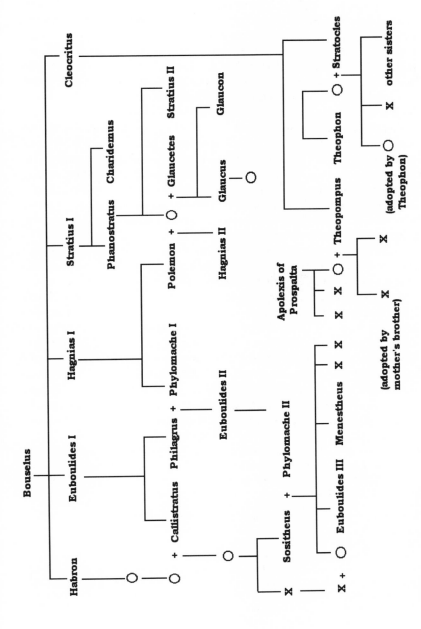

Figure 1. The Bouselidae

The point here, however, is how endogamy was used to encroach on an estate in crisis: the two lines emanating from the brothers Callistratus and Philagrus practiced alternating exogamy and endogamy until in the third generation both lines united maritally. Because Soseitheus married endogamously to an heiress, Phylomache II, and because the marriage was reinforced by the adoption of his son into the estate of Euboulides II, Sositheus, who did not belong patrilineally to the Bouselidae, became the spokesman for the rights of his Bouselid wife and of their son to inherit the estate of Hagnias II. On the other hand, Sositheus did not entirely ignore his original *oikos:* he had his daughter marry a brother's son ([Dem.] 43.74).[7]

Sositheus's machinations were also meant to foil Hagnias II's attempts to hand over control of his estate to his mother's sons by her second marriage. Hagnias II was the product of an endogamous marriage: his mother, the daughter of Phanostratus, a Bouselid, was a first cousin once removed, through the agnatic line, to her husband Polemon. The marriage was endogamous in terms of kinship and deme: both spouses came from Oeum Ceramicum. After Polemon's death, his widow then married a Glaucetes of Oeum Cerameicum, a demesman, though his relationship to the Bouselidae is uncertain (Is. 11.8, 17).[8]

Although the marital career of Hagnias's mother stressed agnation, Hagnias's devotion to his patriline was much more ambivalent. In 396, before Hagnias went on an embassy to Persia that would eventually take his life, he drew up a will stating that his niece be adopted into his estate. The young niece may have been the daughter either of Hagnias's sister (or full sibling) or of one of his matrilateral half-brothers.[9] In any case, it appears that Hagnias stipulated in his will that in the event of the death of his adopted heiress, his homometric half-brother, Glaucon, was to be heir of his estate. This latter bequest would have to imply testamentary adoption of a second heir and not succession per se. If there had been no will, Phylomache I and her descendants, as agnates, would have had the right to assume control of Hagnias's estate, since in intestate succession the patriline took precedence over the matriline. Legally speaking, in terms of succes-

---

construction posits an endogamous union contracted between Hagnias II's matrilineal half-brothers (see below). Humphreys suggests that the endogamy was a result of interests stemming both from the rivalry over Hagnias' estate and from the kin group's religious status, *The Family, Women and Death* (London: Routledge and Kegan Paul, 1983), 110–11. Her suggestion has been taken up by Osborne, *Demos,* 137. For a modern example in which endogamy is high in religious communities, see M. Klat and A. Khudr, "Religious Endogamy and Consanguinity in Marriage Patterns in Beirut," *Social Biology* 33 (1986): 138–45.

[7] See also Davies, *APF,* 80.

[8] See also ibid., 82–83: Hagnias II's mother was Polemon's father's brother's son's daughter.

[9] For the daughter of a sister: Gernet, *Droit et Société dans la Grèce ancienne* (Paris: Sirey, 1955) 129, followed by S. C. Humphreys, "The Date of Hagnias' Death," *CP* 78 (1983): table 1. Davies, *APF,* 82–83, feels that Hagnias's adopted niece was the daughter of a full sibling and that the mysterious Eupolemus, one of the claimants, was her son. But, as Humphreys correctly points out ("Date" 223 n.13), this would give Eupolemus a very clear overriding claim to Hagnias's property.

sion, Euboulides II, the son of Phylomache I, who claimed that she was the homopatric half-sister of Hagnias II's father, would have had every right to claim the estate over Glaucus and Glaucon, the homometric half-brothers of Hagnias.[10] Hagnias flagrantly attempted to undercut the legal norm by naming Glaucon as his second heir and, possibly, by stipulating that Glaucon marry the niece whom he, Hagnias, had adopted as his first heir.[11] Because Athenian law stipulated that an adoptee was severed from his or her *oikos* of origin, and therefore could not inherit from it,[12] Glaucon's marriage to Hagnias II's adopted heiress would leave him in control of two estates, his own which he would inherit from Glaucetes, his father, and Hagnias's. Glaucon's full brother, Glaucus, entered the

[10] A. R. W. Harrison, *The Law of Athens*, vol. 1 (Oxford: Clarendon Press, 1968), 144–46.

[11] The following reconstruction is based upon the theories of Broadbent, *Studies,* 84–89, and following her, Thompson, *De Hagniae Hereditate,* 11–13 and D. M. MacDowell, *The Law in Classical Athens* (Ithaca, N.Y.: Cornell University Press, 1978), 104. However, I have not followed Broadbent's and Thompson's reconstruction that suggests that Hagnias II's mother was the daughter of a Phanostrate, which most of the manuscripts read, rather than of a Phanostratus (I), who is mentioned by one manuscript. Either individual would have been a first cousin to Hagnias II's father, Polemon, as children of Polemon's father's brother. Humphreys, "Date," 222, n. 7, prefers the masculine name, Phanostratus, based on the Phanostratus, son of Stratius of Oeum Cerameicum, who was recorded on a list of councillors for 371/0. Humphreys's contention, however, is that the councillor would be Phanostratus II, son's son to Phanostratus I. This does little to prove the actual gender of the parent of Hagnias II's mother, be it Phanostrate or Phanostratus. Nevertheless, as Humphreys states, the sense of the testimony in [Dem.] 43.22 suggests that all persons there listed, as first cousins of Polemon, should be male; thus, the reading Phanostratus (I) in one manuscript is to be preferred to the reading Phanostrate in the other manuscripts. Further, there is the possibility, as Humphreys states, that the councillor in the inscription was Phanostratus (I), who was serving as a councillor at an advanced age. The hypothesis of a younger homonym is, therefore, not necessary. See Davies' arguments (*APF,* 81–82), who, nevertheless stresses that Phanostratus (I) would be much older than his (half-) brother Charidemus. Yet Isaeus 6 shows that such disparity in the ages of half-brothers was possible. Humphreys ("Date," 223) more recently argues against Thompson's reconstruction, which postulates that the adopted niece had died c. 385, some ten years after the death of Hagnias II. Humphreys counters that, because the first of the court trials concerning the estate is dated to 361/0, there would be a good twenty-five-year gap in which Glaucon was left to hold the estate without challenge. Further, because Sositheus had probably married Phylomache II c. 370, a wait of ten years before Sositheus's first challenge is unlikely. Yet Humphreys herself has provided a possible reason for the long wait: Glaucon may have sired a child (223, n.11), who died in the interim. Furthermore, if Glaucon was the second adoptee, according to Hagnias's will, he would have had solid legal justification for his long tenure. Moreover, to judge from [Dem.] 44, family arbitration did a great deal to postpone conflicts over adoption from reaching the courts. On private arbitration, see most recently: V. Hunter, *Policing Athens: Social Control in the Attic Lawsuits, 430–320 B.C.* (Princeton, N.J.: Princeton University Press, 1994), 43–69.

The fact that Hagnias's heiress was not claimed by other relatives during the time before her death should not pose a problem. Isaeus 7.8–9 (with Wyse's commentary: W. Wyse, *The Speeches of Isaeus* (1904; repr. New York: Arno, 1979), 557, followed by Gernet, *Droit,* 129) shows that a testator, when adopting an heiress, would choose a husband for her precisely so as to prevent her from being ἐπίδικος, to be claimed by a kinsman, preferably an agnate. On this point see now Rubinstein, *Adoption in IV. Century Athens* (Copenhagen, Museum Tusculanum Press, 1993), 95–100.

[12] Harrison, *Law,* 1:82–85, for the laws on adoption and the marrying of the adopter's daughter.

contest because it may have been his daughter who was selected by Hagnias II as heiress; she, in turn, would then be slated to marry her father's full brother, Glaucon. *If* Hagnias's adopted heiress was Glaucus's daughter, then the adoption of Glaucus's daughter outside Glaucus's patriline was followed by her marriage to Glaucon, her paternal uncle; therefore, she would then return to her patriline. One is reminded here of Sositheus's maneuvers: the adoption of his son into the house of his wife's father was accompanied by the marriage of his daughter to his brother's son.

This is all conjectural, but the very least that can be said is that Hagnias definitely ignored all male agnates in his inheritance practices and preferred either the daughter of his sister, a female agnate, or his matrilineal kinsmen. It was a preference that, despite a will, was finally overturned by the court in favor of a male agnate, Theopompus, son of Cleocritus. Theopompus was a first cousin once removed to Hagnias II (a father's father's brother's son) and seems to have been a black sheep in the family: he did not marry endogamously in terms of either kin or deme.

Theopompus had a city residence, but held land at Oenoe (either Hippothontis or Aiantis) and came into possession of his wife's brother's estate at Prospalta by having his son adopted into the estate, which was in the deme of his wife's father Apolexis of Prospalta (Is. 11.49; [Dem.] 43.77).[13] If Theopompus's land at Oenoe was in Hippothontis, then it was located in northwest Attica en route to his brother Stratocles' holdings which were at Eleusis, in the same trittys as Oenoe, and which were also at Thria nearby. Therefore, Theopompus's property may have lain in the same region as that of his brother Stratocles. Unlike Theopompus's marriage, Stratocles' marriage involved his rural neighbor: Theophon, his wife's brother, owned property at Eleusis, the deme in which one of Stratocles' houses lay and close to his *agros* (field) in Thria.[14] In addition, the deme of the Bouselidae, Oeum Ceramicum, may have lain close to Stratocles' holdings, so that proximity of property holdings and the location of the Bouselid deme played a strong role in the formation of affinal ties.[15] Stratocles, moreover,

---

[13] See also Davies, *APF,* 85, 89, for Apolexis; for Theopompus, ibid., 87–88.

[14] Davies, *APF,* 87–88. Thompson, *De Hagniae Hereditate,* 51, conjectures that Stratocles had purchased this land in Thria because the price quoted for it was so out of proportion to the value of Theopompus's own (inherited) farm. This is speculative: Theopompus's whole line of argument in Isaeus 11 is to downplay his wealth and upgrade that of his brother so as to avoid Stratocles' son's claiming part of Hagnias's estate, which Theopompus now possessed. Davies (*APF,* 88) comments on Theopompus's exaggeration. In fact, Thompson admits that Theopompus' figures are suspicious (*De Magniae Hereditate.,* 50). Even if some of Stratocles' property had been purchased, Stratocles was left a patrimony. Some of the property listed in Is. 11.41–42, concentrated in Eleusis and the Thriasian plain, would have to have been part of this inheritance: the wording suggests this, and Theopompus would not have been reticent in pointing out that his brother had sold his patrimony. Thompson's argument that it is difficult to see what Stratocles could have done with the money that had accrued to him from his daughter's adoption other than buy an estate is not a strong one.

[15] Oeum Cerameicum was assigned to the inland trittys of Leontis. If that assignment signifies the general location of the deme, by no means a certain correlation (J. S. Traill, *Demos and Trittys* (Toronto: Athenians, Victoria College, 1986), 131), then the deme of the Bouselidae, if situated on

owned a house at Melite in the western part of the *astu,* the core of the city, on a good communication route to the Thriasian plain where his property was located.[16] The estates of the two men, Stratocles and his brother-in-law, Theophon, were then further united by the adoption of Stratocles' daughter into Theophon's *oikos;* in fact, Theopompus listed Theophon's property under Stratocles' estate (Is. 11.41–42).

There is, possibly, more to say on the use of the neighbor: Sositheus may have been absorbed into the Bouselidae because he was a member of the deme Araphen where Hagnias II's landed estate was located ([Dem.] 43.70).[17] The name Sositheus is very rare in the fourth century; outside of the oration (ibid., 81)[18] it appears only three times, and only once with a demotic: in a list for the phyle Aegeis (*IG* II² 2389 l.10) dating to the mid-fourth century, where the Sositheus listed comes from the deme Araphen, in which Hagnias's estate lay. If Sositheus or a kinsman came from the deme in which a contested piece of Bouselid property lay, then it makes us further appreciate how Sositheus had first-hand knowledge of Theopompus's alleged abuse of Hagnias's estate: Theopompus apparently had chopped down the olive trees on the property (Is. 43.69–70), and those who held neighboring estates in Araphen were summoned as witnesses by Sositheus. Therefore, deme membership in Araphen may well have been a reason for the Bouselid Callistratus's alliance with Sosias and, thus, Sositheus' encroachment on Bouselid land.[19] In the end, however, Sositheus seems to have lost the battle for the property.[20]

---

the western curve of the trittys, would have been situated close to Stratocles' holdings. Note that the eastern end of this long trittys is located close to Aiantid Oenoe, the alternative location for Theopompus's holding. For the Leontid trittys, see ibid., map 1.

[16] On the house, see Davies, *APF,* 87–88.

[17] Davies, *APF,* 87, overlooked this reference to the estate's location, as did Kirchner (*PA* 133) on whom Davies is dependent. See, however, Thompson, *De Hagniae Hereditate,* 101, and Broadbent, *Studies,* 70, table VI, and 71. The passage ([Dem.] 43.70) is also useful for giving us Sositheus's name (*pace* Davies, *APF,* 80).

[18] See Davies, *APF,* 80, for Sositheus's membership in a different phratry. The name "Sositheus" does not appear frequently until the second and first centuries when it is regularly used in two families from Euonymon and Agryle. If Sositheus came from one of these demes, then he was from a city family and encroached on the property of a family from the inland, but which was domiciled in the city. A fifth-century Sosias, the name of Sositheus's father, is attested in the Erechtheid phyle, to which Euonymon and Agryle belong (*IG* II² 929.54), but the name is also attested in Anaphlystus, Hybadae, and the Peiraeus, for instance, in the fourth century (*IG* II² 5683, *SEG* 23.86.187, 24.162.179, respectively).

[19] It is unclear whether the alliance to Sosias occurred contemporaneously with Hagnias's death. Sosias appears to have married c. 390 (Davies, *APF,* 80, for Sositheus's marriage c. 370–360 and, therefore, his birth c. 390). Hagnias's death has been traditionally dated to 396, but the date has been challenged. For the traditional dating, see Davies, *APF,* 82, Broadbent, *Studies,* 81, Thompson, *De Hagniae Hereditate,* 12; this has been challenged by Humphreys, "Date," 219–25, but see my criticisms, above, note 11.

[20] Upon Theopompus's death Sositheus came forward with the claim of Phylomache I's descendants against the claim of Theopompus's line. See Davies, *APF,* 86, for a chronology of these events. That Sositheus lost this round is indicated by an inscription of ephebes dated to 324/3, which bears

SUMMARY

Let us now sum up our findings on the neighbor, kinship endogamy, and its link with adoption. Stratocles contracted a marriage with a woman whose brother, Theophon, was a landed neighbor in northwest Attica, where Stratocles' deme may also have been situated. The marriage yielded a daughter whom Theophon adopted. Therefore, for this branch of the Bouselidae adoption followed and reinforced marriage between two landed neighbors. For other branches of the Bouselidae kinship endogamy and adoption were closely linked. For the Bouselid line descending from Callistratus, Callistratus's daughter was married exogamously to Sosias and their son, Sositheus, married endogamously to his second cousin. His son was then adopted by a Bouselid. Hagnias II's mother married endogamously her first cousin once removed and then she married a demesman. The daughter of her son from this second marriage may then have been adopted by Hagnias II, her son by her first marriage. Essentially we have a balancing act of kinship endogamy with exogamy as families tried to extend ties and consolidate them. Marriage between neighbors, landed and urban, was an important strategy in these maneuvers. Kinship and local endogamy and adoption were closely linked together as adoption could secure an alliance with a nonkinsman or a demesman or neighbor. Endogamy reinforced by adoption kept a balance of interests on both sides of the *ankhisteia,* or extended kin group. It was a balancing act that also formed the strategy of another prominent group in the orations, the kin group of Dicaeogenes I.

THE KIN GROUP OF DICAEOGENES I

The family tree for Dicaeogenes I's kin group (figure 2) is, unfortunately, based upon considerable prosopographical conjecture, which in turn has been subject to debate. If, however, these conjectures are correct, the kin group displays tendencies to both in-marriage and out-marriage, but it also maritally allies with rural and urban neighbors. The kin group of Dicaeogenes I, known to us largely from Isaeus 5, was one of the wealthiest landed families of classical Athens, with an impressive history of liturgical and military activities.[21] The earliest known marriage involving Dicaeogenes I's kin group occurred in the 450s: one of his daughters, of the city deme Cydathenaeum, was given in marriage to an individual of the politically prominent Gephyraei from Aphidna, either to Proxenus

---

the name of Hagnias, son of Macartatus of Oeum (*AE* 1918.75 no. 95 lines 2, 8). Macartatus was the name of Theopompus's son. This Hagnias would have been born c. 344 and, therefore, contemporaneously with Sositheus's lawsuit against Theopompus's son Macartatus (Davies, *APF,* 78). The name of the ephebe, his patronymic, and his demotic suggest that the estate was retained by Theopompus's line: Thompson, *De Hagniae Hereditate,* 106–7. following Broadbent, *Studies,* 62.

[21] Davies, *APF,* 145–49.

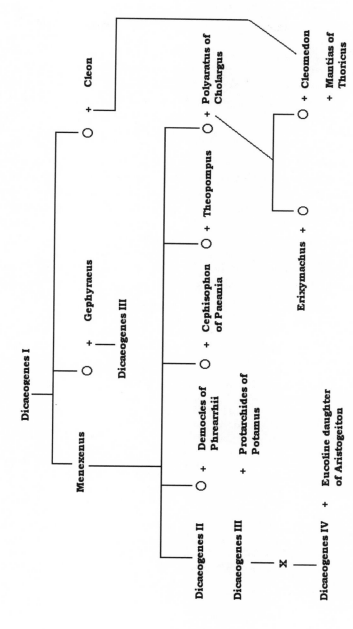

Figure 2. The Kin Group of Dicaeogenes I

I or his father, Harmodius II. A son, Dicaeogenes III, from this union was adopted by Dicaeogenes II who was the grandson (son's son) of Dicaeogenes I (Is. 5.6).[22] Although the neighboring deme did not play a role in these transactions, the urban neighborhood, nevertheless, may have facilitated the association: Dicaeogenes' kin group seems either to have resided, or to have owned property, in the Cerameicus, while members of the Gephyraei may have resided there as well.[23] Further, the marriage alliances, as will be discussed shortly, focused on holdings acquired and networks formed in the northern Athenian plain and in south Attica.

More conjecturally, Dicaeogenes I gave another daughter in marriage in the 440s to his fellow demesman, the statesman Cleon of Cydathenaeum.[24] If this latter marriage of Dicaeogenes' daughter is historical, it was an alliance between two houses, one of which defined itself as landed, while the other was viewed as totally nonlanded.[25] In the next generation, Cleon's son Cleomedon married endogamously, his bride being his first cousin once removed, that is, his mother's brother's daughter's daughter. This endogamous union, then, followed Cleon's exogamous marriage. The purpose of this endogamy will be made clearer in the discussion on Polyaratus below.

Meanwhile, Dicaeogenes I's son, Menexenus, had four daughters and one son, Dicaeogenes II. One of the daughters of Menexenus was married to a certain Theopompus (deme unknown) who lived next door to her brother, Dicaeogenes II, in the city.[26] This proximity allowed Dicaeogenes III, the adopted son of Di-

---

[22] See also Davies, *APF*, 476–77.

[23] See below, note 68.

[24] Davies, *APF*, 145, 319–20. The marriage of Cleon is inferred from the name of Cleon, son of Menexenus, on a bouleutic list dated 390–375 (*Agora* 15.10). Davies, followed by Meritt and Traill (15.10), suggests that this Cleon's father was the son of a daughter of Dicaeogenes I. Bourriot argues that the restored deme name, Cydathenaeum, on the column of the list is merely inferred from the names Cleon and Menexenus. Bourriot states that some names in this column appear in both Cydathenaeum and Paeania, while others appear only in the latter. Thus, Bourriot argues, the column is a list of councillors from Paeania: F. Bourriot, "La famille et le milieu sociale de Cléon," *Historia* 31 (1982): 420–33. Bourriot's criticisms of the stemma are not without their difficulties, however. See C. A. Cox, "Sisters, Daughters and the Deme of Marriage: A Note," *JHS* 108 (1988): 186, n.11, for commentary and bibliography on the stemma. See also, Traill, *Demos,* 38–41, for his objections that the relevant columns should not be reversed, although I do not agree with his exhortation to simplify Cleon's family stemma.

[25] Admittedly, it is difficult to assess the extent of exaggeration in the sources, for Cleon's wealth, which are for the most part found in comedy, but if they can be trusted to any extent, their emphasis is on Cleon's commercial wealth from his tanning business, which was estimated to be around fifty talents: Davies, *APF* 319, for the estimation of Cleon's wealth. On the other hand, Isaeus 5 emphasizes Dicaeogenes I's landed wealth which yielded an income of eighty minae per year. The estate's worth, according to the information from the oration, has been computed at anywhere from ten to thirteen talents: ibid., 146; L. Casson, "The Athenian Upper Class and New Comedy," *TAPA* 106 (1976): 33, n.10, 52, n.55.

[26] This assumes that the city house in which Dicaeogenes III resided originally belonged to his adoptive father, Dicaeogenes II: Is. 5.10–11; Davies, *APF,* 147. Because Dicaeogenes III, the adopted son of Dicaeogenes II, assumed guardianship of Theopompus's children upon the latter's death (Is. 5.10–11), there is a possibility that there were kinship ties between the two men: Wyse, *Isaeus,* 417–18.

caeogenes II, a great deal of influence over the disposal of Theopompus's property. Theopompus appears to have died in debt; Dicaeogenes III paid off the debts, took care of Theopompus's widow and orphaned sons, bought Theopompus' house, demolished it, and used the property as a garden (Is. 5.10–11).

Although the role of the urban neighborhood is clear in this case, the marriages of three other daughters of Menexenus involved, it seems, two regions outside Athens. One of Menexenus's daughters was given in marriage to Polyaratus of Cholargus, a deme in the northern plain. Another daughter married twice: she was married first to Democles of Phrearrhii (Is. 5.5–6), which was a deme in south Attica. Her second husband was Protarchides of Potamus (without modifier) (ibid., 5, 26–27).[27] There were three demes of this name, all three of which were traditionally assigned by scholars to the coastal trittys of Leontis in south Attica, which would make them all neighbors of Phrearrhii; but Upper and Lower Potamus have more recently been assigned to the northeastern portion of the north Athenian plain, while Potamus Deiradiotae is to be located on the southeast coast.[28] If Protarchides' deme was located in the plain northeast of the *astu,* then the deme may have been in the vicinity of a piece of land owned by Dicaeogenes I's line: according to Isaeus 5.22, Dicaeogenes II owned sixty plethra of land ἐν Πεδίῳ, "in the Plain," which, besides meaning the plain of agricultural land south of the city, can mean the upper Cephissus valley in the northern plain where many of the elite families of the fifth century owned land.[29] If so, then it would not have been a coincidence that Menexenus contracted a marriage for a daughter to Polyaratus of Cholargus, a city deme of Acamantis in the northern Athenian plain (ibid., 5),[30] and it may not be coincidence the Gephyraei, the affines of Dicaeogenes' kin group, owned an estate in a deme referred to as Potamus (again, without modifier). According to a Plutarchian tradition, the granddaughter of Aristogeiton, the tyrannicide, was given land in Potamus in the early fifth century (*Arist.* 37.4). In other words the urban neighborhood and holdings in north Attica fostered alliances among members of the kin group of Dicaeogenes I and Gephyraei. The effect of marriage of Menexenus's sister to a Gephyraeus in forging links between the two groups, moreover, was reinforced by the adoption of Dicaeogenes III by Dicaeogenes II.

---

[27] See also Davies, *APF,* 147–48.

[28] J. S. Traill, *The Political Organization of Attica, Hesperia,* suppl. 14 (Princeton, N.J.: American School of Classical Studies at Athens, 1975), 44–46, n.18, following Elliot's suggestion in *Coastal Demes of Attica: A Study of the Policy of Cleisthenes* (Toronto: University of Toronto Press, 1962), 149, n.36; more recently, the conjecture has been incorporated into Traill's map in *Demos.* See also Osborne, *Demos,* 199, table 2a.

[29] The upper Cephissus valley was the part of Attica invaded by the Peloponnesians on their descent from Acharnae. See Thuc. 2.20.1, 55.1 and A. W. Gomme et al., *A Historical Commentary on Thucydides,* 5 vols. (Oxford: Clarendon Press, 1945–81), 2:73, who also cites Hdt. 1.59.4 and *Ath. Pol.* 13.4 for the use of the term *to Pedion.*

[30] See also Davies, *APF,* 149, 461.

Another prominent clan, the Eteoboutadae, and their affines, or in-laws, displayed a similar interest in holdings and marital alliances in the northern plain. Cleombrotus I of Acharnae, if Davies's reconstruction is correct, had allied maritally with a fellow demesman, Menon; possibly, though this is not certain, Cleombrotus's sister was Menon's wife. It may well have been Menon's son, Deinocrates (I), who purchased land at Lousia, northwest of the *astu*. The elder Cleombrotus had a grandson (his son's son), Cleombrotus II, who married the Eteoboutad Callisto; her *genos* was domiciled in the deme of Boutadae, in the same trittys to which Lousia belonged. The marriage was then followed by the adoption of Callisto's son by Cleombrotus (II) into the estate of her father, Lycophron.[31] Thus, the purchase of property was followed by marriage to a member of a household from a nearby deme; and this alliance of two *oikoi* was further secured by adoption.

Besides the northern plain, the kin group of Dicaeogenes I and of the Gephyraei displayed interest in south Attica through their marriages. First, we recall that one of Menexenus's daughters married a man from Phrearrhii. The same woman was then married to a man from Potamus (yet again, without modifier), which could refer to Potamus Deiradiotae in southeast Attica. The Gephyraei also showed interest in the south. *IG* II² 5752 records a kinsman of Dicaeogenes III, a Gephyraeus, Thoutimus, son of Aristogeiton of Aphidna, who is buried with a woman who is presumably his wife, Theosebeia from Anaphlystus, a deme in the mining district of south Attica. Thoutimus appears to have given either his sister or daughter in marriage to a man from Poros—on the gravestone are recorded Androcles, from Poros, and his son, Thoutimus (*IG* II² 5752).[32] The location of Poros has been recently assigned to the coastal trittys of Acamantis in the mining district;[33] if the assignment is valid, then Thoutimus, son of Aristogeiton, married a woman from Anaphlystus in south Attica and gave a kinswoman in marriage into a deme in the same region. Although this discussion can do little to determine which Potamus was the domicile of the affines of Dicaeogenes' kin group and which held Gephyraei land, it does allow us to focus a little more clearly on the interplay between landed property and the selection of marriage partners either in south Attica or in the plain north of the *astu*. In all of this, urban residence clearly facilitated associations of families from disparate demes.

Thus the marriages of Dicaeogenes I's kin group reveal interests in the urban and rural settings. The kin group contracted marriages with the Gephyraei, some of whom lived in the Cerameicus along with Dicaeogenes' group. An adoption

---

[31] Davies, *APF*, 353, 483. For a recent discovery of gravestones belonging to this branch of the Eteoboutadae, Lycurgus's family, see *SEG* 37.160, 161, 162, found near the Academy. For the original discussion, see A. P. Matthaiou, "Ἡρίον Λυκούργου Λυκόφρονος Βουτάδου," *Horos* 5 (1987): 31–44.

[32] See also Davies, *APF*, 474; Humphreys, *Family*, 129, n. 53.

[33] Traill, *Demos*, map, although Poros's precise location is uncertain.

followed this union two generations later when Dicaeogenes II adopted Dicaeogenes III. Dicaeogenes I may also have allied with Cleon, a fellow demesman, while one of Dicaeogenes II's sisters was married to a next-door neighbor. The kin group of Dicaeogenes I also focused on rural demes, particularly in the northern Athenian plain where they and the Gephyraei may have held land. Dicaeogenes' line also contracted marriages to families in south Attica where the Gephyraei were doing the same.

POLYARATUS OF CHOLARGUS

Kinship endogamy and repeated alliances into the same deme also characterize the marriage practices of Polyaratus of Cholargus, the affine of Dicaeogenes II (figure 2). Polyaratus had married out to one of the daughters of Menexenus; she was in turn the sister of Dicaeogenes II of Cydathenaeum. One of Polyaratus's daughters married Cleomedon, son of Cleon of Cydathenaeum; therefore, Polyaratus had married a woman from Cydathenaeum and sent his daughter into that deme for her marriage. His son-in-law, Cleomedon, was not only of the deme of origin of his wife's mother, but also may have been his wife's first cousin once removed, if Cleon indeed married the daughter of Dicaeogenes I.[34] Therefore, Polyaratus balanced his own exogamous marriage with his daughter's endogamous one. Furthermore, Polyaratus's second daughter seems to have followed her sister into Cydathenaeum, by being given in marriage to Eryximachus, son of Eryxias, of Cydathenaeum (Dem. 40.24; IG II² 3063).[35] The daughters' mother married outside her deme of origin and kin group, but one of her daughters may have been married within the kin group, and both daughters were married into her deme of origin.

The marriage of both daughters into Cydathenaeum occurred contemporaneously with their mother's attempts to acquire some of her brother's estate away from his adopted son, Dicaeogenes III (Is. 5.5 ff.). There is a chance as well that some of this property lay in Cydathenaeum itself.[36] To backtrack, Dicaeogenes II had adopted Dicaeogenes III, a son or grandson of his father's sister, but the adoption was contested by his own sisters, their husbands, and their children. By way of compromise, Dicaeogenes III's natural father, the Gephyraeus Proxenus II, may have agreed that his son receive only one-third of Dicaeogenes II's estate, with the latter's sisters receiving the bulk of the estate. This arrangement did defy Athenian law which stipulated that the adopted son inherited all the prop-

---

[34] See Is. 5.5 and Davies, *APF,* 461 for Polyaratus's marriage; [Dem.] 40.24 and Davies, *APF,* 319 for Cleomedon's marriage; for the following discussion, see Cox, "Sisters," 186–87.

[35] See also Davies, *APF,* 462–64.

[36] On the mother's dispute with Dicaeogenes III, see Davies, *APF,* 146; ibid., 476–77, for Dicaeogenes III's relationship to Dicaeogenes II; Osborne, *Demos,* 48, suggests that some of Dicaeogenes II's property lay in Cydathenaeum.

erty of his adoptive father (ibid., 5–6).[37] When he reached his majority, however, Dicaeogenes III challenged this arrangement and, indeed, won back the whole estate. This turn of events was then challenged by Dicaeogenes II's sisters and their sons, and particularly by Polyaratus's wife (ibid., 9 ff.).

We cannot see all the logistics of deme association and its influence on a demesman's property, although Osborne has done a good deal to illuminate the role of demesmen and the workings of deme politics and social networks. What I wish to stress here is how demesmen could be appealed to when an estate of one of them was in dispute; for this, [Demosthenes] 44 is an essential source.[38] In the Demosthenic oration, Meidylides of Otryna, who had married outside his kin group to a woman from Crioa, wished to give his only child, a daughter, to his brother Archiades. The brother refused the offer, and the daughter was given in marriage to a nonkinsman, Aristotle of Pallene. The sister of Meidylides and Archiades had also married out to a Leostratus of Eleusis, whose daughter then married a demesman from Eleusis, who was perhaps a kinsman of her father ([Dem.] 44.13, 17, 21).[39] The son from this union, Leocrates, was then adopted by Archiades into his estate.

One may well wonder how these families met. As with any of the families in this chapter, political activities, business, or war could have provided an opportunity for meeting but interests in locale cannot be dismissed. Although the location of Otryna is unknown, but assigned tentatively to the city trittys of Aegeis,[40] Meidylides and his family were certainly domiciled in the city (ibid., 18); in fact, his grandson was employed in the Peiraeus as a herald (ibid., 4, 10). City residence therefore allowed the alliance with the family from Eleusis, a deme which was quite accessible to the city. Furthermore, the speaker states that, after Meidylides had attempted to contract an alliance for his daughter with his own brother, Archiades, the latter refused and retired to Salamis (ibid., 10, 18). Presumably, Archiades owned some property on this island which lay offshore from Eleusis and the Peiraeus.[41]

Once Leocrates was adopted into Archiades' estate, he sired a natural son, left that son in the estate, and returned to his native deme, Eleusis. Leocrates' son, Leostratus, did the same, leaving his natural son, Leocrates II. When the latter died without issue, however, Leostratus tried to have himself reenrolled into Archiades' estate, and, as a first step, he appealed to the demesmen of Otryna, including the demarch, to reenlist him into their deme. (Leostratus's ultimate goal was to have another son, Leochares, replace Leocrates II in Archiades' estate.)[42]

[37] Wyse, *Isaeus,* 414; on the adoptee's right to inherit the full estate, see Harrison, *Law,* 1:95–96.

[38] Osborne's discussion of this oration concentrates on how the family in the Demosthenic oration married far and wide: *Demos,* 134–35, although the disparateness of these demes is not altogether certain. See below, note 40.

[39] See also Davies, *APF,* 194–95.

[40] Traill, *Demos,* 127. If the assignment indicates location, which is not always the case, then Otryna, as part of the city cluster of Aegeis in the northeastern plain, would have lain close to Pallene. Crioa has also been assigned to the city trittys of Antiochis, but, again, its location is unknown: Traill, *Demos,* map.

It becomes obvious during the course of the oration, however, that the Otrynians, including the demarch, clearly preferred the Eleusinian branch, a preference encouraged by bribery, if the speaker can be believed. The Otrynians were prepared not only to enrol Leostratus back into their deme, but even to reinstate him as the heir. They held back only when it was pointed out to them that the estate was under dispute in court (ibid., 39 ff.).

To judge from the Demosthenic oration, deme membership was an advantage in assuming control of an individual's estate, no matter where that estate lay. Therefore, in the case of Polyaratus, his repeated alliances into his wife's deme, which were contemporary with his wife's interest in the estate of her brother, Dicaeogenes II, are understandable: the marriage alliances to two prominent men of Cydathenaeum would presumably enable influence to be exerted in the deme and would put heirs back into the deme of a family whose estate was contested.

After the death of Polyaratus's son-in-law, Cleomedon, Polyaratus's daughter was given in marriage to Mantias of Thorikos, who has been made famous by Demosthenes 39 and 40 as the paramour of Plango and who, according to his son, was a poor businessman (39.25). One may well wonder why Polyaratus's daughter was given in marriage to such a man.[43] However, the mining activities of Mantias and his descendants in south Attica are well attested, and Mantias may well have been a close associate of Timotheus, the general, and the latter's son, Conon III (40.39).[44] Timotheus' and his son's deme, Anaphlystus, and that of Mantias, Thoricus, lay in south Attica. This was the region where Polyaratus's affines, the Gephyraei, were contracting marriages, in one case, into Anaphlystus, and in the other, into Poros, which was, possibly, in Mantias's trittys. Given these maneuvers, the marriage of Cleomedon's widow makes some sense.[45]

[41] Davies, in his discussion of this family, missed a grave stele that dates to the fourth century and which was found at Laurium. It depicts a young armed man leading a horse. The inscription, *IG* II² 7016, reads simply Λεωκράτης Οτρυνεύς. (Catalogued by G. Kokula, *Marmorlutrophoren AM,* suppl. 10 (Berlin: Gebr. Mann, 1984), 153, no. L6, without prosopographical comment.) Given the youthfulness of the male figure, the *loutrophoros,* which is depicted on the stone, may suggest that Leocrates died unmarried. It would be very tempting to associate the deceased here with the younger Leocrates who had been adopted posthumously into Archiades' estate, but who died without issue. The fact that the stone was found at Laurium adds yet a further dimension to this otherwise shadowy family from Eleusis. See now C. A. Cox, "The Names of Adoptees: Some Prosopographical Afterthoughts," *ZPE* 107 (1995): 251–52.

[42] Davies, *APF,* 194–96, for a discussion of this family's machinations. The appeal to the demarch may suggest that at least some of the property lay in the deme of Otryna. For the demarch as a local figure, see Osborne, *Demos,* 83–87. D. Whitehead, *The Demes of Attica 508/7–ca. 250 B.C.* (Princeton, N.J.: Princeton University Press, 1986), 121 ff., emphasizes that the demarch was the local link with the larger polis.

[43] Davies, *APF,* 366.

[44] Conon III served as a private arbitrator in the dispute between Mantitheus and Boeotus; see also Davies, *APF,* 511.

[45] Recently, D. Rankin, "The Mining Lobby at Athens," *AncSoc* 19 (1989): 201, has suggested that Polyaratus and Mantias were oligarchic sympathizers, a movement supported by mining families who suffered heavily during the latter part of the Peloponnesian War.

Other propertied families with interests in the mines forged kinship links in south Attica. The tyrant Critias's descendants, if not he himself, had mining interests in south Attica; Critias's sister seems to have married Hagnodorus of Amphitrope in south Attica (Lys. 13.55).[46] So also, Nausicles of Oe, who was active in the mining district, seems to have been adopted by a family from Aegilia, in south Attica.[47]

This long discussion of Dicaeogenes' kin group and affines has pointed out the connection between property holdings and demes of (prospective) in-laws. In other families, mining activities seem to have led to marital or adoptive ties with families in demes of south Attica. Once nonkinsmen had been absorbed into the kin group, these relationships could be reaffirmed by kinship endogamy, by adoption, or by repeated alliances into the native deme or into the deme of one's affines. In these maneuvers, although the disparateness of the demes involved may be at first glaring, on closer examination, the alliances reflect a consolidation of interests in a locale or several locales in Attica.

THE FAMILY OF DEMOSTHENES

For the Bouselidae and Dicaeogenes' group, the discussion has centered on interests in demes assigned to coastal trittyes, in the northern plain and in south Attica. There was another prominent family, that of the orator Demosthenes, which was domiciled in the city, with interests certainly in the northern plain, and which made use of social networks in the Mesogeia, the central region of Attica. More will be said in chapters 3 and 4 on the relationships which developed in this family resulting from the will of the elder Demosthenes, the orator's father. This present section will focus on how marriage strategies and inheritance reflect the elder Demosthenes' use of social networks in his deme and in a deme close to it. Aphobus, the younger Demosthenes' enemy, made use of a kinsman who was Demosthenes' demesman. Although the elder Demosthenes came from a rural deme his residence in the city encouraged urban interests and led him to ally with city families. This section will also detail the marriage strategies of the elder Demosthenes' affine Demochares (his wife's sister's husband), who allied with a man whose land lay close to Demochares' deme.

Demosthenes the Elder, although earning most of his income from his workshops in the Peiraeus, was from the rural deme of Paeania and gave his sister in marriage to Mnesibulus of Sphettus ca. 406; Sphettus was close to Paeania. On the other hand, sometime in the 390s, the elder Demosthenes married Cleoboule, the daughter of Gylon of Cerameis, a city deme (Dem. 28.1–3; Aeschin. 3.171–72; Plut. *Dem.* 4.2; [Plut.] *Mor.* 844a; Dem. 27 *hyp.* 1).[48] On his

[46] See also Davies, *APF,* 327.

[47] Ibid., 397; Rankin, "Mining Lobby," 193–94 (Nausicles), 201–2 (Critias).

[48] See also Davies, *APF,* 120–21.

deathbed, the elder Demosthenes willed his widow to his sister's son, Aphobus, and his daughter to his brother's son, Demophon (Dem. 27.4–6, 28.15 ff., 29.31). Aphobus and Demophon also were assigned guardianship of the younger Demosthenes and his sister, thus the elder Demosthenes' marriage outside his kin group was intended to be followed by the unions of both his widow and daughter with his kinsmen. Significantly, the third guardian of the estate was a good friend of the elder man and a fellow demesman, Therippides of Paeania (Dem. 27.4, 12–49, 28.12–16, 29.6, 33, 43–45; [Plut.] *Mor.* 844c). Although these facts are well known, what has not been pointed out is how important Demosthenes' deme may have been for the network formed by Aphobus. In the end, Aphobus did not marry Demosthenes' mother, but rather the sister of Onetor of Melite, who may have had a collateral relative, Onetor, in Paeania, Demosthenes' deme (*IG* II^2 1616.69).[49]

Although the intended endogamous union of the elder Demosthenes's widow with his sister's son and that of his daughter with his brother's son in fact never transpired, it is obvious that with the crisis of the testator's impending death, he turned to two agnates, a brother and a sister, to share in his wealth through marriage (Dem. 27.45). In fact, because the elder Demosthenes' wife, Cleoboule, was the daughter of a traitor, he could well have been responsible for paying some of the debts incurred by his wife's father; in this case he must have turned to the children of his brother and sister to help conceal the full value of his estate.[50] Significantly, although the orator's sister was never given in marriage to her cousin, Demophon, she was finally given to her mother's sister's son, Laches, a public act acknowledging the fact that Laches' father, Demochares, had tried to protect the children's estate against its embezzlement by Aphobus and Demophon (27.14–15). In other words, the marriage through the matriline in this case was a last resort; agnates and their children proved to be rivals.

Little can be said in the elder Demosthenes' case about his landholdings: although he may have had a landed estate, and Aphobus certainly did, the location of these properties is not known.[51] For Demochares, however, the interplay of deme location and landed wealth is a little more apparent. Demochares

---

[49] See also Davies, *APF,* 426.

[50] Davies, *APF,* 128–31; V. Hunter, "Women's Authority in Classical Athens," *EMC* 33 (1989): 40 and n.7.

[51] Davies, *APF,* 135, is not certain of the validity of Deinarchus's statement about Demosthenes' landed estate (1.69) because the land does not appear in the list of property in Demosthenes' orations. Deinarchus, however, does claim that Demosthenes sold off this estate. As Davies himself admits, Demosthenes would not want to own visible property; there is always the possibility that if such land existed, the "sale" was a friendly takeover. For Aphobus's landed estate, see ibid., 119–20. The estate was seized by his brother-in-law, Onetor, in payment for the return of a dowry that Onetor had never given Aphobus. The seizure of the property by Onetor, upon Aphobus's fake divorce from Onetor's sister, was a ruse to prevent Demosthenes from laying claim to the property. For further discussion of the assistance of brothers-in-law, see below, chapter 4. For the "friendly" sale and takeover, see Osborne, *Demos,* 1–3 and "Law in Action in Classical Athens," *JHS* 105 (1985): 45.

gave his daughter to a Lycomid from Phlya, who held land in that deme. Because Demochares' deme was Leuconoeum, possibly a city deme in the northwestern section of the plain, Demochares gave his daughter in marriage to a man owning property in the north Athenian plain and approximately eight to nine kilometers from his own deme.[52] After this marriage to a nonkinsman ended, Demochares' daughter then returned to her deme by being given in marriage to a fellow demesman, perhaps a kinsman, of her father.[53]

The evidence indicates, then, that the elder Demosthenes's deme, Paeania, was rural but his interests lay both in the city and in his own deme in the Mesogeia, and in one close to Paeania, Sphettus. Although he married into a city family, he gave his sister in marriage to a man from Sphettus, and the son from this union, Aphobus, then became one of the guardians of his estate. Although Aphobus intended to marry the elder Demosthenes's widow, he ended up marrying the sister of a man who had a relative in the elder Demosthenes' deme.

For Demosthenes' affine, Demochares, propinquity was likewise important: Demochares' interests reveal expansion into a deme close to his own, but his daughter's marriage out was then followed by a return to the native deme and a marriage, possibly, within the kin group.

To what extent do other families in the orations reveal interests in the Mesogeia and the northern plain? To get some sense of this, let us turn to some families who were from inland demes or owned property in the inland regions of Attica: the families of Deinias of Athmonon, of Ciron and of Euctemon for the northern inland region, and the family of the speaker of Lysias 19 for the Mesogeia.

DEINIAS OF ATHMONON

Interest in the matrilineal deme of origin, brother-sister ties and strong brother-in-law ties mark the practices of Deinias of Athmonon and his affines, the family of a very wealthy banker, Pasio. Despite Pasio's city residence and the location of his bank in the Peiraeus,[54] his son's interest in their rural holdings is evident.

Around 395 Deinias's sister was married to Menecles of Acharnae, the deme into which Pasio was enrolled when he acquired Athenian citizenship.[55] A son, Stephanus, was born from this marriage, who would later become the agent of Phormio, Pasio's manager and guardian of his estate. It was this association with the banking family that probably allowed Stephanus to give his own daughter in

---

[52] Finley, *SLC,* 160, no. 146; *IG* II² 6737a, p. 891; Davies, *APF,* 142.

[53] Davies, *APF,* 142.

[54] Ibid., 431.

[55] Ibid., 430, on Pasio's enrollment in Acharnae; on the marriage of Deinias's sister, see Dem. 45.46, 54; Davies, *APF,* 437–38.

marriage with the very large dowry of 1 talent 40 minae. Deinias, c. 365, then gave his daughter to Pasio's son Apollodorus (Dem. 45.55; [Dem.] 59.2, 8),[56] so that the daughter followed her paternal aunt into the deme of Acharnae, a variation of the strategy in Polyaratus's family, in which a sister followed her sister into the deme of marriage.

After Deinias's daughter followed his sister into Acharnae, his son Theomnestus married his own sister's daughter by Apollodorus ([Dem.] 59.2–3),[57] thereby bringing the daughter back into her mother's deme of origin, Athmonon. It is uncertain what role the proximity of demes played in these unions: the center of Deinias's and Theomnestus's deme, Athmonon, was approximately six kilometers from that of Acharnae, and Pasio seems to have had an estate in or near Acharnae, which was the residence of Apollodorus after Pasio's death.[58] The sources do not reveal, however, to what extent Deinias and his son resided in their deme of origin or whether they owned land there, and therefore whether consolidation of property in this area of Attica was a concern. We do know, however, that kinship exogamy was balanced with endogamy: the out-marriage of Deinias's daughter, which allied the family to the very wealthy Pasio, was followed by the endogamous union of her daughter, a union that allowed Theomnestus and Apollodorus to share each other's wealth ([Dem.] 59.2). As Theomnestus himself declared: "Because Apollodorus was honorable, and useful [ὄντος δὲ χρηστοῦ] toward my sister and us all, and thought that we who were his kinsmen had a share in all that he owned, I took to wife the daughter of Apollodorus, my own niece." Perhaps the fact that the two families could share their wealth so easily implies that they were neighbors.[59] Because they did so, Theomnestus was close to his brother-in-law and eventually prosecuted one of Apollodorus's political enemies, Stephanus (not a relative), who had threatened Apollodorus with a fifteen-talent fine ([Dem.] 59.1–6).

In this family, then, the sister of Deinias of Athmonon married a man from a neighboring deme, Acharnae. The marriage then allowed her son to become the agent of the guardian of Pasio's estate, Pasio being also enrolled in that deme. Deinias's daughter followed her paternal aunt into Acharnae by her marriage to Pasio's son, Apollodorus. The union was then reinforced by the marriage of her brother Theomnestus to her daughter. In this way, kinswoman followed kinswoman into the deme of their marriage and then another kinswoman was sent back to the original deme. The marriage of Theomnestus was endogamous both in terms of kinship and locale and allowed both families to share their wealth.

---

[56] See also Davies, *APF,* 437–38.

[57] See also Davies, *APF,* 437.

[58] Davies, *APF,* 431.

[59] T. W. Gallant, *Risk and Survival in Ancient Greece* (Stanford, Calif.: Stanford University Press, 1991), 150, describing Sahlins's model, which Gallant modifies. The model maintains that such reciprocity between equals, who are bound by kinship and/or affective ties, is often based upon geographical proximity.

Relationships among neighbors who were also in-laws were not always so close and harmonious, as the next examples show.

CIRON AND EUCTEMON

Ciron alternated kinship endogamy with exogamy by marrying first his mother's sister's daughter, with whom he sired a daughter, and then, after his first wife's death, a nonkinswoman, the sister of Diocles of Phlya,[60] where the bulk of his estate lay (Is. 8.7,35). Although it is possible that Ciron's deme was Phlya or one close to it,[61] this is not certain. Rather, Ciron's alliance with an individual from a deme where his own estate lay is one among several strategies for the families of the orations. Furthermore, Ciron's daughter, in her first marriage, was married to Nausimenes of Cholargus, a deme of the northern plain whose center was approximately eight kilometers west of Phlya. For her second marriage, the daughter was married to a man from the deme Pithus, which may have belonged to the same trittys as Phlya (7–8, 19).[62] Thus, there is some indication that proximity of demes and the location of Ciron's estate were the bases for his marital practices, despite his residence in the city (Is. 8.35).[63] The marriages then should have been a means to consolidate Ciron's holdings in the local, rural area.[64]

However, Ciron abandoned his descendants through his mother's sister's daughter and preferred to let the brother of his second wife manage his estate (35 ff.). Ciron's kinship endogamy followed by exogamy seems to indicate an interest in looking outside his mother's affinal kin group and placing his trust in a nonkinsman, who was, nevertheless, a neighbor. This tie with the neighbor was supported by Ciron's agnate, his brother's son. Isaeus 8 reveals that Ciron seems to have preferred his sons by his second wife as his heirs, but when these died his second wife's brother, Diocles, supported the claim of Ciron's brother's son to the estate (1 ff.). Furthermore, Diocles seems to have been able to encroach on Ciron's estate by having his sister, Ciron's second wife, remain in Ciron's house after the death of Ciron's sons by her. The woman, in fact, with little chance of bearing the aging Ciron another son, nevertheless remained with Ciron until his death (36 ff.). Male agnate and brother-in-law colluded to keep Ciron's grandson out of his estate, a grandson descended ultimately from a different patriline.

[60] Davies, *APF,* 313.

[61] Osborne, *Demos,* 49.

[62] See also Davies, *APF,* 314–15. For Traill's hesitation on the exact location of Pithus, see *Demos,* 135, and 136, n.34.

[63] It is difficult to say whether both Ciron and Diocles, Ciron's brother-in-law, resided in the city. The temple leases do record Diocles' son, Polemon, renting property from Athena Polias in Cydathenaeum: Davies, *APF,* 314; M. Walbank, "Leases of Sacred Properties in Attica," *Hesperia* 52 (1983): 124–25.

[64] Osborne, *Demos,* 49, 62–63, for the propensity of Athenians to acquire or build up holdings in the local area.

Ciron's is not the only case in which marriage strategies incorporating the demesman failed. Euctemon of Cephisia is well known to us from Isaeus 6. Although he owned three houses in the city, two of which served as brothels, his marriage to a fellow demeswoman and his daughter's marriage to a fellow demesman betray interests in the native deme; because Euctemon owned a farm in the neighboring deme of Athmonon, local endogamy secured this property (Is. 6.33).[65] In fact, Philoctemon, Euctemon's son, adopted as his future heir the son of his sister, and, therefore, a fellow demesman. When Euctemon, however, informed Philoctemon that he, Euctemon, intended to give one of his estates to his sons by another wife, Philoctemon protested (22–24) and, presumably, would not recognize the legitimacy of his younger half-brothers. Philoctemon relented only when his father threatened to marry the sister of Democrates of Aphidna, a Gephyraeus. Democrates was still resident, occasionally at least, in his native deme which was located around fifteen kilometers from Euctemon's deme, Cephisia.[66] Therefore, in order to settle his dispute with his son, Euctemon resorted to the aid of someone who was outside the immediate rural neighborhood but in the northern region of Attica and who was still resident there from time to time. In general, Euctemon, despite his residence and businesses in the city, focused either on the upper northern plain where his farm lay or in northern Attica.[67] Regional bias occurs fairly frequently in the marriages of the Athenians recorded in the inscriptions, which will be examined in the next chapter. On the other hand, the urban neighborhood also encouraged Euctemon's ties to the Gephyraei: Euctemon owned a lodging house in the Cerameicus, where one branch of the Gephyraei may have been resident.[68]

These examples reveal only too clearly that kinsmen and neighbors could

[65] See also Davies, *APF*, 562–63.

[66] Davies, *APF*, 475–76, for Democrates' residency in Aphidna.

[67] Raphael Sealey was the first to point out Euctemon's regional bias, though Sealey did underestimate the distance between Cephisia and Aphidna: R. Sealey, *Essays in Greek Politics* (New York: Manyland, 1967), 189–90. Euctemon's threat worked, and he did not marry Democrates' sister; she was given in marriage to, probably, Nicandrus from Halae Aexonides (*IG* II² 5733), a coastal deme south of the city and on a clear route between the city and south Attica, where other Gephyraei contracted marriages. The inscription (5733) shows Archedice, the daughter of Democles of Aphidna, buried with Aristoboule, the daughter of Nicandrus of Halae. Because the stone was found at Vari, Archedice clearly migrated to, and resided in, the vicinity of Halae. I have inferred that Aristoboule on the inscription is Archedice's daughter. Davies (*APF*, 475–76) has left the relationship open.

[68] Davies, *APF*, 562, for Euctemon's house. Davies conjectures that Hegeso, the daughter of Proxenus, who was commemorated on a *naiskos* in the Cerameicus, was the daughter of Proxenus I of Aphidna. If so, either her family of origin was resident in or near the Cerameicus, or the family of Cleidemides I of Melite, into which Hegeso may have married, was resident there: Davies, *APF*, 478–79, is silent on the issue of Hegeso's marriage, but see R. Garland, "A First Catalogue of Attic Peribolos Tombs," *ABSA* 77 (1982): 142, for the conjectured marriage. Garland, however, does not posit a connection between Hegeso and the Gephyraei. If Davies's stemma is valid, then Proxenus I's mother (or wife) was the daughter of Dicaeogenes I, whose kin group owned a *synoikia* in the Cerameicus: Davies, *APF*, 145–46, 476–77.

quarrel and that marriages that were meant to consolidate ties and property were not necessarily successful.[69] Ciron balanced exogamy and endogamy by first marrying a mother's sister's daughter and then by marrying the sister of a non-kinsman who was, however, a rural neighbor. But the neighbor encroached on Ciron's estate and eased out Ciron's descendants through the matriline. In Euctemon's case, he married the daughter of one fellow demesman and gave his daughter to another. Nevertheless, Euctemon divorced his wife and married a nonkinswoman; these actions set him in conflict whith his son. Marriage strategies, therefore, with their implicit goal of consolidation in the rural neighborhood, did not always do what they were intended to do.

THE FAMILY IN LYSIAS 19

In the discussion so far, little has been said of the fertile Mesogeia and families with interests there. For this the discussion turns to the individuals known to us from Lysias 19. With the family of the speaker of Lysias 19 and its association with Conon, we have a group of people who were very wealthy and who moved in the circles of the political elite. In this case, therefore, politics had a great deal to do with the formation of marriage ties, but it was politics not totally divorced from ties at the local level.

There is a good chance that the anonymous speaker of Lysias 19 and his father, whose name is also unknown but who was a close friend of Conon, were from the deme of Myrrhinous. The father's nephew Phaedrus, was from that deme; if Phaedrus was a brother's son of the speaker's father, the speaker and his father were from Myrrhinous (Plat. *Phaedr.* 244a, *Conviv.* 176d, *Protag.* 315c; Lys. 19.15).[70]

The marriage alliances of this family centered on the Mesogeia. Although the speaker's father married a woman from the city deme of Melite (the daughter of Xenophon, the son of Euripides), the speaker's sisters married men whose demes were in the Mesogeia, Philomelus of Paeania and Phaedrus of Myrrhinous. Phaedrus was probably his wife's first cousin; he leased some land in his native deme, Myrrhinous, and owned a house in the city. He may be identified as well with the Phaedrus who was a friend of Socrates and suffered political disgrace as a result of the affair of the mutilation of the herms in 415, so that his marriage to his first cousin c. 404 was a gesture of kinship consolidation during a time of political disgrace.[71] Here too, then, the father's exogamous union was followed by his daughter's endogamous one.

As for Philomelus of Paeania, the speaker's second brother-in-law, although

---

[69] Gallant, *Risk,* 158, on neighbor as foe, although some of the references cited by Gallant do not reveal clearly the role of the neighbor.

[70] See also Davies, *APF,* 200–201.

[71] For Phaedrus's exile, see And. 1.15; Davies, *APF,* 200–201.

the nature and location of his property are unknown, the connection with Paeania is repeated in the next generation. The speaker himself married the daughter of Critodemus of Alopece. This Critodemus had a son, Aristomachus, who sent his (Aristomachus's) daughter into the deme of Paeania to marry Diodorus of that deme (Lys. 19.16).[72] Although Diodorus was known for his mining activity, the findspot of his gravestone, which also records the death of his wife, at Liopesi (*IG* II² 7040), suggests that Diodorus owned some property in this area of the Mesogeia around Paeania and that the couple resided there. Therefore, the marriages contracted by the speaker of Lysias 19 and his father reflect both interests in the city, where Phaedrus owned a house, and in the Mesogeia where this family's deme seems to have been located. Interest in the Mesogeia was sustained by the marriage of two sisters and by the speaker's brother-in-law.

Deme associations in Myrrhinous also appear to be operating in the northern plain. Phaedrus, the brother-in-law and cousin of the speaker of Lysias 19, was a member of the Socratic circle. His fellow demesman Eurymedon of Myrrhinous was married to Potone, Plato's sister. Given that Eurymedon's homonymous son or grandson, named as one of Plato's heirs, held a landed estate bordering on that of Plato in the deme of Eiresidae, it is quite possible that this land had belonged to Potone's husband; therefore, Plato and his brother-in-law were neighbors.[73] If the reconstruction is correct, Plato, from Collytus, was a neighbor in the northern plain of a man from the distant deme of Myrrhinous: this proximity of landed estates then facilitated the executorship of Plato's estate by his sister's son, Speusippus, in the next generation.[74]

Perhaps the chapter is still not closed on the local element in Conon's political networks. Eurippides, the son of Adeimantus, also of Myrrhinous, was an

[72] See also Davies, *APF,* 61–62.

[73] Diog. Laert. 3.42–43; Davies, *APF,* 334. The above discussion is similar to that in Cox, "Sisters," 187–88.

[74] Davies, *APF,* 334. Andocides' kin group may have practiced similar maneuvers, which link the city to the Mesogeia. Andocides' deme was in the city, Cydathenaeum. It is possible that his father's father, however, had married a woman from Steiria c. 470 (And. 1.47; Davies, *APF,* 30, 329). If so, then the marriage of Andocides' sister to Callias, son of Telocles, to judge from the rare name Telocles, may have been a marriage to a fellow demesman in Cydathenaeum, or may have been an alliance with a man in Angele or Myrrhinous, both of which belonged to the same trittys as Steiria (Davies, *APF,* 30, 253–54). In other words, Andocides' kin group may have sent two women in marriage to the vicinity of Steiria; their affines, in turn, sent a woman into the city family of Andocides, by having her marry the orator's father's father. Her descendant, Andocides' sister, went back into a family whose deme was close to Steiria. The urban neighborhood facilitated the alliance between two groups who were quite possibly from disparate demes: Andocides and his father lived close to the smithy and house of Callias, son of Telocles, in the *astu* (And. 1.39ff). The family of Nicias the general focused on the eastern section of the Mesogeia as well. The sister of Andocides' brother-in-law, Callias, had married Nicias's brother, Eucrates of Cydantidae. Eucrates' brother's son, Nicias II, married into the vicinity of Angele and Myrrhinous, by marrying the daughter of Thrasybulus of Steiria: Dem. 19.290; Davies, *APF,* 240–41, 404–6.

ambassador to Sicily under the aegis of Conon in 393.[75] Another ambassador with Eurippides was Aristophanes, the son of Nicophemus of unknown deme who, at the insistence of Conon c. 393, became the second husband of Phaedrus's widow, the sister of the speaker in Lysias 19 (7 ff.).[76] Aristophanes held land at Rhamnous, the deme into which Timotheus, the son of Conon, sent his daughter in marriage. Timotheus's daughter married Menestheus, the son of Iphicrates of Rhamnous, c. 362. Because Menestheus and his father had patrilineal kinsmen residing in the deme of Rhamnous in the fourth century (IG II² 7341; [Dem.] 49.66),[77] Iphicrates' kin group still had some property and interests in the local deme.

Thus the members of the family of Lysias 19, who were associates of Conon and were possibly from Myrrhinous, alternated kinship exogamy with endogamy: the father's exogamous union was followed by his daughter's marriage to her first cousin who was from Myrrhinous and who leased land there. Another daughter was given in marriage to a man from Paeania; her brother's brother-in-law sent his daughter into Paeania as well. As for other fellow demesmen and associates of the family of Lysias 19, Eurymedon of Myrrhinous married Plato's sister and was probably a landed neighbor of the philosopher. Conon's associate Aristophanes son of Nicophemus, the brother-in-law of the speaker of Lysias 19, held land at Rhamnous where Timotheus, Conon's son, sent his daughter to a family whose kinsmen still resided in Rhamnous.

These families, from the highest political and economic stratum, with their prestige in Athens and their many ties in Greece and abroad, must have taken many considerations into account when contracting their marriages, but Conon's use of social networks in Rhamnous and Myrrhinous reveals the interplay between local and national, material and political.

A RECONSIDERATION OF THE NEIGHBOR

Osborne has given us a valuable foundation on which to understand social networks in the deme; one of the obvious ways of networking is through marriage. The fellow demesman could be very useful in the formation of kinship ties; the case studies above revealing the use of fellow demesmen are built upon Osborne's discussion and serve to add to it. But the focus here is not just on the fellow

---

[75] Arist. *Rhet.* 1384b15 and scholia; Lys. 19.19f; Davies, *APF,* 202–3. The homonymity of several individuals from Myrrhinous and Plato's family should be noted: the father of Eurippides and Plato's brother had the same name, Adeimantus: Davies, *APF,* 202, 332. The grandson of Plato's brother, another of Plato's heirs, was also given the name Adeimantus. Furthermore, the father of the speaker of Lysias 19 had married the granddaughter (son's daughter) of a Euripides of Melite (Lys. 19.14; *APF,* 199–200). There may be some collateral kinship at play here much like the case of Onetor and Aphobus discussed above.

[76] See also Davies, *APF,* 201–2, for the marriage.

[77] See Davies, *APF,* 250–51, for the marriage and Menestheus's agnates.

demesman: a family can contract a series of marriages into a deme to which the owner of a contested estate belongs; at times a piece of land of the contested estate lies in a deme into which interested kin will maritally ally. At times families will ally with members of a deme close to the estate in question. At times individuals from proximate demes will marry. Or landowners with neighboring plots of land contract marriage alliances, or neighbors in an urban quarter strike up an alliance. In some of this, one may find individuals from disparate demes allying, but at other times there is a focus on the rural deme, either despite urban residence or in conjunction with it. The location of the native deme can be important, but is not always so, in the consolidation of proximate holdings.

Of what use were neighbors and fellow demesmen? Again, Osborne has done a great deal to enlighten us here—neighbors performed services for each other and looked after each others' property when one of them was away. As a consequence, therefore, neighbors could have detailed knowledge of the value of their neighbor's property and how they used or abused it.[78] According to Plutarch, when Themistocles was considering selling part of his estate, he announced that the buyer would have him as a useful neighbor (*Them.* 18.5). The historicity of the remark is not important; the attitude is, of course, indicative of classical views of the helpful neighbor.[79]

Demesmen had knowledge of property held both by each other and by non-demesmen within the borders of their deme.[80] One overlooked example outside of the orations is the statement of Demetrius of Phalerum to the effect that Aristeides the statesman, who was from Alopece, had an estate in Phalerum and was buried there. The reference to burial in Phalerum, though contradicting the tradition about Aristeides' poverty, would suggest that Demetrius knew about activities in his deme (Plut. *Arist.* 1.2, 27.1). Whether an individual owned land in his deme or not, his fellow demesmen voted on membership in his *oikos*—a crucial step if adoption had led to a quarrel among members of the testator's extended kin group.[81] Nor can we assume that the demesmen would look more favorably on a fellow demesman's claim to an *oikos* within their deme: the non-demesman could hope to find support—through bribery, as in the case of Pseudo-Demosthenes 44, according to the speaker, but also through well-placed marital alliances into the deme.

Having discussed in detail how social networks focusing on a region or deme were formed and manipulated, we now turn briefly to the means whereby the newly acquired affine maintained and reaffirmed ties with his kinsmen of ori-

---

[78] Osborne, *Demos,* 146; [Dem.] 43.70, discussed above. For further examples of the use of the neighbor, see below, chapter 6.

[79] Walbank maintains that families even of lower strata, when renting property, would at times try to take over neighboring land: "Leases," 224–25.

[80] For instance: [Dem.] 50.8; Is. 9.16–18; V. Gabrielsen, "ΦΑΝΕΡΑ and ΑΦΑΝΗΣ ΟΥΣΙΑ in Classical Athens," *ClMed* 37 (1986): 113.

[81] See the discussion of [Dem.] 44 above, to which add Is. 7.27–28.

gin and those by his marriage. Frequently, the endogamous union would help to maintain ties with the kin group of origin, but adoption, combined with endogamy, could also be a strong means of consolidation.

MARRYING IN AND ADOPTING OUT

The marriage strategies discussed above attest to the frequent use of kinship endogamy after the expansion of ties through marriages with nonkinsmen. In several of these cases marriage alliances were reinforced by adoption. What emerges with great regularity is the use of the neighbor, whether a fellow demesman or someone from a nearby or even a distant deme. Let us summarize here those adoptions which followed marriages to a neighbor. Themistocles, from Phrearrhii, married into a city family of Alopece; the adoption of his son into that family was facilitated by Themistocles' residence in Melite (see appendix, pp. 217–18). Among the Bouselidae and their affines, Theophon adopted Stratocles' daughter; Stratocles held landed property close to that of Theophon. As well, Hagnias adopted his niece, who was, perhaps, the daughter of his matrilineal half-brother of the same deme. Perhaps, as well, Sositheus was drawn into the Bouselidae and his son adopted by a Bouselid because Bouselid property lay in Araphen, which was either his deme or that of a relative. Araphen was at some distance, however, from Oeum Cerameicum, the deme of the Bouselidae. Adoption and intermarrying linked the Gephyraei with Dicaeogenes' kin group: both lines, although from distant demes, appear to have owned property, or resided, in the Cerameicus and, perhaps, owned land in the northern plain. Callisto's father, an Eteoboutad from Boutadae, adopted his daughter's son, whose own deme was Acharnae, but who held property in Lousia, a neighboring deme to Boutadae. Philoctemon depended on a fellow demesman, his sister's son, as a potential heir. The kin group in Pseudo-Demosthenes 44 from Otryna marrying into, and adopting an heir from, a family in Eleusis may have formed this association because of its urban residence and because of the residence of one kinsman on Salamis. For completeness's sake, if Traill is correct in his intriguing suggestion that Phaenippus's farm in Pseudo-Demosthenes 42 was the amalgamation of both estates which Phaenippus had inherited, his paternal estate and the estate of his maternal grandfather into which he had been adopted, then Phaenippus was the son of parents who held neighboring estates at Cytherus.[82] Further, although Phaenippus's deme is not known, his mother's deme was Colonae—both demes of that name were quite distant from Cytherus.[83] In all of the above listed adoptions for which we have any information, the adoptee was selected through

---

[82] Traill, *Demos,* 48.

[83] Davies, *APF,* 552–53 for the woman's deme. Davies, however, presumes that both estates were distinct. On the demes of Colonae, see Traill, *Demos,* 131 (Leontis), 139 (Antiochis, but assigned to the city trittys).

the female line; the adoptee is chosen from a line outside the adopter's male agnatic line but within his sphere of residence or activity. This adoption practice indicates that marital ties were originally formed on the basis of propinquity—spouses were not wandering far to marry.[84]

How then did a kin group react when one of its own was adopted out? In Themistocles' case, after the adoption of his son into his father-in-law's, Lysander's, *oikos*, his two children by two different wives married, while another daughter married her father's brother's son (see appendix, p. 218). Although these endogamous unions occurred at the time of Themistocles' disgrace and, therefore, could have been prompted by it as well,[85] the case of Sositheus shows that endogamy followed adoption out without the threat of political disgrace: after Sositheus had his youngest son adopted into the estate of his wife's father, Sositheus's daughter married his brother's son. A patriline, then, would practise endogamy as a response to the adoption out of one of its members.

In other cases, however, the adoptee, although adopted out of the patriline, will himself (herself) marry back into the patriline, or a direct descendant will do so. For instance, according to Thompson's reconstruction, Glaucus of Oeum had his daughter adopted by his matrilineal half-brother, Hagnias, of the same deme, but the adoption was followed by the daughter's marriage to her father's full brother.

There are other, more certain cases of the use of this strategy. In Isaeus 10 Aristarchus of Sypalettus had married out of his deme and kin group, his bride being the daughter of Xenaenetus of Acharnae, a nearby deme. Aristarchus secured the fortune of his father-in-law, Xenaenetus, by having his son Cyronides adopted into Xenaenetus's estate (4–7). When Aristarchus's own estate became

[84] Osborne, *Demos,* 128, maintains that propinquity in adoption is secondary to kinship ties. I am stressing here that propinquity was necessary to initiate marriage ties for the families discussed above, and then these ties were reinforced by adoption. Because there is no marriage link recorded for Nausicles of Oe, I have not listed him in this discussion although his mining activities were close to the deme of his adoptive family. Nausicles had been adopted by a family, it seems, from Aegilia (Davies, *APF,* 397). There are two further instances of the adoptee coming from the same deme as the adopter, but, again, no marriage link is explicitly stated in one case, and, in the other, some sort of agnatic kinship between the two families may be indicated. For the former instance: Davies, *APF,* 229: Thudippus had been adopted into another family of the same deme, Araphen. The adoptive family belonged to a different phratry (Is. 9.2, 33) and, therefore, would not have belonged to Thudippus's patriline. The other incident (*APF,* 45) involves the adoption of Thrasybulus of Lousia into the house of Hippolochides, the son of Thrasymedes of Lousia; the similarity of roots in the names may suggest some sort of agnatic kinship: Osborne, *Demos,* 245 n.7, however, states that the kinship is unclear.

[85] The date of Themistocles' birth suggests that his marriages were contracted between 495 and the following decade. His children would have been adult and of marriageable age in the late 470s and 460s, contemporaneous with his exile. In fact, one of Themistocles' daughters, Nicomache, married her first cousin (father's brother's son), after her father's death: see Davies, *APF,* 212 ff., for these dates. The tendency toward endogamy at a time of political disgrace is evident in the practices of other political families (see appendix and bibliography therein).

insolvent (15–16),[86] it fell under the guardianship of his brother, Aristomenes. Moreover, the speaker stated (17) that some families with insolvent estates would try to have their children adopted into other *oikoi* so that the children could avoid the loss of civic rights which necessarily accompanied insolvency. There is the possibility that Cyronides may have been adopted so as to avoid disfranchisement.[87] In any case, Xenaenetus's estate was worth around four talents (10.23), and Cyronides may well have used some of this wealth to pay off his natural father's debts.[88] Cyronides, however, although adopted out, still retained control of his natural father's estate by marrying within his agnatic kin group: his bride was the daughter of Aristomenes, his father's brother, who took with her as a type of dowry title to the estate of Aristarchus (5). The title to the property was then reinforced by the posthumous adoption of Cyronides' sons into his natural father's estate (6 ff.).

If Davies's reconstruction is correct[89]—and in light of the discussion above the reconstruction becomes more likely—then for the son of Polyeuctus of Bate, exogamy, endogamy, and adoption sustained and secured ties with both affines and agnates. Polyeuctus's son married a nonkinswoman, Chrysogone of Erchia, and actually migrated to his wife's deme, possibly being attracted to her family's property there. In fact, Chrysogone was either an only child at the time of her marriage or became the only heir to her father shortly afterward because her son by Polyeuctus's son was adopted into the estate of her father. Polyeuctus's son, however, maintained ties with his original *oikos* by having his son marry his brother's daughter.

In this context, the marriage of Dicaeogenes IV, the son's son of Dicaeogenes III, is illustrative. As noted above, Dicaeogenes III was adopted by Dicaeogenes II (Dicaeogenes III's mother's brother's son or father's mother's brother's son) and, therefore, was adopted out of his patrilineal clan, the Gephyraei. As noted above, these groups might have been neighbors in the Cerameicus and could well have had holdings in the northern plain. Dicaeogenes IV, Dicaeogenes III's son's son, by marrying the daughter of Aristogeiton of Aphidna, married back into Dicaeogenes III's kin group of origin (*IG* II² 6569).[90]

Given such maneuvers, then, Humphreys's reconstruction of a series of gravestones that marked the burial of the family members of Meidon of Myrrhinous is instructive.[91] Two of Calliteles' sons, Meidon II and Meidoteles, married two

---

[86] For which see Wyse, *Isaeus,* 662.

[87] Wyse (ibid., 655) feels that there is a possibility that Cyronides was adopted out before the death of his father.

[88] In the oration the speaker compares Xenaenetus's estate with a disputed piece of land. Was Xenaenetus, therefore, landed?

[89] Davies's stemma for the son of Polyeuctus and his family (*APF,* 172), based on *IG* II² 3455 and 5867, is speculative, but accepted tentatively by Osborne, *Demos,* 132.

[90] See also Davies, *APF,* 147; Osborne, *Demos,* 132–33, states simply that the adoption did not separate Dicaeogenes IV from his genetic family and the deme of Aphidna.

[91] Humphreys, *Family,* 109.

epiklēroi, or inheriting daughters, of Calliteles' wife's brother who was from the same deme, Myrrhinous. From the findspot of the stones at Markopoulo, moreover, both families were resident in their native deme. Although Meidon II and Meidoteles were not necessarily adopted into the house of their mother's brother, one of them, nevertheless, would probably have left a child behind as heir.[92] Thus, this partial absorption of Meidon and Meidoteles into their maternal uncle's line was then followed by the marriage of Meidoteles' daughter to Callimedon, the full brother of Meidon and Meidoteles.

Therefore, in six cases, two affinal families of the Bouselidae, the family of Isaeus 10, the family of the son of Polyeuctus of Bate, of Meidon, and that of Dicaeogenes III, there was an eagerness to accommodate kinsmen outside of the patriline by providing them with heirs, but the interests of the patriline were never far away. Although scholars have maintained that the law severed the adoptee from his or her *oikos* of origin and, therefore, from the patriline,[93] nevertheless, endogamy within or back into the patriline could compensate for the adoptee's absence from the patriline. In most cases, these maneuvers were facilitated by the proximity of both kin groups.

KINSHIP IN-MARRIAGE IN THE ATHENIAN CONTEXT

We must always look carefully at all the rights and obligations that people can hold in property, group membership and in each other, and see how these are distributed. Very often, the lines of division become blurred when this is done, but at least we escape the fallacy that having said of a system that it is 'patrilineal' we have disposed of the most important question about it. We have, in fact, only just begun. All systems are in a sense 'transitional'; change is the law of life in society, as well as in nature. . . .[94]

The Athenians of the orations strikingly exemplify this dictum of the anthropologist Richard Fox. On the one hand, their marriage practices often reveal a strong patrilineal orientation; on the other hand, whenever property is transmitted, it is common for concerns outside the patriline to surface.

In the cases of some of the families and kin groups discussed above, a sibling followed a sibling or a woman followed a kinswoman into a particular deme at marriage in order to secure affinal ties or to reinforce a claim to a kinsman's property. For other families and kin groups, kinship endogamy was resorted to when an estate came into crisis, or, in one case, when a kinsman faced political disgrace, or when a patriline lost a member through adoption. Not all Athenian

---

[92] Harrison, *Law,* 1:132–35.

[93] For example, ibid., 93; MacDowell, *Law,* 99–100; Rubinstein, *Adoption,* 57–60.

[94] R. Fox, *Kinship and Marriage: An Anthropological Perspective* (Harmondsworth: Penguin, 1967), 155–56.

families resorted to kinship endogamy: a rough estimate from the known or inferred marriages in Davies's listing, for instance, indicates a proportion of endogamous unions of 19 percent—not a terribly high figure compared to other agrarian societies that practise kinship in-marriage.[95] However, more instances of endogamy may well lie hidden in the listing; we are at the mercy of texts that do not always detail relationships among members of a kin group. In any case, of the instances discussed above, there was a greater tendency for a man to either contract, or attempt to contract, a marriage through his father's line than through his mother's line; the ratio of such marriages, or attempts, runs about two to one. This ratio is reflected in Davies's listing as a whole, for a possible 37 endogamous unions.[96] Of the 10 unions through the mother's line in

[95] For some agrarian societies kinship endogamy can run as high as 50 percent of all marriages: J.-L. Flandrin, *Familles: Parenté, maison, sexualité dans l'ancienne société* (Paris: Hachette, 1976), 39: Flandrin points out that a high degree of local endogamy fosters kinship endogamy. See also J. Goody, *The Development of the Family and Marriage in Europe* (Cambridge: Cambridge University Press, 1983), 186–87, for the alternation of endogamy and exogamy among the political elite in Europe. Segalen also discusses the pattern for peasant families in France; see below, note 102. H. Rosenfeld, "The Contradiction Between Property, Kinship and Power as Reflected in the Marriage System of an Arab Village," in *Contributions to Mediterranean Sociology,* ed. J. G. Peristiany (Paris: Mouton, 1968), 253–59, records that of eighty marriages made by males in a powerful lineage, 51 percent were to women within the lineage and 23 percent of these with patrilateral parallel cousins. However, there are those who are skeptical of high figures for kinship endogamy: L. Holy, *Kinship, Honour and Solidarity* (Manchester: Manchester University Press, 1989), 17–21. For residual patriliny in endogamy, see E. L. Peters, "Aspects of Affinity in a Lebanese Maronite Village," in Peristiany, *Family Structures,* 33–34, who explains that the marriage of a woman to a stranger will be balanced by her son's marriage to her father's father's brother's son's daughter (fig. 2b), or that two individuals who are distantly related but who share a close friendship must secure this friendship by a marriage in the following generation.

[96] The following list is based on Davies, *APF.* Alliances that have been conjectured by other scholars, and which I have included in my discussions in this chapter and in the appendix, are not listed here; the initials used to denote family relationships will be self-explanatory, except that "Z" stands for "sister." Unions through the father's line: Hipponicus + FZD (19); Polemon + FBSD; Philagrus + FBD; Callistratus + FBDD; Sositheus's brother's son + Sositheus' daughter (FBD; all alliances for the Bouselidae: 77 ff.); Thucritides + FD (94–95, stemma); Demophon + FBD (118 ff.); Diodotus + FBD (151); Polyeuctus + FBD (172); Archiades + BD (194); Phaedrus + FBD (?) (200); Archeptolis + FD (217); Phrasicles + FBD (217); Pyrilampes + ZD (330); Theomnestus + ZD (437); Thrasyllus's son + FBD (Is. 7.11ff—family is mentioned by Davies (43 ff.), but not the intended marriage); Lysias + ZD (589). Marriages in the patriline, but relationship between the spouses is unclear: Hippocleia + Thymocles (142); Dicaeogenes IV + daughter of a Gephyraeus (147); Perictione and Ariston (331); Alcmaeonides + Agariste (383). Through the mother's line: Andocides + MBD (30 ff.); Sositheus + MFBSD (79–80); Leagros + MBD (91); Aphobus + MB's widow; Laches + MZD (118 ff.); Olorus + MZD (235–36: Davies is skeptical); Hipponicus III + MMBD (265); Ciron + MZD (313); Cleomedon + MBDD (320). Relationship unclear and/or distant: Polyeuctus + wife of Ischomachus (6); Alcibiades III + Hipparete (if both related to Pericles) (19); Protomachus + heiress (94); Callias III + daughter of Glaucon (Philaid connection) (91, 263); Xanthippus + Agarista (456, 600 no. 11811, I); Pericles + kinswoman (457). Possible relationship: Polemon's widow + Glaucetes (83); Oinanthe + fellow demesman (87); Leocrates' daughter + fellow demesman (195);

Davies' register, 4 were cases in which a man married an inheriting daughter, and there were, apparently, no male agnates of her father to claim her hand, or willing to do so. Thus, Andocides the orator and his cousin (mother's sister's son) strove to marry Epilycus's daughters, their mothers' brother's daughters, because Epilycus had no brothers or brothers' sons.[97] The same reasoning lay behind Hipponicus III's attempts to marry one of Epilycus' daughters (his mother's mother's brother's daughter).[98] According to Sositheus, no agnatic kinsmen were willing to claim the hand of his wife, a kinswoman through his mother's father (or mother's father's brother's son's daughter). Though the marriages of Meidon II and his brother to their mother's brother's daughters have not been discussed by Davies, Humphreys's reconstruction also shows that the unions were precipitated by a crisis: the daughters' father seems to have had no brothers. In these cases, although the woman's kin group is sending out two women to a man's *oikos,* the man will be leaving his child behind as heir in the woman's original kin group.

Otherwise, marriage to a kinswoman through the matriline could leave the offspring from that union at a severe disadvantage legally: Ciron's grandson from Ciron's first marriage to his mother's sister's son was prevented from inheriting Ciron's estate by Ciron's agnate, his brother's son. Sositheus, in the end, appears to have lost his claim, and that of his son, to the Bouselid property of his wife's patrilineal kinsman, Hagnias II. Noteworthy is the fact that Demosthenes' sister was given to her mother's sister's son only as a last resort, after her intended marriage to a father's brother's son failed so miserably.

The bias in favor of marrying within the patriline reflects the bias of inheritance law. The estate of a man who was without heirs was to be transmitted to his closest male kinsman who was descended from a common male ancestor: in other words, the preferred heirs were a brother of the same father and his descendants. In the absence of these, a sister of the same father and her descendants were resorted to. Only when all kinsmen through the father were absent could the mother's line be eligible for consideration.[99]

Traditionally scholars have agreed that kinship in-marriage is contracted in all

---

Olympiodorus of Phrearrhii + Plathane, daughter of Hephaestodorus of unknown deme (499: Davies does not state the possibility of endogamy; the roots in the spouses' names may suggest kinship ties, but are too common for this to be more than a possibility). In the instances in the orations that were not discussed by Davies, there is one of a marriage to FBD (Is. 10.5), one to ZD (Dem. 41.1ff) and three others of unclear relationship ([Dem.] 48.5; 59.119–20; Lys. 13.1).

[97] Davies, *APF,* 297.

[98] Ibid., 264–65.

[99] For instance, Harrison, *Law,* 1:130–49; MacDowell, *Law,* 92–99; see most recently R. Just, *Women in Athenian Law and Life* (London: Routledge, 1989), 83–89; V. Hunter, "Agnatic Kinship in Athenian Law and Family Practice: Its Implications for Women," in *Law, Politics and Society in the Ancient Mediterranean World,* ed. B. Halpern and D. Hobson (Sheffield: Sheffield Academic Press, 1993), 102–3.

societies in order to consolidate property.[100] Certainly this has been borne out by the Attic orators in all cases except that of Lysias 19, where political disgrace and, perhaps, the confiscation of property which inevitably followed, prompted the marriage of the speaker's sister to her first cousin. Political disgrace, or threat of disgrace, as we will see, may well have been the force behind the endogamous unions of the powerful families of the fifth century (appendix, pp. 216–29). For the orations, in general, as Osborne maintains, "kin determine marriage" to reinforce links and prevent the disintegration of property.[101] Kinship endogamy would be especially effective in a society where equal division of the paternal property among the children (partibility) might eventually reduce holdings to an unprofitably small size.[102] As will be discussed, for Athens the practice of partibility applied only to male children. Theoretically, marriage to a patrilineal kinswoman allowed the woman to reside close to her patriline.[103] Although our sources are not informative about the domiciles of patrilineal kinsmen, the sources do reveal that patrilineal kinsmen tended to depend on each other for moral and material support. Marriage to a father's brother's daughter or brother's daughter was an answer to political threats against the family of Lysias 19, and as will be discussed further in the appendix, the Alcmaeonidae, the Salaminii, and the family of Themistocles.

Among the less prominent families from our orations, in Isaeus 10, Cyronides was adopted into his maternal grandfather's *oikos*, and, therefore, he, presumably, brought his wife (father's brother's daughter) there; their sons, however, were adopted back into the property of Cyronides' natural father. This estate, or rather the line, was being preserved by Cyronides' paternal uncle, his wife's father. In this marriage and the intended one of Demophon, son of Demo, to Demosthenes' sister (father's brother's daughter), the wife's dowry was the means for the (prospective) husbands to control the property of agnates: Cyronides' wife brought as dowry the title to the estate of Cyronides' natural father, and Demophon controlled two talents from his (intended) wife's paternal property. This emphasis on the male agnatic line is clearly seen in the kin group of the Bousel-

---

[100] For a summary of the bibliography, see J. Davis, *People of the Mediterranean* (London: Routledge and Kegan Paul, 1977), 197 ff., although Davis downplays the role of land fragmentation in kinship endogamy. Since Davis, see Goody, *Development*, 31–33, 186–87, and bibliography therein. For the benefits of land fragmentation in ancient Greece, the most recent discussion is in Gallant, *Risk*, 42–46.

[101] Osborne, *Demos*, 135–36.

[102] Martine Segalen, *Historical Anthropology of the Family*, trans. J. C. Whitehouse and S. Matthews (Cambridge: Cambridge University Press, 1986), 120–28. Segalen also discusses the alternation of exogamy with endogamy. Although Davis, *People*, 197 ff., claims that partibility has historically never resulted in overdivision, this ability to offset the crisis may well be due, in part, to the tendencies toward in-marriage. To argue that kinship in-marriage was not practiced to avoid overparceling, on the grounds that such a crisis never occurred in a partible inheritance system, may be putting the cart before the horse.

[103] See, for instance, M. Ottenheimer, "Complementarity and the Structures of Parallel-Cousin Marriage," *American Anthropologist* 88 (1986): 936.

idae where out of the six known or inferred cases of endogamy, five instances reveal that a spouse was sought through the patriline.

In Lysias 32, not discussed above, and in Pseudo-Demosthenes 44, the marriage, or intended marriage, of a man to his brother's daughter would ally the houses of two brothers, who held joint property (Lys. 32.4–7; [Dem.] 44.10 ff.).[104] In fact, in Lysias 32, because Diodotus died several years after his marriage to the daughter of his brother Diogeiton, the latter assumed guardianship of Diodotus's estate, thereby controlling the original wealth and any wealth accrued apart from the original estate (Lys. 32.4–5).

When both spouses came from the same patriline through males the marriage was obviously agnatic in bias. Marriages to a father's sister's daughter or a sister's daughter, although not between spouses of the same patriline through males, did, nevertheless, ultimately involve the descendants of a brother and sister of the same patriline; the implication here is that brother and sister were looking to the interests of their *oikos* of origin. The marriage of the non-Athenian orator Lysias to his sister's daughter may well have brought the wife back to her mother's original *oikos,* or, at the very least, to her original kin: Lysias lived with both his wife and his widowed mother ([Dem.] 59.22). The one certain instance of marriage to a father's sister's daughter in Davies, the marriage of Callias III's son, Hipponicus III, to the daughter of Hipparete and Alcibiades, balanced Hipparete's marriage out to Alcibiades.[105] Furthermore, Hipparete's daughter took up residence in the house of Hipparete's brother's son (Lys. 14.28). This latter union would have reinforced two *oikoi* that were suffering severe financial problems during the Peloponnesian War, and may well have been intended to bring some of Hipparete's vast dowry back to her *oikos* of origin (see appendix, pp. 225–27). In the case of Deinias's family, Theomnestus's marriage to his sister's daughter allowed for the fluidity of boundaries between his *oikos* and that of Apollodorus as the two men shared their wealth. This fluidity is reflected in Demosthenes 41, not discussed above. In this oration, although Leocrates' marriage to his sister's daughter accompanied his adoption by his wife's father and led to his residence in his wife's *oikos,* the situation would probably have been temporary. Leocrates' wife was an inheriting daughter; her husband was adopted so as to provide an heir to her father's estate, and most adoptees, after leaving a natural son in the

---

[104] I disagree with Davies (*APF,* 195–96), followed by Osborne (*Demos,* 136), who believe the speaker's statement that Archiades' refusal to marry his niece left the estate undivided. See the discussion in chapter 4, below, pp. 110–11.

[105] Lys. 14.28; Davies, *APF,* 19. The frequency of marriage to FZD would have been impeded by a common marriage strategy in Athens: the earlier marriage of a sister would make the sister's fraternal nephew younger than her daughter. See, for instance, J. F. Martin, "Genealogical Structures and Consanguineous Marriage," *Current Anthropology* 22 (1981): 401–6. Marriage to FZD would take place only if the husband's father and his wife's mother, the brother and sister of the original *oikos,* had married contemporaneously. Indeed, Callias III and his sister, Hipparete, were rather unusual in that they both married around the same time, in the late 420s: Davies, *APF,* 263. For the earlier marriage of a sister, see below, chapter 4.

oikos of adoption, returned to their original line.[106] Nevertheless, because of the endogamous union and adoption, Leocrates had brought some of his property into the marital residence (4–5).

There was, therefore, a strong patrilineal bias in Athenian law, and in a greater number of cases Athenians tended to contract marriages that reflected this bias. If an individual married within the kin group he preferred marriage with a kinswoman through his father or brother. That this preference did not always result in consolidation of kinship ties and property is evident from the orations recording Demosthenes the orator's dispute with his guardians: although the elder Demosthenes turned to his brother and sister to provide husbands for his widow and daughter, the intended marriages never transpired, the guardians embezzled the estate, and the daughter was finally given to the son of her mother's sister. In Isaeus 7, which was not discussed above, Thrasyllus[107] married out, but it seems that his son was intended to marry one of his brother's daughters. But the brother, Eupolis, tried to embezzle his nephew's estate, so that a dispute erupted between uncle and nephew. No marriage was contracted between the cousins, even though the parties involved knew that endogamy would have bound the wealth of both houses together, by increasing the uncle's hold on the nephew's estate (11 f.). In fact, Thrasyllus's son turned to his matrilineal kin, his half-sister and her son, to carry on his line (ibid., 9–13).[108] Isaeus 7, therefore, shows that the ideal of endogamy was not realized because of disputes among agnatic kin. Isaeus 7 is hardly exceptional in its depiction of feuding kin.

Later chapters will show how the agnatic bias in inheritance laws could make rivals of the very individuals who had the right to inherit, a friction that often resulted in their coming to depend on female kin of the patriline or on kin through the matriline.[109] Hence, there was a basic contradiction between kin-

---

[106] The one exception to this practice is the speaker's claim in Is. 9.1 ff. that Cleon and his father had passed into another *oikos* through adoption. A whole line severing itself from its patriline was unusual, if not un-Athenian. Cleon's son and the speaker were both claiming the right to be adopted into the estate of Astyphilus, who was an agnate of Cleon and his son. Therefore, by claiming that Cleon's father, Cleon himself, and Cleon's son all were members of another *oikos*, the speaker has effectively severed them from their patriline and from Asyphilus's estate. The speaker's allegation may be suspect: Cleon probably had other sons (*APF,* 229). The speaker's rival might never have been adopted into another house, but may well have stayed in the patriline. In the case of the family in Demosthenes 41, Spudias, who married Leocrates' ex-wife after Leocrates and Leocrates' father-in-law, Polyeuctus, had quarreled, seems to have left heirs in Polyeuctus's estate: see below, chapter 3.

[107] For Thrasyllus, see Davies, *APF,* 43–44.

[108] Wyse, *Isaeus,* 557; Osborne, *Demos,* 136.

[109] For other societies see: Fox, *Kinship,* 121; I. M. Lewis, "Problems in the Comparative Study of Unilineal Descent," in *The Relevance of Models for Social Anthropology,* ed. M. Banton (London: Tavistock, 1965), 105. Lewis argues that even in systems that appear to have dual descent, patrilineality may be strongly stressed. In this regard, see also S. Chojnacki, "Kinship Ties and Young Patricians in Fifteenth-Century Venice," *Renaissance Quarterly* 38 (1985): 243. V. Hunter, "Agnatic Kinship," is the most recent discussion based on the Attic orators.

ship endogamy, which stressed inheritance through the patriline, and adoption practice, in which the adopter often selected his heir through a female relative. Disputes among kinsmen, particularly male agnates, as will be discussed later, had a direct effect on domestic relationships and *oikos* composition.

Town and Country, Marriage and Death

OUR EXAMINATION of the literary sources has shown to what extent locale, though not necessarily the native deme, played a role in the marriages of the propertied elite. From time to time urban domiciles facilitated alliances among families in neighboring demes or owning neighboring estates, and at other times propinquity in the city encouraged alliances among prominent families in disparate demes. Once two families were united in marriage, kinsmen and kinswomen acted so as to reinforce those ties and consolidate property and wealth. But these strategies were not restricted to the families in the orations. The present chapter will deal with individuals in the grave inscriptions, many of whom were socially or politically obscure both in their demes and in the larger, formal structures of the polis. Whether or not these people were also poor is a highly debated question. The standard view claiming that the purchase of gravestones could be afforded only by well-to-do families is now being challenged.[1] On both sides of this issue, however, the estimates of the cost of gravestones, including inscription and sculpted reliefs, are quite speculative. It would be safest to say at this point that the maneuvers outlined below may describe the strategies of rich and poor alike, though this is far from certain. Furthermore, because the study of marriage strategies is dependent on the full record of both the husband and wife, indicating the deme from which they come, the most informative of the grave stelae are those dated to the fourth century, which often give the demes of both spouses. Therefore, our conclusions are restricted to the fourth century, although in some cases the marriages recorded may date to the late fifth century.

The social commentaries of Humphreys, Garland, and Osborne on the gravestones are by now well known. Humphreys and Garland, however, focused primarily on burial and burial groups and not specifically on marriage practices.[2] Humphreys argued that large extended groups and clan plots were not the norm. Although she is correct in showing that the choice of burial plot was highly individual, it was individual in an Athenian way: as Humphreys' description of groups itself shows,[3] those extended group burials that did occur generally em-

---

[1] See the works cited below, in notes 10 and 14.

[2] R. Garland, "A First Catalogue of Attic Peribolos Tombs," *ABSA* 77 (1982): 125–76. For Humphreys and Osborne see below, notes 3 and 7.

[3] S. C. Humphreys, *The Family, Women and Death* (London: Routledge and Kegan Paul, 1983), 111–17.

phasized kinship through the father. Therefore, brothers' sons, father's brothers' sons and their descendants make up the majority of individuals recorded in group burials. It did also happen that cross-siblings were also buried together, at times with the spouse of one sibling and their descendants or with the spouses of both and their children. As will be shown in chapter 4, the display of ties between cross-siblings is a manifestation, not a contradiction, of agnation. Sisters were also buried together in the plot with other original family members or, in one case, with their mother's brothers' sons, who may also have been their husbands (*IG* II² 5811). In two cases, sisters were buried together in plots isolated from their families, without their children (*IG* II² 5673 + 5681; 6025 + 6045). Therefore, children descended from two sisters were not buried together, or, at the very least, the extant gravestones do not show, or refuse to show, this relationship. The omission is again pertinent. Only in one instance, in the literary sources, were sisters' sons buried together. According to Pseudo-Plutarch, Isocrates' maternal aunt and her son were buried in his plot, along with Isocrates' mother, brother, adopted son and other relatives ([Plut.] *Mor.* 838b–c).[4] No other source tells us that a woman could extricate her son from his father's plot and be buried with his mother and her sister's family of marriage. Certainly, this unique burial practice of Isocrates' kin may reflect the orator's great reputation, with marginal kin gravitating toward his burial spot.[5] Because, however, Pseudo-Plutarch admitted that stones in the plot were missing or had been destroyed ([Plut.] *Mor.* 838b–c), he was not able to give the full story to posterity. In short, burial, as a public statement, tends to focus on the nuclear family, and then on the patriline; the larger number of individuals in the patriline consists of brothers and their descendants, but cross-siblings and their descendants can be represented. Representation of kinship ties through strictly female lines is very rare.[6]

Robin Osborne, in his discussion of the use of kin and neighbors in marriages, concludes from his study of the gravestones that locale was not a decisive consideration in the choice of marital partners.[7] Those stones that record marriages between individuals of neighboring demes are in the minority, while the occurrences of neolocality outstripped even those of virilocality.[8] (Neolocality would be defined as residence close to neither spouse's deme, while virilocality is residence in or closer to the husband's deme.) However, Osborne studied the role of migrations in marriage in only a handful of cases, and he did not con-

---

[4] See also C. Tuplin, "Some Emendations to the Family-Tree of Isocrates," *CQ* 30 (1980): 288–305; Humphreys, *Family*, 116.

[5] Ibid.

[6] Besides the possible ties through sisters represented in Isocrates' group above, see the discussion of *IG* II² 5753 below, note 58.

[7] R. Osborne, *Demos: The Discovery of Classical Attika* (Cambridge: Cambridge University Press), 127–53.

[8] I interpret Robin Osborne's rubric "neither viri- or uxorilocal" (ibid., 130) as neolocal, though Osborne may have included those spouses who remained in their native demes and married within them. Again, definitions need refinement here.

sider findspots in detail, for, as we will see, the practices of those domiciled in the city, regardless of demotic, could be quite different from those of residents of rural areas, where deme and locale played a larger role. One example in which the findspot of the gravestone can make a substantial difference is in the case of Aexone. Osborne maintains that this deme seems to have had no connection with the Peiraeus, yet the findspots of gravestones recording men from this deme show that seventeen out of twenty of these men, who were domiciled in the city, resided in the Peiraeus.[9]

More recently, Damsgaard-Madsen's investigation of migrations, based on a thorough study of the findspots of the gravestones, has reinforced a theory cautiously proposed by Gomme that the classical era witnessed heavy migration from the country to the city.[10] Unfortunately, Damsgaard-Madsen's study was a preliminary one and did not consider marriage ties or women's migrations, though it noted briefly that women were less stationary than men.[11]

The basis of the present chapter will be the corpus of grave inscriptions compiled by the Copenhagen team of Mogens Herman Hansen, Lars Bjertrup, Thomas Heine Nielsen, Lene Rubinstein, and Torben Vestergaard.[12] Although the corpus includes inscriptions of Hellenistic and Roman date, the present study will focus on those inscriptions of the classical era, dating from before c. 300 B.C. The purpose here will be to study the marriages contracted by both the wealthy and the less wealthy, and to determine to a greater extent than hitherto into what demes Athenians married, as well as whether their marriages involved migration or kept them, more or less, in their demes of origin. Of prime importance to this study is H. Osswald's investigation of the town of Porto in northern Portugal, in the first half of the seventeenth century. Porto lay a few kilometers from

---

[9] Ibid., 2–3. I focus on men alone, as the women whose names precede a male name in the genitive and who are not buried with other males may be either daughters or wives.

[10] A. Damsgaard-Madsen, "Attic Funeral Inscriptions: Their Use as Historical Sources and some Preliminary Results," in *Studies in Ancient History and Numismatics Presented to Rudi Thomsen,* ed. A. Damsgaard-Madsen, E. Christiansen, and E. Hallager (Aarhus: Aarhus University Press, 1988), 55–68. Migration is denied by Osborne, *Demos,* 16, 41–42; and D. Whitehead, *The Demes of Classical Attica 508/7–ca. 250 B.C.* (Princeton, N.J.: Princeton University Press, 1986), 352–57, who, however, appear not to have studied the findspots of gravestones in detail. See M. H. Hansen et al., "The Demography of the Attic Demes: The Evidence of the Sepulchral Inscriptions," *AnalRom* 19 (1990): 44, n. 36, for bibliography on the issue.

[11] Damsgaard-Madsen, "Attic Funeral Inscriptions," 63.

[12] Database at Copenhagen University, Institute of Classics, compiled by L. Bjertrup, M. H. Hansen, T. Heine Nielsen, L. Rubinstein, and T. Vestergaard. I am indebted to Bob Develin for sending me a copy of this corpus. At the time of receipt the file consisted of the inscriptions dating to the classical era and culled from *IG* II² 5228–7861, 7862–13085, and the addenda in W. Peek, "Attische Inschriften," *AM* 67 (1942): 77–217; G. Stamiris, "Attische Grabinschriften," ibid., 218–29; W. Peek, *Attische Grabinschriften,* vol. 2 (Berlin: Akademie-Verlag, 1957); D. W. Bradeen, *The Athenian Agora: Inscriptions: The Funerary Monuments,* vol. 17 (Princeton, N.J.: American School of Classical Studies at Athens, 1974); *SEG* 12–35 (1955–85); M. J. Osborne, "Attic Epitaphs. A Supplement," *AncSoc* 19 (1988): 5–60. I have since consulted the current issues of *SEG* to volume 40.

the coast and had extensive trade connections but its economy depended heavily on agriculture. Osswald studied migrations from the countryside to the city and compared marriage practices in the city with those in the country. Her conclusions were that the city encouraged a high degree of heterogamy—marriages between families from disparate villages. The farther one got from the city, the less frequent heterogamy became, and the rural inhabitants tended to marry locally, either in the same village or with families of villages nearby; only then, as a third choice, were spouses chosen from the city. In the most homogamic (marriage within a class or profession) and endogamic area women had to move more than men.[13]

In order to determine to what extent locality played a role in the marriages of those recorded in the grave inscriptions, in the calculations below I have ignored all inscriptions where the findspots are not known. This can be frustrating in some instances, because there are intra-deme marriages recorded on stones in cases where findspots have not been noted. Although the intra-deme marriage in such a case clearly indicates some attention to locale, we cannot assess the extent to which rural or urban domiciles encouraged these alliances. I have also ruled out any stones where the deme of a woman's father is not stated, for this information is also essential to a discussion of marital locale. Nor, in the tabulations below (tables 1a–d, 2a–d), have I considered the stones whose findspots are vaguely given as "Athenis"; this term does not indicate either an urban or a rural locale. Therefore, of the approximately 1,330 men and 721 women in the corpus compiled by the Copenhagen team for the fourth century,[14] I have estimated and inferred a minimum of 112 marriages for individuals whose demes and deme locations are fairly certain. A static number is impossible here because the excavations in the rural areas are still yielding stones, and the stones at Rhamnous suggest, rather than actually record, marriages among families of that deme.[15] Altogether the number 112 and more is, nevertheless, disappointingly small, so that I offer the following statistics as only a possible guide to ancient behavior in marriage strategies. Of the more than 112 marriages in the stones, 60 were con-

[13] H. Osswald, "Dowry, Norms and Household Formations: A Case Study from North Portugal," *Journal of Family History* 15 (1990): 201–2, 208–9; heterogamy in this study was defined as marriage between individuals of different social and occupational backgrounds, though Osswald maintains that marriage tended to be within the group or profession (ibid., 207).

[14] Hansen et al., "Demography," 27; T. H. Nielsen et al., "Athenian Grave Monuments and Social Class," *GRBS* 30 (1989): 411, who calculate the numbers of Athenians mentioned in these sources from ca. 400 B.C. to 250 A.D. Nielsen et al. argue that many of the people in the inscriptions were not from the wealthier, elite strata.

[15] Note that the study refers to marriages rather than number of inscriptions, because several stones can belong to one family and record one or two marriages. I depart slightly from the Danish team who record a marriage only when a woman is specifically termed a *gynē* to a man on a stone. Rather, I have assumed that if a woman's name is followed by a male name in the genitive and a demotic, and the woman is also commemorated with another man, then the male name in the genitive is the woman's patronymic and the man with whom she is buried, her husband.

tracted between individuals domiciled in the city or its environs, while a minimum of 52 were between individuals domiciled in rural areas.[16] Of the 60 urban
marriages, only 18 (30 percent) could be said to have occurred between individuals who came from the same deme or from demes close to each other, that
is within an eight- or ten-kilometer radius. Significantly, 42 of the 60 marriages
(70 percent) were contracted between individuals of disparate demes, over ten
kilometers apart. Logically enough, therefore, as many as 61 percent of all urban
marriages (37 unions) were neolocal, with both spouses immigrating to the
urban center, while virilocal and uxorilocal unions constituted only 17 percent
and 14 percent respectively.[17] These figures suggest that when people migrated
to the city, there was ample opportunity to contract marriages either with families from city demes or with others who had migrated to the urban center from
rural areas in Attica that were at times far-flung.

If we view the rural marriages, the 52 or more marriages taking place between
individuals who did not migrate to the city, or in two cases spouses from city demes
migrating a small distance into the country (*IG* II^2 6193, 6748), the percentage of
marriages between individuals from disparate demes is reduced: 21 unions, or 40
percent of the rural marriages, involved families from disparate demes, and of these,
16 were virilocal, 1 was neolocal, and 4 uxorilocal, that is, in the wife's deme or
close to it. Therefore, in the disparate alliances, which make up slightly less than
half of the rural marriages, women were generally sent out to distant parts of Attica—a pattern suggesting division of labor by gender: men stayed in their demes
to till the land, while the women, who were for the most part relegated to household management, were sent out some distance from their original home to manage another man's *oikos*. The tendency for men to stay put is also reflected in the
very low percentage of neolocality for all rural marriages—in only 8 percent of
the marriages did both spouses move to a region away from their demes. To judge
from all inscriptions recording rural marriages, a large percentage was virilocal (44
percent), whereas uxorilocal marriages consituted a mere 8 percent.[18]

[16] Since I received a copy of the Copenhagen team's list, two other gravestone inscriptions have
appeared in *SEG* and have been included in the following estimates. *SEG* 39.25 may record a marriage between Charippus of Halae and Damostrate of Icaria. The stone was found in the Peiraeus.
SEG 40.216 records an intra-deme marriage of either Diotheides or Socrates of Halae to Anesagora.
The stone was found at Voula, in southwest Attica.

[17] Besides these, on six stones found in the city (*IG* II^2 5560, 5822, 7372, 7525, 7786, Agora
17.56) the married women were commemorated apart from their family of marriage; in one case
(Agora 17.56) the woman was buried with a member of her original family. It may well be that the
stones commemorating the woman's husband and her children were lost. This is probably the case
in 7786 where a woman from a city deme was commemorated alone but was buried in her husband's
deme, Peiraeus. Therefore, the findspot could well reflect marital residence. There is the possibility,
however, in the case of the remaining stones that the woman left her marital residence on termination of the marriage and returned to her family in the city, in which case marital residence might
not necessarily have been urban.

[18] Besides these, three so-called uxorilocal marriages, or more specifically neo-uxorilocal—closer
to the wife's deme than the husband's—were actually uxorilocal burials, the woman again being com-

Besides these 21 unions of partners from disparate demes, what then do we make of the remaining 31 marriages (60 percent)? Ten of these marriages involved individuals from proximate demes while a minimum of 21 were intra-deme alliances. Thus, the incidence of marriages among neighbors, that is, local endogamy within the deme and with proximate demes, rises when families remain in rural areas, while heterogamy and neolocality are encouraged by the urban center.[19]

These bald numbers, which reflect a difference between urban and rural behavior, reveal little of actual interests. For these we must look a little more closely at the inscriptions themselves, particularly the group burials, to see to what extent the urban setting or its environs undercut or reinforced rural ties, and to see how various families extended and then consolidated kinship ties through exogamy and endogamy (local and kin). It will be one of the chief ironies of the present discussion that, although the inscriptions can give us some idea of the marital practices of the obscure people they record, too often strategies can be gleaned only from the burial practices of the elite. Let us, then, look first at the urban setting, which is here defined as not just the *astu* but the city harbor, the Peiraeus, as well as those demes near the urban center which were assigned to city trittyes. The discussion will show that some of these families appear to have been interested in locale—a region, the native deme or rural neighborhood—but this can only be inferred from the inscriptions. There are no literary sources giving us the motivations behind the marital alliances.

THE FAMILIES BURIED IN THE CITY DEMES:
LOCALE AND AFFINES

Some of the larger burial groups (tables 1a–d) reveal that certain families contracted alliances either with families of their own or neighboring demes or with those whose sphere was fairly localized in the urban center. In other cases, local endogamy accompanied exogamy as families attempted both to localize and to extend affinal ties. Let us begin with the groups in the Peiraeus (table 1a).

---

memorated without her husband or members of her marital family (*SEG* 21.831; *IG* II² 5407, 6045). As in the urban cases, the stone for the wife's husband may have been lost, or the woman returned to her native deme, or to a deme close to it, after the death of her husband. This certainly seems to be the case in 6045, where the woman is buried with or near her sister (6025). One marriage which may have been neolocal again is based on the solitary burial of the wife (7376), while three virilocal marriages (7231, 7259, Osborne no. 39) are again solitary burials but in the husband's deme. Therefore in these three cases marital residence was probably virilocal. The argument above assumes that women were ideally relegated to the household, although it is quite likely that women helped out in the field certainly from time to time: R. Brock, "The Labour of Women in Classical Athens," *CQ* 44 (1994): 343–46; W. Scheidel, "The Most Silent Women of Greece and Rome: Rural Labour and Women's Life in the Ancient World (I)," *GaR* 42 (1995): 202–17.

[19] See below, note 51, for a woman, perhaps from Rhamnous, who was buried in that deme but apart from her husband (it seems), who in turn was from Tricorynthus close by: *SEG* 30.219.

TABLE 1a
City Burials: The Peiraeus

Inscription*	Husband's Deme	Wife's Deme	Type of Residence*
SEG 25.243	Acharnae	Oenoe	n
5783	Acharnae	Xypete	u
5404	Aexone	Peiraeus	u
6476	Aexone	Cothocidae	n
5450	Aexone	Anagyrus	n
5327	Athmonon	Athmonon	n
6306	Ceiriadae	Xypete	—
5607	Cephale	Amphitrope	n
6391	Cydantidae	Cerameis	n/u
6028	Eleusis	Eleusis	n
7702	Ericeia	Phlya	n
SEG 39.256	Halae	Icaria	n
7189	Peiraeus	Acherdous	v?
7695	Phlya	Oeum	n
7702	Phlya	Teithras	n
7717	Phrearrhii	Colonus	n/u
7717	Phrearrhii	Erchia	n
7230	Pithus	Phalerum	u
7269	Potamus Deiradiotae	Halae	n
7277	Prasiae	Anagyrus	n
7412	Sunium	Sunium	n
7415	Sunium	Lamptre	n
7418	Sunium	Euonymon	u
7456	Steiria	Steiria	n
6926	Xypete	Eleusis	v
6934	Xypete	Coprus	v

*See notes to table 1d.

TABLE 1b
City Burials: The Cerameicus

Inscription*	Husband's Deme	Wife's Deme	Type of Residence*
6715	Acharnae	Lamptre	n
5376	Aegilia	Aegilia	n
5678	Anaphlystus	Agryle	u
5678	Anaphlystus	Acharnae	n
5725	Aphidna	Sunium	n
6609	Cydantidae	Marathon	n
6609	Cydantidae	Cettus	u
6609	Cydantidae	Bate	n
5633	Halae Aexonides	Anagyrus	n
6746	Leuconoeum	Aexone	n/v
6746	Leuconoeum	Scambonidae	—
6746	Leuconoeum	Cettus	—
5753	Phalerum	Aphidna	v
5728	Phalerum	Aphidna	v
7449	Sunium	Gargettus	n
6230	Sphettus	Thoricus	n
5633	Thria	Halae Aexonides	n

*See notes to table 1d.

In one case, *IG* II^2 5450, Alcimache, the daughter of Callimachus of Anagyrus, may have been married to one of the sons or grandsons of Philon of neighboring Aexone. This inscription is part of a group burial in the Peiraeus commemorating Philostratus and Callipus the sons of Philon, their parents (?), their sisters and Callipus's two sons.[20] Although residence for these people was in the port deme, they had kinsmen in the native, rural deme: the brother of

---

[20] Davies, *APF,* 276, does not know where in the stemma Hedeline the daughter of Philon is to be placed (as the daughter of either Philon I or Philon II the son of Callipus II). The Aristagora named with Hedeline on 5408 may well be the daughter of Phanagora, the mother of Philon I and his brothers. Davies does conjecture that Alcimache was a relative; therefore, some marriage link is certainly possible.

TABLE 1c
City Burials: Elsewhere in Athens and Environs

Inscription*	Husband's Deme	Wife's Deme	Findspot	Type of Residence*
6767	Sunium	Marathon	Phalerum	n
7414	Sunium	Marathon	Xypete	n
Agora 17.196	Cropidae	Cropidae	Agora	n
Agora 17.191	Conthyle	Cephisia	Agora	n
SEG 21.890	Melite	Cydanthenaeum	Agora	—
SEG 14.174	Prasiae	Paeania	Agora	n
5396	Aethalidae	Cephale	Cypseli	n
5479	Halae	Cothocidae	Sepolia	n
5753	Phlya	Aphidna	Patissia	n
7528	Sphettus	Aethalidae	Ambelokepi	n
Osborne no. 19	Acharnae	Phyle	city	n
SEG 35.255	Melite	Halae	city	v
SEG 29.207	Cerameis	Cerameis	city	n
6077	Hermus	Acharnae	Daphni	v
6054	Peiraeus	Eleusis	Trachones	v
5533	Halimous	Alopece	Trachones	v
5533	Halimous	Halimous	Trachones	—
Stamiris no. 6	Oe	Peiraeus	Rouf	n?

*See notes to table 1d.

Philostratus and Callipus, Philocrates son of Philon, was buried separately in his native deme of Aexone (5448).

A similar interplay between native deme and city is evident for a family from Acharnae. In 5822 (table 1d) Nausistrate, the daughter of Hieron of Acharnae, was married to Protimus of not too distant Cephisia; she was buried in the Peiraeus, without her husband it seems, while her brother, who was wealthy enough to perform a trierarchy,[21] was also buried in the city (findspot in the area

[21] Ibid., 243.

TABLE 1d
City Burials: Wives Buried Alone

Inscription*	Husband's Deme	Wife's Deme	Findspot	Type of Residence**
Agora 17.56	Acharnae	Halae	Agora	n?
5822	Cephisia	Acharnae	Peiraeus	n?
7372	Gargettus	Rhamnous	Olympieion	n?
7786	Peiraeus	Cholargus	Peiraeus	v
5560	Thoricus	Alopece	Agora	u
7525	Thria	Sphettus	Peiraeus	n?

*Numbers without source indication refer to *IG* II².
**n = neolocal; u = uxorilocal; v = virilocal; — = in native deme.

of the Dipylon gate—5810). The siblings' father, on the other hand, was buried in their native, rural deme (5809).[22]

For another family buried in the Peiraeus, marriages were focused in the region of the northern plain and the northern Mesogeia, despite residence in the Peiraeus. In 7702 Polycles of Phlya has married Themisto from Teithras, a deme approximately ten kilometers to the south and east of Phlya. Polycles gave his daughter in marriage to Calliades from Ericeia, which, according to the conjectured location, was situated about five kilometers to the south and west of Phlya.[23]

As for the families from Eleusis in the extant gravestones, whose findspots were in the city demes, the sample is hardly large so that firm conclusions are impossible: there are alliances with families of the port demes Peiraeus and Xypete (6054 [table 1c], 6926 (table 1a) respectively). One further stone, 6045 (table 2d), has a woman from Eleusis married to a man from Halimous. The alliances involving families from Eleusis go no further south than this. Whether the alliances with the families in Peiraeus and Xypete indicate quarrying interests—there were quarries in both Eleusis and Peiraeus—or whether the alliances with families from Peiraeus/Xypete and Halimous suggest religious connections pertaining to the Demeter cult, is uncertain. For this latter point, Eleusis's role in the worship of Demeter hardly needs explanation, but Phalerum, close to Peiraeus, was one

[22] They seem to have another (agnatic?) kinswoman buried in the city as well, if Nausistrate, daughter of (?) Naucydes of Acharnae, is related (5823). See ibid., 243.

[23] Themisto's father was named Apollodorus, a very common name, but one attested in Teithras: Apollodorus son of Onesiphon rented property in his native deme (*SEG* 24.152.5); if this Apollodorus was Themisto's father, or a relative, then Themisto had family members who still retained a hold in the rural deme.

deme, among others in Attica, that had an Eleusinium, while Halimous was the starting point for the procession of the Thesmophoria. The deme had also been a site of an ancient cult of Demeter.[24] In all alliances except that with the man from Halimous, residence was in the Peiraeus. The findspot of 6045—the woman from Eleusis married to a man from Halimous—at Menidi (Acharnae), and the fact that she was not buried with her husband but close to her sister (6025), suggest that her original family's interest lay inland north of the city. So far Eleusinians have not wandered too far to form their alliances, which tend rather to concentrate on the Peiraeus, its environs, or Halimous.[25]

At times families from coastal demes reveal shipping interests or associate with individuals who have such interests. This appears to be the case for two families from Prasiae allying with families in Anagyrus and Peiraeus. In 7277 (table 1a) Alciades and his two sons are buried with his wife in the Peiraeus; for two generations thereafter the family resided in the city port. One of Alciades' sons, Demochares, married Democrateia daughter of Archeidamus of Anagyrus. Her brother is recorded in Demosthenes 35.14 as a witness for and associate of the speaker, who has given a loan on a shipping contract in the Peiraeus.[26] 7286, on the other hand (table 2b), records a man who had interests in the Peiraeus but did not migrate permanently there, and, in fact, brought his city wife to his rural deme. Poseidippus of Prasiae brought a woman from Peiraeus to his own deme (findspot at Markopoulo). Poseidippus was propertied with land in Prasiae and performed two syntrierarchies. His brother appears on a list of amphictyons on Delos leasing temple property there.[27]

Sunium with its five intra-deme marriages has already been discussed by Osborne who attributes endogamy there as a reaction to the influx of non-locals

[24] For the quarries at Eleusis and in the Peiraeus and around it, see Osborne, *Demos,* 96; for the Eleusinium at Phalerum, ibid., 177; 170 f. for Halimous's role in the Thesmophoria. There was one other marriage in which the spouses resided in the Peiraeus: 6028 may be recording the intra-deme alliance of possible kinsmen.

[25] In 6054 Philoumene, daughter of Gnathon of Eleusis, appears to have migrated to Trachones (the city deme, Euonymon), perhaps for her marriage to the father of Nicomachus of Peiraeus, Nicomenes. Philoumene's brother, on the other hand, was active in Eleusis, attested in *IG* II² 1188.2 as honoring a hierophant. However, see Whitehead, *Demes,* 427, no. 159 for his conjecture that Philoumene was the mother of the proposer in 1188.2. The deme Coprus, which was in the same trittys as Eleusis, displays in one case a strong tendency toward alliance with a city family and residence in the Peiraeus. In 6929 and 6934 the group burial shows that Praxilla of Coprus was buried with her husband, Nicippus of Xypete, and his brother and the latter's children, a son and a daughter. The latter was named Praxo after Praxilla, the wife of her father's brother, Nicippus.

[26] Archenomides, Democrateia's brother, is otherwise unknown and therefore belongs to the group of men described by Mossé as individuals of modest means involved in commercial transactions: C. Mossé, "The 'World of the Emporium,' in the Private Speeches of Demsothenes," in *Trade in the Ancient Economy,* ed. P. Garnsey, K. Hopkins, and C. R. Whittaker (Berkeley: University of California Press, 1983), 57.

[27] Davies, *APF,* 469. Osborne, *Demos,* 2 for Eupolemus of Myrrhinous as amphictyon of Delos, whose brother has a home base in the Peiraeus but associates closely with his fellow demesmen in the port.

into the deme;[28] indeed four out of five of these intra-deme alliances occurred at Sunium (7425, 7442, 7448 [2 instances]: table 2a), while in the fifth case (7412) residence was in the Peiraeus. But a closer look at how people behaved in an urban setting is equally instructive, particularly since there was extensive migration from Sunium to the city: of the 21 men from this deme recorded on the gravestones, 11 resided in the city (7 of these in Peiraeus and 2 in Phalerum). Other individuals who resided in the city but were from Sunium married far and wide: there was a marriage alliance with a family from Euonymon (7418: table 1a), one with a family from Lamptre (7415: table 1a), two alliances with separate families from Marathon (6767, 7414: table 1c), and one with a family from Gargettus (7449). All families concerned, except the case of 7449 (table 1b) with its location in the Cerameicus, resided in the Peiraeus or in Xypete nearby.

In one instance we have an idea of why a man from Sunium migrated to the Peiraeus (table 1a). In 7415 Ameinonicus of Sunium, who was commemorated with, presumably, his wife Hegesippe of Lamptre, was a member of the Salaminii, a *genos* which had, among others, two centers, at Porthmus (Sunium) and Phalerum, close to the Peiraeus, where Ameinonicus and his wife were buried. Although the Salaminii had centers in demes such as Melite and Alopece in the city, their centers at the port demes of Phalerum and Sunium suggest maritime interests; perhaps there was even a ferrying route between Sunium and Phalerum. In any case, Ameinonicus gravitated to Peiraeus, adjacent to Phalerum, and married a woman whose coastal deme lay half way between Peiraeus/Phalerum and Sunium.[29] Therefore, for individuals buried in the Peiraeus, residence in the port deme provided an opportunity to pursue maritime interests. At times these interests were combined with religious duties and duties to one's *genos*.

In another family from Sunium local ties were reinforced by local endogamy, which in turn was balanced by exogamy. In 7425 (table 2a) Demagora of Sunium was married to Menestratus of Sunium, with residence in Sunium, and their great grandson then married a woman from Sunium (7442: table 2a).[30] Demagora's sister, on the other hand, was given in marriage to a man from Aphidna, and they were both buried in the Cerameicus (5725: Table 1b). Either

[28] Osborne, *Demos,* 140–41, 247 n. 39 for the inscriptions. In 7434 Theomneste is cited as the wife of Theodorus, son of Diodorus of Sunium. Given the roots of the names, these people might be related and therefore from the same deme. If so, this would be a second intra-deme marriage of spouses from Sunium whose residence was in the Peiraeus.

[29] Ameinonicus's association with the Salaminii is based on the appearance of a kinsman, perhaps even Ameinonicus's son, Philoneus son of Ameinonicus, on an inscription concerning the arbitration of a dispute between the Salaminii of Heptaphylae and Sunium: *SEG* 21.527.71; W. S. Ferguson, "The Salaminii of Heptaphylai and Sounion," *Hesperia* 7 (1938): 1–74, and esp. 14, 18 ff., 44–45. Also, S. C. Humphreys, "Phrateres in Alopeke, and the Salaminioi," *ZPE* 83 (1990): 243–48, and particularly 247, where Humphreys emphasizes that originally the urban center lay at Alopece and branched out to Phalerum as trading interests in the *polis* grew.

[30] See also Kitchner, *PA* 9960, for the conjectured stemma.

Demagora's sister was sent to the city for her marriage, or, equally likely, both women were resident in the city, with one sister being sent back to her father's native deme, while the other was sent to a deme whose location was practically at the opposite end of Attica.

IG II² 7414 (table 1c) is instructive for how urban residence encouraged heterogamy. In the inscription either Alexus or his son Stratocles of Sunium married Philoumene, daughter of Theoxenus of Marathon. The fact that both father and son were buried in Xypete with Philoumene may suggest that residence in the city began with the father and was continued by his son, Alexus. Philoumene, moreover, had a sister. In 6609 (table 1b) Mnesiptoleme, daughter of Theoxenus of Marathon, was married, possibly, to Deinias, son of Phormus of Cydantidae.[31] She was buried in the Cerameicus with, perhaps, her husband, Deinias, his brother, Procleides and the latter's wife, and the men's parents and grandparents (father's father and mother). The family from Cydantidae seems to have resided in the city for two generations as well; burial of several generations in the Cerameicus suggests that Phormus and his son Procleides resided in the city; urban residence was then followed by the marriages of both Phormus and his son Procleides to women from city demes (Bate and Cettus).[32]

Outside of this family group, in 7717 (table 1a) the family of Theodorus of Phrearrhii, that is, his father and grandfather, had been resident in the Peiraeus for one generation at least before Theodorus' marriage to Philoumene of Colonus.[33] This migration to the city port followed by urban marriage is not unlike that recorded for the famous Themistocles (appendix, p. 217): the politician's domicile in the city allowed him to marry a woman from Alopece.

Turning to the burials in the Cerameicus (table 1b), families here can display similar inclinations to extend and contract. One of the most famous of the periboloi is that marked by the monument of Hipparete, granddaughter (son's daughter) of Alcibiades, the famous politician (5434, 6719, 6723, 6746, 7400). If Kirchner's stemma is correct,[34] Hipparete, from Alcibiades' deme of Scambonidae, married Phanocles, son of Andromachus of Leuconoion of the same city trittys of Leontis. Furthermore, Phanocles' father, Andromachus, and

---

[31] She is not included in Kirchner's stemma, *PA* 14963.

[32] The name Mnesiptoleme is reminiscent of Themistocles' family (Davies, *APF,* 217). The name Themistocles itself appears in a family also from Marathon. *IG* II² 6794, edited by Kyparisses in 1927 but not seen by Kirchner in 1935, recorded a Themistocles son of Themistocles commemorated with his son Themistocles. Neither Kirchner nor Davies hazard any connection with the famous politician. Either there is some sort of marital connection with the famous Themistocles' family, or the names are being used for propaganda in a deme whose significance in the Persian Wars needs no discussion.

[33] Theodorus's grandfather, Antibios (father's father), had married Glyce daughter of Aeschines of Erchia. Theodorus's brothers Antimachus and Antibios are commemorated in 7718, also found in the Peiraeus.

[34] His stemma is followed by Davies, *APF,* 21–22, and Humphreys, *Family,* 117, but is questioned by Garland, "First Catalogue," 142.

mother, Critolea, daughter of Phanocles of Cettus, were also of the same trittys. Phanocles' son's son, Phanocles, the son of Aristion, then married Cleo from Aexone, about ten kilometers from the city and on a good communication route along the west coast. In other words, the city family of Phanocles for two generations allied with members of its own trittys and in the third generation allied with a family from a coastal deme to the south. For comparison's sake, in 5533 (+5541, 5579: Table 1c), the reverse is the case; a woman from Alopece, just south of the walls of the *astu*, travels due south to her husband's deme, Halimous, where her son, also recorded on the stone, marries within the deme.[35]

To return to the Cerameicus, there is a group burial recording Archippe's marriage to a fellow demesman, Procleides of Aegilia; the latter is commemorated with his parents, with Procleides and Archippe's son, and with Archippe's brother and brother's son (5374, 5376, 5378, 5379).[36] *IG* II² 5633 records a Micion of Anagyrus and Demostrate from neighboring (?) Halae—presumably his wife—together with Ameiniche, daughter of Micion of Thria. Ameiniche may be the mother of Micion of Anagyrus. Therefore, the younger Micion's father from Anagyrus and his mother, Ameiniche, from Thria were from disparate demes. Their son, the younger Micion from Anagyrus, then married a woman of a neighboring deme, Halae, if the Halae in our inscription refers to Halae Aexonides.

Outside of the Cerameicus, 5479 (table 1c) shows that Exopius of Halae, perhaps to be identified with a landowner in the mining district,[37] is buried with his wife, Democleia of Cothocidae and one of her brothers in the city at Sepolia, but her two other brothers are buried on Salamis, where the family property may have been located.[38] If so, the deme of Democleia's family is known, being of liturgical standing, with a syntrierarchy to its credit.[39] In the case of Exopius, therefore, his marriage alliance, besides focusing on the mining district, focuses as well on the island of Salamis and the city, very similar to the practice of the family in Pseudo-Demosthenes 44 outlined earlier, where Archiades resided on Salamis, his brother's family resided in the city, and their sister was married to a man from Eleusis.

Our survey indicates that among the members of several families buried in the Peiraeus, although some members were buried in the city and presumably resided there, others resided in the native, rural deme. In some cases we could

---

[35] Humphreys, *Family,* 112. The son's cousin, a father's brother's son perhaps, appears to be buried with the group.

[36] Ibid., 114, 129, n. 57, who notes that 5374 and 5378 were not specifically discovered in the Cerameicus and therefore these stones may not originally have stood with 5376 and 5379.

[37] According to Robin Osborne's findings for landowners and lessees in the mining district, there is a strong likelihood that Exopius was from Aexonides, because the people from the east coast are markedly absent from the mining district: *Demos,* 122, 207–8, tables 9 and 10.

[38] *IG* II² 6474, 6480, with perhaps their cousin (father's brother's son) in 6475. See, however, Davies's stemma (*APF,* 176). Davies believes that the two "brothers" Silanion and Execestides are really father's brother and father's brother's son respectively.

[39] Davies, *APF,* 176.

tell why individuals resided and were buried in the Peiraeus. Some individuals displayed commercial interests, while for one man from Sunium the Peiraeus lay close to the cult center of his *genos,* and he married a woman from a deme on a sailing route to Sunium. People from Sunium who lived in the city tended to marry far and wide, while for some families a marriage in a rural deme, which was locally endogamous, was balanced by an exogamous union in the city. Migration to the city and its port was frequently followed by urban marriage. For the families buried in the Cerameicus, there was also a balancing of local endogamy with exogamy: marriage for two generations within the same trittys was then followed by marriage outside the trittys.

The statistics suggest that there was a difference between rural and urban behavior when an individual, or his family, selected a marriage partner. Some of the urban families seem to have considered locale, the native deme or rural neighborhood, while others focused on a region. These interests can only be inferred as there are no literary sources to explain motivation, nor can random exogamy be entirely dismissed either. However, the intra-deme marriages recorded on stones in the city certainly, and probably also the marriages between families of proximate demes, suggest that for some of these "urban" families the native deme and the neighboring demes were not entirely forgotten. This is evident in the burial of some family members in the city while other members were buried in the native deme. Once domiciled in the city, Athenians could still look to the native deme or its close environs for spouses, but there was also a good likelihood that the urban center provided an opportunity to go far beyond the native deme or region and to contract marriages with families from disparate parts of Attica. Some families balanced local endogamy with exogamy: one sibling, for instance, will marry within the native deme, while another marries away from it. This maneuver reflects an interest in extending and then consolidating alliances.

Let us now turn to the rural families, to see to what extent the rural neighborhood played a role in their marriages.

THE FAMILIES IN RURAL AREAS

Our survey will begin with the rural demes of the west coast, will proceed to south Attica and then up the east coast, and thence to the inland demes (tables 2a–c). Included under the rubric "coast" will be those demes well inland from the coast but assigned to a coastal trittys.

The sample of inscriptions for Eleusis is small, 28 stones, but they seem to indicate that the men in this deme, if they had not migrated to the city, did not migrate to any part of Attica for marriage. Rather, their wives came to them, at times from great distances, while women were sent out of Eleusis as well. The great distances involved in some of these marriages may well indicate that Eleu-

TABLE 2a

Rural Burials: Northwestern, Southern, and Western Attica

Inscription*	Husband's Deme	Wife's Deme	Findspot	Type of Residence*
		THE NORTHWEST		
6022	Eleusis	Acharnae	Eleusis	v
6972	Oenoe	Pergase	Thriasian plain	v
		THE SOUTHWEST		
6193	Euonymon	Euonymon	Koropi	n
5525	Halae Aexonides	Halae Aexonides	Zoster	—
SEG 40.216	Halae Aexonides	Halae Aexonides	Voula	—
5733	Halae Aexonides	Aphidna	Vari	v
Osborne no. 32	Lamptre	Lamptre	Koropi	—
Osborne no. 32	Lamptre	Thorae?	Koropi	v
6366	Cephale	Cephale	Ceratea	—
7725	Cephale	Phrearrhii	Ceratea	—
5977	Deiradiotae	Oe	Ceratea	v
7425	Sunium	Sunium	Sunium	—
7442	Sunium	Sunium	Sunium	—
7448	Sunium	Sunium	Sunium	—
7448	Sunium	Sunium	Sunium	—
SEG 34.202	Thoricus	Thoricus	Thoricus	—

*See notes to table 2d.

sis, as a major cult center, attracted people from all over Attica. When families from Eleusis allied with those from inland demes, the latter tended to be in the northern region, between the Aigaleus and Pentelieum ranges: in two cases men from Eleusis married women from Acharnae (6022: table 2a) and Pithus (7231: table 2d) and brought their wives to their deme.[40] In 6405 (table 2c) a woman

[40] This assumes that Pithus belonged to the inland trittys of Cecrops. For 7231 see above, note 18. Recently, Traill does not show the deme in his map (*Demos and Trittys* [Toronto: Athenians, Victoria College, 1986], map), conjecturing either a city or inland trittys assignment. See also P. Siewert, *Die Trittyen Attikas und die Heeresreform des Kleisthenes, Vestigia* 23 (Munich: Beck, 1982), map 4, for a possible inland location, though here as well Pithus has not been placed on the map.

TABLE 2b
Rural Burials: Eastern Attica

Inscription*	Husband's Deme	Wife's Deme	Findspot	Type of Residence*
5228	Angele	Angele	Markopoulo	—
5280	Hagnous	Phegaea	Markopoulo	v
Humphreys**	Myrrhinous	Myrrhinous	Markopoulo	—
Humphreys**	Myrrhinous	Myrrhinous	Markopoulo	—
Humphreys**	Myrrhinous	Myrrhinous	Markopoulo	—
SEG 35.178	Oe	Hybadae	Markopoulo	n
SEG 35.178	Oe	Angele	Markopoulo	u
SEG 35.178	Oe	Angele	Markopoulo	u
SEG 35.178	Oe	Angele	Markopoulo	u
7286	Prasiae	Peiraeus	Markopoulo	v
SEG 30.228	Rhamnous	Oenoe	Rhamnous	v
6006	Rhamnous	Eitea	Rhamnous	v
SEG 26.301, 304	Rhamnous	Pithus	Rhamnous	v
SEG 21.855	Thorae	Pallene	Rhamnous	n

*See notes to table 2d.
**S.C. Humphreys, *The Family, Women and Death* (London: Routledge and Kegan Paul, 1983), 109 and table 1.

from Eleusis was sent out to Cephisia, with residence there, to marry a man from a liturgical family.[41]

Further down the west coast, two intra-deme marriages are recorded for Halae Aexonides (5525, *SEG* 40.216: findspots at Zoster and Voula respectively). In 5525 (table 2a) Chaerelea, daughter of Chaereas of Halae, was married to her fellow demesman Eupolis. Both families were prominent in their demes; the fathers of both spouses along with Eupolis and his brothers cooperated in erecting a statue of Aphrodite. Eupolis's father is also known as moving a decree in the deme, while Eupolis's brother was a syntrierarch.[42] Also, according to

[41] Davies, *APF,* 25. There is one recorded marriage of a woman from Conthyle to a man from Eleusis (Osborne no. 39), with residence at Eleusis (table 2d). See also 6972, in which a woman from north inland Pergase migrates to the Thriasian plain where her husband's deme, Oenoe, one of two homonymous demes, probably lay. Also, *SEG* 35.178, the Goulandris stele, has Themyllus of Oe married to a woman from the north inland and not too distant deme of Hybadae.

[42] Davies, *APF,* 197–98; Osborne, *Demos,* 85–86, 134.

TABLE 2c
Rural Burials: Central Attica

Inscription*	Husband's Deme	Wife's Deme	Findspot	Type of Residence*
		THE MESOGEIA		
5658	Anaphlystus	Anaphlystus	Liopesi	n
5867	Bate	Erchia	Spata	u
6097	Erchia	Cydathenaeum	Liopesi	v
6834	Erchia	Melite	Spata	v
6100	Erchia	Erchia	Liopesi	—
6135	Erchia	Erchia	Spata	—
6131	Erchia	Phlya	Spata	v
7087	Paeania	Oe	Spata	v
7820	Paeania	Oa	Liopesi	v
7060	Paeania	Paeania	Liopesi	—
7095	Paeania	Paeania	Karela	—
7098	Paeania	Acharnae	Liopesi	v
7527	Sphettus	Ceiriadae	Koropi	v
5817	Acharnae	Deceleia	Menidi	v
5848	Acharnae	Aexone	Menidi	v
5349	Athmonon	Alopece	Marusi	v
6405	Cephisia	Eleusis	Cephisia	v
6430	Cephisia	Cephisia	Cephisia	—
6437	Cephisia	Cephisia	Cephisia	—
6437	Cephisia	Phegous	Cephisia	v
5983˙	Deceleia	Phegous	Tatoi	v
6748	Leuconoeum	Leuconoeum	Menidi	n

*See notes to table 2d.

TABLE 2d
Rural Burials: Spouses from Different Demes

Inscription*	Husband's Deme	Wife's Deme	Findspot	Type of Residence**
	SPOUSES FROM DISTANT DEMES			
5848	Acharnae	Aexone	Menidi	v
5349	Athmonon	Alopece	Marusi	v
5867	Bate	Erchia	Spata	u
6405	Cephisia	Eleusis	Cephisia	v
5977	Deiradiotae	Oe	Ceratea	v
6022	Eleusis	Acharnae	Eleusis	v
6097	Erchia	Cydathenaeum	Liopesi	v
6834	Erchia	Melite	Spata	v
6131	Erchia	Phlya	Spata	v
5280	Hagnous	Phegaea	Markopoulo	v
5733	Halae Aexonides	Aphidna	Vari	v
SEG 35.178	Oe	Angele	Markopoulo	u
SEG 35.178	Oe	Angele	Markopoulo	u
SEG 35.178	Oe	Angele	Markopoulo	u
6972	Oenoe	Pergase	Thriasian plain	v?
7087	Paeania	Oe	Spata	v
7098	Paeania	Acharnae	Liopesi	v
7286	Prasiae	Peiraeus	Markopoulo	v
SEG 26.301, 304	Rhamnous	Pithus	Rhamnous	v
7527	Sphettus	Ceiriadae	Koropi	v
SEG 21.855	Thorae	Pallene	Rhamnous	n
	WIVES BURIED ALONE			
5407	Anaphlystus	Aexone	Karela/Liopesi	n/u
7231	Eleusis	Pithus	Eleusis	v
Osborne no. 39	Eleusis	Conthyle	Eleusis	v
6045	Halimous	Eleusis	Menidi	n/u

TABLE 2d (*Continued*)

Inscription*	Husband's Deme	Wife's Deme	Findspot	Type of Residence**
7259	Paeania	Potamus	Guba	v
SEG 21.831	Phegaea	Aexone	Glyfada	u
7376	Thoricus	Rhamnous	Cephisia	n
SEG 30.219	Tricorynthus	Rhamnous	Rhamnous	—

*Numbers without source indication refer to *IG* II².
**n = neolocal; u = uxorilocal; v = virilocal; — = in native deme.

Michael Osborne's reconstruction, Aresias I of perhaps Thorae[43] sent his daughter to neighboring Lamptre to marry Philocedes I. The latter's brother's son, Amoebichus III, married within his deme of Lamptre (Osborne no. 32: table 2a).

For south Attica (table 2a), besides the four intra-deme marriages which had the spouses buried in Sunium, 5658 records an intra-deme marriage for Anaphlystus in which both spouses moved to the Mesogeia (findspot at Liopesi: table 2c). For Cephale marriages are contracted with members of Phrearrhii (7725 + 11873: table 2a) and there is one intra-deme union recorded (6366: table 2a), with marital residence for both families being in or near Cephale.[44]

At Thorikos SEG 23.134 records the name Chaerephon of Thorikos with the names of Charinus and Sosippe, perhaps his daughter; these may well be related to the people in SEG 34.202, recording a Sosigenes son of Sosippus of Thoricus, who married Chaerylla, daughter of a Chaer[-] of Thoricus. This is speculative, but given the roots of the individuals' names there is a strong likelihood that two families of Thoricus intermarried and, as the findspots may indicate, stayed in their native deme.[45]

---

[43] The other possibility to Aresias's demotic Θορ[---] would be Thoricus, at some distance from Aresias's affines in Lamptre: M. J. Osborne, "Attic Epitaphs," 12–14. To Osborne's stemma I would add the Amoebichus of Lamptre attested for the mid-fifth century in *IG* I³ 433.32.

[44] One further marriage between a man from Cephale and a woman from Amphitrope has the partners residing in the Peiraeus (*IG* II² 5607). The one marriage involving disparate demes has a residence on Salamis: a man from Cephale buried with his three sons is married to a woman from Probalinthus (6355). The findspot was at Ambelaki on the east coast of the island across the strait from Peiraeus.

[45] These families may be related to the group recorded in *IG* II² 6218 where a Sosigenes, son of Euthippus, was buried with his brother Charmides of Thoricus. Given the name Sosigenes and, the root *hippus* in his patronymic and the fact that the root "Char" also appears in the Chaerephon group, I would speculate that there was a kinship tie with the groups in SEG. Unfortunately, the findspot of 6218 is given only as "Athenis." According to Kirchner's reconstruction Sosigenes married the sister of Demochares, son of Attabus of Thoricus, and Sosigenes and his brother were buried with Sosigenes' wife and her family of origin (her brother and sister). Demochares, Sosigenes' brother-in-

If we move up the east coast from south Attica (table 2b), an intra-deme marriage is recorded for Angele (5228), with residence in the deme, while the famous Goulandris stele, as noted by Robin Osborne, displays local endogamy despite the disparate demes of the spouses. The stele, *SEG* 35.178, records Themyllus son of Themyllus of Oe married to a woman, Nausistrate, from the not too distant inland deme of Hybadae. However, also commemorated on the stone are his son Antiphanes and the latter's wife, the daughter of Dionysius of Angele, Antiphanes' son Themon and Themon's wife Cleopasis from Angele. A space is left to record Themon's son's name with the latter's wife, Archestrate daughter of Meletus of Angele. Because the findspot of the stone was at Markopoulo, Antiphanes, his son and grandson certainly migrated to the deme of Angele,[46] a migration that suggests that the men were attracted to property in their wives' deme. Moreover, the deme of Oe experienced a great deal of emigration during the classical period. Of twenty-one men recorded in the gravestones, eleven certainly migrated to or became resident in other parts of Attica. A father and his sons and a daughter or wife, for instance, were buried at Rhamnous (*SEG* 30.203, 204). Three inscriptions record men (two of whom appear to be related) in southwest Attica at Koropi (6954, 6967, *SEG* 17.103),[47] while seven men are recorded on stones found in the city and another on a stone found two kilometers west of the Agora (Stamiris no. 6). Another man migrated to Salamis (6950).[48] Women were sent out as well: Lysimache of Oe, who was the

---

law, also from Thoricus, however, married a woman from Aphidna, whose father, Paramythus, was also buried with her. Although the findspot of 6218 is unknown, one can infer from the reconstruction that Demochares was also interested in extending and contracting alliances through the intra-deme marriage of his sister and through his own marriage to a woman from Aphidna. For a discussion of 6218 see Humphreys, *Family,* 114.

[46] R. Etienne, "Collection Dolly Goulandris, II: Stèle funéraire attique," *BCH* 99 (1975): 379–84; Humphreys, *Family,* 116; Osborne, *Demos,* 131. Archestrate's father, Meletus, could be related to the Meletus, son of Menestratus, on a list of prytaneis in Agora 15.47.23 dated c. 330 B.C. Meletus's father may well be identified with or related to Menestratus, priest of Asclepius in *IG* II² 4353, 4354.

[47] One of these inscriptions, 6954, records the marriage of Calliphantus of Oe to Callistrate of Kedoi. The name on 6967, Calliphon, has been restored by Peek: *SEG* 13.112. Although Traill (*The Political Organization of Attica, Hesperia,* suppl. 14 [Princeton, N.J.: American School of Classical Studies at Athens], map 1) had first tentatively assigned Kedoi to the coastal trittys of Erechtheis, he more recently (*Demos,* map) assigns it to the city and locates it on the map. Siewert (*Trittyen,* map 4) also assigns the deme to the city without, however, putting it on the map. M. K. Langdon, "The Topography of Coastal Erechtheis," *Chiron* 18 (1988): 51, though finding a coastal location attractive, feels that Kedoi should be left off the map of Attica.

[48] For a discussion of the migrations of individuals from Oe, see Etienne, "Collection Dolly Goulandris II," 379–84. I would like to thank Dr. Judith Binder for her kind help in locating the findspot of Stamiris no. 6. It is with great caution that I include this stone among those recording a marriage (table 1c). The woman's name was inscribed later and more carelessly than the man's, and the stone gives no explicit statement of marital ties. There is the possibility that the stone was reused. Other stones, however, on which the woman's name is added carelessly and at a later date do show that the woman is related to the men with whom she is listed: for example, *IG* II² 6131.

wife of a Leocrates, was buried at Rhamnous.[49] In another case (5977: table 2b), a woman from Oe was sent to Deiradiotae on the east coast; residence was decidedly virilocal, as indicated by the findspot of the inscription at Ceratea.[50] Another woman from Oe was given in marriage to a man from Paeania, with residence in that deme or close to it (7087, findspot at Spata + 12665: table 2c). The migration to the Mesogeia, certainly, and that to Deiradiotae, probably, suggest interest in landed property.

The most dramatic display of deme and kinship solidarity comes from the grave inscriptions at Myrrhinous and Rhamnous (table 2b). The peribolos of Meidon of Myrrhinous and the reconstruction of the family tree by Humphreys, followed by Robin Osborne, have already been discussed (see above, pp. 30–31). In summary, the peribolos may record the marriages of two brothers Meidon and Meidoteles, sons of Calliteles, to their mother's brother's daughters. One of these brothers, Meidoteles, sired a daughter, Cleoptoleme, who was married to her father's brother, Callimedon. Thus the marriages of Meidon and Meidoteles to women of their matriline were followed by sending Cleoptoleme back into her father's patriline. The series of gravestones marking this family's plot were found at Markopoulo, near the ancient deme of Myrrhinous.

Much further up the coast at Rhamnous, the large cemetery, which is still being excavated, reveals from its stones a high incidence of local endogamy, marriages both within the deme and into neighboring ones. Among the latter appear to be Oenoe, Eitea, and perhaps Tricorynthus.[51] Otherwise, the family periboloi so far published reveal that one woman came from the distant deme of Pithus, presumably as a bride.[52] Two stones do record marriages of women from

---

[49] Garland, "First Catalogue," 165.

[50] There is a liturgical family from this deme that owned farmland, presumably, in the deme, the family of Philopolis, son of Polystratus. Polystratus was a politician of some note in the latter part of the fifth century, Lys. 20.1 ff.; for his family, see *IG* II² 12499, 12658, 12967, and Davies, *APF,* 467–68.

[51] For Oenoe and Eitea, see Osborne, *Demos,* 247, n. 41; there was also a Cleonicus son of Eunicides of Eitea buried at Rhamnous as well as an Aristonice daughter or wife of Phanodemus of Eitea: *SEG* 31.194, 197. For the two demes called Eitea and the controversy concerning which one was located in northeast Attica, see Traill, *Demos,* 141–42; for Tricorynthus, *SEG* 30.219 records a Callistomache daughter of Cephisius of unstated deme who had been married to a man from Tricorynthus and was then buried at Rhamnous. Callistomache was buried with, and therefore belonged to, the family of Cephisius son of Lyceas of Rhamnous (*SEG* 21.916); therefore, she probably came from that deme. (Note that *SEG* 30.219 updates the stele *SEG* 21.916 from the third to the fourth century.) If this reconstruction is correct, then it could undercut Osborne's suggestion that women whose demes were not mentioned on the stelae came from their husband's deme (*Demos,* 130–31). Garland, "First Catalogue," 165–66, does not mention Callistomache's husband in his stemma. The name of Callistomache's father, Cephisius, also appears in Tricorynthus, the deme of Callistomache's husband: *IG* II² 1618 b 85, 1625.10.

[52] Pheidostrate, daughter of (?) Eucolus of Pithus, is buried in the Diogeiton peribolos (Garland, "First Catalogue," 164). In the same peribolos, inscribed on the wall, is the name Olbius, son of Timotheus of Aphidna, a deme at no great distance from Rhamnous (ibid.); perhaps Timotheus was also a relative or affine.

Rhamnous with men from distant demes (7372, 7376); in both cases the women seem not to have been buried with their husbands. In 7376 (table 2d) the woman from Rhamnous, married to a man from Thoricus, was buried at Cephisia. This burial may suggest the marriage of landed neighbors and therefore the migration of both families to Cephisia, but this is speculative. In 7372 (table 1d) the woman from Rhamnous had been married to a man from Gargettus but was buried in the city. Again the urban setting may have provided an opportunity for families from distant demes to ally.

Thus in demes in the coastal trittyes of Attica except at Eleusis, there was a high incidence of local endogamy. Individuals married within their deme or married individuals from proximate demes. This was especially true for south Attica with its intra-deme unions and for Rhamnous with its locally endogamous marriages. Especially noteworthy was the large family burial of Themyllus of Oe and his descendants in Angele. Themyllus's migration from Oe was then followed by the repeated marriages of his descendants to individuals from Angele. Again we see an extension out to Angele followed by consolidation within the deme. In Myrrhinous the large family burial of Meidon reveals a good deal of kinship endogamy with two brothers marrying heiresses. A daughter from one of these unions was then married to her father's brother.

Generally, if men stayed in their deme they married locally, either within their deme or with individuals of neighboring demes; if anyone moved a great distance, it was women, although the Goulandris stele shows that men could migrate as well; migration appears to have been a common occurrence for the deme of Oe. Perhaps the search for land in other rural parts of Attica drew men from their deme, while the city provided men with business and trading opportunities. The high incidence of local endogamy in the coastal demes and the demes in south Attica is reflected again in the inland demes, in both the Mesogeia and the northern plain.

THE INLAND DEMES OF THE MESOGEIA AND THE NORTH

Besides these marriages contracted by families from coastal demes in the Mesogeia, there are twelve marriages, to judge from findspots, linking families who from inland demes who resided in the rural area (table 2c).[53] In all except two marriages the spouses came from nearby and sometimes contiguous demes; and several intra-deme marriages are recorded. For instance, in Erchia there is one intra-deme marriage recorded (6135), while 6100 also records an intended (?) marriage within the deme for another apparently unrelated family; both groups

[53] The relevant inscriptions are: *IG* II² 5817, 5983, 6100, 6131, 6135, 6430, 6437 (2 instances), 7060, 7095, 7098, 7820.

were of liturgical status and resided in the deme of origin.[54] 7820 records an alliance among families of Paeania and Oa in the same trittys and therefore neighboring; residence was near Paeania (findspot at Liopesi). Two intra-deme marriages are also recorded (7060, 7095) for Paeania; in these alliances, residence was
in the Mesogeia, at Spata and Liopesi.

The families of the Mesogeia did not marry solely among themselves, but did
marry into the northern inland demes: 6131 records a marriage that had a
woman from Phlya migrate some ten kilometers to her husband's deme of Erchia. On the other hand, 7098 records the long-distance marriage of a woman
from Acharnae who migrated to Paeania, her husband's deme. Otherwise
women from distant coastal and city demes by and large migrated to the inland
for their marriages.[55]

The northern inland demes (table 2c) also show a great tendency for families
to form marital alliances with ones from the same or neighboring demes. For
instance, a woman from Deceleia joins her husband's family at Acharnae (5817),
while 5983 records the marriage of Nicodemus, son of Phanias of Deceleia, to
a woman from Phegous—a nearby deme, if the conjectured trittys assignment is
correct—with residence in Deceleia, the husband's deme. Nicodemus, the proposer of a decree for the phratry Demotionidae, was a wealthy and important
man in both his phratry and his deme—Deceleia, the center for the Demotionidae.[56] Another family in Phegous (6437) sent their daughter to a man in

---

[54] For the stemma of 6135, see Davies, *APF,* 402; for 6100, ibid., 361–62, where Davies, following Kirchner, feels that because there is a *loutrophoros* depicted on the stone Anticrates, son of Call-
icrates of Erchia, named on the stone, actually died before his marriage to Aristaechme, daughter of
Lysis of Erchia, who is commemorated with him. Davies is followed by Osborne, *Demos,* 134. For a
more cautionary note, see Garland, "First Catalogue," 130, n. 20, who, citing *IG* II² 5614, demonstrates that *loutrophoroi* could be used on the graves of married people.

[55] Eleven such marriages are recorded, all decidedly virilocal, and only in one case is there the
possibility that proximity was an issue: 7259, recording the solitary burial of a woman from Potamus, also states that her husband was from Paeania. The findspot was in the Mesogeia; if Potamus
here refers to one of the city demes, then the demes of the spouses were not far removed. For women
from city demes, see, for instance: 6097, 6834, 7527. 6097 will be discussed further below. In 7527
Timesylla's father, Euthycrates of Ceiriadae, may be commemorated on a gravestone found in Athens
(*SEG* 32.279). The stone was reused but if its findspot reveals that it originally stood in the city, then
Timesylla was from an urban family and had migrated to the Mesogeia for her marriage. In other
alliances linking families from disparate inland demes or linking families from inland demes with others from disparate parts of Attica, the families resided in the city: 7702 (Teithras and Phlya), 7717
(Erchia and Phrearrhii). Outside of these instances, neolocality is recorded for perhaps four marriages. 5658, 6193, 6748, all intra-deme alliances, have the couples moving from Anaphlystus, Euonymon, and Leuconoeum, respectively. The couple from Anaphlystus moved to the Mesogeia, that
from Euonymon moved slightly southward down the coast, and the couple from Leuconoeum
moved into the northern plain around Acharnae. 7376 is a solitary burial at Cephisia of a woman
from Rhamnous who had been married to a man from Thoricus. One, final, uxorilocal marriage is
recorded in 5867—the migration of the son of Polyeuctus of Bate to his wife's deme, Erchia.

[56] C. W. Hedrick, Jr., *The Decrees of the Demotionidai* (Atlanta, Ga.: Scholars' Press, 1990), 55–56.

Cephisia nearby, and their son married a woman from Cephisia, his own deme. Residence for all was in Cephisia.[57]

Even when there are alliances of families from distant demes of the northern inland, there may well be a local element. We recall the discussion of the Gephyraei from Aphidna (above, p. 13), who may have had property in the northern plain. Similar strategies may be indicated in the stone 5753 (table 1c), which commemorates two brothers and a sister from Aphidna who were buried near Patissia, a suburb of Athens stretching toward the northern plain. If Charidemus of Phlya, who is recorded on the stone, is the sister's husband, then the stone not only records a uxorilocal burial, but may indicate as well that the proximity of the husband's deme to the siblings' residence encouraged a marriage tie.[58] For other families from Aphidna who married far and wide, residence was in the city (5725, 5728: table 1b).[59]

On the other hand, some families from northern city demes allied with families of inland demes in the northern plain, so that proximity of demes may have played a substantial role. 6748 records spouses from Leuconoeum migrating to Acharnae (table 2c), while another stone records the migration of a woman from Acharnae to her husband's (city) deme of Hermus, five kilometers away (6077, findspot at Daphni: table 1c).[60]

In the Mesogeia and in the northern inland demes, then, there was a high incidence of local endogamy. For the most part rural folk, if they stayed in their deme, had a greater tendency to marry locally, though not necessarily in their own deme. The extensive migration of women, on the one hand, allowed men to stay put and farm their land, but, on the other hand, allowed farmers to ally with families outside their own locale. In the event of a crisis affecting a farmer's crop in one locale, but not affecting his affines' crop in another locale, disaster

---

[57] In another intra-deme marriage in Cephisia, the spouses resided in their deme as well (6430).

[58] There are, however, other names recorded on the stone. Humphreys, *Family*, 112, states that the stone probably records the names of the spouses of one brother and the sister, but also states that two women's names were later added to the stone. She does not conjecture a relationship between these women and the siblings from Aphidna. If we ignore these women, then Humphreys is incorrect in stating that the spouse of one brother is recorded; besides the two brothers, their sister and her husband, the remaining individual on the stone is [Apole]xis son of Tauriscus of Amphitrope, whose mother and father may be recorded on 5614. Given that the name of Apolexis's mother in the latter inscription was Hierocleia of Alopece, and given that the name of the siblings' father in 5753 was Hierocleides, I would conjecture that Apolexis has been attracted to kinsmen through a female line. To confuse matters even more, one of the women whose names were added later was Hierocleia (Peek *AM* 67 (1942) no. 365). I would also conjecture that, given the strongly religious names of some of these individuals (Hierocleides the father and Asclepiodorus the son-in-law), this could be a priestly family.

[59] However, the daughter of Democles of Aphidna, a Gephyraeus, migrated to Halae Aexonides for her marriage. She was originally going to marry Euctemon of the northern deme, Cephisia, who, like the Gephyraei, was active in the city (see above, chapter 1, p. 23).

[60] In contrast, one woman from Alopece, south of the *astu*, traveled to her husband's deme of Athmonon, with at least one son remaining in the region (5348, 5349).

could be averted. Exogamy, therefore, allowed farmers to spread their risks.[61] Whatever reaction to nonlocal influx may be behind local endogamy at Sunium and Rhamnous, and in the large and numerous periboloi in the latter deme, this kind of behavior cannot be isolated from rural behavior in general. It is quite clear that in the case of many rural demes, including Sunium, when demesmen migrated to the city, they could contract marriages with members of their native deme, but were equally as likely, indeed more likely, to contract marriages with families from distant demes.

MARRIAGE STRATEGIES: THE ROLE OF KINSHIP ENDOGAMY

More often than not the inscriptions do not inform us whether spouses were related to each other; only in instances of homonymity can the scholar detect the possibility of kinship in-marriage. But even in cases of local and kinship endogamy, frequently the marriage and the married couple are isolated from any record of the extended kin group. Therefore, this section will concentrate on two families where the significance for the family's or kin group of a woman's marriage out can be appreciated. These strategies will be quite familiar by now, for they are evident in the practices of some of the families discussed in chapter 1. As with the study of many of these stones, considerable prosopographical conjecture is involved.

In the previous chapter, we noted how families extended their ties only to consolidate by marrying endogamously, within their kin. For instance, Demochares' daughter, Hippocleia, married out, but her second union was endogamous. Besides the orations of Demosthenes, a horos stone and a grave lekythos (Finley, *SLC*, no. 146, and *IG* II² 6737a respectively) inform us that Hippocleia, the daughter of Demochares from the deme Leuconoeum, married a man from Phlya with property in that deme. She then returned to her own deme to be remarried to a fellow demesman and perhaps kinsman. The marital practice found in the orations, therefore, is paralleled by the marriage of a family in the inscriptions, which was from a northern city deme and which allied with a family in a northern inland deme; in Hippocleia's case, furthermore, her endogamous union was probably roughly contemporaneous with the marriage of her brother to their mother's sister's daughter.[62]

The practice of sending a woman out and bringing her descendant back, or the woman herself back, as in Hippocleia's case, may be seen in the case of another family in the grave inscriptions. In 5811, whose findspot is given vaguely as "Athenis," Cleostrate, the daughter of Deximenes of Acharnae, was married to Sostratus, son of Eratocles of Daedalidae, and was buried with him. Also com-

---

[61] T. W. Gallant, *Risk and Survival in Ancient Greece* (Stanford, Calif.: Stanford University Press), 154–55.

[62] Davies, *APF,* 142. The findspot of Hippocleia's lekythos, 6737a, is unfortunately unknown.

memorated on the stone are Cleostrate's sister, Sostrate, and the latter's husband, Eratocles, son of Sostratus of Daedalidae. The feminized form of Sostratus for one woman's name and the root *stratē* in the other woman's name suggest that they are related to Sostratus and Eratocles, son of Sostratus. Also, because Sostratus's father was also named Eratocles, and the younger Eratocles' father was named Sostratus, I would infer that the two husbands were related to each other; they may well have been father's brother's sons to each other. In other words, the elder Sostratus and the elder Eratocles were brothers. Because the women came from a different deme from that of their husbands, but had similar names to their husband or husband's father, the women may well have been related to their husbands through a woman. If so, it is more than likely that a female ascendant of the women's husbands had been given in marriage to Deximenes, the women's father. Therefore, the ascendant, a kinswoman of Sostratus and Eratocles, went to Acharnae, but her daughters were brought back to Daedalidae.[63]

A similar strategy has the family reacting to the departure of a kinswoman by marrying within its deme. If Davies's reconstruction is correct, Metagenes of Cydathenaeum was himself married to a fellow demeswoman (6587); Metagenes' brother's daughter, Delias, the daughter of Nicias, was sent out of her deme Cydathenaeum to marry (possibly) Apolexis, son of Euaeon of Erchia; the findspot of the stone on which she is recorded (6097) was at Liopesi, and therefore may indicate that Delias migrated out and resided in her husband's deme. This migration out, however, was followed by a good deal of intra-deme consolidation on the part of her agnates and her own descendants. Davies surmises that Delias's brother's son married a woman of his own deme and that Delias's own grandson (son's son), Phrasisthenes, son of Eualcides of Erchia, married a woman from his deme of Erchia (6135).[64] In other words, the marriage of a woman out of her city family and her introduction into a rural family was followed by intra-deme marriages in her families of both origin and of marriage.

POSTSCRIPT: THE DOTAL HOROI

There has been no systematic study to date on the relation between findspots of horoi defining secured property for a dowry and the deme of the woman to be married. Methodologically, this study may seem hazardous as the sample is very

---

[63] See, C. A. Cox, "Sisters, Daughters and the Deme of Marriage: A Note," *JHS* 108 (1988): 187.

[64] The findspot of 6587 is, however, unclear: *IG* cites it as Athens, but *SEG* (35.173), without explanation, cites it as Attica, while G. Kokula, *Marmorlutrophoren, AM,* suppl. vol. 10 (Berlin: Gebr. Mann, 1984) lists its findspot in the index (232) as unknown, again without explanation. The stone is in the British Museum, as the *SEG* editors and Kokula (193–94, no. 37) point out. Davies, *APF,* 401–2, cites the other inscriptions outlining the family tree, 6109 and 6110. Davies suggests that either Delias's brother, Epigenes II, gave his daughter in marriage to a demesman, Conon, son of Metrodorus I of Cydathenaeum, or that Metrodorus I gave his daughter in marriage to Epigenes' homonymous son, Epigenes III.

small; only fifteen of the stones recording the woman's deme have findspots that are known. Moreover, many of these stones have no date and are not necessarily of the classical era; in fact some can be dated as late as the second century B.C. In addition the stones are biased toward the wealthy, so that again the practices of the "average" family cannot be assessed.[65] Nevertheless, there are some advantages to these documents, the chief one being that the dotal horoi always mention the woman's name and often her father's deme, though not that of her husband. Furthermore, although only a small number of these stones can be securely dated to the classical era, in general they seem to affirm the findings from the classical grave stelae: the extensive mobility of women in the rural area and the high rate of heterogamy in the city. Because postclassical documents seem also to show this pattern, the mobility of women is a general trend not confined to chronological limits.

In bald numbers, of the ten stones found in rural areas, six record property secured for a woman in an area at a great distance from her deme, while in the remaining four, the secured property lay close to the woman's deme. However, a closer look at the stones indicating great distance reveals that two of the six women were from the city, from the deme of Cerameis to be exact (Finley, *SLC*, no. 135A; Millett no. 137A), with land and a house being secured for the bride at Icaria and Brauron respectively. The number of women from rural demes who married men owning rural property at a great distance from the woman's deme is equal to the number marrying men whose property lay close by (four each). If the secured property in these stones gives some indication of the whereabouts of the husbands' demes, then rural women of the wealthier families were equally likely to be sent out to distant demes as to remain in their local area.

Noteworthy as well is the correlation in these rural stones between the distance of the property secured and the woman's urban deme, a correlation reaffirmed by the horoi found in the city. Of the five stones found in city demes (though not necessarily in the *astu*), one at Trachones (Euonymon) records property secured for a woman from Phegaea (Finley, *SLC*, no. 138), while two found in the Agora record secured property for women from Deceleia and Phrearrhii (Finley, *SLC*, no. 151; Millett no. 148A, respectively), and a fourth stone, found close to the temple of Amynus on the Acropolis (Finley, *SLC*, no. 148), records property secured for another woman from Phrearrhii. Only one stone (Finley, *SLC*, no. 21A) shows that a woman, whose *kyrios* was from Melite, had property secured for her in or near the Agora, close to her *kyrios*'s deme.[66] If the *kyrios*

---

[65] The stones to be used are Finley, *SLC*, nos. 132, 134, 135, 135A, 136, 137, 138, 140, 146, 148, 151, 21A; Millett nos. 137A, 146B, 148A. On the bias of the stones, see Millett, xi. All horoi found in the Agora have now been edited by G. Lalonde et al., *Inscriptions: Horoi. Poletai Records. Leases of Public Lands. The Athenian Agora*, vol. 19 (Princeton, N.J.: American School of Classical Studies at Athens, 1991).

[66] Finley, 183, points out that this stone was one of five linking the dowry with *prasis epi lysei* as opposed to *apotimēma*. Millett, xviii, notes that *apotimēma* is found for transactions other than pupil-

was her appointed guardian there is a good chance that the woman herself was from Melite; her deme, however, is not known.

Although the horoi seem to affirm the thesis that city conditions encouraged heterogamy, one stone found in the city may indicate that a rural locale was, nevertheless, a force behind the marriage. In horos no. 148A (Millett = *Agora* 19.H81) the woman from Phrearrhii, Cleitarete the daughter of Scythes, who had property secured for her dowry in the city, has been identified tentatively with Pyrrhus's mother, Cleitarete, in Isaeus 3.30.[67] If the identification has any validity, this woman's daughter's son, the speaker of the oration, was evicted by his rival from an *ergastērion* in the mining district at Besa (ibid., 22–23). The implication of the eviction is that the property belonged to Pyrrhus, Cleitarete's son and mother's brother to the speaker. Pyrrhus's father, therefore, although owning a house in the city according to the horos, seems to have married a woman whose native deme was proximate to Pyrrhus's sphere of activity, and therefore perhaps to that of Pyrrhus's father himself, in south Attica.

To conclude generally, then, the behavior witnessed in the wealthier families of the orations is observed once again in the "average" families of the inscriptions. For the families of the orations, alliances among fellow demesmen or repeated alliances into certain demes were meant to secure an estate, which was frequently contested. Although urban neighborhoods encouraged marital alliances among families from disparate demes, some attention to locale, particularly in the northern plain and in south Attica can be seen. In other words, families from neighboring rural demes could ally or landed neighbors could contract marriages. The grave inscriptions recording 112 or more marriages and the fifteen dotal horoi can complement this literary material by demonstrating the real difference between urban and rural marriage patterns, patterns which might well cut across wealth and status. Though small in number, the inscriptions suggest that the urban setting allowed families from the same deme or from neighboring demes to contract marriages, but heterogamy and neolocality dominated: the

---

lary or dotal obligations. See Harris's argument that *apotimēma* is no different than other types of security used by the Athenians: E. M. Harris, "*APOTIMEMA*: Athenian Terminology for Real Security in Leases and Dowry Agreements," *CQ* 43 (1993): 73–95.

[67] For the identity of Cleitarete, see Millett's commentary ad loc. based on S. Miller, "Mortgage Horoi from the Athenian Agora," *Hesperia* 41 (1972): 274, no. 4. I am not in agreement with Miller's interpretation of the events in Isaeus 3, however. The identity of Cleitarete may nevertheless may gain some justification by the fact that the father of the Cleitarete on the stone was named Scythes, a rare name but one which is known from [Dem.] 45.8 in a list of witnesses for Phormio the banker. Also witnessing with Scythes (of Cydathenaeum) was a man by the name of Endius (of Lamptre); Endius, not a common name for the fourth century, was the name of the speaker's brother, Pyrrhus's adoptee, in Isaeus 3. This Endius of Lamptre, moreover, had a brother who owned land and perhaps as well an *ergastērion* at Besa (Davies, *APF,* 178), the same deme in which Pyrrhus's workshop had been located. Endius of Lamptre, however, had sons (ibid., 179–80), and as the actor in Isaeus 3 appears not to have had children, the two homonymous men could not have been identical, though they certainly could have been related.

migration of families, often from distant regions of Attica, then allowed for a marital alliance. Whether such heterogamy also reflects at times social heterogamy, that is, alliances between families of different social status, cannot be known. Nevertheless urban and rural biases can be observed: an individual in the city was in some cases married to a spouse from a distant deme, while his or her kinsmen (kinswomen) remaining in the native deme married locally. The inscriptions suggest that the rural setting encouraged a higher rate of local endogamy, particularly for men, while the mobility of women could be marked by the practice of sending a kinswoman out to follow another into a certain deme, or by bringing a woman's descendant back to her kin group and native deme. In yet other instances, a woman's marriage out could be followed by a family member's endogamous union within the deme, if not within the kin group. Sometimes concerns in a family or kin group regarding marriage and the selection of partners could span generations, as the family attempted to spread its risks and consolidate what it had.

Marriage strategy, however, is only half the picture, for in this discussion our participants, and particularly the women, appear as no more than pawns. The dynamic half of the picture, domestic relationships, needs yet to be discussed, to determine first to what extent marriage strategies were successful in securing wealth and keeping kinship ties intact, and second to what extent the model of the nuclear family accurately reflects the complexity of interests in the *oikos*, the basic domestic unit prompting marriage and in turn being affected by it.

Harmony and Conflict within
the Household

THE INVESTIGATION so far has focused on the kinds of interests motivating marriage alliances among the elite and among the less well known, and hence the emphasis has been on the patriline, the formal genealogy. The patriline, however, is only part of the picture. Marriage is only part of the history of two *oikoi,* for with marriage came the family and the interests of individuals in the family. Accordingly, we now turn to the relationships among dyads in the nuclear family; that is, among pairs of individuals who held either conflicting or mutually beneficial interests, such as parent and child or brother and brother. Through the examination of dyads, affective ties among family members can be better understood.[1] In particular, it will become clear how property interests could consolidate but also disrupt ties among family members, and this will provide a balance to the often seemingly rigid schemes in the marriage strategies previously examined. In this chapter, the discussion will focus on the transmitters of property and wealth, the husband as chief transmitter and his wife, and will then examine how each parent interacted with his or her child. The next chapter will examine the role of property interests in sibling relationships.

The chief sources throughout will be again the orations with their almost constant concern for inheritance. Again I must point out that the orations have problems as sources with their incessant distortions of the truth, denigration of opponents as unworthy citizens, and depiction of the speaker's side as good citizens. As David Cohen has recently stated, in an agonistic society the orations on inheritance provided an arena for an ongoing pursuit of conflict so that rhetoric and kinship ties were manipulated to fit the needs of the moment.[2] The picture of inheritance drawn by the orations was frequently the conventional one: the

---

[1] A. Plakans, *Kinship in the Past: An Anthropology of European Family Life 1500–1900* (Oxford: Basil Blackwell, 1984), 159.

[2] D. Cohen, *Law, Violence and Community in Classical Athens* (Cambridge: Cambridge University Press, 1995), 163. The following chapters, though focusing on the orations, will rely from time to time on other sources, for instance Plutarch's biographies. Plutarch's essays on affection toward children and on brotherly love, however, will not be considered as they rarely pertain to Athenian individuals. Plutarch in general is a difficult source to use because of his late date. In addition, the motives he ascribed to the actions of individuals were shaped by his moral concerns: he concentrated on an individual's qualities rather than on the wider historical significance of that person's actions. See D. A. Russell, *Plutarch* (London: Duckworth, 1973), 102–3. For bibliography on the contradictions in Plutarch, see A. G. Nikolaides, "Plutarch's Contradictions," *ClMed* 42 (1991): 154 and n. 4.

focus was on the downward transmission of wealth and, given the legal bias, on downward transmission among males. This bias had a direct effect on emotions and needs among family members, which in turn structured and were structured by property concerns.[3]

No discussion of property interests would be complete without first stating that ancient Athens was a shame culture, that is, one in which there was a tendency to evaluate oneself according to the way one was seen by others. Shame was caused by the fear of external sanctions. Shame and honor in Athens were closely linked as honor was fundamental to one's reputation and social worth. Honor for a man could be public honor gained through his political reputation or his benefactions to the city. A man's reputation also depended on the proper conduct of his family members, so that honor was also tied in with behavior at the private level. Here the women of a man's family were important. A woman's honor was bound up with her public display of sexual modesty. Whether married or unmarried, she was expected to manifest reserve in her dealings with the opposite sex. In many cultures, the reputation of a woman depends upon her fulfillments of community expectations of chastity. Her movements, dress and behavior must fit a standard of modesty.[4] In Athens, behind the woman's public display of modesty, her interest in property use and transmission could influence relationships among close family members as well as among extended kin.

HUSBAND AND WIFE

Social historians and anthropologists studying European societies are now acknowledging that women could have a great deal of informal power at the private level of the household. A woman's chastity was indispensable to the honor of her family of marriage, and, therefore, she could gain leverage by threatening to trespass against chastity. Furthermore, women's interests were reflected and expressed in succession practices and in the successful management of the household economy. Particularly important to the status of women was the dowry, because of its place in the conjugal household and the negotiations over its use and

---

[3] H. Medick and D. Sabean, introduction to *Interest and Emotion* (Cambridge: Cambridge University Press, 1988), 2, argue that property should not be reified, but rather understood in the context of emotions and needs.

[4] The bibliography on shame culture is vast. For some discussion of shame culture in antiquity, see K. J. Dover, *Greek Popular Morality in the Time of Plato and Aristotle* (Berkeley: University of California Press, 1974), 226 ff.; D. L. Cairns, *Aidōs: The Psychology and Ethics of Honour and Shame in Ancient Greek Literature* (Oxford: Clarendon Press, 1993), 15 ff., 120 ff., for cross-cultural bibliography. Cairns, however, would downplay the antithesis between shame and guilt cultures. For further bibliography, see D. Cohen, *Law, Sexuality and Society* (Cambridge: Cambridge University Press, 1990), 60 ff. Two classic discussions on female honor in modern Greece are: J. K. Campbell, *Honour, Family and Patronage* (Oxford: Oxford University Press, 1974), esp. 270; J. du Boulay, *Portrait of a Greek Mountain Village* (Oxford: Clarendon Press, 1974), 104 ff.

transmission. A large dowry ensured the woman an important role in the decisions of the marital household; it helped to stabilize the marriage and to encourage marital intimacy. Because the dowry, as the property of the woman's natal kin, would ideally be transmitted to the man's children, the man could become involved in the property interests of his wife's family of origin.[5]

In classical Athens, the male sphere of activity was predominantly the outdoor and public one—the fields, the lawcourts, the Agora, the council, and the assembly. The woman was relegated to the indoors—her chief function was the managing of the *oikia,* the house, and as such her role was acknowledged as indispensable.[6] Marriages in Athens were arranged: the selection of a prospective husband for a woman was a matter of great concern for her parents as she was supposed to marry a man of satisfactory status.[7] Generally the bride was about fourteen years of age, whereas her husband tended to be in his thirties—an age difference that can be attributed first to the importance of the dowry and second to delayed transmission of property from father to son.[8]

---

[5] For the woman's influence on her husband and his interest in her kinsmen, I cite here only a few references. The series of essays in M. Erler and M. Kowaleski, eds., *Women and Power in the Middle Ages* (Athens, Ga.: University of Georgia Press, 1988) were very helpful, and in particular, S. Chojnacki, "The Power of Love: Wives and Husbands in Late Medieval Venice," 126–48. Also valuable are the essays on modern Greece in J. Dubisch, ed., *Gender and Power in Rural Greece* (Princeton, N.J.: Princeton University Press, 1986), and especially E. Friedl, "The Position of Women: Appearance and Reality," 42–52. Friedl insists that a large dowry must include land, the most valued form of productive wealth, in order to enhance the woman's position. See also S. D. Salamone and J. B. Stanton, "Introducing the *Nikokyra:* Ideality and Reality in Social Process," 97–120, for the economic success of the household. P. Sant Cassia and C. Bada, *The Making of the Modern Greek Family* (Cambridge: Cambridge University Press, 1992), 18, argue that urbanization was conducive to devoting attention to one's affines. These societies of course do not parallel ancient Athens in every instance, but I use them here as a means to understand the motivations of the ancient Athenians. The sources suggest how property concerns unite the husband with his affines.

[6] See the sections in Xenophon cited in below, chapter 5, p. 130. The most recent discussion on spatial segregation is Cohen, *Law, Sexuality,* 70 ff., who argues that spatial categorization can shift; for example, symposia took place within houses, and were seen as private as compared to conversations in the Agora. However, they were also seen as public when compared to the activities of the free women of the house. On the isolation of the woman, see S. Pomeroy, *Goddesses, Whores, Wives, and Slaves* (New York: Schocken, 1975), 71–73; also, more recently, R. Just, *Women in Athenian Law and Life* (London: Routledge, 1989), 13–25. Cohen, *Law, Sexuality,* 133 ff., however, questions the reality of this rigid ideal.

[7] See, for instance, Dem. 20.57. For some discussions of arranged marriages: W. K. Lacey, *The Family in Classical Greece* (Ithaca, N.Y.: Cornell University Press, 1968), 107; R. Sealey, *Women and Law in Classical Greece* (Chapel Hill: University of North Carolina Press, 1990), 25; Just, *Women,* 43 ff.; R. Garland, *The Greek Way of Life* (Ithaca, N.Y.: Cornell University Press, 1990), 217 ff.

[8] For the age difference, see Just, *Women,* 151–52; for the attention to the dowry, see below, pp. 116–20. For the delayed transmission of the estate to the son, see on fathers and sons, below, p. 86. Age differences between spouses have been noted for Tuscany from the thirteenth century onward, where the father was reluctant to have his son marry at too early an age and be thereby led to question the older man's authority: C. Klapisch-Zuber, *Women, Family, and Ritual in Renaissance Italy,* trans. L. Cochrane (Chicago: University of Chicago Press, 1985), 19.

Once a marriage took place, it created a strong and lasting bond. In itself, divorce was an easy procedure: the husband merely dismissed his wife, while the woman, if initiating the divorce, had to present herself to the archon.[9] The orations, however, give little indication that divorce was indeed common. For instance, in the corpus of Isaeus approximately fifty marriages are recorded, but only two divorces are mentioned.[10] This probably does not reflect the divorce rate of ancient Athens; because a woman's divorce could lead to gossip about her behavior and thereby bring shame on her,[11] the reluctance of the orators to discuss divorce may represent the normative view, the social ideal. In Isaeus 6 the speaker, the alleged adopted son of Euctemon's son by a first wife, strengthens his claim by hiding the fact that Euctemon had divorced his first wife;[12] the obfuscation was meant to weaken the claims of legitimacy of Euctemon's sons by a second marriage.

Indeed, a look at the divorces recorded in Isaeus and elsewhere reveals that although the husband could merely dismiss his wife, the woman was not necessarily passive or mute. Isaeus, for one, was quite careful to portray a divorce in acceptable terms.[13] Isaeus 2.6 ff., which describes a divorce initiated by an older man from his young wife, details how the husband, Menecles, concerned that his wife should produce children, approaches her brother with the suggestion that she should be divorced and remarried to someone who can sire offspring. The husband is not only careful to praise the woman's virtue and character, but also, with the brother, approaches his wife to obtain her consent. The woman at first refuses but, reluctantly, with the prodding of both her brother and her husband, agrees to the divorce.[14] In another oration, the young wife does not leave

[9] See, for example: Lacey, *Family*, 108–9; A. R. W. Harrison, *The Law of Athens*, vol. 1 (Oxford: Clarendon Press, 1968), 38–44; Pomeroy, *Goddesses*, 64–65; D. M. MacDowell, *The Law of Classical Athens* (Ithaca, N.Y.: Cornell University Press, 1978), 88.

[10] That of Euctemon from his first wife (Is. 6 and Davies, *APF*, 563), and that of Menecles from the speaker's sister (Is. 2.6–8). Sant Cassia and Bada note the same phenomenon for nineteenth-century Athens: although nullifying a marriage was easy, the divorce rate was low because the need to produce offspring created a strong moral basis for the union: Sant Cassia and Bada, *Making*, 199, 201.

[11] A. Scafuro, "Witnessing and False Witnessing: Proving Citizenship and Kin Identity in Fourth-Century Athens," in *Athenian Identity and Civic Ideology*, ed. A. Boegehold and A. Scafuro (Baltimore: Johns Hopkins University Press, 1994), 163.

[12] Davies, *APF*, 563.

[13] The following are the divorces mentioned in the texts: Plut. *Per.* 24.5 (Pericles' wife); And. 1.124 ff. (Callias's second and third wives); Lys. 14.28 (Hipponicus III's wife); Is. 2.6 ff. (Menecles' wife); Is. 6 (see also note 10 above) (Euctemon's first wife); Dem. 30–31 (Onetor's sister, divorced twice); 39–40 (Mantias and Plango); Dem. 41.3 ff. (Leocrates' wife); Dem. 57.41 ff. (Protomachus's wife); Dem. 59.50 ff. (Phrastor and Neaera's daughter); Lysias 1, passim (the speaker's wife) (suggested but not actually stated in the oration). For completeness' sake I mention the tradition, of dubious reliability, of Cimon's divorce from his sister Elpinice before her marriage to Callias II (Plut. *Cim.* 4.7; Nep. *Cim.* 1.2).

[14] Given the active role, therefore, of the woman in this divorce, the Plutarchian tradition stating that Pericles' wife agreed to their divorce, and that Pericles gave her to another man, is credible (*Per.* 24.5).

her older husband, Ciron, although their two young sons have died and there is little chance, given her husband's age, that they can have any more children (Is. 8.36).

Although Mantias divorced Plango, he continued his relationship with her and finally, after some coercion from Plango, acknowledged the paternity of his sons by her. When Callias dismissed his third wife, the widow of Ischomachus, and denied his paternity of her son, her kinsmen induced Callias to reconsider; Callias in the end swore to his paternity and in fact took Ischomachus's widow back into his house.[15] This is similar to the divorce of Phrastor of Aegilia from his wife, who was, as it turned out, not a citizen but the daughter of a prostitute. Nevertheless, when Phrastor was ill and he feared that he was dying, he reconciled himself with his pregnant ex-wife, albeit temporarily ([Dem.] 59.50 ff.). In another case, Protomachus, a poor man, divorced his wife when he had the chance to marry a wealthy heiress. Because his first wife was also poor, and therefore would have had a difficult time remarrying, Protomachus took it upon himself to have an acquaintance marry her (Dem. 57.41 ff.). This second marriage lasted until the husband's death. Finally, Onetor's sister registered a false divorce in an attempt to save her husband's property from confiscation (Dem. 30. and 31).[16]

The general view of the orations, no doubt idealized, is that husband and wife try to make a marriage work. There may be some distrust of the wife at first, but when she begins to bear children for the *oikos* a deep respect and trust develops between spouses (Lys. 1.6, 14), which is based on open communication (Lycurg. fr. C 11–12). Likewise, husbands and wives are supposed to settle their differences for the sake of the children ([Dem.] 40.29). Certainly in myth and drama this ideal prevails—the domestication of women allows for their incorporation into society as the wives of men.[17] On the other hand, although some of the ancient sources do admit that a husband can be romantically and sexually intimate with his wife,[18] other sources consider it in poor taste to display too much affection for one's wife, indeed such behavior can lead to gossip that the woman is not the man's wife but a hetaera (Is. 3.13–14; see also Plut. *Cim.* 4.8–9).[19]

---

[15] On the sordid details of Mantias's and Callias's divorces, see Davies, *APF,* 264–65 (Callias), 365–67 (Mantias).

[16] On brothers and sisters, see below, chapter 4, pp. 123–24.

[17] Just, *Women,* 232.

[18] D. Cohen, "The Social Context of Adultery at Athens," in *Nomos: Essays in Athenian Law, Politics and Society* ed. P. Cartledge, P. Millett, and S. Todd (Cambridge: Cambridge University Press, 1990), 163.

[19] J. Rossiaud, *Medieval Prostitution,* trans. L. G. Cochrane (Oxford: Blackwell, 1988), 75, points out that among the medieval moralists a husband's excessive love for his wife was considered adulterous. Emotional abandon was a worse fault within marriage than outside of it. Likewise, in late eighteenth- and early nineteenth-century Athens, romantic love was viewed as threatening the collective interests of the family: Sant Cassia and Bada, *Making,* 195. The concern, therefore, of classicists like Just, *Women,* 103, 135 ff., and Cohen, "Social Context," 163, *Law, Sexuality,* 167–68, as to whether Athenian spouses were close may reflect modern north European and American values.

Spouses do show genuine concern when the other is ill (Dem. 30.34, 50.61, 59.56) and in one case a husband instructs his wife to have their yet unborn son avenge the husband's upcoming execution at the hands of political foes (Lys. 13.42).[20]

Men were allowed extramarital sexual activity, but they should not bring the concubine or hetaira into the household out of respect for their wives ([Dem.] 40.9–10, 59.21–22). For the wife, however, absolute fidelity was the rule, as men had to be certain that their heirs were their own children. Furthermore, the children had to be true Athenians in order to participate in the *polis*, their citizenship defined by the Athenian citizenship of both parents and the formality of the parents' union.[21] Consequently, the husband was obliged to divorce his adulterous wife (Lys. 1, passim), and she could suffer public humiliation and be barred from the religious rituals of the *polis*.[22] In his diatribe against Demosthenes, Aeschines was unique in asserting that Demosthenes put his wife in bed with his associate, Cnosion (Aeschin. 2.149). Women were strongly discouraged from displaying improper behavior (Is. 3.13–14; Hyp. fr. D 9–10); and the ideal was for the husband to keep his wife in the house away from the eyes of other men.[23] Also, if the woman turned out to be a noncitizen passing as a citizen, by the fourth century the man was required to divorce her and she could lose any dowry brought into the union ([Dem.] 59.51 ff., 81–83). Although the woman's duty not to shame her husband is a recurring theme in the orations, and is a typical attitude of shame cultures, men as well were not supposed to shame their wives' by supporting measures or approving of actions detrimental to their wives' physical safety (Lycurg. 1.1–2, 141; Lys. 12.69–70; Dein. 3.1) or by supporting measures that would jeopardize their modesty ([Dem.] 59.110, 114). To do so, it was feared, would encourage women to abandon their modesty ([Dem.] 59.111–12). Also, so as not to shame his wife, a man should be responsible in his financial affairs (Dem. 22.53).

One oration tells of how a wife defended the honor of her late husband. The husband, the speaker's father, had been away on military service under Thrasybulus (Dem. 57.42) during which time the woman hired herself out as a wet nurse to Cleinias son of Cleidicus, the young child of an old and noble family. Years later, after the death of her husband, the woman was obliged to defend her

---

[20] See also Is. 6.65, where it was the husband's duty to perform the burial rites for his wife.

[21] On the definition of marriage, see below, chapter 6, pp. 178 ff.

[22] MacDowell, *Law*, 88, 124–25; Harrison, *Law*, 1:35–36; Pomeroy, *Goddesses*, 81–83; Sealey, *Women*, 28–29; Just, *Women*, 68–70. Aeschin. 1.107 claims that many men are too ashamed to admit their wives' adultery: S. Cole, "Greek Sanctions Against Sexual Assault," *CP* 79 (1984): 106; Cohen, "Social Context," 163, argues that sources do state that adultery destroyed the *philia* between husband and wife. Although traditionally classicists have believed Lys. 1, which states that rape is a lesser crime than seduction, this view and Lysias' arguments have been recently challenged: E. M. Harris, "Did the Athenians Regard Seduction as a Worse Crime than Rape?" *CQ* 40 (1990): 370–77.

[23] Cole, "Greek Sanctions," 97.

late husband's citizenship, her own citizenship and that of her son, and one of her witnesses was the adult Cleinias (Dem. 57.40–44).[24]

Close cooperation and respect between spouses are reflected in the active interest a husband and wife took in each other's property. The wife could not inherit from her husband except for any additions to her dowry he might make in the event of his early death and her subsequent remarriage. Nevertheless, the wife knew the financial details of her husband's *oikos* to the point, particularly after his death, of having managerial control of the estate (Dem. 27.40, 29.40–48, 36.14 ff., 55.24–25),[25] even though sons legally acquired control at their majority and guardians were assigned control of the estate during the sons' minority. The orations frequently attest to the widow's strenuous efforts to keep her husband's estate intact against encroachment by kinsmen or neighbors.[26] Such concern in one case led a woman into a dispute with her own father (Lys. 32.10 ff.) and in two other cases with her own son (Aeschin. 1.98–99; Dem. 36.17–18). And in her husband's lifetime a wife might try to guard her husband's property from creditors (Dem. 30.4 ff., 31.10, 47.57–58), and was cognizant of her husband's attempts to pay off debts (Dem. 47.57–58).

In some cases, however, if a wife or widow had minor sons, she could be at a legal disadvantage, literally dependent on male kin or even nonkinsmen to protect her and her children.[27] In Demosthenes 47, an oration concerned with a wife whose husband was away in the Peiraeus, the husband's creditors barged into the house while the wife was within with her minor children and a beloved freedwoman. The creditors proceeded to seize the furniture, some of which apparently belonged to the woman's dowry, assaulted the freedwoman, and seized the couple's son, thinking that he was a slave (57–58). Surely the woman tried to explain that the boy was her son, for this woman was not mute, but vigorously defended furnishings she claimed to be items in her dowry and informed the creditors that her husband had deposited money for them at the bank. Surely the boy himself cried out for his mother. But the creditors did not release the boy until one of the neighbors, an adult male citizen, accosted them and informed them of the child's identity (61). This deliberate dismissal of the wife's statement was reinforced by law: when the speaker, the husband in question, went to the religious interpreters (*exēgētai*) for advice on how to prosecute his creditors, he was told not to mention the assailants by name, as his charges relied only on the testimony of his wife and children (69–70).

Informally, therefore, a woman actively pursued the preservation of her marital *oikos* because, as is stated frequently in the sources, marriage was a kind of

---

[24] For Cleinias, see Davies, *APF,* 12–15.

[25] V. Hunter, "Women's Authority in Classical Athens," *EMC* 33 (1989): 39–48; C. A. Cox, "Incest, Inheritance and the Political Forum in Fifth-Century Athens," *CJ* 85 (1989): 45.

[26] V. Hunter, "The Athenian Widow and Her Kin," *Journal of Family History* 14 (1989): 300.

[27] On the widow's vulnerability, see ibid., 299.

fusion of two estates, that of her husband and that of her *oikos* of origin (for example, Is. 2.4–5; Dem. 27.5, 30.12, 59.2–3). This was not merely rhetoric; the husband could be a vociferous defender of his wife's claims to her father's estate, should she be an heiress, or to her brother's estate, should he die without heirs (Dem. 43.3 ff., 63 ff.; Is. 3.22 ff.; 5.9 ff.; 7.3; 8.41–42; 10.18–20; 11.41–42, 49).[28] Furthermore, a wife could influence her husband either to adopt one of her kinsmen (Dem. 41.3 ff.; Is. 2.7 ff.) or to send one of their sons or daughters into her brother's estate as its heir (see discussion below, pp. 126–27). The law acknowledged a wife's influence on the use of her husband's wealth by trying to limit her power: a man, when drawing up a will, could not be influenced by a woman (Is. 2.1; Dem. 48.56; Hyp. *Athen.* 5.17; *Ath. Pol.* 35.2). In the orations (Demosthenes and Hyperides, ad loc.) the emphasis is on the influence specifically of the wife and the *hetaira,* that is the type of woman who had sexual relations with the man.

In a material sense, the wife's dowry allowed for the cohesion of two *oikoi.* More will be said about the dowry in the next chapter; the point to underline here is that the dowry, in legal terms, belonged to the woman's natal *oikos,* as it had to be returned to her original family either on divorce or on the death of her husband and her remarriage (see the references cited below, pp. 119–20). To judge from the orations and dotal horoi the wealth of the dowry for elite families on average was valued around thirty to forty minae, though there are instances of dowries given to the woman which were well above this range and below it as well.[29] Because the wife's dowry could be inherited by the children,[30] it was worth fighting for, especially if she had not received her full share (Dem. 41, passim). Therefore, the potential loss of a substantial amount of dotal wealth would inhibit divorce (Is. 3.28), and the fear of this loss was a recurring theme in the drama of the day (Eur. *And.* 864 ff.).[31] Certainly the dying husband realized the power of the dowry when he gave his widow one the value of which was far above the value of most dowries given to the young bride of an elite family.[32] In one case, that of Cleoboule, Demosthenes' mother, part of the dowry given to her by her dying husband consisted of items she had brought into her first marriage (Dem. 27.4, 13; Aeschin. 3.172).[33] Her first dowry had been given to her by her mother (Demosthenes and Aeschines, ad loc) and had allowed her

[28] V. Hunter, "Agnatic Kinship in Athenian Law and Athenian Family Practice: Its Implications for Women," in *Law, Politics and Society in the Ancient Mediterranean World,* ed. B. Halpern and D. Hobson (Sheffield: Sheffield Academic Press, 1993), 103.

[29] Finley, *SLC,* 79; W. Wyse, *The Speeches of Isaeus* (Cambridge: Cambridge University Press, 1904; New York: Arno, 1979), 243; L. Casson, "The Athenian Upper Class and New Comedy," *TAPA* 106 (1976): 54–55.

[30] See the sections on mothers and sons and mothers and daughters below, pp. 99–104.

[31] For further references, see D. M. Schaps, *Economic Rights of Women in Ancient Greece* (Edinburgh: University of Edinburgh Press, 1979), 76, 142–43, nn. 26–27.

[32] Finley, *SLC,* 266–67, n. 29; see also Hunter, "Athenian Widow," 307, n. 7, for the values of the dowries given to widows.

[33] Hunter, "Women's Authority," 40.

to reenter Athenian society after her father's political disgrace and exile and to be married to a wealthy Athenian.[34] In another case, the speaker argues that his mother's dowry, after the end of her first marriage, would have been increased by her brothers to ensure a proper second marriage for her. The importance of the dowry is the basis for the speaker's argument that his father, Mantias, had not actually married Plango, Mantias's presumed first wife, but only intended to. Though the speaker is incorrect, it is significant that he bases his argument on the premise that Plango had brought no dowry, and, for that reason, Mantias married the speaker's mother ([Dem.] 40.19–27).

Although the dowry was valued in cash, it frequently consisted not just of cash, but also of movable items—furniture, jewels, plated ware—and, perhaps, land (see below, p. 117), and could be amalgamated with the husband's estate. Thus in his list of his father's property Demosthenes included his mother's jewelry and gold-plated objects (27.9–11). Although this was not productive wealth, the prestige associated with these items allowed Demosthenes' mother a good deal of influence in discussions on their use.[35] Another oration tells of a wife making loans to family members from, possibly, her dowry, though this is not explicitly stated (Dem. 41.9). In some cases, dotal wealth was so integrated in the marital *oikos* that a wife's dowry was confiscated to pay off her husband's debts (Is. 8.8–9; Lys. 19.32; Dem. 47.57–58), although whether this practice was legally permitted is subject to debate.[36] In Isaeus 8 Ciron gave his daughter in marriage to Nausimenes, but on the latter's death did not receive his daughter's dowry back, presumably because it had been expended (whether legally or not) to meet some debts incurred by Nausimenes (8–9). As I noted above, in Demosthenes 47.57–58 the speaker's wife tried to plead with her husband's creditors not to confiscate furniture that was part of her dowry. That the creditors ignored her may indicate their rapaciousness, but there is the possibility—and this is strictly conjectural—that they suspected that the woman was deliberately lying in an attempt to save some of her husband's property. In Isaeus 10, the speaker's mother, according to the speaker, did not inherit her father's estate as was her due as an heiress, but was given in marriage to a nonkinsman with a dowry. When the woman's husband protested to his wife's kinsmen about their disregard for his wife's rights, they then threatened to initiate a divorce between the two and have her marry a close kinsman of her father, in accordance with the laws governing heiresses (for which, see below, p. 95). Although the speaker states that his father could not bear the emotional loss, the effect of the divorce would have been the

[34] For Cleoboule's background, see Davies, *APF,* 121–22.

[35] Hunter, "Women's Authority," 41; on the prestigious symbolism of cash in dowries, see Sant Cassia and Bada, *Making,* 81.

[36] Just, *Women,* 82 f.; See V. Hunter, *Policing Athens: Social Control in the Attic Lawsuits, 420–320 B.C.* (Princeton, N.J.: Princeton University Press, 1994), 19 ff., for a discussion of the dotal wealth's integration into the conjugal fund. For the legality of confiscating the woman's dowry to meet her husband's debts, see Schaps, *Economic,* 75–76.

forced return of the dowry to the woman's patriline, not an attractive prospect for the husband who may well have been experiencing financial difficulties.[37] The binding effect of the dowry and its amalgamation into the husband's *oikos* could, however, prove dangerous to a woman, if gossip is at all trustworthy: the extremely large twenty-talent dowry brought by Hipparete led Alcibiades, her husband, to prevent her physically from filing a divorce with the archon ([And.] 4.13 ff.; Plut. *Alc.* 8.1–4).

Although the sources at times underplay ardent love between husband and wife, they do emphasize the close cooperation between spouses which could result in the wife's detailed knowledge of her husband's estate and his interest in her natal *oikos*. Close cooperation was also necessary to ensure that sons inherited well and daughters were dowered fittingly. Cooperation, therefore, was basic to a woman's status, but her status was situational, dependent on many variables, including the length of her residency in her husband's *oikos,* the wealth of her dowry, and the presence of adult males, preferably kinsmen, to protect her rights.

FATHERS AND SONS: CURRENT RESEARCH

The current trend in psychoanalytical analyses of father/son relationships in Western society is to emphasize the distance of the father from his family, his emotional separation from his children, and the role of the mother as chief caregiver.[38] The separation of the Athenian male citizen from his *oikos* will be a concern in chapter 5, but the studies that have shaped the following discussion are those that focus on the interaction of material and emotional concerns, particularly in those societies in which honor and shame determine behavior. In his recent work on fathers and sons in Athens, Barry Strauss has argued that examples from modern Greece are instructive. Among the pastoral Sarakatsani of Epirus, for instance, there is a great deal of tension over the timing of transmission of property. In ancient Athens, although postmortem transmission of property was the ideal, in fact sons could at least assume the management of the estate before the father's death.[39] As in ancient Athens, Sarakatsani fathers and sons are careful to present themselves in a unified way, with the son constantly displaying respect for paternal authority.[40] Behind this public unity, however, the relationship between father and son is delicately balanced for the Sarakatsani; in

[37] His son, the speaker, was certainly in debt to the state (20) and claimed to have given meager dowries to his sisters (25).

[38] For instance, S. H. Cath, A. Gurwitt, and L. Gunsberg, eds., *Fathers and Their Families* (Hillsdale: The Analytic Press, 1989); M. Lamb, *The Father's Role: Cross-Cultural Perspectives* (Hillsdale: Lawrence Erlbaum Associates, 1987).

[39] P. Strauss, *Fathers and Sons in Ancient Athens* (Princeton, N.J.: Princeton University Press, 1993), 67–70. See further the discussion below, p. 86.

[40] Campbell, *Honour,* 160–61, 170–72.

return for his son's respect, a father is forced by social pressure to hand over management of the estate to his eldest son when the latter has reached thirty; any
failure to do so could lead to the public airing of the resultant quarrel between
father and son. Any physical or mental feebleness of the father would also prompt
the son to question the older man's authority.[41] In other communities outside
Greece, inheritance systems in which there is a delayed transmission of property
betray a mistrust on the father's part of his children—the father is uncertain that
his children, once they own the land and a house, will care for him properly.[42]
In seventeenth- and eighteenth-century Haute-Provence, all sons in peasant and
artisanal families inherited shares of movables and cash, but one son was selected
to inherit the residence and the land of the father. Legal authority over the father's estate, however, did not enter into effect until the father's death. The inheriting son could not sell the estate, dispose of its wealth, or make a will until
his father's death; only then could the son legally own the property. Because of
such late transmission of ownership, the inheriting son lived in the same house
with his father and mother and brought a wife into the residence. If the father
and son found the situation intolerable and there was an agreement on physical
separation, such separation would deprive the son of any further right to inherit
the chief estate and its residence. The father still did not hand over the son's full
share of the patrimony, a move that would make the father's economic position
too tenuous. In the end, physical breaks rarely occurred despite tensions that
could arise among members of the household, which could consist of the inheriting son, his wife, his parents, and any unmarried siblings.[43] To what extent
does the ancient case, where strict partibility among sons was the rule, display
similar attitudes and motivations? To what extent did public unity hide conflict
at the private level, conflict that could result from late transmission of property?

FATHERS AND SONS IN ANCIENT ATHENS: PUBLIC UNITY

Barry Strauss's recent book on the ideology of the father-son relationship argues
that conflict between father and son was a social and political construct of the Peloponnesian War era. The ideal of the rebellious son, however, was quickly suppressed
at the end of the war after Athens had suffered her disastrous defeat.[44] My purpose
here will be different from that of Strauss: this chapter will take a synchronic approach to the conflicts that developed from material interests. The focus here will
be on how the ideal of father-son cooperation was undercut by tensions and ri-

---

[41] Ibid., 161–62; 187–89.

[42] R. Behar and D. Frye, "Property, Progeny and Emotion: Family History in a Leonese Village,"
Journal of Family History 13 (1988): 27.

[43] A. Collomp, "Tensions, Dissensions, and Ruptures Inside the Family in Seventeenth- and Eighteenth-Century Haute-Provence," in Medick and Sabean, *Interest,* 151–56.

[44] Strauss, *Fathers,* passim.

valries between transmitter and heir. Therefore, individuals who stood outside this formal dyad of father and son—formal in the sense of politics and inheritance—could have a good deal of influence over the legal heir and his estate. Rather than duplicate Strauss's admirable assemblage of sources, I will cite instances mostly from the orations that are meant merely to complement his discussion.

The Athenian male was constantly preoccupied with maintaining the honor of his family members—his parents and his siblings. The need to present a unified front between father and son was a key element to preserving one's honor. The ideal of the obedient son obeying his father's injuctions and learning from the older man's memories is a standard theme in the orations.[45]

In public a father, as his son's nearest adult male agnate, could defend the son on charges of homicide or bring his son's murderer to trial (Antiph. 3.1; Lys. 12.83). At the end of the fifth century, Andocides, returning from exile, declares that he is without refuge in his home city because his father is dead and he has no brothers (And. 1.148). Andocides actually had affines through his sister's marriage,[46] but the stress here in Andocides' rhetoric is on male agnatic responsibilities in the lawcourts and political forum. In turn, the son was supposed to obey his father while the latter was alive and preserve his memory after he died (Lys. 12.82–83, 13.42; Lyc. 1.2, 136–37).

The close link between father and son in terms of material inheritance was reflected in the language used to describe political disgrace and personality makeup. Fathers bequeathed their character to their sons. Demosthenes 54, describing a dispute between two men that began over a *hetaira,* is a comparison between the speaker's services to the state and those of his father, on the one hand, with the debauchery of Conon, which was inherited by his sons, on the other (47.7–8, 14 ff., 39, 44).[47] Also, sons were censured if they did not live up to their father's standards: as Isocrates states, sons could ill afford being worse than their fathers (7.72). This attitude takes a humorous turn in an oratorical fragment where the speaker, charging Demosthenes the orator with cowardice, declares that Demosthenes did not even have a sword inherited from his own father—a pointed remark, as a large part of Demosthenes Senior's estate was based on his sword manufacturing (P. Oxy. 6.858 and commentary). Further, it was assumed that a son inherited his father's attitude toward the state; therefore, a son was judged by his father's political stance (Lys. 12.65–66; 26.4, 21) and by his munificence to the state (Dem. 28.22, 54.44; Antiph. 5.20, 74 ff. [a metic]).[48]

---

[45] Ibid., 72.

[46] Davies, *APF,* 30, 253–54.

[47] M. Golden, *Children and Childhood in Classical Athens* (Baltimore: Johns Hopkins University Press, 1990), 101, for this case and the recurrent theme in comedy that bad behavior breeds bad behavior. For other examples of inherited behavior, see Dem. 25.54, Lys. 26.21, Lys. 30.1. For similar beliefs in a modern Greek community, see Campbell, *Honour,* 166–67.

[48] However, in Dein. 3.17 and [And.] 4.33 sons are not given special concessions simply because of the many great deeds of their famous fathers.

Moreover, the son's reputation could be marred by his father's deceptive behavior towards the deme or the *polis* (Dem. 57.18 ff., 60; Isoc. 16.1 ff.) and thus could be, along with his father, charged with treason or illegal activity (Dein. 1.62–63; Lys. 18.1–5, 20.1 ff.; Dem. 57.18 ff.; 58.1 ff.; Isoc. 16.1 ff.; And. 1.22 ff.); consequently, under the law the son inherited his father's disfranchisement (Dem. 58 passim; [Plut.] *Mor.* 833e–834b). One of the most famous instances was that in which both Andocides and his father were implicated in the profanation of the Mysteries prior to the Sicilian expedition. The prosecution, however, accused Andocides of turning informer against his father, a charge Andocides repeatedly denied in his public speeches on his return to Athens from exile at the end of the fifth century (1.19–20, 23–24; 2.6–7).[49]

The private life of the father was a source of honor or shame to the son: several orations attest to an individual challenging the citizenship status of a rival's father or his morals (Dem. 18.129, 261; 19.281, 22.61, 24.125, 25.65), thereby undermining the civic rights of both father and son. Aeschines defended his father from such charges (Aeschin. 2.78, 147), because the common attitude held that a bad father could not be a good guide to the people (Aeschin. 3.78).

Reinforcing the attitude that sons inherited the political bents and attributes of his father was the tendency in Athens for a son to inherit his father's friends and enemies (Isoc. 1.2–3).[50] Strauss has noted that the orations are full of examples.[51] A father's friend could argue in a lawcourt for the inheritance rights of that father's two sons (Is. 4.1) or a speaker could defend a foreign friend of his father (Lys. 5.1). Deinias of Acharnae supported Pasio's grant of citizenship and gave his daughter in marriage to Pasio's son Apollodorus. Deinias's son Theomnestus then defended Apollodorus against the latter's political enemy, Stephanus ([Dem.] 59.2).[52] Appropriately, Aeschines uses his outrage to great rhetorical effect when he declares that his enemy Demosthenes did not hesitate to be one of the accusers of Cephisodotus the general, an old friend of Demosthenes' father (3.52). At the private level, sons marry off their sisters to old friends of their father (Is. 2.3–4) or borrow money from paternal friends (Dem. 50.56).[53] Aeschines (1.41–42) argues that Timarchus lived with an older man who was not even his father's friend; the absence of paternal association in this liaison further adds to Timarchus' long list of excesses.

---

[49] There might be a possibility that Andocides had denounced his father: there were traditions that claimed Andocides informed against his father to gain immunity, but then helped to defend him in court against Speusippus, the prosecutor: D. M. MacDowell, *Andokides on the Mysteries* (Oxford: Clarendon Press, 1962), 170–71. See also Strauss, *Fathers,* 187 ff.

[50] Although Isocrates in his speech written to Demonicus, the son of Hipponicus, may be writing to a non-Athenian, the orator's sentiments reflect Athenian attitudes and behavior.

[51] Strauss, *Fathers,* 77.

[52] Relations between Apollodorus and Deinias, however, do not seem to have been smooth all the time: see below, chapter 4, p. 122.

[53] The friends are *xenoi* at Tenedos. For the role of monetary assistance at Athens, see G. Herman, *Ritualised Friendship and the Greek City* (Cambridge: Cambridge University Press, 1987), 22, 92–93.

Concomitantly, a son inherited his father's enemies—so much so that in one case a young man tried to shame an opponent by stating that their fathers had never quarreled (Dem. 55.1 ff.). In Lysias 14, the speaker is prosecuting the younger Alcibiades because the fathers of both men were enemies: the speaker is arguing for Alcibiades' punishment for his father's crimes (ibid., 2, 16–17, 30–31) and ends the speech with a catalogue of crimes committed by Alcibiades' ancestors (ibid. 39 ff.). In Isocrates 16 the younger Alcibiades must defend himself against allegations of extortion by another of his father's enemies; rather than answer the charge directly, Alcibiades calls the roll of his father's impressive ancestors (1 ff.).[54]

This unity between father and son in the public sphere was ideally supposed to be reflected at the private level. Common sentiment acknowledged that close affective ties should exist between father and son (Is. 7.14; Lys. 19.55), and any known case of enmity was used against an individual's character (Lys. 14.26–27). Responsibility was enforced by law, which protected both father and son against egregious abuse: a son could not beat or abuse his parents at the risk of losing his civic rights (atimia—Aeschin. 1.1 ff.),[55] and the father who prostituted his son could not expect to be supported by the son, although the son was required to bury his father (Aeschin. 1.13–14). Charges of abuse against a father or a son were meant to undermine their worth as responsible citizens,[56] but examples of abusive sons outnumber those of abusive fathers,[57] a bias that seems to reflect a general reticence to criticize an older man's behavior as a father.

The primary focus of Athenian law, and hence of the private orations, was on the son as his father's heir, and for that reason laws strove to ensure the transmission of property from father to legitimate son. The interest of the state in a son's inheritance was underscored at the end of the Peloponnesian War and of the *stasis* in Athens by the decree of Theozotides, which guaranteed state assistance to the orphans of a man who had died violently under the oligarchy (*P.*

---

[54] Two other orations attest to the enmity between two men being carried on by their sons; the stakes are not small, for in both cases there is the risk of disfranchisement (Dem. 57.60 ff.; 58.1 ff.). I find Osborne's dismissal of the inherited feud in Demosthenes 57 curious (*Demos: The Discovery of Classical Attika* [Cambridge: Cambridge University Press, 1985], 150). Although the speech, a defense for the speaker's right to be considered a demesman of Halimous, may reflect the deme's suspicions of the outsider, such suspicions could certainly fuel a private vendetta.

[55] Harrison, *Law,* 1:77–78.

[56] B. Strauss, "*Oikos/Polis:* Towards a Theory of Athenian Paternal Ideology 450–399 B.C.," in *Aspects of Athenian Democracy,* ed. W. Connor et al., *ClMed Dissertationes* 11 (Copenhagen: Museum Tusculanum Press, 1990), 108.

[57] For examples of abusive sons, see Dem. 24.7–8, 25.54; Lys. 10.1–2, 11.7–8; Dein. 2.14, 18. Given that the orators were not reluctant to slander a rival's father, the virtual absence of charges of paternal neglect or abuse is remarkable. See Dem. 19.230 where there is a charge that a man prostituted his son to gain Philip's favor. See now V. Hunter, "Gossip and the Politics of Reputation in Classical Athens," *Phoenix* 44 (1990): 324 for further examples.

Hibeh 1.14; Lys. fr. 6 [Gernet]).[58] If a father had sons he was required by law to bequeath his estate to them in equal portions. Only in the absence of sons could the estate devolve upon a daughter.[59] Furthermore, laws mandated the responsible transmission and use of wealth: although the state frequently took large portions of a man's wealth in the form of liturgies, a father could not squander his estate to the detriment of his legitimate sons. Two laws, the *graphē argias,* against idleness, and the *graphē paranoias,* against mental incapacity, stated that a father could be prosecuted by his sons, or by anyone representing them, for mismanagement of his estate.[60] In turn, a son could not squander his patrimony on pain of forfeiting his civil rights (Aeschin. 1.28 ff.; Isoc. 12.140).

Because inheritance was so concerned with legitimacy, which in turn depended on marriage, legally, paternal authority was supreme over both the production of legitimate heirs and their proper marriage. In the *amphidromia,* a ceremony on the fifth or seventh day after a child's birth, a father declared before witnesses whether a child was his and whether that child would live and be reared in his *oikos.*[61] Although law and custom accorded the father such power over a child, a man stood the chance of shaming himself if he tried to renounce a son considered his own or tried to legitimate a son he had formerly renounced or had claimed was his by only an informal union. Renunciation of a child followed by acceptance often led to suspicions that the man had been duped or coerced by the child's mother (And. 1.124 ff.; [Dem.] 39.3–4, 59.59–61). Responsibility toward a son as legal heir and the downward transmission of wealth remained a father's concern throughout his son's adulthood. Although the arrangement of a young girl's marriage by her father has been frequently discussed in works on social history (see below, pp. 92–93), it should be emphasized here that if a father was still alive when his son reached marriageable age, he was careful to see that his son married properly and actively arranged the match (Lys. 19.16; [Dem.] 40.12; Is. 2.18 [adoptive father]).

It was a matter of honor, therefore, for father and son to appear united in the protection of the property of their *oikos.* Fathers and sons were frequently seen in court trying to preserve their property or that of a kinsman (Is. 5.9, 9.3–4; Lys. 19.1–2; [Dem.] 44.40–41), or the son could plead in court to have property, whether in land, goods, or money, returned to his dead father's estate (Is. fr. 33; Lys. 17.3 ff., 19.1 ff.; Dem. 27–29, 38.1 ff., 44.3–4, 49.1 ff.). A closer look at some of these cases is instructive.

In Isaeus 10, Cyronides, though adopted out of his father's financially en-

---

[58] R. Stroud, "Greek Inscriptions: Theozotides and the Athenian Orphans," *Hesperia* 40 (1971): 280–301, and esp. 287.

[59] Lacey, *Family,* 125; MacDowell, *Law,* 92–93; Just, *Women,* 85–86.

[60] Harrison, *Law,* 1:79–80; Strauss, *Fathers,* 64.

[61] For instance, Harrison, *Law,* 1:70–71; MacDowell, *Law,* 91; Lacey *Family,* 111–12; J. K. Davies, "Athenian Citizenship: The Descent Group and the Alternatives," *CJ* 73 (1978): 109–10; Strauss, *Fathers,* 64; Golden, *Childhood,* 23–24.

cumbered estate, strove not to let the *oikos* die out. When he sired sons, he had them posthumously adopted into his deceased father's estate. These adoptions were contested by his sister's son, the speaker, who was continuing the cause of his father, Cyronides' sister's husband. The husband, while alive, had claimed that his wife was an heiress to the estate of her father.[62]

In Lysias 19, the speaker is in a predicament: when asking the state to hand over to him his sister's dowry from the confiscated property of his brother-in-law Aristophanes, son of Nicophemus, he does not want to portray himself or his father as rapacious; he therefore emphasizes that his father, when contracting his own marriage as well as the marriages of his children, did not consider the wealth but the ancestry of his prospective affines (8, 12 ff.). Furthermore, his father's wealth now being demanded of the state is of small consequence compared to the wealth devoted to the state by both father and son (ibid., 57 ff.).

The lengthy lawsuits over Demosthenes' estate are by now famous and much discussed.[63] The emphasis here will be on a son's attempts to uphold the image of his father as an innocent victim of scheming kinsmen and friends in order to justify the son's struggle to regain his paternal estate. Three orations (Demosthenes 27–29) survive in which Demosthenes details the wealth in his father's estate and the terms of the older man's will. All three carry the same theme: Demosthenes the elder put his estate into the hands of men he trusted and who were all present when he made his will. In the will Demosthenes the Elder gave his widow in marriage to his sister's son, Aphobus, and his five-year-old daughter to his brother's son, Demophon (Dem. 27.4 ff., 55–57; 28.4 ff.; 29.47 ff.). He selected a third guardian for the estate, an old friend and demesman, Therippides of Paeania: "His intention," Demosthenes insists, "was that if he joined these men to me by still closer ties, they would look after my interests all the better because of this added bond of kinship" (27.4–5). In the end, the guardians extorted the wealth, leaving Demosthenes only seventy minae from an estate of around fourteen talents (27.6 ff.). All three orations emphasize that this betrayal was sudden and unjustified.[64]

It is likely, however, that Demosthenes the elder did not entirely trust the men to whom he willed guardianship of his estate. The bequest may well have been an attempt to hide much of Demosthenes Senior's estate from the state to avoid having it encumbered to pay for the treason of Demosthenes Senior's father-in-

[62] In the preliminary examination of the case, the archon may well have sided with the speaker's opponents, forcing the speaker to declare that his mother was the sister of Aristarchus II (Cyronides' son who had been posthumously adopted into the estate of Cyronides' birth father, Aristarchus I). In essence this step acknowledged Aristarchus II's right to inherit the estate of Aristarchus I: Wyse, *Isaeus,* 650–51.

[63] See the bibliography in Davies, *APF,* 113; for a more recent discussion, see Hunter, "Women's Authority," 39–48.

[64] Golden, *Childhood,* 52, argues that the choice of a friend might have seemed imprudent. It was not totally unknown for nonkinsmen to be selected as guardians: see below, chapter 4, n. 26.

law, Gylon of Cerameis.[65] Demosthenes admits that his father gave large sums of money to Therippides and Demophon because, if they should prove to be dishonest, they would not be treated leniently by a jury (27.65). Also, according to Aphobus, Demosthenes Senior kept four talents hidden in his house for his son and put his widow in charge of it; this hidden wealth soon became a source of conflict between Aphobus and his intended wife, Cleoboule (27.52–53; 29.46–47).[66] The orator hotly denies Aphobus's allegation, for it would have shown a poor face to Athenian society to portray his father as handing his estate, widow, and children over to men he did not trust (27.55–57; 29.47 ff.). Rather, Demosthenes states that his father gave substantial sums of money to the guardians, but certainly not all his wealth—he would not have left his son destitute (27.44–45). The father's death played a pivotal role in the disputes that followed: after Demosthenes the Elder's death his nephews reneged on their promises, and his children were stripped of protection until Demosthenes came of age.[67]

To sum up, the unity of father and son was frequently described by the metaphor of inheritance: sons inherited their father's character, his attitudes towards the state, his political leanings, his friends and foes, as well as his estate. This public display of loyalty justified a son's inheritance of his father's estate as well as his entry to the male public sphere. Yet despite these constant attempts to portray a unified front in both the public and private spheres, the orations are riddled with references to conflict between fathers and sons, to which we now turn.

FRICTION BETWEEN FATHER AND SON

The well-known scene in Plato's *Euthyphro* (4a ff.) in which the character by the same name is informing Socrates of his intention to prosecute his father is by now a cliché: in philosophy, mythology, and tragedy father/son conflict is a common theme.[68] Even in the orations, where the unity of the father and son is obsessively displayed, there are indications that unity in the private sphere could be merely an ideal. Explicit statements of hatred between father and son are rare, though the famous Alcibiades was said to have hated his son (Lys. 14.26–27). The emphasis in the sources is rather on neglect, and failure to perform filial duties publicly and privately. Deinarchus tells of a son who did not care for his father while the latter was in exile nor gave him a proper burial (2.8)—omissions that are mentioned with disapproval even though the father was a criminal. Or a father, now dead, would be a stern judge if he knew his son, who had fled Athens, left behind the ancestral images to be mutilated by an invading enemy (Lyc.

[65] Davies, *APF*, 122; Hunter, "Women's Authority," 41 and n. 12.

[66] Ibid., 43.

[67] Ibid., 42, emphasizes that Cleoboule's case demonstrates the vulnerability of the widow no matter how detailed a will might be to protect her future.

1.136 f.); or a son did not care for the elderly brother of his dead father (Aeschin. 1.102). A true son, one speaker states, although quareling with his father while the latter was alive, should not slander him after his death ([Dem.] 40.46–47). Appropriately enough, the speaker in Lysias 19 brags that he and his father never had a dispute (19.55). An oratorical fragment states that there should be unity between a father and his son and between the son and his grandfather (*P. Lond. Lit.* 140).

Historians have before now noted that inheritance could be a source of such conflict, although they have not focused on the orations in detail.[69] What do these sources have to say? First, although a father was required by law to leave his estate in equal shares to his sons, the sons did not always inherit the expected amount from their father (Lys. 20.32 ff., 24.6; Isocr. 8.125–26, 15.161): the ravages of war, over which a father had little control, could leave an estate impoverished (Lys. 20.32 ff.; Isocr. 15.161). Further, a wealthy man, in order to be considered a good citizen, was expected to expend a great deal of his property on liturgies, although a father was certainly expected to leave enough for his son's maintenance, preferably in the liturgical class (Is. 11.39; Lys. 19.9, 57–59, 61–62; Dem. 27.44–45, 28.22, 29.43–45). Isocrates states that Pericles, because of his state services, did not bequeath to his son as much as he himself had inherited from his father (Isoc. 8.125–26). Liturgies can partially explain the depleted fortunes of other prominent Athenians: Ischomachus, Nicias, Callias III, and Alcibiades (Lys. 19.46–52).[70] Also there was a fear that the son would dissipate his father's fortune. There is a tradition, the reliability of which is unknown,[71] that Pericles and his son quarreled over the son's use of money and the father's behavior. Pericles was afraid that his son spent too much, and in turn, Pericles' son seems to have criticized his father, spreading gossip that Pericles spent too much time with sophists (Plut. *Per.* 36.2–3).[72] Hipponicus II, one of the wealthiest men in Greece, was said to have feared that his son Callias III would ruin his livelihood (And. 1.130–31). The theme of a son's squandering his patrimony appears elsewhere as well. Timarchus was notorious for having sold off all his inheritance to pay his gambling debts (Aeschin. 1.97 ff.), and when Demosthenes sold some landed property of his father, he too came under suspicion as a wastrel (Dein. 1.71).[73]

---

[68] J. Bremmer, "The Importance of the Maternal Uncle and Grandfather in Archaic and Classical Greece and Early Byzantium," *ZPE* 50 (1983): 183, who emphasizes the emotional and physical separation of fathers and sons; Strauss, "Oikos/Polis," 115; Golden, *Childhood,* 106.

[69] Golden, *Childhood,* 106; Strauss, "Oikos/Polis," 115, and *Fathers,* 220, where Strauss places the oratorical references to conflict in a different ideology after the 420s. From this time onward the ideology enforced paternal authority.

[70] The liturgical activity of these individuals is recorded: Davies, *APF,* 20–21 (Alcibiades), 261–62 (Callias III), 266 (Ischomachus), 403–4 (Nicias). Callias III's depleted fortune was also attributed to the collapse of the Laurium mines c. 413: Davies, *APF,* 261–62.

[71] Golden, *Childhood,* 109.

[72] For expenditures on sophists, see Davies, *APF,* 262, 336.

[73] See the appendix to Hunter, "Gossip," 324–25 which lists the references to the various themes of gossip.

Although the law mandated transmission of property at the father's death, at which time the sons succeeded to the property, the father's estate could be managed by his sons, and even divided among them, prior to his death. Aristophanes' *Wasps* depicts the struggles between a frivolous, incompetent father and the son who must manage the estate.[74] From other sources we find that a father's estate could be divided up before his death and some control, if not total control, given to the sons. Such is the case in Demosthenes 47.35–36, in which two brothers live in separate residences with the one brother living with his parents. Nevertheless, there was the feeling that a man could not trust his sons with full management. Lysias 19.36–37 declares that, when a man divides his inherited estate among his sons for their use while he is alive, he should keep a good amount for himself: in that way, a man who still had wealth would be guaranteed care from his children, whereas the impoverished person (i.e., one who had relinquished his wealth) would be depending upon his children.[75]

Isaeus 6 illustrates that division of an estate before the father's death does not necessarily indicate a father's desire to hand the management of that estate over to his son. The oration describes the quarrel between Euctemon and his son Philoctemon, when the former attempted before his death to bequeath part of his estate, a small farm, to Philoctemon's half-brother, Euctemon's son by a second union (23–24). In the end, Euctemon won the argument by threatening to marry a third time—implying that he would sire more sons and thereby divide the estate up even more (ibid.). It is noteworthy that the conflict between Euctemon and Philoctemon is made explicit only with Euctemon's increasing incompetence as a result of old age, at which time he began a relationship with a prostitute (18 ff.). It is also significant that Philoctemon did not bring his father to court; in fact, the speaker, Philoctemon's adopted son, waited to prosecute Euctemon's younger sons only after the death of both Euctemon and Philoctemon (39 ff.).

There is also evidence of a father who abandoned his children because of property concerns. Demosthenes 39 and 40 detail a series of quarrels between the sons of Mantias: Boeotus and his full brother, Pamphilus, on the one hand, and their half-brother Mantitheus on the other.[76] Although the details in the two orations are deliberately confused, it appears that Mantias first married Plango, but then divorced her when she was pregnant with Boeotus and at a time when her father had become a state debtor. Mantias then married Mantitheus's mother but continued his relationship with Plango. After the death of Mantias's second wife, Plango gave birth to Boeotus's full brother Pamphilus; although Mantias at first refused to acknowledge his paternity of

[74] Lacey, *Family,* 128–29.

[75] Ibid.; MacDowell, *Law,* 92.

[76] On the family of Mantias, see Davies, *APF,* 364–68; J. Rudhardt, "La reconnaissance de la paternité, sa nature et sa portée dans la société athénienne," *MusHelv* 19 (1962): 43–60; S. Humphreys, "Family Quarrels," *JHS* 109 (1989): 182–85; Hunter, *Policing Athens,* 63–64.

Plango's two sons, she nonetheless tricked him into swearing to it (39.3–4; 40.10).[77]

By modern standards Mantias's rejection of his sons by Plango seems harsh, and indeed Boeotus instituted lawsuits against Mantias which finally led to Plango's trick (40.8 ff.). But if Mantias had previously acknowledged the legitimacy of Boeotus, he would have been admitting to the formality of the union. Because Plango's father was a state debtor, Mantias had not received a dowry from her father's estate and would have run the risk, as Plango's husband, of being saddled with at least some of the debts of her paternal estate[78]—too much responsibility for a man, who, even Mantitheus admitted, mishandled his financial affairs (39.25–26).[79] For the sake of financial security, therefore, Mantias married a second woman from a solid background and with a wealthy dowry on hand.[80] For that reason, he would not have Boeotus in his house and established his line of descent through Mantitheus (40.4, 12). When Boeotus continued to press his claim, Mantitheus appealed to the jurors' traditional emotions by depicting Boeotus as the bad son always quarreling openly with his father (39.25–26; 40.49). He, Mantitheus, was the respectful and obedient son (40.4, 12), although, as Mantitheus himself admits, Mantias continued to have relations with Plango while married to his second wife and lavished a great deal of wealth on her (40.8–9, 50–51). Indeed, Manthitheus's statement (40.46–47) that trueborn sons quarrel with their fathers while the latter are alive may indicate the reality behind the idealistic picture he paints of himself. Finally, it is again typical behavior, that, with the death of Mantias, his sons take their quarrel into the lawcourt: Boeotus, tried, against Mantitheus's resistance, to have his own name changed to Mantitheus, the name of Mantias's father, so that he, Boeotus, could display his link with his patriline. Also, Boeotus and Pamphilus successfully sued their half-brother for two-thirds of Mantias's estate (40.2, 48–49). It is little wonder, then, that in Lysias 10 and 11 the speaker insists that he did not murder his father after his brother allegedly received a larger portion of the estate (10.1–5; 11.1–2).

To sum up briefly, the ancient Athenian strove very hard to present a united front of himself and his father: certainly, in public, father protected son and son protected father in conflicts with political or social rivals. In fact, the father could wield such authority that feuds among his sons, his son's descendants, or their collaterals erupted and were aired in the lawcourts only after his death. Ties between father and son could be strained, however, over property concerns, even though such quarrels were considered bad form and the forgiveness of fathers was a cultural given (Dem. 25.88–89). Sons, for their part, were reluctant to admit that such arguments ever occurred and justified them only on the grounds

---

[77] For Plango's trick, see S. Todd, "The Purpose of Evidence in Athenian Courts," in Cartledge, Millett and Todd, *Nomos,* 35–36.

[78] Davies, *APF,* 365; Humphreys, "Family Quarrels," 182–83 and n. 4.

[79] Davies, *APF,* 367–68.

[80] For Mantias' second wife, see ibid., 319, 366.

of incompetency. Despite these arguments, sons in the orations and historical sources maintain an image of steadfast loyalty, a loyalty that solidified their claims as heirs and as citizens.

It was such loyalty that lay at the basis of relationships between younger men and older men who became substitute father figures—the adoptive father and the stepfather.

THE ADOPTIVE FATHER

In the classical era there were strict rules concerning adoption. Only a man who had no legitimate sons could adopt. If the adopter had a daughter, the adopted son had to marry her, a stipulation very closely linked to the epiclerate, as we shall see in dealing with fathers and daughters. Furthermore, by the classical era, adoptees had to leave a natural son in the estate of their adoption before they could return to the estate of origin (Dem. 44.63, 67).[81] As for the adoptee, he was severed from his paternal *oikos,* though there were ways around this rule (see above, pp. 28–31, and below, pp. 150–51). An equally great, if not greater, impediment to adoption than this severance was the jealousy of the adopter's kin, particularly those of the patriline (male and female). No fewer than ten instances in the corpus of Isaeus alone refer to contested adoptions in which both the adoptee and the adopter's agnates justify their claims to wealth on the basis of emotional ties.[82] In Isaeus 2 the testator's brother and son contest the adoption of the testator's ex-wife's brother, while the adoptee in his turn argues that his devotion to his adoptive father, an old friend of his natural father, was like that of a birth son. In Isaeus 7 the speaker emphasizes the deep emotional ties between his adoptive father, Apollodorus, and his mother, who were matrilineal half-siblings. These ties developed because Apollodorus had been saved from the rapacity of his guardian, an agnate, by the speaker's mother's father, Apollodorus's stepfather. It is the descendants of this guardian who are now contesting the speaker's claim to have been adopted by Apollodorus (17). This insistence on emotional ties is perhaps a direct response to Athenian attitudes that adopted sons were not as close to their adoptive fathers as to those who had sired them.[83]

For their part kinsmen tried to use the force of the law in their attempts either to be adopted into an estate or to wrest it from another claimant (Is. 6.18 ff.), but emotional appeals were also resorted to so as to strengthen legal claims.

---

[81] A corollary to this law was that the adoptee could not return to his original *oikos* until his adoptive father had sons of his own: Antiph. B10. There has been some debate on whether the restriction that an adopted son could not in turn adopt applied to every type of adoption, *inter vivos,* by will, and posthumous: Harrison, *Law,* 1:85–87; cf. Lacey, *Family,* 146, and L. Rubinstein, *Adoption in IV. Century Athens* (Copenhagen: Museum Tusculanum Press, 1993), 18, who see the restriction as all-encompassing.

[82] Hunter, "Agnatic Kinship," 106.

[83] Golden, *Childhood,* 143.

In Isaeus 1 sister's sons of Cleonymus, whose own father told him they should inherit (4), have to admit that Cleonymus was an enemy of their guardian, their father's brother, although Cleonymus had never had a conflict with them per se (9–11). This argument is used to obstruct the claim of their rivals, nonkinsmen, who were adopted into Cleonymus's estate by will and who in turn claimed close affective ties to the deceased (ibid., 9–10, 30–32).[84] In other cases kinsmen as claimants compared their munificence to the state with the miserliness or criminality of the adoptee (Is. 4.25–26, 5.37 ff.).[85]

THE STEPFATHER

Because property interests could have a direct influence on interpersonal relationships, our sources are divided as to whether the stepfather was a benevolent or malevolent figure. Essentially, if the stepfather was viewed as helping the stepson secure his paternal inheritance or the property of another kinsman, the stepfather was benign; if, on the other hand, the stepfather somehow impeded the son from getting his full share of the paternal estate, vicious quarrels could be made public.[86]

Stepfathers are attested as being close to their stepsons. Astyphilus was brought up by his stepfather, his mother's second husband, even though children were often left behind by the widow to reside in the paternal *oikos*.[87] While Astyphilus was a minor, his stepfather tilled the land Astyphilus would inherit and doubled its value. The stepfather, by bringing Astyphilus along with his own son, Astyphilus's half-brother, to religious festivals, publicly displayed unity with his stepson. It was taken for granted that in turn Astyphilus would ignore his agnates and adopt his half-brother, thereby bequeathing his estate to him (Is. 9.3 ff., 27–30).[88] Likewise, one can infer that, because Hagnias II preferred his matrilineal half-brother as heir, relations were probably close between Hagnias II and his mother's second husband. In this particular case, Hagnias's bequest precipitated a dispute among his agnates that would not be resolved for generations.[89]

[84] Hunter, "Agnatic Kinship," 106.

[85] Hunter, "Gossip," 315.

[86] D. Nicholas, *The Domestic Life of a Medieval City: Women, Children, and the Family in Fourteenth-Century Ghent* (Lincoln: University of Nebraska Press, 1985), 116, for the stepfather as an ambiguous figure. Although deep affective ties could exist between stepfather and stepchildren, conflict was much more likely to erupt between them than between blood kin. Because of the small sample of instances pertaining to the Athenian stepfather, no discussion is possible on frequency of conflict.

[87] Hunter, "Athenian Widow," 296–98.

[88] For amicable ties, see also Dein. 1.58–59 (Polyeuctus of Cydantidae who visited his stepfather exiled in Megara).

[89] On Hagnias II's maneuvers, see Davies, *APF,* 83; M. Broadbent, *Studies in Greek Genealogy* (Leiden: Brill, 1968), 86; W. E. Thompson, *De Hagniae Hereditate: An Athenian Inheritance Case, Mnemosyne,* suppl. 44 (Leiden: Brill, 1976), 11–13. I am less certain of the relationship between Diocles and his stepfather (Is. 8.40–42), for which see the section below, p. 98, on inheriting daughters.

So too, Callias III, who was appointed guardian of Ischomachus's sons, also became their stepfather: it was in his role as guardian that he took the lessees of his minor stepsons' estate to court.[90] Isocrates' adoption of his wife's son by her previous marriage implies strong trust between stepfather and stepson ([Plut.] *Mor.* 838a, 839b), a trust reflected on a public level when both men cooperated in several trierarchies.[91]

On the other hand, whether from good intentions or bad, the stepfather could encroach on the stepson's estate. Demosthenes 58 tells of Polyeuctus, who was apparently in collusion with the speaker's father: the latter proposed a decree that would ultimately have severed Polyeuctus' stepson from the estate into which the boy had been adopted, that of his maternal grandfather. The maneuver would then allow Polyeuctus managerial control of the estate to which his wife, the boy's mother, would be the only heir (Dem. 58.30–31). However, given the possibility that Polyeuctus might have been related to his wife's father, as she was her father's heiress,[92] this particular conflict of interest might have led to the undermining of the boy's rights.

The most famous stepfather in our sources is Phormio, the ex-slave of Pasio the banker. The latter, before his death, had acquired Athenian citizenship, and Phormio himself won the honor in later years.[93] In his will Pasio assigned guardianship of his estate to Phormio and stipulated that his trusted assistant marry his widow, Archippe. Demosthenes 36 and 45, the former a defense of Phormio and the latter a prosecution of one of his witnesses, detail the reasons why Pasio's elder son, Apollodorus, one of the most litigious individuals in the orations, came into conflict with Phormio over the latter's guardianship. First, Phormio was given managerial control of the bank and was given guardianship of Pasio's estate, even though Apollodorus was an adult of around twenty-four years of age. Apparently Pasio did not trust his elder son because of the young man's profligacy (36.7–8). Second, this profligacy prompted Phormio, as guardian, to divide the estate before Apollodorus's younger brother Pasicles had reached his majority: Apollodorus' expenditures from the undivided estate necessitated the move (36.8–9, 36). Third, Phormio and Archippe had two sons, who then inherited some of their mother's possessions which were taken from the original estate of Pasio (36.14, 45.28, 50.60).

To obstruct these maneuvers, Apollodorus contended that the will was a forgery: no father with sons could write a will (Dem. 46.15, 25). It is unclear whether Apollodorus's assertion was correct: in the fourth century men with legitimate sons are known to have made wills, particularly so as to provide for the

---

[90] Cox, "Incest," 44.

[91] On the adoption, see L. Gernet, *Droit et société dans la Grèce ancienne* (Paris: Sirey, 1955) 129; Davies, *APF,* 247 for the list of liturgies.

[92] Davies, *APF,* 6–7; for the rules on heiresses see the section directly below, p. 95.

[93] See Davies, *APF,* 430, 436, for Pasio's grant of citizenship between 391 and 371 and Phormio's in 361/0.

needs of their widows and unmarried daughters.[94] Essentially Apollodorus was angry because he wanted to be treated as an Athenian citizen whose rights were defined strictly by Athenian inheritance laws. Pasio's inheritance strategies and the marriage of his widow to his ex-slave, however, were customary practices in the banking world (36.28 ff.), a world dominated by slaves and metics. This was basically the argument of Phormio's defender, and it won the jury over.[95]

It was especially annoying to Apollodorus, and certainly revealing of Phormio's ability as a guardian, that Pasicles never joined Apollodorus his brother in prosecuting Phormio. In retaliation, Apollodorus resorted to slander which is revealing in its bias: he claimed that Phormio had seduced Archippe, his mother, while Pasio was still living and that Pasicles was the product of this union (45.35, 39, 83–84). The accusation was not simply the result of the wild anger of a rather unsavory character against his insupportive brother or against a mother who, while alive, had prevented her son from prosecuting Phormio. Rather, it went to the heart of attitudes toward father/son relationships: it implied that the reason Pasicles did not come into conflict with Phormio was that he was in fact Phormio's natural son. It is of course dangerous to argue from silence, but Pasio's bequests seem to have angered Apollodorus; in fact the defender in Demosthenes 36 states that Apollodorus is acting against his father's will (52). Yet Apollodorus nowhere blames his father. Rather, blame is put elsewhere—on the supposed forgery of the will, on the false testimony of the witnesses to this forged will, on his mother's gullibility and lack of virtue, and on his mother's attempts to hide the *grammata,* or writings, upon which the will was based (36.18–19).[96]

Older men were testators and younger men were heirs; as a consequence the transmission of property could be fraught with fears and tensions lasting for years, culminating in a will that could as easily be ignored as observed. Frequently upon the father's death tensions surfaced in the courtroom; the very law that protected male heirs led to those heirs' threatening family unity.

Thus we see a dichotomy emerging between marriage practice and inheritance: the planning that could go into marital alliances, and which we have viewed earlier, was effective only to a certain point and was challenged by the very transmission of property that it was meant to protect. To what extent, then,

[94] Harrison, *Law,* 1:151–52; Rubinstein, *Adoption,* 83–85. Lacey *Family,* 132–33, 295, n. 43, conjectures that Apollodorus was absent on a trierarchy when his mother married Phormio. If so, the will, Pasio's death, and Archippe's marriage all occurred within a very brief span of time. Davies conjectures Pasio's death to have occurred c. 370/69 and Apollodorus's trierarchy, his second, to have taken place in 368: *APF,* 429, 440. J. Trevett, *Apollodorus the Son of Pasion* (Oxford: Clarendon Press, 1992), 10, 33, n. 17, agrees with the dating of the trierarchy though he takes issue with Davies's conjectured first trierarchy for Apollodorus in 373. Trevett also dates the year of Archippe's death to 362, shortly after Apollodorus's return from another trierarchy, and admits that Pasio's will was strictly speaking illegal: ibid., 13, 27.

[95] For the practices of the banking world, see Davies, *APF,* 427–28, and further in chapter 6, below, pp. 193–94.

[96] Finley, *SLC,* 214–15, n. 59, on the *grammata.*

could tensions or affective ties also be seen between fathers and daughters, who were not the preferred heirs in succession law?

FATHER/DAUGHTER RELATIONSHIPS

One scholar has recently noted that in Western society the father is the figure associated with the contracting of marriages for women. "Woman" in this context does not mean a man's wife, who sexually belongs to him, nor his sister, who falls under the bestowal rights of her own father, but rather the man's daughter. Although the exchange of the daughter is fundamental to the formation of kinship structures, which in turn form culture, the woman as daughter is least discussed in many primary sources. The primary dyad is that of father and son, and although in this dyad the linking role of the mother is frequently acknowledged, the father-daughter dyad is ignored. The one major exception to this lack of interest in the daughter is Roman society where the father/daughter relationship was given cultural prominence. Fathers and daughters were especially close, and while fathers demanded deference and allegiance from their daughters, daughters in turn looked to their fathers for protection.[97] In contrast, although the Attic orations depict the man as the exchanger of his wife and sister, the lack of information on the father-daughter relationship is striking. As for affective ties, the orations tell us that a father was expected to grieve for the death of his daughter, and if he did not do so for a proper length of time he could bring shame on himself and could be depicted as a bad citizen incapable of feeling much responsibility toward the *polis* (Aeschin. 3.77–78). As for the daughter, there is only one reference to her feelings: a daughter commonly worried about her father's fate in battle (Lyc. 1.40). In addition there is one reference to a daughter's contribution from her dowry to the funeral service for her father (Dem. 41.11). Only in drama is there any treatment of affective ties; here father/daughter relationships are seen as close.[98]

Besides the few references to emotions, the emphasis in the texts is rather on the role of the father as the daughter's *kyrios*. As the defender of his daughter's virtue (Aeschin. 1.182–83; [Dem.] 40.57, 59.65 ff.),[99] the father gave his daughter away in marriage by the act of *engyē,* the handing over of one man's daughter

---

[97] For the lack of interest in the woman as daughter, see L. E. Boose, "The Father's House and the Daughter in It: The Structures of Western Culture's Daughter-Father Relationship," in *Daughters and Fathers,* ed. L. E. Boose and B. S. Flowers (Baltimore: Johns Hopkins University Press, 1989), 19–74. For Roman society, see J. Hallett, *Fathers and Daughters in Roman Society: Women and the Elite Family* (Princeton, N.J.: Princeton University Press, 1984), esp. 62–149.

[98] Humphreys, *Anthropology and the Greeks* (London: Routledge and Kegan Paul, 1978), 202; Golden, *Childhood,* 94–97.

[99] In [Dem.] 59.65 ff., Stephanus pretended Neaera's daughter was his—the attitude, not the actual fact, is relevant here (ibid., 12–13); Pomeroy, *Goddesses,* 86.

to another man's son ([Dem.] 44.49; Dem. 40.57, 59.65 ff.).[100] By classical times, the rite was integrally connected with the notion of legitimacy and citizenship. The father ensured that his daughter married a trustworthy man of her own status and of good repute.[101] In one instance, Hipponicus II is portrayed as using poor judgment in giving his daughter away to Alcibiades ([And.] 4.13; Plut. *Alc.* 8.1–5), but the latter's son cast the match in a positive light, stating that Hipponicus gave his daughter to a man whose status was considered higher than that of the greatest citizens (Isoc. 16.31). Indeed, marrying a daughter to a man of bad repute could bring shame upon the father (Hyp. *Eux.* 31). As will be discussed in the next chapter, an integral part of the marriage negotiations was the dowry. Anthropologists have noted that the dowry is typically present in the marriage transactions of plow-agricultural societies where women and their kin are competing for wealthy husbands whose wealth is not being shared contemporaneously with other wives.[102] In Athens, the dowry was given to a daughter so that she could marry a fitting husband (on brothers and sisters, see below, pp. 116–20), but little is stated in the orations about discussions between father and daughter concerning her dowry.

One exception is Lysias 32: Diogeiton gave his daughter in marriage to his brother Diodotus; after Diodotus's death, according to the terms of his will, his widow and daughter received substantial dowries (a talent each with some extra cash going to the widow), while Diodotus's two minor sons were put under the guardianship of Diogeiton (Lys. 32.4 ff.). It was not until Diogeiton embezzled the boys' estate (ibid., 8–9, 15), paying his liturgies from it, supporting commercial ventures (ibid., 24–25) and even taking some of the cash from his daughter's dowry for these expenses (ibid., 8), that the woman assembled a group of kinsmen and friends and with the help of her son-in-law confronted her father (ibid., 1 ff., 10 ff.). In this case, the woman, as a widow whose son had just reached his majority, was entering into contention with her own father who would have acted as her *kyrios* as well. In her accusation she claimed that her father had jeopardized her sons' inheritance for his own needs (ibid., 11 ff.) and for the needs of the children by his second wife (ibid., 17).

Although the outcome of this case is unknown, the daughter, so as to damage her father's reputation, might have deliberately inflated the value of her hus-

---

[100] See also Harrison, *Law,* 1:3–9; Lacey, *Family,* 105–6; MacDowell, *Law,* 86–87. See C. Patterson, "Marriage and the Married Woman in Athenian Law," in *Women's History and Ancient History,* ed. S. Pomeroy (Chapel Hill: University of North Carolina Press, 1991), 48–72, for a recent discussion of marriage and betrothal, although I do not agree with Patterson's insistence that Athenian inheritance was nonagnatic.

[101] Note that in Isaeus 7.11 Eupolis refused to marry any of his daughters to his brother's son because of a feud between the two men. For a father's care in betrothing and marrying his daughter to a trustworthy ally, see chapter 4, below, p. 119. In [Dem.] 47.9 Theophemus and his brother were aided by a *kedestēs,* perhaps their sister's husband; if so, because their father was still alive (ibid., 35), one can infer that the alliance to the trusted affine was the result of the father's arrangement.

[102] See most recently S. Gaulin and J. Boster, "Dowry as Female Competition," *American Anthropologist* 92 (1990): 994–1005.

band's estate. Furthermore, Diogeiton's guardianship occurred at the end of the fifth century, when fortunes, especially those based on commerce as was Diodotus's, were being lost in the Peloponnesian War.[103] Looking at the accusations, we may be able to pinpoint the source of the friction between father and daughter. The daughter seems to have been Diogeiton's only child for some time until Diogeiton remarried and had children by his second wife.[104] Second, the father lost or spent one thousand drachmae from the dowry bequeathed to his daughter by her late husband: the stress which the speaker lays on this point implies the daughter's resentment.[105]

The woman's concern in Lysias 32 about her father's behavior toward his maternal grandchildren was not, however, unwarranted, to judge from Isaeus 8, where the speaker's maternal grandfather, Ciron, preferred his sons by his second marriage as his heirs. Even after the death of these sons, Ciron's second wife and her brother tried to keep control of the estate from Ciron's daughter's son with Ciron's approval and with the help of his agnates after his death (8.3 ff., 36 ff.).[106] Indeed, the stepmother is a pervasively disagreeable character: her quarrels with her husband's daughters were a cliché (Is. 12.5), while her sons could threaten the inheritance rights of her husband's sons by a previous marriage (see below, pp. 112–13).

Although one can scarcely generalize from these two examples, father/daughter relationships could be tested by the transmission of property. The same may be true of relations between father and son-in-law: both men could work smoothly in performing public liturgies (Antiph. 6.12–13), but a speaker could argue that his father and the latter's son-in-law were not close (Lys. 19.18–19), and relationships were strained if the younger man did not think his father-in-law was protecting his property rights ([Dem.] 45.56).[107]

If the rights of the daughter and her children were so precarious, how would she fare if she were the only heir to her father? Although there were strict rules governing the marriage of young heiresses, Athenians frequently disregarded them.

THE DAUGHTER WHO INHERITED

Although Athenian law preferred the downward devolution of property onto males, that is, sons of the same father, sometimes no sons but only daughters were

---

[103] Davies, *APF,* 152–53.

[104] Ibid., 151–52.

[105] Campbell, *Honour,* 172, states that among the Sarakatsani, although breaches of trust and respect between father and daughter were rare, the suspicion that the father stinted on his daughter's dowry would result in her resentment.

[106] On the precarious legal position of the daughter, see Rubinstein, *Adoption,* 102–103.

[107] See also the discussion on sororal relationships chapter 4, below, p. 113. In [Dem.] 49.66 Timotheus, who had contracted a marriage between his daughter and Iphicrates' son, had, nevertheless, at one time charged Iphicrates with *xenia.*

born or left to the father. An *epiklēros,* in the strictest sense, was a daughter who had no brothers and was unmarried at her father's death,[108] or perhaps she was married but without children at her father's death. There were strict laws governing the *epiklēros,* as it was her son who would carry on her father's line. The heiress was required to marry her father's closest agnate, preferably his eldest brother, but in his absence, another brother or brother's son, and in their absence, a sister's son. The daughter's sons would then inherit her dead father's estate. In the event that a married woman had several sons and was married to a man not adopted by her father, one of the sons would be adopted into the father's estate.[109]

The laws maintaining and defining the epiclerate were codified by Solon on his *axōnes,* according to Pseudo-Aristotle (*Ath.Pol.* 9.2), and presumably they stipulated that the heiress was to marry her dead father's next of kin. The situation in which a daughter without brothers was unmarried at the time of her father's death, however, is rare in our sources (And. 1.117 ff.; Dem. 57.41; Lys. frr. 23, 26[?] [Th]).[110] Normally the father, before his death, would fully realize that the daughter would be his only heir and could attempt to marry the daughter off to his brother ([Dem.] 44.10),[111] or adopt a son who then must by law marry the daughter,[112] or would simply give the daughter in marriage to an outsider (Dem. 42.21, 27; 44.10; 58.30–31; Is. 8.1 ff., 40–41; 10.4, 7). In the latter case, the daughter's son could then be adopted into the estate of her father which would prevent the extinction of the *oikos* (Is. 10.4 [Cyronides]; Dem. 42.21, 58.30–31).[113] At times, however, the daughter's son simply inherited the estate,

---

[108] Gernet, "Sur l'epiclérat," 338, is the classic discussion of the strict regulations and the narrow definition of the *epiklēros.*

[109] On the laws regulating the epiclerate, see L. Beauchet, *Histoire du droit privé dans la république athénienne,* 4 vols. (Paris: Chevalier Marescq, 1897), 1:398–487; Gernet, "Sur l'epiclérat," 337–77; Harrison, *Law,* 1:132–38, and bibliography 132, n. 2; Lacey, *Family,* 139–45; J. Karnezis, *The Epikleros* (Athens: n.p., 1972), 195 ff.; Schaps, *Economic,* 25 ff.; Just, *Women,* 95 ff. Cf. Rubinstein, *Adoption,* 98–100, who feels that a married daughter with sons at the time of her father's death could be considered an *epiklēros* and could be forced to divorce in order to be married to an agnate. On the adoption of just one son, see Harrison, *Law,* 1:135. There were probably legal stipulations or social attitudes that prevented too broad a disparity in the ages of the spouses: Plut. *Sol.* 20.2–3; E. Ruschenbusch, *Solonos Nomoi, Historia Einzelschriften* 9 (Wiesbaden: F. Steiner, 1966), 46, 88–89, F52a; Gernet, "Sur l'epiclérat," 363; Schaps, *Economic,* 36. On the discouragement of marriage between individuals of vastly disparate ages, see S. Isager, "The Marriage Pattern in Classical Athens: Men and Women in Isaios," *ClMed* 33 (1981–82): 86.

[110] Karnezis, *Epikleros,* 206–12, is one of the few scholars who have discussed at any length how rarely the true *epiklēros* appears in the sources. See Dem. 37.45, where unmarried daughters whose father was living are referred to as *epiklēroi.*

[111] The doings in Lys. 32.4–5 may also have been the result of such concerns, but Diogeiton, the woman's father, subsequently remarried and seems to have sired children (Davies, *APF,* 151).

[112] On the law and practice, see Dem. 41.3 ff. For the close association between the epiclerate and adoption, see Gernet, "Sur l'epiclérat," 362. Cf. Rubinstein, *Adoption,* 87, who argues, against the general consensus, that the adopted son was not required to marry the adopter's daughter.

[113] See further note 152, below.

or attempted to, without being adopted into it (Is. 8.1 ff.; 10.4 ff. [the speaker]). This latter move meant the termination of the maternal grandfather's *oikos* as such and its amalgamation with the heir's own patrimony.[114] Also, if the heir's father had not been an agnate of his maternal grandfather, the testator's estate would then devolve onto an individual who did not belong to that testator's patriline: such a move could be hotly contested by the testator's agnates.[115]

Certainly in the case in which a woman had been married to a nonkinsman, her son who was adopted into her father's estate would not be her father's agnate. However, when the testator adopted a husband for his daughter, although the adoptee was frequently a kinsman, he was not necessarily an agnate.[116] What was the cost to agnates of such a maneuver? First, in general, despite kinsmen's objections, an adoption could result in a long tenure of the estate—there are several instances of an adopted line holding on to an estate for at least two or three generations.[117] Demosthenes 41 may provide evidence, with the aid of inscriptions, of long tenure through a daughter. In the oration, Polyeuctus of Teithras had two daughters and no sons. He gave one daughter in marriage to the speaker, whose relationship to Polyeuctus, if any, is unknown. Polyeuctus gave his other daughter to his wife's brother, whom he had adopted. When, however, a dispute erupted between Polyeuctus and his adopted son, Leocrates, Polyeuctus initiated a divorce between his daughter and her husband and gave her in marriage to Spudias of Aphidna, who was a nonkinsman and whom Polyeuctus appears not to have adopted.[118] Nevertheless, it appears from inscriptional evidence that Spudias had descendants adopted into the estate: *SEG* 32.118 II 37, a list of donors dated to 244/3, records a Spudias of Teithras,[119] while another inscrip-

[114] Rubinstein, *Adoption*, 88 ff. Lin Foxhall ("Household Gender and Property in Classical Athens," *CQ* 39 [1989]: 28–29) is quite right in stating that there was an overwhelming desire to leave property to the next generation, and therefore most Athenians had children or adopted them.

[115] Is. 8.1 ff. is a clear case. Is. 7.30–32 depicts a sister who did not have her son adopted into her brother's estate, thereby terminating his *oikos*.

[116] Gernet, "La loi," 131 ff.; Rubinstein, *Adoption*, 98–99.

[117] Theopompus, Theopompus's son, and his son's son held on to the estate of the brother of Theopompus's wife. Dicaeogenes II's adoption of a nonagnate resulted in a three-generation tenure as did the adoption of Archiades of his sister's daughter's son: see Davies, *APF*, 85–86 (Theopompus and his descendants), 146–47 (Dicaeogenes II), 195 (Archiades). See also ibid., 229, for the possibility that Thudippus, his son Cleon, and the latter's son had all been adopted into another *oikos*.

[118] Although Polyeuctus's deme is given as Thria in the manuscripts, the discovery in the Agora of a dedication to Demeter and Core by Polyeuctus of Teithras, his daughter, and her husband Spudias of Aphidna, leaves little doubt that Polyeuctus's deme must be changed to Teithras. For the dedication, see T. L. Shear, "The Campaign of 1936," *Hesperia* 6 (1937): 341–42, and the emendations in *SEG* 17.83 giving Spudias's deme. For the probability that Spudias was not adopted, see Harrison, *Law*, 1:152; Rubinstein, *Adoption*, 56, argues that an adopter could not annul an adoption, despite the clear statement in Demosthenes 41 that Polyeuctus did exactly that. Rubinstein feels that this case was exceptional.

[119] These inscriptions have been discussed in terms of the break in the secretary cycle in the third century: B. D. Meritt, "Athenian Archons 347/6–48/7 B.C.," *Historia* 26 (1977): 163–64, 176. For a discussion of Spudias and Demosthenes 41, see: C. A. Cox, "The Names of Adoptees: Some Prosopographical Afterthoughts," *ZPE* 107 (1995): 249–54.

tion eighteen years later records a Spudias of Aphidna (*SEG* 25.106.7). If Spudias of Teithras is a direct descendant of the actor in Demosthenes 41, then the implication is that a line of descendants from the fourth-century Spudias was adopted into Polyeuctus's estate for a century and a half. The Spudias of *SEG* 25.106.7 is intriguing. He could be a member of a collateral branch or he could be identical with Spudias of Teithras; in that case, the third-century Spudias would have left a son in Teithras and returned to Aphidna. This reconstruction is, of course, speculative, but if it is at all accurate, it gives us a good idea why these people were so litigious: marriage to an heiress would give the victor in these squabbles added wealth that could be retained by himself and his descendants for generations. The hand of an heiress was well worth fighting for, even though the moment of transmission was filled with tensions and concerns over whether the daughter had received her full share (Dem. 41.17).

Gernet, in his study of the epiclerate in 1921,[120] remarked on the instability of the institution, although he did not elaborate on the reasons for this. First, as just discussed, although the father could attempt to marry his daughter to a close agnate, it could happen that she was married to an outsider. Second, agnates were not always available or willing to marry the (potential) heiress. Third, an heiress was at the mercy of her male relatives' willingness to comply with the law, and although there were strict laws overseen by the archon protecting the heiress from abuse, illegal machinations appear in the claims to the heiress, or indeed in avoiding claims to her. Pseudo-Demosthenes 44 relates how Archiades refused to marry his brother's only daughter and child; the brother was forced then to give his daughter in marriage to an outsider (10). Neither Mantitheus son of Mantias nor Apollodorus son of Pasio wanted their daughters to marry their brothers ([Dem.] 40.5 ff., 45.75).[121] At times the woman herself would not marry her father's agnates because she was already married (Is. 10.19–20). In Isaeus 6 one of the daughters of Euctemon was considered a possible heiress of her father's kinsman, Androcles, only after she was widowed (Is. 6.46, 58).[122]

Complications resulted when agnates were neither available nor willing to claim the hand of an heiress. In one case, a nonkinsman tried to claim an heiress's hand (Lys. fr. 23 [Th]). Epilycus's two daughters, true *epiklēroi* at their father's death, were claimed by their father's sister's sons because Epilycus had no brothers. However, one of the cousins, Leagros II, was allegedly bribed by his brother-in-law Callias III to drop his claim so that Callias's son, a more distant kinsman, could put in his claim (And. 1.117–21).[123] From the protracted conflicts among the Bouselidae, Sositheus alleged that he was adjudicated Phylomache II as her

---

[120] See above, note 109.

[121] Apollodorus actually shuddered at the thought of his daughters marrying Phormio's sons by Archippe, Apollodorus's mother. Resorting to the mother's side was legally permitted only after all possibilities on the father's side were exhausted. That Apollodorus refused to consider his full brother, Pasicles, underscores the fraternal conflict: see chapter 4, below, p. 110.

[122] Wyse, *Isaeus*, 533–34; Davies, *APF*, 563.

[123] See also Davies, *APF*, 31, 91, 265.

nearest kinsman although he was only her second cousin (father's father's brother's daughter's son—[Dem.] 43.55),[124] not a true agnate, and there were agnates closer in line. Sositheus's claim should not be taken at face value: despite his claim of adjudication, his wife's father was clearly alive at the time of the marriage and therefore no adjudication was warranted. Second, as Sositheus declares, no close agnate wanted to marry Phylomache II: in Theopompus's case (43.55) he was already married and probably unwilling to divorce. Furthermore, the legitimacy of Phylomache's father's mother, Phylomache I, was questioned (Is. 11.8–10; [Dem.] 43.49).[125]

Other cases attest to individuals simply ignoring the law, although kinsmen who did so could be reported to the archon (*eisangelia kakōseōs*) and punished, in extreme cases, with confiscation of their estate (Is. 3.46–47, 62).[126] Moreover, there was no penalty for the prosecutor or informant should he lose his case. In Isaeus 10, if the speaker is at all reliable, although his mother was an heiress after her brother's adoption out of the paternal estate (4 ff.), she was not married to a kinsman. The laws may have been ignored in this case, however, because the paternal estate was insolvent (ibid., 15).[127] Indeed, the law recognized that kinsmen would not wish to marry a poor heiress (of the thetic class), though they were required to dower the woman.[128] In this context it is worth repeating that Gylon, a state debtor whose estate was confiscated, gave his two inheriting daughters in marriage to nonkinsmen.[129]

Isaeus 8 tells us that within the decade 420–410 or shortly afterward (8.40 ff.),[130] Diocles, the brother-in-law of Ciron, had himself adopted into his stepfather's estate. According to law, however, Diocles was the very person the stepfather could not adopt. The law stated that if the testator had daughters, the adoptee had to marry one. Diocles' stepfather had daughters who were Diocles' homometric sisters, and whom, therefore, by law Diocles could not marry.[131] We have no idea whether Diocles forcibly usurped the rights of his homometric sisters, as the speaker claimed, or whether his stepfather willingly adopted him during his lifetime so as to assure himself of a male heir. In any case, the daughters violently defended their lost status as potential *epiklēroi*, to the point that one husband was killed, apparently by Diocles, during the conflict (Is. 8.40 ff.).[132]

For the fourth century, Isaeus 3[133] tells of an adopted son, Endius, a sister's

---

[124] See also ibid., 80.

[125] Thompson, *De Hagniae Hereditate*, 89 f.

[126] MacDowell, *Law*, 94–95, 98; Karnezis, *Epikleros*, 226–27, suggests that it might be rash to assume that the maltreatment of the *epiklēros* was punishable.

[127] Wyse, *Isaeus*, 651, 662; Gernet, "Sur l'epiclérat," 346.

[128] On the dowering of thetic heiresses, see Harrison, *Law*, 1:135–36; MacDowell, *Law*, 96.

[129] Davies, *APF*, 121–22.

[130] On these events, see ibid., 313–14.

[131] Marriage to a homopatric, not a homometric, sister was allowed: Harrison, *Law*, 1:22.

[132] See Thalheim fr. 6 for another reference to the rivals for their property.

[133] Wyse feels that the oration is one of Isaeus's later works: *Isaeus*, 276–77. Wevers dates it to 389: R. F. Wevers, *Isaeus: Chronology, Prosopography and Social History* (Paris: Mouton, 1969), 16.

son to the adopter Pyrrhus, who did not marry his adoptive father's daughter, Phile. Rather, Endius married her off to a nonkinsman, because, according to the speaker (Endius's brother), Phile was illegitimate, the issue of her father by an *hetaira*. Though there is some strong evidence to question the allegation of illegitimacy (Is. 3.26–30, 32–34), Endius was unwilling to marry Phile because her mother had a bad reputation (ibid., 10 ff.) and there may have been a considerable age difference between Endius and Phile.[134] Consequently, it was difficult for Phile to acquire her father's estate for her children, or for one of them (ibid., 55).

The cases above have shown how the patrilineal bias in claims to inheriting daughters was ignored because agnatic kin refused to marry the (potential) heiress or because the father married her to an outsider. The adoption of an *epiklēros* could also undermine the agnatic bias. In the 390s Hagnias adopted his niece, perhaps the daughter of his homometric brother, although this relationship is not certain.[135] Hagnias's kinsman, Stratocles, who had only one son, allowed one of his daughters to be adopted by her maternal uncle (Is. 11.41),[136] while Apollodorus had adopted his homometric sister as heiress, stipulating that she marry a Eumolpid, a nonkinsman (Is. 7–9).[137] Although it was rare to adopt a woman as heiress, the move allowed the adopter to marry her to someone upon whom he wanted his estate to devolve. In this case, the groom could manage the adopter's estate while legally remaining a member of his natural *oikos*.[138] This type of adoption presumes a close, trusting relationship between the birth and adoptive fathers.

The father/daughter relationship, as described by the orations, was ambivalent. There are indications of affective ties, but the orations also depict the father as a stern authoritarian who could stint on his daughter's dowry or even cheat her descendants of their rights to inherit. Nor was the daughter's position as heiress secure, despite legal strictures. Often relying on kinsmen who did not necessarily want to marry her but who did want her father's property retained in the patriline, the heiress could be married to an outsider, and when her children claimed her father's estate, they could face the opposition of his patriline.

MOTHERS AND SONS

Much of the discussion of this type of relationship is based on Virginia Hunter's studies of the widow in Athens,[139] in particular of her role as a mother of sons.

---

[134] Wyse, *Isaeus,* 310, 322.

[135] This is the theory of Thompson, for which see chapter 1, above, pp. 7–8.

[136] Broadbent, *Studies,* 94; Davies, *APF,* 84; Thompson, *De Hagniae Hereditate,* 12.

[137] Thompson, *De Hagniae Hereditate,* 12–13.

[138] Ibid., 12 f.

[139] Hunter, "Women's Authority," 39–48; "Athenian Widow," 291–311.

The orations commonly acknowledge that the mother/son relationship was close and affective. A son was not reluctant to tell the jury that while on trierarchic service, he was devastated to learn that his mother lay dying in Athens ([Dem.] 50.60), or a mother could become hysterical when her son was wounded in a brawl ([Dem.] 54.9, 20). Another speaker is concerned that if he is exiled his mother will live in poverty (Lys. 7.41), a common plea in a defendant's argument for acquittal.[140] In Lysias 1 a mother may even be cognizant of her son's relationship with a married woman (20). The sons in Antiphon 1 steadfastly maintain their mother's innocence when she was prosecuted for poisoning their father (1.4 ff.), although they seem, according to the speaker, to have difficulty in proving it. Mothers, like fathers, could also inform their sons of an individual's ancestry, information passed on by their sons to the lawcourts ([Dem.] 57.37).

Any rift between mother and son was perceived as the result of the son's personal and civic irresponsibility: because the law, attributed to Solon, protected both mothers and fathers from abuse by their children, any allegation against an individual of abuse underlined that person's baseness as an Athenian citizen. Timarchus, who had squandered his patrimony and prostituted himself, thereby depriving himself of the right to the franchise, also allegedly denied a proper burial to his mother (Aeschin. 1.98–99). Dicaeogenes III, who "robbed" his adoptive father's sisters of their share of their brother's estate and who was miserly with liturgical services, was anathema to his mother (Is. 5.39). In Lysias 31 the speaker, who is prosecuting Philon for cowardice, treason, and robbery in Philon's scrutiny for public office, relates that Philon's mother refused to let her son bury her, but gave the task to a nonkinsman (20–21)—a brutal insult, as it was a son's duty to bury his mother.[141] The implication is that the son's misdeeds must have been truly terrible, because a mother ordinarily forgives most injuries done to her out of love for her children (ibid., 22). In the sources outside the orations a mother's love is a common theme.[142]

Just as the orators stress the public unity between father and son, the public and private support a mother gave her children was her symbol of honor—here defined in terms of her Athenian ancestry and her conduct. Discussions on modern Greek cultures have noted the deeply affectionate ties between mothers and sons; sons must protect the honor of their mother, and she in turn maintains the honor of her marital family through her modest conduct. Such conduct is frequently defined in terms of sexual activity.[143] In classical Athens, sons were sure not to offend the private space of the mother—they defended her against in-

---

[140] Golden, *Childhood*, 100.

[141] Hunter, "Athenian Widow," 301; "Women's Authority," 48 and n. 44.

[142] Golden, *Childhood*, 97–98, for references and for a discussion of Philon's case.

[143] Campbell, *Honour*, 169–70; M. Herzfeld, *The Poetics of Manhood* (Princeton, N.J.: Princeton University Press, 1985), 124, who states that the male self is defined by protecting his family in general from sexual and verbal threats.

truders in the household (Dem. 21.78–79, 120–21) or they did not bring a *het-aira* to live in the household out of respect for both mother and wife ([Dem.] 59.21–22). If there were attacks against an individual's female kin, these attacks were directed against the individual himself by a political or social rival. Often the women referred to remained nameless;[144] in fact, sons ideally were not to mention the names of their own mothers in court ([Dem.] 45.27).[145] Demosthenes lists the common types of slander hurled at women: they were unchaste, or they smuggled in a changeling to pass for their child, or they were not citizens. Although Demosthenes hastily adds that men who stoop to such lies and insults are themselves despicable (Dem. 22.61), he nevertheless seems to have used them himself. Thus, he charged that Aeschines' mother had behaved improperly in her function as a cult priestess; and in response Aeschines charged that Demosthenes' maternal grandmother was not Athenian, in stark contrast to Aeschines' own citizen mother (Aeschin. 2.148).[146] Indeed, slandering the mother's citizenship was very common because female citizenship was difficult to prove. Women's names were not entered in lists of citzens, and even though witnesses were present at the girl's birth and her marriage, such testimony could be refuted.[147]

In the private orations, the unity between mother and son was especially obvious in their claims to and interests in two, sometimes three, *oikoi:* the *oikos* of the woman's husband, that of her natal kin, and, if the woman remarried, that of her second marriage. Much of the woman's role as wife and her interest in her husband's property has been discussed above: for instance, the widow represented in Lysias 32 as well as Demosthenes' own mother were women who knew the details of their husband's estates and had their sons defend that estate.

Only when a son perceived that his mother was obstructing his chances to acquire his full share of the paternal estate, or to use that estate as he saw fit (Aeschin. 1.98–99), did conflicts arise. Such was the case with Apollodorus and his mother, leading to his claim that she had had an affair with Phormio prior to the death of Apollodorus's father, Pasio. Appropriately enough, this is the only recorded instance of a son's slandering his mother, and Apollodorus waited until his mother's death to indulge in his diatribe ([Dem.] 45.3, 27, 34, 39, 74–75, 83–84).

A woman could also be a link between the sons of her first marriage and those she bore in a second marriage. As noted above, in Isaeus 7 and 9 sets of homometric siblings shared in each other's property: in Isaeus 7 Apollodorus adopted his half-sister's son, thereby ignoring his agnates, and in Isaeus 9 the son of Theophrastus claims on the basis of emotional ties his right to inherit the estate

[144] Hunter, "Gossip," 317–20.

[145] D. Schaps, "The Woman Least Mentioned: Etiquette and Women's Names," *CQ* 27 (1977): 323–30; see also Cox, "Incest," 34 for the use of slander as a political weapon.

[146] Cox, "Incest," 37 and n. 11.

[147] Hunter, "Gossip," 317–18.

of his mother's son by a former marriage. Hagnias II preferred his homometric brothers as his heirs, while Archippe's attempts to have her children by Phormio inherit her dowry given to her by Pasio met with no opposition from Pasicles, though Apollodorus successfully opposed her wishes.[148]

A chief concern for the son was the mother's dowry. Inextricably bound up with his honor and hers, it was a key element in formalizing a marriage, and therefore establishing the legitimacy of a woman's children.[149] The speaker in Isaeus 8 was forced to explain why his mother was remarried with a small dowry, since small dowries could cast suspicion on the nature of the union (7–8).[150] The speaker in Lysias 19 goes to great lengths to explain why his father married his mother without a dowry—his father gave greater importance to her lineage than to her wealth (14–15). Furthermore, as stated above, the dowry was absorbed into the conjugal fund and therefore the son could use the wealth and inherit it.[151] Nevertheless, dotal property belonged to the woman's natal *oikos,* so the son would be quite careful to protect the dowry from confiscation (Dem. 42.27, 53.28–29). Because the dowry was the mother's material link to her patriline, her son would be very interested in protecting her inheritance rights, should she suddenly find herself eligible to inherit, that is, if the male heirs in her patriline had died leaving her as heiress to her father or brother, even if, as noted above, these claims could be opposed. Frequently such inheritance took the form of adoption, the woman's son being adopted into her father's or brother's estate. At other times, however, the son inherited as the closest in line; his mother's brother had no male agnates so that heirs were sought through the line of the deceased's sister. The son, in other words, defended his mother's right to inherit as a female agnate; there is no case in which a son is defending his mother's right, and thus his right, to inherit property strictly through the mother's matriline. A son, therefore, could not inherit an estate through his mother's mother or even his mother's sister.[152]

One of the most ironic statements in the private orations deals with the individual's interest in the property of his matrilineal kin. Sositheus, the speaker of Pseudo-Demosthenes 43, was not a Bouselid on his father's side but only on his

---

[148] Hunter, "Athenian Widow," 308, n. 21.

[149] Ibid., 301; Just, *Women,* 44–45, emphasizes that marriage was a "bundle of rights"; see also 70–75 for a discussion of the dowry.

[150] Wyse, *Isaeus,* 594.

[151] Hunter, "Athenian Widow," 301.

[152] For the cases of adoption into a mother's father's estate, see Is. 10.4, 7 (Cyronides); Dem. 42.21; Dem. 43.11–15; Dem. 58.30–31; cases in which the role of adoption is not stated: Is. 3.55; 8, passim; Is. 10., passim (the speaker). For instances outside of the orations: Rubinstein, *Adoption,* 88. For the adoption of a woman's son into the estate of her brother, see below, chapter 4, pp. 125–28. There is no indication whether the speaker in Isaeus 3 is planning to be adopted into Pyrrhus's estate, as his brother had been, or whether he would simply inherit it. For the inheritance of part of a mother's brother's estate without adoption, see Is. 5.13; 7.19, 31. In the latter case the same woman is arguing for the right of her son to inherit the estate of her father's brother's son.

mother's. He had married a Bouselid, Phylomache II, and had his son adopted into his wife's father's estate in the hopes of having that son adjudged the estate of the Bouselid Hagnias II. Thus Sositheus spent much time and energy in securing and laying claim to property belonging to an agnate of his wife and mother. In his speech, however, Sositheus strenuously defends his claim by impugning his rival Macartatus for the latter's unswerving interest in matrilineal property (Macartatus had been adopted into his mother's brother's estate).[153]

Although fathers and sons could conflict, there is rarely any indication that the mother and son collaborated against the father. In only one case, when the father is perceived as spending too much of his time and his wealth on a *hetaira,* do a woman and her sons take him to task for his behavior (Is. 6.21). The implication here is that the woman was justified in voicing her concern to her husband for his misuse of wealth, since it would ultimately threaten the inheritance of their sons.

Once absorbed into the marital *oikos,* a mother could have a good deal of influence, resorting to either husband or son as spokesman in the lawcourts.[154] By contrast, the relationship between mother and daughter is rarely seen in our sources because this particular link was not essential in an inheritance system that enforced transmission of property among males.

MOTHERS AND DAUGHTERS

One of the most informative orations on mothers and daughters is Demosthenes 41, which deals with inheriting daughters. The oration reveals a great deal of cooperation between the mother and her two daughters—the mother's brother at first was adopted into the father's estate and married to one of the daughters. Even on the divorce of the woman's brother from her daughter, relations between mother and daughter were close, as this daughter seems to have taken her mother in after the death of the father (3 ff.).[155] Also, the mother continued throughout her life to make small private loans to the husbands of both daughters, and it appears that on her death, the mother left her dotal wealth to her daughters and their husbands (ibid., 9–11).

This interest of the mother and daughter in the older woman's dowry is evident in a second case, that of Demosthenes' mother, Cleoboule. Cleoboule had brought into her marriage a dowry of fifty minae, consisting of jewelry and plated objects, items that appear to have been given to her from her own mother's dowry (Aeschin. 3.172 f.). However, Aphobus, Cleoboule's intended second husband, embezzled the dowry when he took over guardianship of the elder

---

[153] Davies, *APF,* 80; Broadbent, *Studies,* 75, for Sositheus's interest in matrilineal and uxoral wealth.

[154] For women's private influence in disputes, see Hunter, *Policing Athens,* 53.

[155] Hunter, "Athenian Widow," 309, n. 23.

Demosthenes' estate. Furthermore, the orator himself was being pressured on his majority to expend money on state services.[156] Therefore the statement in Demosthenes 28.20–21 may not be pure rhetoric: the orator was charged by his mother to ensure that he receive compensation for his sister's dowry when he sued Aphobus. The mother, faced with the encumbered estate of her late husband, was concerned that an adequate dowry be provided to her daughter so the latter could marry well.

Otherwise, a woman, although divorced from her husband, could collaborate with her daughters by her ex-husband to ensure that they gained access to some of his property on his death (Is. 6.40); or a mother could look to a daughter's husband to protect her sons from their abusive guardian (Lys. 32.9–10); and it was the sign of bad character for a man to embezzle his mother-in-law's wealth (Dem. 45.70). The one case in which mother and daughter appear at odds, the case in which Chrysilla allegedly stole her daughter's husband, was the product of considerable rhetorical embellishment.[157]

To sum up the discussion on domestic relationships, the law emphasized the downward transmission of property from male to male. With that succession bias in mind, marriage strategies were formed. Even in the case of an inheriting daughter, the assumption was that she was to provide her father's estate with a male heir. Although the woman as wife or mother could have a great deal of managerial control over a man's estate, the law did its best to limit actual ownership of substantial property over generations of women. A woman could express a very active interest in property of her patriline, for instance, but interest did not necessarily guarantee access or ownership. At the same time, however, the legal emphasis on downward transmission resulted in ambivalent relationships between the father and his children, particularly his sons, so that the woman as mother could be seen as supportive and usually nonthreatening. Thus there was conflict in the very dyad, father and son, that lay at the heart of the agnatic bias in inheritance law. It was a conflict that was never really resolved and continued into the next generation of inheriting siblings, the brothers, while sisters were often very close to their brothers.

---

[156] For Aphobus's embezzlement of Cleoboule's dowry, see Hunter, "Women's Authority," 41; on Demosthenes' being targeted in an *antidosis* challenge to perform a trierarchy: Davies, *APF,* 135 and chapter 6, below p. 196, on friends.

[157] Cox, "Incest," 42–45.

CHAPTER 4

Sibling Relationships

THE BREAKDOWN at times of the father-son relationship was a breakdown of the formal genealogy, or the genealogy recognized and protected by inheritance law. According to that law property was transmitted downward, ideally from an older male to a younger one. Precisely because this was the preferred form of transmission, father and son could argue over the moment of transmission and the amount of property involved. Just as fathers and sons could argue, so too male heirs, or brothers, could become rivals over property. As we will see, this rivalry could extend along the line of agnatic kin, so that mistrust among agnates was very much a reality. Within this context of rivalry relationships among members of the less formal genealogy should be examined. Included in this less formal genealogy are sisters and maternal kin, those individuals who were not preferred heirs in inheritance law.

In recent years there has been a proliferation of historical studies of medieval and early modern European households and the effects of transmission practices on familial relationships. These studies suggest that in countries such as France, Germany, and England, it was customary in some regions—usually among the upper classes—to bequeath the bulk of the estate to one son, most often the eldest; whereas in other regions of the same country, or in other classes, the estate was divided among several, if not all, children. Even within these areas and groups, local customs varied or changed over time; strict impartibility or partibility was not always practiced. In Southern Europe, partibility was the norm, as it was in classical Athens, but for males alone.

As regards women, on the other hand, in areas of partibility, after receiving a dowry of cash, movables, or land (depending on local custom or the social class), could either be excluded from any further inheritance of the paternal estate, or could inherit along with their brothers, at times receiving an equal share and sometimes a lesser one. Of particular interest for the present discussion are the studies done on central and north Italy of the Renaissance era where a daughter's dowry ensured the honor of the bride's family, proclaimed the social status of the couple, defined the legitimacy of the union and symbolized the young woman's virtue. A daughter's dowry was probably not equal to the shares of inheritance received by her brothers and effectively denied her further rights of inheritance in the paternal estate. Likewise, in classical Athens, the dowry was a *pre mortem* inheritance which was crucial for making a good marriage but which tended not to be equal to the wealth inherited by a young woman's brothers.

Outside of Renaissance Italy, in both partible and impartible systems, the woman's dowry after marriage could be bound inextricably to the conjugal fund, but at times the husband had little say over the dowry, particularly if it took the form of land. As with Athens the wife was only a temporary member of her husband's house, taking the dowry with her to her original house on termination of her marriage. As for sibling relationships, in the areas where unigeniture was the norm, relations between the inheriting son and his noninheriting brothers would naturally be tense, but in partible systems tensions could arise as well, and they certainly arose in ancient Athens. In regions where males and females inherited equally, brothers-in-law became the focal point: they could cooperate in agricultural or building activities or in feuds with third parties who threatened their property. Yet relations could be competitive, with conflict between brothers and their married sisters.[1]

The present chapter has been influenced by anthropological studies of present-

---

[1] H. Medick and D. Sabean, "Interest and Emotion" in *Interest and Emotion,* ed. Medick and Sabean (Cambridge: Cambridge University Press), 13, who stress that property transmission affects sibling relations. For impartible systems in northern Europe, see J.-L. Flandrin, *Familles: Parenté, maison, sexualité dans l'ancienne société* (Paris: Hachette, 1976), 75–79; E. LeRoy Ladurie, "Family Structures and Inheritance Customs in Sixteenth-Century France," in *Family and Inheritance: Rural Society in Western Europe 1200–1800,* ed. J. Goody, J. Thirsk, and E. P. Thompson (Cambridge: Cambridge University Press, 1976), 37–70; L. Berkner, "Inheritance, Land Tenure and Peasant Family Structure: A German Regional Comparison," ibid., 71–95; J. P. Cooper, "Patterns of Inheritance and Settlement by Great Landowners from the Fifteenth to the Eighteenth Centuries," ibid., 215–21. For partible systems in south Italy, see D. Kertzer and C. Brettell, "Advances in Italian and Iberian Family History," *Journal of Family History* 12 (1987): 96–101. Kertzer and Brettell point out that in some regions of southern Europe, however, (e.g. Portugal and Spain) impartibility was resorted to in order to avoid severe fragmentation of property. In Italy, among the elite, partible inheritance for males was preferred, but sons often lived together and shared the patrimony. Partibility was abandoned by the Italian elite after the mid-sixteenth century in favor of impartibility, which in turn was abandoned in the nineteenth century. For the woman's exclusion from her paternal house or her ties to it, see LeRoy Ladurie and Kertzer and Brettell above. For discussion on Renaissance societies in Italy, see C. Klapisch-Zuber, *Women, Family, and Ritual in Renaissance Italy,* trans. L. Cochrane (Chicago: Chicago University Press), 214–18. Unlike in the case of Renaissance Italy (219 ff.), there appears to have been no counterdowry given by the husband in classical Athens. As to whether the dowry was considered property belonging to the conjugal house, or remained in the possession of the wife's original family, see: D. Sabean, "Aspects of Kinship Behaviour and Property in Western Europe 1200–1800," in Goody, Thirsk and Thompson, *Family and Inheritance,* 107–11; R. Wheaton, "Affinity and Descent in Seventeenth-Century Bordeaux," in *Family and Sexuality in French History,* ed. R. Wheaton and T. Hareven (Philadelphia: University of Pennsylvania Press, 1980), 124; A. MacFarlane, *Marriage and Love in England: Modes of Reproduction, 1300–1840* (Oxford: Basil Blackwell, 1986), 274, 287. For fraternal tension in impartible systems, see Sabean, "Aspects," 100–101; A. Collomp, "Tensions, Dissensions, and Ruptures inside the Family in Seventeenth- and Eighteenth-Century Haute-Provence," in Medick and Sabean, *Interest,* 166–68; Kertzer and Brettell, "Advances," 100–101. For fraternal tension in partible systems, see R. M. Smith, "Families and Their Land in an Area of Partible Inheritance: Redgrave, Suffolk 1260–1320," in *Land, Kinship and Life Cycle,* ed. R. M. Smith (New York: Cambridge University Press, 1984), 191–92. On relations between brothers-in-law, see D. W. Sabean, "Young Bees in an Empty Hive: Relations between Brothers-in-Law in a South German Village Around 1800," in Medick and Sabean, *Interest,* 171–86.

day Greece. There are variations from region to region, between the mainland and the islands, and among the various occupations, farming, pastoralism, and fishing;[2] our study focuses on those agrarian systems that stress either equal inheritance by all siblings or a preference for sons. The two worlds, modern rural Greece and ancient Athens, have many differences. Most obviously, the ancient sources deal with the slave-owning elite, whereas the anthropological studies deal with the average peasant or shepherd. Another large difference between ancient and modern Greece is religion: Christianity can have an effect on marriage practices. For instance, both the Civil Code and the Greek Orthodox Church forbid close-kin marriages and exchange marriages,[3] the intermarrying between family groups over generations. In ancient Athens, on the other hand, both types of marriage practices were common. Therefore the modern material is merely suggestive of the motivations behind ancient behavior.

Local customs in present-day Greece vary as to how or when the property is divided: sons can inherit at the father's death, or each son inherits at his own marriage, or at the marriage of the eldest child. In most Greek societies, relations between brothers are often potentially competitive and tense.[4] In many of these societies, daughters are dowered at or before marriage; but in some, daughters thereafter have no further claim to inherit, whereas in others, they can inherit along with their brothers at their father's death. Equal distribution, however, may be only an ideal; for instance, some sons can receive an education in lieu of inheritance. The custom in which sons are left virtually propertyless because of the priority given to daughters' dowries is the polar opposite of the classical Athenian situation.[5]

[2] For an excellent summary of these variabilities, see P. Sant Cassia and C. Bada, *The Making of the Modern Greek Family* (Cambridge: Cambridge University Press, 1992), 16–18, which describes how pastoralists, continental farmers, island farmers, and fishermen transmit property to their children in different ways. The fishermen, for instance, tend to emphasize the daughter's dowry to the detriment of the sons.

[3] E. Friedl, *Vasilika: A Village in Modern Greece* (New York: Rinehart and Winston, 1962), 64–65.

[4] Ibid., 63; J. G. Peristiany, "Honour and Shame in a Cypriot Highland Village," in *Honour and Shame: The Values of Mediterranean Society,* ed. J. G. Peristiany (Chicago: University of Chicago Press, 1966), 180–81; J. K. Campbell, *Honour, Family, and Patronage* (Oxford: Oxford University Press, 1964), 173–78; M. Herzfeld, "Social Tension and Inheritance by Lot in Three Greek Villages," *Anthropological Quarterly* 53 (1980): 91–92; and "Dowry in Greece: Terminological Usage and Historical Reconstruction," *Ethnohistory* 27 (1980): 230.

[5] Friedl, *Vasilika,* 48–70; Campbell, *Honour,* 154–84; P. Loizos, "Changes in Property Transfer among Greek Cypriot Villagers," *Man* 10 (1975): 503–23; Herzfeld, "Social Tension," 91–100; Herzfeld, "Dowry," 225–41; P. Sant Cassia, "Property in Greek Cypriot Marriage Strategies," *Man* 17 (1982): 643–63; Friedl, Campbell, and Herzfeld ("Social Tension") discuss societies in which the dowry is the only share of the inheritance that the daughter receives. Friedl states that for a son an education can be a substitute for an inheritance (49), while Sant Cassia (650) discusses how dowries are the ultimate priority. Sant Cassia and Bada have shown that, although for most women in nineteenth-century Athens the dowry was equal to their brother's inheritance, the women of the upper class (*arkhontes*) tended to have dowries whose worth did not equal the inheritance of their brothers. The tendency to limit the amount of dowries among the *arkhontes* reinforced agnation: *Making,* 46–54.

Of particular relevance to the ancient situation, in which the daughter was dowered and married before her brothers were adult, are the modern communities where the daughter is dowered ideally before the death of the household head and the division of the property of her natal household.[6] The dowry, always linked to male honor,[7] stimulates concern for the woman's welfare and her proper marriage, and reinforces strong ties between brothers and sisters.[8] In many modern communities, and in ancient Athens, as we will see, this concern results in a tendency for sisters to marry earlier than their brothers.[9] Especially interesting are those communities that allow a female to inherit her share of the paternal property only through the dowry. As in the ancient case, this form of inheritance prevents conflicts between brothers-in-law because the husband has absolutely no claim to the property of his wife's natal household. In other Greek societies, however, where a married woman shares in the patrimony along with her brothers, there is a tendency toward conflict between the brother and the sister's husband.[10]

The purpose here is to investigate how sibling relationships in classical Athens were molded by concerns for the paternal property, and whether such relationships adhered to or defied the patrilineal bias of Athenian inheritance law.[11] The primary focus will be on the orations, although other sources, such as historical biographies, will be considered as much as possible. All sources are, unfortunately, biased toward the Athenian elite and, although informative about relations between brothers and between brothers and sisters, they say very little about relations between sisters.

TIES BETWEEN BROTHERS

As with fathers and sons, the public display of unity between brothers was important (relations between half-brothers will be discussed separately). Affection did exist between brothers; such sentiments were deeply entrenched in the Athenian desire to save face and to preserve one's honor and familial property. A brother's death or the prospect of his death was said to be a sorrowful occasion

---

The authors further note that although by the mid-nineteenth century all siblings by law could inherit equally, brothers frequently urged their sisters not to claim any of the paternal property outside of their dowries (55, 63).

[6] Friedl, *Vasilika,* 59–60; Campbell, *Honour,* 188–89; Herzfeld, "Social Tension," 96.

[7] Friedl, *Vasilika,* 69.

[8] Sant Cassia and Bada, *Making,* 174–75.

[9] Campbell, *Honour,* 82; Loizos, "Changes," 512; Herzfeld, "Dowry," 230; Sant Cassia, "Property," 644, 650.

[10] Herzfeld, "Social Tension," 95–97.

[11] Medick and Sabean, introduction to *Interest,* 13, presume that property holding and transmission affect sibling relations.

for his brothers (Lys. 2.71–72; Aeschin. 2.179). A brother was expected to avenge any injury done to a brother (Is. fr. 9; Lys. fr. 75 [Th]), or avenge his brother's death (Lys. 12.17 ff., 13.41–42; Antiphon 6.20–21; [Dem.] 58.28–29). The reputation of a man was frequently bound up with the reputation and activities of his brother (Lys. 18.1 ff., 20.28–29; Aeschin. 1.63–64).[12] Consequently brothers worked together not only in the political sphere (Aeschin. 1.71; [Dem.] 25.55), but also in business deals ([Dem.] 35.6) and in performing liturgies (Lys. 18.20–21; Isoc. 18.60). Brothers could also cooperate with each other in their disputes with third parties, whether resulting from belligerent name-calling or from competitiveness in contests (Dem. 21.62; 54.3 ff., 14 ff.). Private conflicts often resulted from the desire to retrieve property owed to a brother, to protect the brother's property against confiscation, or to embezzle the property of a third individual (Dem. 21.78; 29.3, 15 ff.; 47.45 ff., 62 ff.; 53.6 ff., 55.2). Brothers could also work together to maintain or acquire the property of a kinsman, either an agnate or a cognate (Is. 1.1 ff., 4.1–3, fr. 4; [Dem.] 43.7), or to try to hold on to property belonging to the paternal estate which was threatened with confiscation (Lys. 17.2 ff.) or was in danger of being embezzled by a greedy guardian (Dem. 38.1–2; Lys. 32.1–2, 9–10, 20). What was the private world, however, behind this unity?

PATERNAL PROPERTY: CONFLICTS BETWEEN BROTHERS

As we saw, Athenian inheritance law placed highest priority on the inheritance of the paternal estate by sons of the same father. In the absence of sons, daughters of the same father inherited, and in their absence, kin of the patriline were preferred to those of the matriline.[13] Although the bulk of the estate was ideally left to male heirs and divided equally among them,[14] at times, when sons inherited, rather than split up the estate, they shared it jointly (Is. 2.28 ff.; [Dem.] 44.10 ff.; Lys. 32.4; Aeschin. 1.102).[15]

A son's concern for his own inheritance from the paternal estate, however, could lead him into conflicts, sometimes violent, with his brother. Socrates' well known reprimand of Chaerecrates and his urging the latter to consider his brother of greater value than his own possessions (Xen. *Mem.* 2.3.1 ff.) signifies only too clearly that the Athenians generally acknowledged where the source of

[12] See also S. C. Humphreys, "Kinship Patterns in the Athenian Courts," *GRBS* 27 (1986): 73 ff.

[13] A. R. W. Harrison, *The Law of Athens*, vol. 1 (Oxford: Clarendon Press, 1968), 130–49; see most recently, R. Just, *Women in Athenian Law and Life* (London: Routledge, 1989), 83–104.

[14] W. K. Lacey, *The Family in Classical Greece* (Ithaca, N.Y.: Cornell University Press, 1968), 125; D. M. MacDowell, *The Law in Classical Athens* (Ithaca, N.Y.: Cornell University Press, 1978), 92–93; for the patrilineal bias in Athenian law, see E. Karabélias, "La succession *ab intestat* en droit attique," *Symposion* (1982): 41–63; Just, *Women*, 89 ff.

[15] See also Dem. 57.19, 29, for paternal uncles who held on to their nephew's property.

fraternal friction lay.[16] In Isaeus 9, two brothers, Thudippus and Euthycrates, quarreled over the division of land, a confrontation which led to Euthycrates' death at the hands of Thudippus; Euthycrates instructed his son to carry on the feud with Thudippus's descendants (16–17). In Isaeus 2, two brothers quarreled over the attempt of one of them to sell part of the paternal estate, which was shared jointly, and give the money to an orphan under his guardianship (28 ff.).[17] In Lysias 10, an elder brother became guardian of the younger one and therefore had control over the estate, but, according to the speaker, would not hand over the younger brother's half when the latter reached his majority (4–5). This situation led the younger brother to wish ruefully that his father were still alive, implying that the father would have resolved the conflict.[18] And in Lysias 16.10 the speaker asserts that he allowed a larger portion of the estate to go to his brother so as to avoid a conflict.

Apollodorus's feud with Phormio, the guardian of his father's estate, has already been noted, though the role of his brother, Pasicles, in these disputes needs some discussion. From Pseudo-Demosthenes 45 we find that Apollodorus fell out with his younger brother over the inheritance of their father's estate, the property of the wealthy banker Pasio. The dispute reached such a pitch that Apollodorus claimed in court that his brother was illegitimate, the son of his father's slave assistant Phormio (83–84). In turn, Apollodorus's enemies claimed that he was defrauding his brother of part of the paternal estate (Dem. 36.36–37). That Apollodorus's charge of illegitimacy was indeed slanderous is indicated in another, earlier speech delivered by Apollodorus in which he is dependent upon his brother's testimony regarding a loan conducted by their father ([Dem.] 49.42–43); no mention of the brother's illegitimacy is made here. It is little wonder, then, given the animosity between the two brothers, that Apollodorus did not give one of his daughters, a potential heiress, to his brother Pasicles in marriage.

We can also infer from Pseudo-Demosthenes 44 that two brothers, Meidylides and Archiades, had quarreled over the paternal estate. Meidylides had offered his only child, an heiress daughter, in marriage to his brother Archiades (10).[19] The intended marriage alliance, as with any form of kinship endogamy through the patriline, was meant to consolidate the two *oikoi*.[20] For example, in Lysias 32.4 two brothers shared the paternal estate; one brother married the only child of the other, a daughter, and became guardian of all of his brother's fortune, including even that part of it that had accrued separately from the inherited wealth

---

[16] M. Golden, *Children and Childhood in Classical Athens* (Baltimore: Johns Hopkins University Press, 1990), 119.

[17] Lacey, *Family*, 126.

[18] Humphreys ("Kinship Patterns," 75) without explanation declares that these two brothers were "patrilateral stepbrothers." The text offers no such evidence.

[19] See the discussion above in chapter 3, p. 97.

[20] This fact contradicts the assertion of the speaker, Meidylides' daughter's son's son, that the marriage would have resulted in a division of the estate (10).

(4–5). In Pseudo-Demosthenes 44, however, Archiades not only refused to marry his brother's daughter, but even in his lifetime adopted the grandson of their sister. The adoption angered Meidylides, and it split up the joint estate. ([Dem.] 44.19–20, 46).[21] However, Meidylides eventually agreed to the adoption and was persuaded by relatives not to prosecute his sister's grandson. Archiades' estate remained in the grandson's line for three generations (ibid., 18 ff.).

In this case, a sister's descendants, if not the sister herself, helped out her brother, but by so doing incurred the wrath of her other brother. Other orations show that a sister, or her descendants, might actually ally with one of her brothers against another one. Pseudo-Demosthenes 25.55, 79 points out that Aristogeiton's brother prosecuted him for the manner in which Aristogeiton contracted a marriage for their uterine half-sister.[22] The conflict was put aside, temporarily in all likelihood, when the brother defended Aristogeiton against the speaker in the Demosthenic oration (ibid., 55).

Brother and sister also allied against another brother in the case of Demosthenes' estate. Demosthenes the elder, the father of the orator, had married Cleoboule, the daughter of Gylon of Cerameis. The latter had been convicted of treason, had his property confiscated, and been sent into exile. The sister and brother of Demosthenes the elder had probably colluded with him to prevent his estate, which included his wife's dowry, from being confiscated to pay Gylon's debts.[23] Demosthenes the Elder, on his deathbed, willed his widow to his sister's son, Aphobus, and his daughter to his brother Demo's son, Demophon. Aphobus and Demophon were also to be guardians of the estate and the two children, Demosthenes the orator and his five-year-old sister. Aphobus and Demophon, however, appropriated the dotal property and refused to marry their betrothed kinswomen (Dem. 27–30, passim). Furthermore, Aphobus allied with both Demo, his mother's brother, and Demo's son, Demophon, to embezzle Demosthenes Senior's estate (Dem. 27., 4 ff.; 29.19–20). In other words, sister and brother colluded to acquire a second brother's estate. The collusion was frustrated, however, once Demosthenes the orator began his lawsuit: Aphobus's testimony was not consistent with that of Demophon (28.14), and Aphobus reluctantly gave testimony against Demophon's father, Demo (29.20).

[21] L. Gernet, *Demosthène: Plaidoyers civils*, 4 vols. (Paris: Les Belles Lettres, 1954–60), 2:137, n. 2; Davies, *APF,* 195–96. Davies (ad loc.) suggests that Archiades had inherited the bulk of the estate and did not want to share it by marrying his niece. Such an inheritance practice, however, would defy the standard Athenian custom of equal division.

[22] The Greek (25.55) states that Aristogeiton sold his sister for export (*ep' exagōgē*), the same phrase used in Dem. 24.202–203 to indicate that a brother gave his sister in marriage to a non-Athenian without a dowry but with a gift of money from the groom. Although Humphreys ("Social Relations on Stage: Witnesses in Classical Athens," *History and Anthropology* 1 [1985]: 338) contends that Aristogeiton and his brother were half-siblings, there is no evidence for this. In fact, the oration states that they were twins (25.78–79). Standard prosopographical studies view them as full siblings: For instance, Kirchner, *PA,* 1775 + 5863.

[23] Hunter, "Woman's Authority in Classical Athens," *EMC* 33 (1989): 41 following Davies, *APF,* 122.

In other orations, an individual who served as a guardian was charged either with mismanagement or with depriving his brother's son or daughter of his or her share of an inheritance from either the paternal estate or the estate of a male agnate (Is. 7.8, 11; 10.4–6, 11.5 ff., 36 ff.; Lys. 32.1–10; Dem. 38.23).[24] In fact, in two of these cases (Is. 7.8, 10.4–6) kinship endogamy was thwarted as a result of the alleged mismanagement and consequent disputes. In one oration (Aeschin. 1.102) a man is accused of abusing his paternal uncle: Timarchus is charged with depriving his father's brother Arignotus, a blind man, of his right to assistance from the joint estate bequeathed to both Arignotus and his brother Arizelus, the father of Timarchus. Stephanus is also accused of depriving his father's brother of his house (Dem. 45.70).[25] In contrast to these quarrels between brothers and by extension between the testator's children and their father's brother, we have only one certain case in which the natural brother of a woman, her uterine brother, was criticized for his guardianship of her child (Is. 8.40–42).[26] In other words, tensions between brothers could extend to their children. On the other hand, close ties between children and a maternal uncle reflect the ties between cross-siblings, to be discussed shortly.

Thus quarrels over the estate between full brothers and between brother and brother's descendants could be vicious; those between homopatric half-brothers were practically guaranteed because of the brothers' unwillingness to share the paternal wealth. In one case, this animosity reached international proportions. Boeotus was a friend of a foreign tyrant, Cammys of Mytilene, who was a personal enemy of Boeotus's half-brother Mantitheus ([Dem.] 40.37). An individual might charge his half-brother with being the product of an informal union between their father and another woman, or the son of a non-Athenian mother, or with being supposititious, which would create a presumption that he was the son of an alien (Dem. 39.4, 40.8–13; Is. 6.1–26). Any of these charges, if upheld, would deprive the half-brother of his right to inherit. Philoctemon and his sisters allied to keep their half-brothers from inheriting Philoctemon's estate (Is. 6.5 ff.). Callistratus and Olympiodorus (wife's brother) were in collusion to exclude Callistratus's homopatric half-brother from receiving any share of a kinsman's estate ([Dem.] 48.20 ff.: relationship of kinsman is unspecified). Finally, there is one oration in which two sets of half-brothers argue over whether their father's second wife poisoned him (Antiphon 1.1–13). Conflict between homopatric brothers, especially over inheritance, was so taken for granted that in an exceptional case where a man defended his half-brother against charges of

---

[24] See also J. Bremmer, "The Importance of the Maternal Uncle and Grandfather in Archaic and Classical Greece and Early Byzantium," *ZPE* 50 (1983): 177, 182.

[25] Ibid., 182.

[26] Although Davies (*APF,* 416) assumes that Aristaechmus, who was sued by his wards for mismanagement in Demosthenes 38, was their mother's brother, the oration nowhere states Aristaechmus's relationship to the boys. In fact, appointments outside the family were not uncommon: Harrison, *Law,* 1:99–101; MacDowell, *Law,* 93.

alien citizenship, the man declared: "But as for myself, no man would consider me so insane as to lie under oath for this man [his half-brother] just so that I would share my patrimony with more heirs (Is. 12.4)."[27]

On the other hand, matrilineal half-brothers could not inherit from each other if the testator had living agnates, yet as discussed above (on mothers and sons, pp. 101–2), the homometric brother did try at times to gain control of his half-brother's estate, with the latter's approval.

The antipathy between full and homopatric brothers can, ironically, be further illustrated by a brief examination of the relationships between sisters. Although the orations are not very informative about these, it is clear that sisters could be allies. In the quarrels over Demosthenes' estate, Demosthenes' mother's sister, Philia, was concerned about the fate of both Demosthenes' mother and her children, if the actions of Philia's husband are any indication: at one point during the quarrels with the guardians, Philia's husband, Demochares, remonstrated with Aphobus and was later a witness for Demosthenes in the latter's lawsuit against the guardians (Dem. 27.14–15). This loyalty was followed by the marriage of Demosthenes' sister to the son of Philia by Demochares.[28] In another case, sisters' sons could combine forces to undermine the inheritance of another first cousin, the adopted son of their mothers' brother. Afterwards, however, the sisters' sons turned against one another, each in the hope of getting a greater share of their uncle's estate (Is. 5.12–13). Similar tensions marked Andocides' relationship with his mother's sister's son, as the two men were both candidates to marry one heiress, their mother's brother's daughter (And. 1.117 ff.).

The most informative oration on sororal relationships, however, and one that indirectly underscores the argument on fraternal conflicts above, is Demosthenes 41. The oration deals with two sisters who had no brothers and therefore were the sole heiresses to the estate of their father, Polyeuctus, as well as, it seems, to the dowry of their mother. Although both sisters were supposed to receive equal dowries (5 ff.) and to inherit equal shares of their father's estate (ibid., 26), the husbands of both sisters argued over the actual items given in the dowries: the speaker felt that the dowry given his wife was less in value by one thousand drachmae. The husbands also quarreled over the private loans given them by their mother-in-law. One husband claimed that the other was favored by the women's parents (ibid., 9, 12, 20). Also, the speaker hints that at the division of the estate upon the father's death there was potential for unpleasantness—the sisters would have told their husbands of their suspicions of an unfair bequest (ibid., 17). In other words, when women became the main heirs to an estate, their husbands certainly, and probably the sisters themselves, began to act like inheriting males.

[27] For one further example, see P. Oxy. 2538; Humphreys, "Kinship," 75–76.
[28] Davies, APF, 141–42.

Thus far, then, heirs quarrel among themselves, and these conflicts can be transmitted to their descendants. We will now see what takes place between siblings who are not rivals.

TIES BETWEEN BROTHERS AND SISTERS

Bonds between siblings of opposite sexes, whether full or half, were generally very strong. In fact, one scholar has suggested that because young girls and women were segregated so strictly from males who did not belong to their immediate family, intense bonding naturally developed between cross-siblings.[29] Orators used all their resources to invoke pity for a sister's bereavement, when she was deprived of her brother by death in battle (Lys. 13.45–46; Lycurg. 1.40; Hyp. *Epit.* 27) or by murder (Lys. fr. 22 [Th]). Brothers and sisters were also concerned with each others' honor. The orations state that the brother (either full or half) and his sons were expected to protect his sister from sexual abuse, from charges of alien citizenship[30] or from verbal abuse frequently laced with sexual innuendo (Dem. 21.78–79, 24.202–3, 25.55, 57.38–39; Hyp. *Lyc.* 4 ff; Lys. 3.29).[31] In turn, a sister and her husband could defend her brother from charges of alien citizenship (Dem. 57.43, 68; Is. 12.5).[32]

Sources other than the orations, moreover, testify to close social and political alliances between cross-siblings. For instance, supposed abuse of sisters was an important item in hostile gossip concerning the politicians Cimon and Alcibiades: both Cimon and his sister Elpinice and Alcibiades' daughter and son were accused of incestuous relations.[33] Furthermore, Plutarch states that when Cimon was charged with bribery by his rival Pericles, Cimon's sister Elpinice intervened and influenced Pericles to drop the charges (*Per.* 10.4–5). Elpinice later denounced Pericles' military actions and contrasted them with those of her brother (ibid., 28.4–5). Although the veracity of these stories is uncertain,[34] nevertheless, when Cimon was threatened with ostracism, a voter wrote on his ostrakon that when he left Athens he should take Elpinice with him.[35] In addition, the fact that Elpinice was buried with members of her original family (Plut. *Cim.*

---

[29] P. Walcot, "Romantic Love and True Love," *AncSoc* 18 (1987): 5–33.

[30] Aliens or non-Athenians in classical Athens could not produce offspring considered to be Athenian citizens (Harrison, *Law*, 1:25–26; Lacey, *Family*, 100–101).

[31] For preclassical Athens, see B. M. Lavelle, "The Nature of Hipparchos' Insult to Harmodios," *AJP* 107 (1986): 323–28.

[32] See also *P. Iand.* 81, a fragment possibly of Isaeus, which appears to be concerned about the children of cross-siblings providing testimony for each other. The fragment may also mention the collaboration between homometric half-brothers.

[33] Eupolis fr. 208 (Kock) = Plut. *Cim.* 15.3; *FGrHist* 107 F4 (Stesimbrotus); schol. Arist. 3.446 (Dind.); [And.] 4.33; Suda s.v. *Kimon;* Lys. 14.28, 41.

[34] Davies, *APF,* 303–4.

[35] J. Holladay, "Medism in Athens 504–480 B.C.," *GaR* 25 (1978): 186.

4.2) and not with her family of marriage,[36] suggests that there was a real bond between siblings here, which was the source for further embellishments. Likewise, when Hipparete, the wife of Alcibiades, attempted to divorce her husband, she sought refuge at her brother's house, but was forced by her husband to return to his house ([And.] 4.14; Plut. *Alc.* 8.1–5). Indeed, Alcibiades allegedly attempted to assassinate Callias, Hipparete's brother, to gain control of the latter's estate ([And.] 4.15), for if Callias had died childless, his estate would have devolved upon Hipparete, leaving Alcibiades in managerial control. In the short term Callias was powerless against Alcibiades' right as a husband, but eventually, not long after Hipparete's death, he had the satisfaction of seeing Alcibiades accused of profaning the Eleusinian Mysteries, the very rites overseen by Callias as a chief priest, and forced to flee Athens.[37]

To return to the orations, a major concern for the brother was the material welfare of his sister. The orator Demosthenes states that the chief aim in contracting a marriage for a sister or daughter is to give her the greatest amount of security (Dem. 30.21). Therefore, when Demosthenes' own sister was defrauded of her dowry by her guardians, Demosthenes in his lawsuit against the guardians lamented that his sister would not be able to marry well (Dem. 27.61, 28.21). Also, a brother could be concerned for his sister's childlessness after marriage, and at the instigation of her husband and with the consent of the sister, agree to his sister's divorce. The latter might make sure to return the dowry so that the woman could remarry (Is. 2.4 ff.). Another source reveals a brother's anxiety about the confiscation of a widowed sister's dowry along with her late husband's property: the dowry was needed to provide for his sister and her children (Lys. 19.32–33). Theomnestus was eager to prosecute the political rival of his sister's husband after the rival had persuaded the people to impose a fifteen-talent fine on the husband. In his speech Theomnestus declares his concern for his sister's welfare and for that of one of her daughters who, he says, may not be able to be dowered ([Dem.] 59.7–8, 12); hence he was aiding his brother-in-law in prosecuting the rival. Another oration informs us that a woman was divorced by her husband because she could not provide a dowry from her father's impoverished estate: she and her sons were cared for by her brothers (Dem. 39.24–25, 28).[38] Other orations reveal that the married woman returned with her children to her brother's house on the termination of a marriage, and in one case was given in a second marriage by her brother (Lys. 3.29; Hyp. *Lyc.* 1 and 2, passim). In another case, a brother avoided contracting a marriage for his sister to a family enemy (Lys. fr. 8 [Th]).

---

[36] See Humphreys, *The Family, Women and Death* (London: Routledge and Kegan Paul, 1983), 111–12, for examples of married women with their original kin: such burials suggest close bonds between siblings.

[37] On the assassination attempt, see J. Hatzfeld, *Alcibiade,* 2d ed. (Paris: Presses universitaires de France, 1951), 137; on Alcibiades flight and condemnation: And. 1.11–16; Thuc. 6.27 ff.; Isoc. 16.6; Plut. *Alc.* 19.2; 22.4; Nep. *Alc.* 3 ff.; Davies, *APF* 19.

[38] Ibid., 366.

By extension, therefore, relations between an individual and his mother's brother could be very close:[39] exceptions will be discussed further below. Charmides, Andocides' patrilineal cross-cousin, was reared by his mother's brother, Andocides' father, and was his confidant in prison during the affair of the mutilation of the herms (And. 1.48–50).[40] Both Andocides and Aeschines spoke with pride of their maternal uncles (And. 3.29; Aeschin. 2.78): Andocides' admiration was equaled only by his interest in marrying his uncle's heiress and thereby acquiring managerial control of his uncle's estate (1.120 ff.). In other orations, a mother's brother often appears as a valuable ally in legal battles (Is. 3.26, 30, 71; 12.5–6).[41] In Isaeus 1 two brothers were reared by their maternal uncle, Cleonymus, despite the latter's quarrel with the boys' paternal uncle, Deinias, and perhaps with their father (1 ff.).

Emotional embellishments aside, the sources reveal a brother's concern for his sister's welfare at and after marriage, concern for her children, and concern particularly for the dowry which originally belonged to the woman's paternal estate. Although uterine half-siblings could not marry, homopatric half-siblings, offspring of the same patriline, could do so.[42] This marital strategy reflects concern for immediate sibling control over the paternal property.

BROTHERS, SISTERS, AND DOWRIES

Dowries mentioned in the orations were, of course, provided by elite families. Givers of dowries appearing in Attic descriptions were probably also prosperous. Athough smaller amounts than those mentioned in the orations appear in inscriptions listing property mortgaged for dowries, the amounts cited there may

---

[39] Bremmer, "Importance," 173–86, was an important early study on the role of the mother's brother, although as Bremmer himself admits (174), his discussion is incomplete. Nevertheless, Bremmer has some useful bibliography (173, n. 2) of classic studies by social anthropologists on the maternal uncle. For Athens one cannot discount demographics. Given the difference in ages of marriage for men and women an individual would more likely have maternal uncles to depend on than paternal uncles.

[40] D. M. MacDowell, *Andokides on the Mysteries* (Oxford: Clarendon Press, 1962), 175.

[41] See also Humphreys, "Kinship," 63.

[42] Harrison, *Law,* 1:22. The Athenian taboo against the marriage of homometric siblings may not have been an incest taboo. Sparta, for instance, allowed homometric sibling marriage. Because women in Sparta could inherit as well as men, the marriage of homometric siblings allowed the property from the siblings' matriline to be combined with the estates from two different patrilines. This combined property devolved on the children of the married siblings, so that, technically, property consolidation was delayed a generation. In the Athenian pattern, property consolidation would have been more immediate. For the marriage pattern in Sparta, see S. Hodkinson, "Inheritance, Marriage and Demography: Perspectives upon the Success and Decline of Classical Sparta," in *Classical Sparta: Techniques Behind Her Success,* ed. A. Powell (Norman: University of Oklahoma Press, 1988), 81 ff. and particularly 92.

not reflect the entire amount;[43] hence, it is unsafe to assume that the inscriptions reflect the practices of poorer people. In any case, the Athenian *oikos*, which was always concerned with the devolution of property, practised an extreme form of male inheritance by excluding daughters from any share besides the dowry. Brothers shared equally in the paternal estate, while daughters were given a dowry as a pre-mortem inheritance. The dowry, consisting of cash or real estate and movable items valued in cash, was meant to take care of a woman's needs in her marital *oikos* and to consolidate the ties between her children and her natal *oikos*. Apart from this, a woman had no further material claim on the paternal estate, if she had brothers who themselves had sons.[44] Furthermore, the daughter's dotal wealth never seems to have been equal to the wealth inherited by any one brother. Table 3[45] compares known values of elite estates with known dotal outlays: dowries from these estates never exceeded one-third of the estate's value and rarely exceeded one-fifth.[46] The largest percentage of wealth devoted to a dowry comes from one of the smallest estates in the orations (Is. 8.7–8): from an estate of approximately one and a half talents, Ciron dowered his daughter with twenty-five minae or about 28 percent of the estate's value. He then gave her in a second marriage with a smaller dowry of ten minae or 11 percent of the estate. Because a one-and-a-half-talent estate was well below the income of wealthier families who were required to perform state services (three to four tal-

---

[43] D. M. Schaps, *Economic Rights of Women in Ancient Greece* (Edinburgh: University of Edinburgh Press, 1979), Appendix 1.

[44] H. J. Wolff, "Marriage Law and Family Organization in Ancient Athens," *Traditio* 2 (1944): 62; H. Levy, "Inheritance and Dowry in Classical Athens," in *Mediterranean Society: Essays in the Social Anthropology of the Mediterranean,* ed. J. Pitt-Rivers (Paris: Mouton, 1963), 141; Harrison, *Law,* 1:45–60, 130–32; Lacey, *Family,* 109–10; Schaps, *Economic,* 23, 74–84. R. Osborne, *Demos: The Discovery of Classical Attika* (Cambridge: Cambridge University Press, 1985), 137, states that land was not normally given as a dowry, and that it is impossible to determine from the stelae how many of the uxorilocal marriages were unions with heiresses. See V. Hunter, "The Athenian Widow and Her Kin," *Journal of Family History* 14 (1989): 306, n. 3, for further thoughts on this issue. As Hunter notes, some horoi reveal that women could own landed property, though the stones are not dealing with dowries per se.

[45] The table is based on L. Casson, "The Athenian Upper Class and the New Comedy," *TAPA* 106 (1976): 55, who however, includes the dowering of two sisters by their brothers in Isaeus 2.3, 5. Casson claims that each woman received twenty minae from a one-and-a-half-talent estate. However, Isaeus specifically states that this estate is that into which one of the brothers was adopted (2.34–36; Davies, *APF,* xxiii), and not the paternal estate from which the sisters were dowered but for which we have no figures. Therefore, I have not included this case in table 3. Furthermore, Casson's chart values the estate in Lysias 19 at five talents. The original estate, before payments to the state, however, was worth around thirteen talents (Davies, *APF,* 200). I am well aware of the inaccurate use of figures in antiquity, particularly given that individuals tended to hide the full value of their estates (see below, chapter 6, pp. 168–70). On the other hand, these figures must either stand or fall together: the unanimous impression given by the sources is that a daughter never received wealth equal to that of any one son.

[46] For our purposes, 1 talent = 60 minae.

TABLE 3

Dotal Outlays for Daughters and Sisters

Source	Estate Value	Number of Women with Dowries	Number of Brothers	Dotal Outlay	Dotal Outlay as Percent of Estate Value
Lys. 32.6	15 tal.	1 daughter	2	1 tal.	6.6
Dem. 27.4, 28.15–16	14 tal.	1 daughter	1	2 tal.	14.3
Is. 5.5, 26	13 tal.	4 sisters	1	40 min. each	5.1
Lys. 19.16 f.	13 tal.	2 daughters	1	40 min. each	5.1
Is. 8.7–8	1½	1 daughter	2	25 min. 10 min.	27.7 11.1
Dem. 29.48, 31.6–9	30 tal.	1 sister	2	1 tal. 20 min.	4.4
And. 4.13; Plut. *Alc.* 8	200 tal.	1 daughter	1	20 tal.	10.0

ents minimum),[47] Ciron was giving a large dowry relative to his means to se-cure a suitable marriage for his daughter.[48]

A larger number of the families in the table had estates ranging from thirteen to fifteen talents with each daughter or sister receiving anywhere from 5 percent to 14 percent of the estate's wealth. One of the wealthiest men in the orations, Onetor, worth around thirty talents, dowered his sister with one talent and twenty minae, a very substantial dowry but only 4.4 percent of his own wealth (Dem. 29.48, 31.6–9).[49] In fact, because Onetor had a brother,[50] Onetor's thirty talents may have been his share of the paternal estate, which could have been worth as much as twice that amount before the sons inherited. If so, the dowry would have been worth only 2.2 percent of the value of the original estate's. The largest known dowry in Athenian history, twenty talents, was given to Hipparete the daughter of Hipponicus, who was worth around two hundred talents, upon her marriage to Alcibiades. Hipparete thus received 10 percent of her father's wealth, with the rest going to her brother Callias (Plut. *Alc.* 8.1–5; [And.] 4.13;

---

[47] Davies, *APF,* xxiv.

[48] Because Ciron had two sons by a second marriage (Is. 8.7–8), his daughter's share, 28 percent of his estate's value, almost one-third, comes very close to the shares of each of his sons. However, the one and a half talents is the figure estimated from the real property of the estate, and Ciron also had an unspecified amount of money out on loan (Davies, *APF,* 314).

[49] On Onetor's wealth and the size of the dowry, see ibid., 423; Schaps, *Economic,* 78.

[50] Davies, *APF,* 423.

Isoc. 16.31).[51] Thus, although Isaeus 11.39 states that a father should endow his daughters well and that his son was not less wealthy from what remained, most elite fathers ensured the greater wealth of their sons. The practice of giving a smaller dowry to the sister in classical Athens was also followed by the highest social class, the *arkhontes,* in Athens in the early nineteenth century. In both cases, smaller dowries allowed for patrilineal transmission of property among males and let women marry endogamously within their status group.[52]

Even though a woman did not inherit equally with her brothers, a great deal of attention was directed to the dowry. Brothers were concerned about the recovery of the dowry after termination of the sister's marriage (Lys. 19.32–33), or ensured that she was remarried with a dowry equal in value to the one initially set aside by the father for her first marriage (Dem. 29.48 + 30.7 + 31.6–9; 40.6–7). In most cases, the father set aside the dowry, or attempted to, before his death.[53] Demosthenes the elder went so far as to make a will bequeathing two talents of his fourteen-talent estate to his five-year-old daughter and specifically stating whom she was to marry (Dem. 27.5; 28.15–16, 19; 29.43–45).

Historians have known for years that the dowry, which always remained the property of the woman's original *oikos,* served to prevent the woman from being separated from the paternal estate. This can certainly be seen in Athenian laws that mandated the return of the dowry to the woman's natal family on the dissolution of her marriage by death or divorce.[54] The dowry could, it is true, be estimated as part of the husband's wealth (Dem. 27.4, 9–11; 42.27) and be included in the confiscation of his property by private creditors or by the state.[55]

---

[51] Ibid., 19, 260. Incidentally, the speaker in Isaeus 3 (49–51) tries to prove the illegitimacy of Pyrrhus's daughter by stating that she was given a very small dowry, ten minae, from the estate. However, Pyrrhus's estate was worth about three talents; his daughter's dowry was, therefore, about 5.5 percent of his wealth, well within the range of the shares given to respectable women. For the controversy on the legitimacy of Pyrrhus's daughter, see W. Wyse, *The Speeches of Isaeus* (Cambridge: Cambridge University Press, 1904; New York: Arno, 1979), 333; D. M. MacDowell, "Bastards as Athenian Citizens," *CQ* 26 (1976): 89–91; P. J. Rhodes' response: "Bastards as Athenian Citizens," *CQ* 28 (1978): 89–92; C. Patterson, "Those Athenian Bastards," *ClAnt* 9 (1990): 70–73. The one exception to the rule of the smaller value of the dowry is that given to Phaenippus's mother in Demosthenes 42, which seems to have been one of over one talent (Davies, *APF,* 554). Phaenippus's estate had the combined value of the estates of both his maternal grandfather and his own father, and Phaenippus's wealth was estimated at four and a half talents; hence his maternal grandfather was worth somewhat less than that amount. Therefore, the dowry of Phaenippus's mother was worth a large percentage of her father's estate. However, because Phaenippus had been adopted into his maternal grandfather's estate, Phaenippus's mother was an heiress and without brothers: Golden, *Childhood,* 133.

[52] Sant Cassia and Bada, *Making,* 52–55.

[53] Lys. 19.14–15, 32.6; Is. 8.7–8, 11.39; Dem. 27.5, 28.15–16, 29.43; 40.6–7, 20–22, 56–57; 41.3, 6, 26, 29; 45.66, 59.7–8; Plut. *Alc.* 8.1–5 + [And.] 4.13 + Isoc. 16.31.

[54] Wolff, "Marriage Law," 50, 53; Levy, "Inheritance," 141; Harrison, *Law,* 1:55–60; Schaps, *Economic,* 81–83; Just, *Women,* 72–73.

[55] On husbands and wives, see above, chapter 3, pp. 74, 76.

But apart from this case, Demosthenes declared, a dowry was the woman's property, and that by giving a dowry, a brother made the woman's husband his kinsman (30.12; see also Is. 2.4–5). That the dowry belonged to the woman's natal family is clearly demonstrated by the dowry given to a sister of Dicaeogenes II. The woman was dowered with a city house instead of cash (Is. 5.26–27),[56] and she and her husband took up residence there. In the course of surveying the property of Dicaeogenes II, his adoptive son Dicaeogenes III demanded and received the house back.

Although the dowry was never legally required, it was a social obligation:[57] not only could a marriage be suspect without it, but also the prestige of the family depended on a good match made through a substantial dowry.[58] The orations reveal that dowries were needed to attract prestigious husbands (Lys. 19.15–16; [Dem.] 40.6), while the giving of a large dowry was an indication of a family's good standing and that of its affines (Dem. 39.32–33, 40.20–22).

TIES BETWEEN BROTHERS-IN-LAW

Besides the disparity in the amount of the *oikos*'s wealth inherited by sisters and brothers, there was another difference between them which also reflected marriage strategy: in many cases, the daughter married before—in some cases well before—her brother of comparable age. In Davies's listing alone, there are eighteen instances in which the brother married after his sister, or sisters, as opposed to six in which roughly contemporaneous marriages occurred.[59] Of the fami-

---

[56] Wyse, *Isaeus,* 446; Davies, *APF,* 146; Osborne, *Demos,* 247, n. 30.

[57] Harrison, *Law,* 48–49; Finley, *SLC,* 79; MacDowell, *Law,* 87; Karabélias, "Succession," 54.

[58] Lacey, *Family,* 109–10.

[59] Many of the dates for the following marriages are calculated from the birthdates of the offspring: Davies, *APF,* 30–31 (Andocides IV and his sister); 91 (Leagros II and his sister); 118–21 (Demosthenes Senior and his sister); 138, 143 (Demosthenes the orator and his sister); 145, 147 (Menexenus and one sister; from Isaeus 5); 152–53 (= Lys. 32.9–10); 194 ff. (= [Dem.] 44.9–10); 200–201 (Lys. 19.15–16, one sister married before her brother); 296–97 (Epilycus and his sisters); 319–20 (Cleon's son and daughter: Cleon's daughter was married c. 422, but her brother's wife was not born until c. 420–415; Cleon's son married before the death of his wife's father in 399: Davies, *APF,* 462); 329–30 (Pyrilampes and his sister); 333–34 (Plato, who never married, and his sister); 379–81 (Megacles IV and Agarista); 437–38 (Deinias and his sister; Theomnestus and his sister). Of less certainty: Davies, *APF,* 230 (= Is. 9.29) for a daughter's being betrothed after her brother's majority; there is no indication of the brother's having married; 256–57 (Hipponicus II and a possible sister); 326–27 (Critias IV and a possible sister; Critias seems never to have married). For the contemporaneous marriages: Davies, *APF,* 30 (Andocides III's daughter and son); 93 (Damostratus's son and daughter); 200–201 (= Lys. 19.15–16, a brother and one sister); 263 (Callias III and Hipparete); 303–5 (Cimon and Elpinice and possibly a second sister (235) who married a man of the deme Halimous). In her article on marriages in Isaeus, S. Isager ("The Marriage Pattern in Classical Athens: Men and Women in Isaios," *ClMed* 33 [1981–82]: 91), shows twelve men who died single but who had married sisters. This is conjectural; Isaeus's text in all cases states only that these men died childless, and there are instances of married men dying without issue (Is. 6.3–7, for example). In one of

lies in the orations not listed by Davies, register, there are six more instances of later marriages for brothers (Lycurg. 1.17 ff.; Is. 2.3 ff.; Lys. 3.29 ff.; Dem. 41.3, 48.53 ff.; Lys. fr. 43 [Th]), and there is only one explicit reference to a brother's marrying before his sister (Is. 10.5–6). Significantly, in this latter case, that of Cyronides, the paternal estate was probably insolvent (ibid., 15).

Earlier age of marriage of women and later age of marriage for men was the norm for ancient Athens. This pattern of marriage is generally known as the Mediterranean type and is evident not just in Athens but in the later society of the Roman empire.[60] In Athens, there were several reasons for this practice. One of them was that property transfer occurred ideally at the death of a man's father, and it made sense for a man to postpone marriage until he had control, if not actual ownership, of his paternal estate. As a consequence, there was often a large gap in age between father and son and between husband and wife.[61] In the latter situation a young wife, as in Xenophon's *Oeconomicus,* would ideally be under the tutelage of her husband, receiving guidance from him on household management while bearing his children.

In addition, the earlier marriage of a sister would secure a beneficial alliance for the woman's natal family, and in particular for a later-marrying brother. Among the political families, for instance, before Epilycus the Philaid married, he and his father gave Epilycus's sisters in marriage to some of the most powerful politicians of the day: the great *stratēgos* Glaucon of Cerameis, the son of Pericles, and the father of Andocides the orator. These alliances brought the family out of political obscurity.[62] In Lysias 19.15–16, one of the speaker's sisters married her first cousin well before her brother's first marriage; the marriage consolidated the kin group after the cousin's political disgrace (see above, p. 24). Although Andocides' sister was married by 415, Andocides remained unmarried at the end of the century. During this time he vied with his mother's sister's son, Leagros II, for the hand of his uncle's (mother's brother's) daughter, an *epiklēros.* In fact, Leagros himself had remained unmarried some twenty years after the marriage of his own sister to Callias III, the son of Hipponicus II, one of the wealthiest Athenians of his day and a priest of the Ceryces, a prominent priestly clan overseeing the rites in the Eleusinian Mysteries (And. 1.117 ff.).[63] Furthermore, Leagros relinquished his claim to the heiress on behalf of his brother-in-law Callias III, machinations which brought both men into direct conflict with Andocides. The rivalry reached the political forum when Callias III, in an at-

---

Isager's cases, that of Hagnias II, it is uncertain whether he even had a sister. For the conjectured relationship of the *adelphidē* whom Hagnias II adopted, see discussion above, chapter 1, p. 8.

[60] For Roman society, see R. Saller, "Men's Age at Marriage and Its Consequences in the Roman Family," *CP* 82 (1987): 21–34.

[61] On this pattern in Athens and its consequences, see B. Strauss, *Fathers and Sons in Athens* (Princeton, N.J.: Princeton University Press, 1993), 67–70.

[62] Davies, *APF,* 296–97.

[63] Davies, *APF,* 30, 91, 254 ff., 297, for Andocides and his kin group.

tempt to extricate Andocides from the claimant pool, charged him with profanation at the end of the fifth century and attempted to have Andocides put to death for the alleged crime (And. 1.110–21).

The strategy of the earlier marriage of sisters was not restricted to these politically powerful, fifth-century families. It was noted earlier how a neighbor often became an affine, often as a result of the earlier marriage of his sister. Although Plato never married, his sister's marriage allowed him to ally with a landed neighbor, thereby consolidating two landed estates in Eiresidae.[64] Both Deinias and his son Theomnestus married after their sisters, thereby allying with the wealthy banking family of Pasio: Deinias's sister had married c. 395 and bore a son, Stephanus. Deinias's daughter married Pasio's son, Apollodorus, c. 362. In fact, when Apollodorus sued his guardian Phormio, the latter was assisted by Stephanus, the son of Deinias's sister.[65] Deinias, although called by Apollodorus, his own daughter's husband, to testify, would not testify against Stephanus, his sister's son ([Dem.] 45.54–56).[66] Despite this conflict with Deinias, Apollodorus remained on good terms with his wife's brother, Deinias's son, Theomnestus, who prosecuted one of Apollodorus's political enemies ([Dem.] 59.7–8, 12). The pattern of later marriages for brothers accords with the arrangements of Demosthenes' father in his will; he made detailed provisions regarding the marriage of his daughter, but no terms were laid down for the marriage of his son (Dem. 27.4–5).

Sources for other families demonstrate the trust that developed between affines linked by the marriage of a sister. There are references to brothers who married after their sisters, in one case to pursue a military career, and then were adopted as heirs into the house of the sisters' husbands (Is. 2, passim; Dem. 41.3). In the latter oration, however, the wife's husband, Polyeuctus, and her brother quarreled and a divorce ensued between the brother and Polyeuctus's daughter (4 ff.). However, because the wife's brothers witnessed and approved her finan-

---

[64] Ibid., 201.

[65] Ibid., 430, 437–38.

[66] Humphreys, "Kinship Patterns," 77 ff., tends to think that because an individual was called upon by the prosecution he was necessarily against the defendant. Therefore, Deinias is against Stephanus, and in cases to be discussed further in our text, Timocrates conflicted with his ex-brother-in-law, Onetor (Dem. 30), and Timochares with his brother-in-law, Leocrates (Lycurg. 1.22 ff.). However, in the orations witnesses are at times called upon by, but are hostile to, the prosecution (Is. 9.18–19, Dem. 29.20, Lyc. 1.20). (The spuriousness of Dem. 29, although insisted upon by Humphreys, "Kinship Patterns," 84, is debatable: Harrison, *Law,* 1:105–6, n. 4.) Furthermore, witnesses in Athens were constrained to give testimony under threat of punishment (MacDowell, *Law,* 243). If a witness did not wish to swear to the written statement, often prepared by the litigant (ibid., 243), he could take an oath disclaiming the facts, which as Humphreys admits, could make him look foolish or possibly leave him open to a charge of perjury: "Social Relations," 321. For *atimia* resulting from perjury, see M. H. Hansen, "ATIMIA in Consequence of Private Debts?" *Symposion* (1977): 113–20, where Hansen conjectures that in cases of perjury in private suits, a fine may well have been paid to both plaintiff and state. See now A. Scafuro, "Witnessing and False Witnessing: Proving Citizenship and Kin Identity in Fourth-Century Athens," in *Athenian Identity and Civic Ideology,* ed. A. Boegehold and A. Scafuro (Baltimore: Johns Hopkins University Press, 1994), 170–80.

cial transactions with the daughter's second husband, Spudias, the quarrel between the families may have been patched up. The wealthy estate prompted the speaker in Lysias 32 to defend the property of his wife's unmarried brothers against the alleged misappropriation of the estate by their maternal grandfather (1 ff., 20, 28). Trust between brothers-in-law is clearly evident in Lycurgus 1 where Leocrates, who had a concubine but apparently no wife (17), married his two sisters to Amyntas and Timochares of Acharnae (ibid., 21–23). After the defeat of the Athenians at Chaeronea, Leocrates went into self-exile to Rhodes and then to Megara (ibid., 21). While in Megara he sold his estate to one brother-in-law, Amyntas, who in turn sold the slaves to Leocrates' other brother-in-law, Timochares (ibid., 22–23). Leocrates seems to have owned the same slaves again on his return to Athens (ibid., 30 ff.): he was asked to hand over his slaves for interrogation under torture about his departure from Athens. Logic would dictate that the slaves in question were those who helped him to pack his belongings into a boat and leave Athens secretly (ibid., 17)—the very slaves bought by his affines. Therefore, the implication here is that Leocrates' property was bought by his brothers-in-law for safekeeping during his sojourn.[67] Finally, in Pseudo-Demosthenes 47 Theophemus uses his brother and a *kedestēs* (in-law) to help him confiscate property to settle a debt (9 ff.). Because Theophemus was not married (ibid., 38), the *kedestēs* may have been the husband of a sister.[68]

Collusion is again evident in other orations, although in them there is no information as to whether a brother married after his sister. Onetor married his sister first to Timocrates and gave her away with a dowry of one talent and twenty minae. Onetor then instigated a divorce between the two, and in collusion with Timocrates did not hand the dowry over to Aphobus, his sister's second husband (Dem. 30.7 ff.). Rather, Aphobus secured, or hypothecated, his farm and a house in Onetor's name for the dowry he had never been given. Dotal hypothecation was the securing of property equal in value to the dowry; the property in question was secured should the return of the dowry on the dissolution of the marriage be necessary. If the dotal property itself was not returned, the hypothecated property was seized by the woman's natal kin.[69] Both moves, the absence of dotal

---

[67] Humphreys, "Kinship," 77–78, feels that because Timochares, one of Leocrates' brothers-in-law, admitted in court that he bought the slaves from Leocrates' other affine, Amyntas, Timochares was deliberately attacking Leocrates. However, Timochares could well have been a hostile witness: Lycurgus anticipates (1.20) that some of the witnesses he will call upon, among them Timochares, will not be eager to testify. Otherwise, the testimony of a willing witness could be a sociopolitical act, a witness's public declaration of whose side he was on: S. Todd, "The Purpose of Evidence in Athenian Courts," in *Nomos: Essays in Athenian Law, Politics and Society* ed. P. Cartledge, P. Millett, and S. Todd (Cambridge: Cambridge University Press, 1990), 19–39.

[68] Humphreys, "Kinship," 77. I focus only on those instances where the word *kedestēs* (in-law) is clearly either a wife's brother or sister's husband. Humphreys, ad loc., 76 ff., interprets the word as generally meaning wife's brother or sister's husband, although this translation at times is not certain from the context of the orations and other historical sources.

[69] Finley, *SLC*, 44–52; Harrison, *Law*, 1:284–86.

transaction and the hypothecation of the farm, were maneuvers to save both the dotal and landed property when Aphobus lost the lawsuit brought against him by Demosthenes and was threatened with confiscation (Dem. 30.26, 31.1–7). Neither was Onetor's sister passive in these machinations: she and her brother registered a false divorce with the archon so that Onetor could seize the hypothecated farm when Aphobus fled Athens to escape further prosecution (30.26 ff.). Demosthenes acknowledged that both Onetor and his sister were actively involved in the machinations to gain control of his, Demosthenes', estate (31.11–12).

Other orations reveal the encroachment of a wife's brother on her husband's estate, with, it seems, the testator's approval. Diocles was said to have maintained his hold on Ciron's estate by encouraging his sister, Ciron's second wife, to stay in the house of Ciron even after her sons by him had died. Furthermore, Diocles backed the claim of Ciron's *adelphidous* (brother's son) to Ciron's estate against the claim of the son of Ciron's daughter by a first marriage (Is. 8.3 ff., 36 ff.).[70] The complexities of brother-sister ties and brother–in-law relations are clearly evident in Isaeus 9, where Euthycrates was killed by his brother, Thudippus. As he lay dying Euthycrates charged his sister's husband to keep Thudippus's descendants from his, Euthycrates', estate (19–20). Astyphilus, Euthycrates' son, may have defied his father's orders and adopted one of his paternal uncle's descendants. The executor of Astyphilus's will was his mother's brother, who in turn conflicted with Astyphilus's uterine half-brother; the latter had anticipated inheriting Astyphilus's estate (ibid., 1 ff., 18 ff.).[71] This is one of the rare instances of a public dispute between nephew and maternal uncle. There are other instances of a brother-in-law's protecting a testator's will: in Lysias 13.2, 41, where a woman was married to her first cousin, her brother witnessed her husband's will and was asked to avenge the husband's death at the hands of one of the Thirty. In Isaeus 6.3 ff., a sister's husband was the executor of Philoctemon's will,[72] which insisted on the adoption of another sister's son to the exclusion of Philoctemon's homopatric brothers.

Collusion between brothers–in-law could at times break down. Polyeuctus quarreled with his adopted son, who was his wife's brother (Dem. 41.3 ff.); Cleonymus quarreled with the brother of his sister's husband, and perhaps the husband himself (Is. 1.1 ff.);[73] and a man was accused of breach of guardianship by his wife's brothers (Lys. fr. 43 [Th]). Finally, in Pseudo-Demosthenes 48 an unmarried brother, Olympiodorus, contracted a marriage for his sister with a certain Callistratus. Both men conspired to share the estate of a deceased relative and to exclude all other relatives from the property (1 ff., 53). A quarrel, however, developed between the two men when Olympiodorus claimed and

---

[70] Davies, *APF,* 314.

[71] Wyse, *Isaeus,* 626, 640; Davies, *APF,* 229.

[72] Humphreys, "Kinship," 77.

[73] Wyse, *Isaeus,* 176; Humphreys, *Family,* 8.

won the whole estate for himself after a series of suits against the other relatives (ibid., 25–31). Olympiodorus's victory led his brother-in-law Callistratus to berate him for abandoning his sister and her daughter and devoting his extra wealth to his concubine (ibid., 53), thereby equating a quarrel between affines with the abandonment of a sister's needs. In other words, collusion broke down when the two affines became rivals for the same estate, as also happened when the statesman Alcibiades allegedly tried to assassinate his brother-in-law Callias to gain control of his property.

The sources for both the politically prominent and the private families reveal, then, a clear tendency for trusting relationships between brothers-in-law. It is difficult to generalize the reasons for a breakdown of this trust, but certainly the fact that two affines were vying for the same estate or encroaching on each other's property could precipitate a feud. Could a marital alliance endure a feud between affines? The sources are not very informative.[74] In Demosthenes 41.3 ff. the oration does not state why Polyeuctus quarreled with his wife's brother but only that the quarrel resulted in a divorce between Polyeuctus's daughter and the brother-in-law, not between Polyeuctus and his wife. On the other hand, in the case of Alcibiades, his wife's attempt to divorce him on the grounds of sexual promiscuity was contemporaneous with his dispute with her brother Callias ([And.] 4.14, Plut. Alc. 8.1–5).

The obvious implication of this trust between brothers-in-law is the concern for the sister's welfare and her marriage, and more often than not her early marriage to a trusted ally. This trust is reflected in yet another inheritance practice, that of adoption.

ADOPTION

Athenian law stipulated that if a man had no heirs, his estate would devolve upon his brothers and their descendants; in the absence of these the sister and her descendants had the right to inherit.[75] Therefore, in Isaeus 1.4–5 the testator was instructed by his father to leave the estate to the testator's sister and her descendants. In Isaeus 3 Pyrrhus's sister, through her son the speaker, attempted to inherit his estate after the death of her other son Endius, who had been adopted by Pyrrhus. The move was contested by Pyrrhus's daughter, who claimed to be legitimate, a claim denied by Pyrrhus's sister and her son but defended by the daughter's mother's brother (8 ff.) and by the brothers of Pyrrhus's mother (ibid., 26, 71).

In any case, the law permitted the heirless man to adopt whomever he wished as heir so that his *oikos* would not be extinguished.[76] In most cases the adoptee

---

[74] See, S. Dixon, "The Marriage Alliance in the Roman Elite," *Journal of Family History* 10 (1985): 370, for a discussion of the fact that in Roman society such conflict would definitely lead to divorce.

[75] Harrison, *Law*, 1:144–46; MacDowell, *Law*, 98.

[76] Harrison, *Law*, 82–96.

was adult so that the focus of adoption was on the needs of the adopter: to carry on his *oikos* and to provide him with future heirs.[77] However, as Louis Gernet pointed out in a study originally published in 1920, the majority of adoptions concerned the man's adoption of descendants through the female line,[78] either that of the sister or that of the mother. Of thirty-one instances of adoption,[79] ten certainly involve the adoption of a son or descendant of the testator's sister or his father's sister.[80] Sisters were under a great obligation to provide an adoptee for their brother and were severely criticized if they could not, or would not, do so.[81] In one case, Philoctemon, whose two brothers had died, relied on his two married sisters to ensure that his estate had an adopted heir. One of the sisters, the wife of Chaereas, had only one daughter, but the other sister had one of her sons adopted into her brother's estate. In the meantime the wife of Chaereas and Chaereas himself were entrusted with Philoctemon's will stipulating the adoption (Is. 6.5–7). In another oration, the speaker admits publicly that his wife persuaded him to have one of their sons adopted into the estate of her two dead brothers (Is. 11.49). In the same oration, the wife of the speaker's brother, instead of having her only son adopted into her brother's estate, had one of her daughters adopted (ibid., 41–42). These cases, it could be argued, simply reveal the sister's right to inherit her brother's estate after all her brothers are dead: in Is. 11.41–42 the speaker states that the adoption of the woman's daughter reinforced the woman's ability to inherit her brother's estate and her husband's ability to manage it.[82] In other cases, however, individuals were chosen who were not

---

[77] L. Rubinstein, *Adoption in IV. Century Athens* (Copenhagen: Museum Tusculanum Press, 1993), 13, 22. The following are instances in which an infant may have been adopted: Is. 5.6–7; 11.8 ff., 41; [Dem.] 43.12, 58.31, and possibly [Dem.] 43.77 and Davies, *APF,* 86.

[78] Gernet, *Droit et société dans la Grèce ancienne* (Paris: Sirey, 1955), 121–49, esp. 129–31.

[79] Gernet's list of adoptions (ibid., 129) is now superseded by Rubinstein's catalogue of thirty-six adoptions (*Adoption,* 117–25); for five of these the relationship between adopter and adoptee is unknown and therefore they have not been included in the above discussion (Is. 4.8, 4.10, 7.23; 9.2, 33; Dion. Hal. *De Din.* 12). To the remaining thirty-one cases, we might add the possible adoption of Polyeuctus's son's son into the estate of Xanthippus of Erchia (mother's father) (*APF,* 172). See also V. Hunter, "Agnatic Kinship in Athenian Law and Athenian Family Practice: Its Implications for Women," in *Law, Politics and Society in the Ancient Mediterranean World,* ed. B. Halpern and D. Hobson (Sheffield: Sheffield Academic Press, 1993), 103–8, 117–18.

[80] Is. 1, passim; 3.1 (son of a sister); 5.6–7 (the son or grandson of a father's sister; see Davies, *APF,* 145–46, 476–77); 6.4 ff. (the son of a sister); 7.9 (the adoption of a half-sister and then her son); 11.41 (the daughter of a sister); 11.49 (the son of a sister); [Dem.] 44.19, 46 ff. (the grandson of a sister and the grandson's descendants). In Is. 11.49 above, the adoption of a woman's son into her brother's estate may have been an attempt to block a possible claim from a collateral to the estate (W. E. Thompson, *De Hagniae Hereditate: An Athenian Inheritance Case, Mnemosyne,* suppl. 44 (Leiden: Brill, 1976), 58).

[81] Hunter, "Agnatic Kinship," 107–8.

[82] There is some debate as to whether a woman was actually the heiress to her brother's estate or to the paternal estate from which the brother's property devolved. See most recently Hunter, "Agnatic Kinship," 109–10, who argues that the woman was *epiklēros* to her brother. Is. 3.58–59 may be support for such a view.

in a direct line to inherit (Is. 7.9, fr. 4; [Dem.] 44.19, 46): in Pseudo-Demosthenes 44.19, 46, Archiades adopted his sister's daughter's son, while in Isaeus 7.9 the testator chose his uterine half-sister and then her son as adoptees in a deliberate attempt to exclude all living male agnates. In the latter case, the woman's natural father had aided her half-brother Apollodorus in preventing Apollodorus' agnates from embezzling the estate (ibid., 6 ff.). In gratitude, Apollodorus later used his wealth to recover his stepfather's insolvent estate (ibid., 9). Therefore, the adoption solidified the trust between the two *oikoi* and consolidated their wealth.

Outside the ten cases of adoption through a sister or father's sister, there are two instances of the adoption of a wife's or ex-wife's brother into the estate of her husband (Is. 2.14; Dem. 41.3); in one case (Is. 2.14, 21) the adoption thwarted the succession rights of the deceased's brother and the latter's son. Therefore, in twelve out of thirty-one instances of adoption (over a third of the cases) brother-sister ties play a dominant role in the provision of heirs to the testator. On the other hand, in five instances out of the thirty-one we have a male agnate through the male line adopted, or attempting to be adopted.[83] In one of these instances, Isaeus 10, Cyronides had originally been adopted by his maternal grandfather, that is, out of his paternal estate, to which he should therefore have had no claim (4, 7 f.). The estate's insolvency, however, allowed him not only to marry his father's brother's daughter, but also, with the help of his wife's brother, to purchase the estate and reestablish it in his father's name. By posthumous adoption Cyronides introduced his natural sons as the estate's heirs (ibid., 6 ff.). These maneuvers were challenged by the son of Cyronides' sister, who laid claim to the estate as the son of an heiress (ibid., 4–5, 12 ff.).[84]

This is one of three instances in which a nephew openly opposed the actions of his maternal uncle. Such conflicts erupted when the testator did not adopt a direct descendant of his sister. Disputes between brother and sister, or between their descendants, might develop as a result of the desire for more property or the wish to reestablish succession links with the original paternal *oikos*. In Isaeus 5 the sisters of Dicaeogenes II and their sons quarreled with Dicaeogenes II's adopted heir, Dicaeogenes III. The latter was not a direct descendant of the sisters, but rather the son or grandson of the sister of Dicaeogenes II's father.[85] In other words, Dicaeogenes II's attachment to the marital family of his father's sister conflicted with the strong attachment of his own sisters and their sons to the women's paternal estate. Even here, however, throughout the dispute the speaker, the son of one of Dicaeogenes II's sisters, was careful not to lay the blame at his uncle's feet, but rather at those of the adopted son (7 ff.).

---

[83] Is. 6.36, 44 (two brothers posthumously adopted into their father's estate; Is. 10.6 (two brothers posthumously adopted into their paternal grandfather's estate); and Is. 9.1. For a possible sixth example, see Is. 7.9 and Davies *APF,* 45–47, in which Thrasybulus is adopted by the son of Thrasymedes. The roots of the men's names may suggest agnatic kinship, although this is not certain.

[84] Wyse, *Isaeus,* 649–52.

[85] Davies, *APF,* 145, 476–77.

Finally, there is the exceptional case of Diocles, who was a rival to his uterine half-sisters as a claimant to their father's estate. Diocles' assertion that he had been adopted by his stepfather indicates that the latter had no natural son (Is. 8.40–41). The adoption, however, was underhanded at best, illegal at worst, because Diocles as adoptee was required by law to marry one of his stepfather's heiresses; these women, however, were Diocles' homometric sisters, and marriages between uterine siblings were forbidden.[86] Furthermore, because the sisters had married and one of them seems to have had a son before the adoption took place (ibid., 42), their father's estate may well have by law devolved upon that son.[87] Because the adoption of Diocles would have prevented the women and their children from inheriting, violent conflicts erupted between Diocles and his half-sisters' husbands (ibid., 41–42).

CONCLUSIONS

Our investigation of sibling relationships has shown an important side-effect of the agnatic bias in inheritance law: it often made male heirs rivals so that men looked to kinsmen through female lines as allies. The complexities of sibling relationships resulted from struggles for the acquisition of property and wealth, which led to alliances, realliances, and misalliances. In Athens, brother could often cooperate publicly with brother in political struggles or social conflicts in which a third party threatened the property of one brother or the paternal estate of several brothers. When the time came to inherit, however, succession laws and practice could often pit brother against brother, or brother against brother's child. As brothers became rivals, they turned their attention to the welfare of sisters. Brotherly concerns often focused on whether or not the sister was dowered adequately. Because the dowry was always considered the property of the woman's original *oikos,* and had to return with the sister on the termination of her marriage, a brother made sure that his widowed or divorced sister would return to his house with an intact dowry. The care devoted to the dowry and the contracting of a suitable marriage for the sister went hand in hand with a brother's concern for the prestige of his original family, which was reinforced by ties with trustworthy allies. Because the sister ideally had little claim to the paternal estate outside the dowry, frequently she was not a rival to her brother, and as such she and her husband could work with her brother in a trusting relationship for the benefit of her estate of origin or that of her brother. In other words, in her role as female agnate, the woman was constantly concerned about her original *oikos* and its property. These interests which focused away from the male

---

[86] See the discussion of inheriting daughters, chapter 3, above, p. 98. Wyse, *Isaeus,* 621; Harrison, *Law,* 1:22; Davies, *APF,* 313. This interpretation is contrary to that of J. Karnezis, *The Epikleros* (Athens: n.p., 1972), 221 (where Diocles is incorrectly called Androkles).

[87] Harrison, *Law,* 1:11–12.

agnate are again evident in the institution of adoption; a sister was socially pressured into providing heirs for her deceased brother's estate, while brothers often sought adoptees through a sister's line. On the other hand, if a testator had not chosen his sister's son as heir, squabbling could erupt between the sister's son and the adoptee. Hence, trust broke down when brother and sister, or more typically their descendants, became rivals for the original paternal estate: common interests between brother and sister were liable to survive only in their generation. No system was perfect, especially not for the litigious families of Athens. Ironically, however, a legal system that emphasized the male actually promoted the role of the woman in the preservation of the paternal and/or fraternal estate: a sister and her brother worked together to protect her dotal property, or, in order to protect her brother's estate, she could ally with him against another brother. It was the tie between brother and sister that could prove essential in the machinations of the typical affluent Athenian, who constantly strove to make other Athenians less wealthy than himself.

The same type of relations between siblings as we have seen from the orations and historical sources may also be found in fifth-century tragedy, most notably in Antigone. In the play we see feuding brothers who have actually killed each other, and Antigone's devotion to her dead brother Polyneices is striking. She willingly dies for her chance to bury Polyneices properly and she willingly gives up any chance for marriage and children. As noted by one scholar, the play sets up a conflict between two types of families, the blood family and the family of marriage.[88] Antigone's devotion to her brother reflects fifth-century attitudes and would not have seemed excessive to the audience of her day.

In dealing with domestic relationships we have discussed how interests in inheritance and the use of wealth before and after inheritance could shape and change relations among the various members of the family: male kin were at odds, while female kin were usually supportive of male kin. It would be inaccurate, however, to leave the discussion of the *oikos* with the nuclear family. For this hardly gives any idea of the complexity of the *oikos*, despite the insistence of the ancient sources that laws defined that unit in terms of the nuclear family. We now turn to an examination of how the boundaries of the *oikos* included both kinsmen outside of the nuclear family and nonkinsmen, among whom could be included the kind of individual legally disqualified from inheritance rights.

---

[88] M. Neuberg, "How Like a Woman: Antigone's Inconsistency," *CQ* 40 (1990): 66–67.

CHAPTER 5

What Was an *Oikos?*

IN THE OPENING remarks to his work entitled the *Oeconomicus,* Xenophon has Socrates the philosopher exchange views with Critoboulus, an Athenian citizen and fellow demesman,[1] on the *oikos.* During the conversation, Socrates poses the question "What do we mean by '*oikos*'?" Is it the same thing as the *oikia,* the physical building, the house, or does it include all the property one possesses outside the *oikia*? In the course of answering these questions, Socrates and Critoboulus agree that a man's *oikos* is the same as a man's property, even if some of that property lies outside the city in which the man resides. Everything a man possesses is his *oikos;* furthermore, by "property" is meant all those items useful to him in increasing his wealth (Xen. *Oec.* 1.5–11).

Once these definitions have been established, it becomes quickly apparent that the ideal form of property is land, a source of wealth often associated in the discourse with war (5.12–14, 6.7, 11.12–17). These definitions are given a living example, as Socrates relates his story of Ischomachus, a fine and noble man (*kalos kagathos*), whose wealth and enviable reputation are based upon his successful management of his property, both the produce of the fields and the possessions within his *oikia,* his house (6.13–14, 7.15 ff.). Within the *oikia,* Ischomachus's wife, as the mother of their future children, meticulously supervises the storage of the produce from the fields, keeping enough for a year and watching that the food is consumed with care. She is also in charge of storing in an orderly fashion linens, blankets, weapons, and utensils, and she supervises and teaches the slaves at the loom, pounds the grain to make bread, tends to the sick slaves, sends the field servants outside, and segregates male slaves from female slaves (7.21–9.11). In her work, the wife chooses a *tamia,* a slave housekeeper, to help her supervise, and rewards such loyal service with food and goods from the household (9.11–13).

Ischomachus's duties are relegated to the outdoors (7.22): he meticulously tends to his crops and trees (11.15 ff.). He assigns slave stewards to keep the field slaves in line and to see that the fields are well tended (12.2 ff.).[2] As a reward for

---

[1] Davies, *APF,* 336–37. For a good overview of Xenophon's *Oeconomicus,* see S. Pomeroy, *Xenophon's Oeconomicus: A Social and Historical Commentary* (Oxford: Clarendon Press, 1994).

[2] Ellen Meiksins Wood, *Peasant-Citizen and Slave* (London: Verso, 1989), 75–76, who downplays the role of slave labor in agriculture, admits that these passages can refer to a slave bailiff, although she warns that presumably the *tamia* in the earlier passages may not have been a slave (49). Her point that not all bailiffs or *oikētai* in general were slaves cannot be the focus of this study. For a recent dis-

their service, the stewards will receive a share of the produce. In the meantime, Ischomachus exercises for war with his horse (11.12–18), and then conducts business in town where his house is situated at some distance from the fields (11.18).[3]

In Xenophon's account, therefore, the *oikos* is viewed as a unit of production, a unit of consumption and as a unit of reproduction, to use the social scientist's terms, and is based on landed wealth. An integral part of the *oikos* is the nuclear family—husband, wife, and (intended) children (7.21)—and the marital union forming this family was carefully arranged between the husband and his young wife's parents, both sides having made certain that this was the best possible choice (7.11).

To what extent, however, is Xenophon's ideal reflected in other sources on the Athenian *oikos*? Several aspects of his account should alert us to a hidden side of the *oikos*. First and foremost, Xenophon admits that individuals outside the family proper have some influence in the *oikos* and on its wealth, namely the so-called "bad friend" (1.20), the *hetaira* or prostitute (1.13), and the trusted slave (9.11–13, 12.3–13.9). Second, he briefly acknowledges the existence of non-landed occupations such as builder and smith (6.13–14). Third, he sees as integral to the activities of the gentleman farmer the aspect of war and the necessity to train for the more than likely event of war; in fact, war can increase the wealth of an *oikos* (5.13–15). But what one must ask of Xenophon, is how war or business ventures, both of which involved travel, affected the makeup of an *oikos*. Further, how would the scattering of landed holdings, frequently outside of Attica proper, affect the makeup of the *oikos* and its decisions? Both these questions serve to cast some suspicion on Xenophon's unswerving equation of the household with the nuclear family unit.[4]

---

cussion, see T. W. Gallant, *Risk and Survival in Ancient Greece* (Stanford, Calif.: Stanford University Press, 1991), 30–33, who argues that slave assistance might have been required for the common farmer during periods of peak labor. Pomeroy, *Xenophon,* 65, 316, assumes that the housekeeper and steward are slaves.

[3] See L. Foxhall, "Household Gender and Property in Classical Athens," *CQ* 39 (1989): 29–31, for a discussion of *oikos* property in Xenophon's treatise, emphasizing the integrative gender framework of the private world of the household. See also P. Cartledge, *The Greeks* (Oxford: Oxford University Press, 1993), 86–87. On the distance of the fields from the house or settlement, see R. Osborne, *Demos: The Discovery of Classical Attika* (Cambridge: Cambridge University Press, 1985), 16–19.

[4] The following discussions in this chapter and the next have been influenced by the essays in R. McC. Netting, R. R. Wilk, and E. Arnould, eds., *Households: Comparative and Historical Studies of the Domestic Group* (Berkeley, Calif.: University of California Press, 1984). Although the editors (xiii ff.) are critical of theories on the domestic life cycle that are relied upon in the following discussion, they do admit that concerns about reproduction, marriage strategies, and the transmission of property could influence the make-up of some households. Their insistence that the nonkinsman cannot be ignored in discussions of the household will be an obvious influence on the discussion in chapter 6 below.

THE USE OF THE TERM *OIKOS*

Although there was no ancient equivalent for the modern phrase "nuclear family,"[5] the word *oikos* in sources outside Xenophon agrees closely with his definition of the nuclear family unit and its property. The most obvious instance is Aristotle in his *Politics,* who assumes that the formation of the *oikos* is based upon the principle of reproduction and therefore must consist of parents and children. This natural desire for children leads to partnership among several *oikoi,* a partnership which then forms the *polis.* In fact, the *polis* as a whole is naturally prior to its parts, the *oikoi.* For this reason, knowledge pertaining to household management, which includes master-slave relationships, marital relationships, and parental rule, is the most elevated type of knowledge (*Pol.* 1252a25 ff.).

Concomitantly, the use of the term *oikos* in other sources can center on the Athenian interest in bequeathing property downward to direct heirs. Thus in Isaeus, for example, the *oikos* can be the term used for both "house," the physical residence, and/or property attached to it. In Isaeus 3.8 the speaker complains that his opponent's sister did not bring a dowry into Pyrrhus's *oikos*—a three-talent *oikos*—and when she left that *oikos,* she took no dowry with her (see also 3.78). Clearly this passage shows how all three aspects of the term *oikos,* family, property, and house, can overlap; a reading of the orations will reveal countless instances of such overlapping.[6] Outside of the orations, *oikos* can also mean a large house used as a meeting place for demesmen or phratry members.[7] In a similar way the term *oikia,* literally house, can also be extended to mean family, household, and property.[8] For instance, Andocides (1.147) described his *oikia* as the oldest and most courteous to someone in need. Clearly the sense here of *oikia* is lineage or descent group.

Although scholars have always been aware that *oikos* was a complex term, meaning more than "family," historical interpretations have, nevertheless, in practice reduced the *oikos* to the nuclear family. Indeed, Xenophon's concept of the *oikos* has dominated legal and sociohistorical research throughout this century. A few quotations from various scholars, regardless of methodological approach, will suffice to demonstrate the traditional equation. In 1920, the French scholar

---

[5] See, for instance, M. I. Finley, *The Ancient Economy* (Berkeley, Calif.: University of California Press, 1973) 18–19, who, however, is dependent on Xenophon's ideal and stresses that the word *oikos,* originally meaning a peasant household, was slanted toward landed property.

[6] See D. M. MacDowell, "The *Oikos* in Athenian Law," *CQ* 39 (1989): 10, for a brief discussion of the definitions.

[7] C. W. Hedrick, Jr., *The Decrees of the Demotionidae* (Athens, Ga.: Scholars Press, 1990), 50–51, where he discusses the *oikos* of the Deceleieis. Cf. S. D. Lambert, *The Phratries of Attica* (Ann Arbor: University of Michigan Press, 1993), 117–18, who feels that *oikos* in this instance may not be an actual building but rather the local base and hereditary membership of a subgroup of a phratry.

[8] For examples in Isaeus, see W. A. Goligher and W. S. Maguinness, *Index to the Speeches of Isaeus* (Cambridge: Heffer, 1961), 170; see more generally, MacDowell, *"Oikos,"* 11.

Louis Gernet declared: "Car tout Athénien mâle et adulte, du vivant même de son père, représente un οἶκος en puissance. . . . A la notion concrète et comme solidifiée de la maison qui ne meurt pas, s'oppose l'idée des maisons qui naissent et qui recommencent à chaque génération."[9] According to Hans Julius Wolff, writing in 1944, "The οἶκοι, i.e., the organized family units, were the basic groups which in their totality made up the πόλις. . . ."[10] And again: "in the democratic era the οἶκος, i.e., the "little family" of the individual citizen, took the place of the clan."[11] More recently, Sarah Pomeroy stated: "The principal duty of citizen women toward the *polis* was the production of legitimate heirs to the *oikoi,* or families, whose aggregate comprised the citizenry. . . . In effect the interest of the state coincided with the interest of the family in seeing that individual families did not die out. . . . In families in which a son was lacking, the daughters were responsible for perpetuating the *oikos.*"[12] In 1978 MacDowell, in his study of Athenian law, entitled his sixth chapter: "The Family: Control of Dependents and of an 'Oikos.'"[13] In her series of essays published in 1978 and 1983, S. C. Humphreys explicitly equated *oikos* with household, and household in turn with the nuclear family. In the earlier book, under a subsection entitled "Household," Humphreys writes that the nuclear family was the normal residential unit as early as Homer. In classical Athens, "The *oikos* . . . was a closed space, architecturally functional rather than ornamental. Its relationships were hierarchic: husband–wife, parent–child, owner–slave. . . . Entry to the household emphasized the control of its head—he decided whether to rear a child or not, purchased slaves, and arranged marriages."[14] Quite recently, Sinclair has stated: "The maintenance of the *oikos* (the 'house' or the family living together in the house) was fundamental to the thinking of Athenians,"[15] while Roger Just declares that: "The *oikos* was, in short, the basic Athenian family unit."[16] Various aspects of this consensus have found their way into standard textbooks on social history: "[The *oikos*] means something more like our 'household' and has a far wider range of reference than our 'family' . . . the Athenian *oikos* extended beyond our nuclear family to include property. . . . But the *oikos* also embraced the instruments needed to work the land and service the property generally. Thus tools, animals and slaves . . . all fall within the definition of the *oikos.* At the head

---

[9] Gernet, *Droit et société dans la Grèce ancienne* (Paris: Sirey, 1955), 149.

[10] H. J. Wolff, "Marriage Law and Family Organization in Ancient Athens," *Traditio* 2 (1944): 83–84.

[11] Ibid., 90.

[12] S. Pomeroy, *Goddesses, Whores, Wives, and Slaves* (New York: Schocken, 1975), 60–61.

[13] D. M. MacDowell, *The Law in Classical Athens* (Ithaca, N.Y.: Cornell University Press, 1978), 84–108.

[14] S. C. Humphreys, *The Family, Women and Death* (London: Routledge and Kegan Paul, 1983), 2.

[15] R. K. Sinclair, *Democracy and Participation in Classical Athens* (Cambridge: Cambridge University Press, 1988), 50.

[16] R. Just, *Women in Athenian Law and Life* (London: Routledge, 1989), 27.

of this composite entity stood the *kurios,* the male master of the household. . . ."[17] Thus Xenophon's depiction of the *oikos* still reigns supreme: it acknowledges that the *oikos* includes elements beyond the house, but insists that these elements in the end serve the needs of the nuclear family.

Certainly scholars are not incorrect in pointing out the rigidity of Athenian legal and social ideals pertaining to the definition and makeup of the *oikos.* Laws defined explicitly the basis for rightful membership in the *oikos,* that is, who could inherit its property and pass that wealth on to future heirs. At the basis of the *oikos,* as the law defined it, was marriage, the agreement between two household heads that one man's daughter was to be given to another man's son. This agreement, or betrothal, was known as *engyē* and culminated in the act of consummation (e.g. [Dem.] 44.49; Pl. *Leg.* 774e).[18] Along with the act of betrothal, social custom required the transaction of the dowry, and a wedding feast given by the groom for his *phrateres* as a public acknowledgment of the bride. After the birth of a child, the ten-day ceremony was the father's formal acceptance of the infant as his own and as his potential heir.[19]

By the classical era, and particularly after 450, Athenian citizenship was the basis of defining the inheriting members of an *oikos:* only the children of formally married Athenians were considered eligible to inherit or own property.[20] Legally speaking, a man's property devolved upon his sons in equal shares, with his daughters receiving a *pre-mortem* inheritance in the form of the dowry. If a man lacked natural male heirs, he was allowed to adopt whomever he wished, provided that the (male) adoptee was a citizen whose birth conformed to the citizenship law. If a man had only female heirs, he could adopt a son on the understanding that the adoptee marry the daughter (see above, p. 95).

Only in the past few years have scholars begun to acknowledge that *oikos* boundaries went beyond the nuclear family and that use of *oikos* wealth have little or nothing to do with laws on ownership and inheritance. Foxhall maintains that household boundaries were not tidy, defined concepts and that the state might define household membership quite differently from the individuals liv-

---

[17] Joint Association of Classical Teachers, *The World of Athens* (Cambridge: Cambridge University Press, 1984), 150.

[18] The bibliography on *engyē* is extensive: for example, A. R. W. Harrison, *The Law of Athens,* vol. 1 (Oxford: Clarendon Press, 1968), 3–9; M. Broadbent, *Studies in Greek Genealogy* (Leiden: Brill, 1968), 155 ff.; L. Gernet, *The Anthropology of Ancient Greece,* trans. J. Hamilton and B. Nagy (Baltimore: Johns Hopkins University Press, 1981), 196; Wolff, "Marriage Law," 75 ff.;, MacDowell, *Law,* 86–87; R. Sealey, *Women and Law in Classical Greece* (Chapel Hill: University of North Carolina Press, 1990), 25; Just, *Women,* 45–50, 71–73.

[19] On the *gamēlia: FGrHist* 325 F 17 (Phanodemus) and Jacoby's commentary and references; Harrison, *Law,* 1:7–8; Lambert, *Phratries,* 181–86. On the dowry, see, e.g., H. J. Wolff, "Προίξ," *RE* 23:136; Finley, *SLC,* 79; Harrison, *Law,* 1:48; MacDowell, *Law,* 87–88.

[20] The whole question whether children from two Athenian parents not formally married were considered citizens and could inherit has plagued the discipline of classics throughout its history. See below, chapter 6, notes 22–23.

ing day to day within a particular household. Despite legal restrictions on ownership of wealth, the use of wealth in a household could often override such strictures.[21] Golden, in his recent work on children and childhood, warns that household boundaries were fluid enough to include even outsiders.[22] Gallant has emphasized the complexity of household membership—that the nuclear family is actually seen rather rarely in our sources and that the extended family was a vital part of the life cycle of the household.[23]

The present discussion will begin where Foxhall, Golden, and Gallant have left off. Through a detailed study of the orations, and illustrative examples from historical sources such as the biographies, a discussion of the nature and use of wealth in the household will enable us to see how the model of the nuclear family does not fit the complexity of Athenian life. On the contrary, as family members married and died, the family assumed a multiplicity of forms.

THE INFLUENCE OF *OIKOS* WEALTH ON *OIKIA* COMPOSITION

I begin with the physical unit, the *oikia*. For clarity's sake, and because English words can obscure the meaning of the Greek, *oikia* in the following discussion will mean the physical building, the house. True, as was stated in the former section, Andocides referred to his descent group as an *oikia*, but in the same oration, besides this one instance, the word *oikia* defined a house, a place of private residence, including Andocides' own house (1.11, 17, 40–41, 47, 48, 62, 124–25, 130). The quotation in 1.130 from a folk tale in which *oikia* means "house" demonstrates that common usage equated *oikia* with domestic residence.

The orator Aeschines defined the *oikia* as a building where one man lives; implied here is one man as head of one household (Aeschin. 1.124). But the passage also reveals that such a building's use could change depending on the needs of the individuals who purchase (or rent) it. Thus, if one man purchases and dwells in a house it is referred to as an *oikia;* if several men live there, dividing it among themselves, it is a *synoikia*.[24] In the same breath Aeschines then discusses *ergastēria,* "workshops" or, less appropriately, "factories." These *ergastēria* and the building which can house them (*oikēsis*) can change names as well depending upon the occupation of the man running the establishment or depending upon how the man uses the premises. Thus, a shop can become a surgeon's office, then a bronzesmith's workshop, then a laundry, then a carpenter's workshop and finally a brothel. Thus, by the way he used many places (*polla*), Timarchus, the tar-

---

[21] Foxhall, "Household," 22–44.

[22] M. Golden, *Children and Childhood in Classical Athens* (Baltimore: Johns Hopkins University Press, 1990), 141–42.

[23] Gallant, *Risk,* 22 ff.

[24] For the definition of *synoikia,* see W. K. Pritchett, "The Attic Stelai II," *Hesperia* 25 (1956): 268.

get of Aeschines' notoriously vitriolic attack, has made many establishments into brothels (1.124). Aeschines' close equation of *oikia* with commercial establishment is not idiosyncratic—inscriptions dealing with leased property show that shops in the *astu* could be referred to as *oikiai*.[25]

Architecturally, the *oikia* as a domestic unit was a closed space: the standard architectural design for both moderate-sized and large houses was a group of rooms built around a central courtyard. In the city, due to the irregular plan of the streets, rooms in houses tended to be irregular in shape, and a narrow corridor off the street into the courtyard served as the entrance.[26] Often, in the houses in southwest Athens there were workshops with, at times, their own separate entrances.[27] Near the Agora, houses with workshops were especially irregular in design, adapting to the contours of streets leading into it.[28] In the Peiraeus, there are remains of large house complexes which were spacious and luxurious, but these existed close by many smaller multiple dwellings.[29] In the rural areas, an *oikia* could be a building that was not primarily residential but served agricultural needs and only secondarily provided temporary residence for agricultural laborers and perhaps the landowner himself.[30] As for houses per se, they could be more regular in plan than their urban counterparts, with the central courtyard constituting as much as one-third of the total area. There might be an external courtyard as well for penning livestock, or a tower for storing produce in or near the courtyard.[31] Many of these larger houses may well have been the living quarters for a single family, conforming therefore to Xenophon's ideal of the family unit contained within the self-sufficient landed *oikia*. Other sources, however, tell a different story.

First and foremost, not all *oikoi* (property and residence) of wealthy familes were composed of a single residence: the *oikos* as property could consist of sev-

---

[25] M. B. Walbank, "Leases of Sacred Properties in Attica," ibid., 52 (1983): 223.

[26] G. Morgan, "Euphiletus' House: Lysias 1," *TAPA* 112 (1982): 122–23.

[27] R. S. Young, "An Industrial District of Ancient Athens," *Hesperia* 20 (1951): 135–288, esp. 187–267.

[28] For a good overview of town and country domestic architecture, see J. E. Jones, "Town and Country Houses of Attica in Classical Times," in *Thorikos and the Laurion in Archaic and Classical Times, Miscellanea Graeca* 1 (1975): 68–71 for the Agora houses; 71 ff. for the houses in southwest Athens.

[29] R. Garland, *The Piraeus* (Ithaca, N.Y.: Cornell University Press, 1987), 142–43.

[30] R. Osborne, "Buildings and Residence in Classical and Hellenistic Greece," *ABSA* 80 (1985): 125–27.

[31] For the rural house, see for instance, J. E. Jones, L. H. Sackett, and A. J. Graham, "The Dema House in Attica," ibid., 57 (1962): 75–114. Recently the excavation of a house at Rhamnous has revealed the presence of an external courtyard: H. W. Catling, "Archaeology in Greece," *JHS* 109 (1989): 18. For the towered sites at Sunium, see J. H. Young, "Studies in South Attica, Country Estates at Sounion," *Hesperia* 25 (1956): 122–46; Jones, "Town and Country Houses," 116–19; 105–6 for an irregularly shaped house at Ano Voula. For a general discussion of houses, see R. E. Wycherley, *The Stones of Athens* (Princeton, N.J.: Princeton University Press, 1978), 237–46. For a review of the discussion of houses in Greece, see J. Pečirka, "Homestead Farms in Classical and Hellenistic Hellas," in *Problèmes de la terre en Grèce ancienne,* ed. M. I. Finley (Paris: Mouton, 1973), 113–78; M. Jameson, "Domestic Space in the Greek City-State," in *Domestic Architecture and the Use of Space,* ed. S. Kent (Cambridge: Cambridge University Press, 1990), 92–113.

eral *oikiai*. A survey of the propertied families in Davies's listing will suffice to demonstrate that elite families often owned several houses: the Bouselid Stratocles owned two, one at Melite and one at Eleusis, both of which were rented out—presumably after Stratocles' death, but the Greek is not explicit (Is. 11.44–45). One should note here that a fragment of Lysias (1.3–4 [Th]) states that Athenians could lease houses they owned and rent the house in which they lived.[32] Demon of Paeania may have had a *synoikia* as well as an *oikia* with a garden; the latter were, however, donated to the cult of Asclepius so that Demon could become its priest. Aphobus had a *synoikia* as well as a farm with a house. Dicaeogenes II owned a city house, a *synoikia,* and two *oikidia* outside the city wall. Phaedrus of Myrrhinous had a rented house as well as another in the city, which he seems to have owned prior to its confiscation. Hagnon of Steiria apparently owned land and houses, while Callias III owned a house in the Peiraeus and one in Melite. Ciron owned a farm at Phlya and two houses in the city, one of which was rented out. Pasio the banker owned two *synoikiai,* one of which included his bank premises. The orator Hyperides owned a townhouse in Athens, a house in the Peiraeus, and a house and estate at Eleusis. Euctemon had three residences—two in the city, one of which was rented out, and a rented lodging in the Peiraeus.[33]

Furthermore, many landed families owned scattered holdings throughout Attica and even outside of it. A cursory overview of the families in Davies's listing will suffice to demonstrate this point. Among the fifth-century politicians, Themistocles held land in his own deme, property in the Peiraeus, a house in Melite, property in Phlya, and perhaps property in Magnesia in Asia Minor—at least, he received large amounts of revenue from the latter. Cimon possessed fields in Laciadae, and had mining interests in Thrace and perhaps property in the Chersonese. Alcibiades owned property in Scambonidae and Erchia in Attica as well as three garrisons in Thrace and the Hellespont. A relative of Alcibiades, Alcibiades of Phegous, held land at Oropos, while a certain Oionias owned property in the Lelantine Plain, and at Diros in Euboea. Nicides also owned property in Attica as well as at Diros.

To consider prominent individuals of the late fifth and the fourth centuries, the generals Nicophemus and Conon both resided in Cyprus and had families there. Conon gave his son Timotheus a largely cash bequest which was then converted by the latter to purchase land in Attica. Timotheus, however, appears to

[32] See P. Millett, *Lending and Borrowing in Ancient Athens* (Cambridge: Cambridge University Press, 1991), 1–2 on this fragment.

[33] For the houses of the men discussed, see Davies, *APF,* 87–88 (Stratocles); 117–18 (Demon: Demosthenes allegedly stated that the *synoikia* was wrongly attributed to Demon (Aeschin. 1.125)); 119–20 (Aphobus); 146 (Dicaeogenes II); 201 (Phaedrus); 228 (Hagnon); 260 (Callias III); 313–14 (Ciron); 431 (Pasion); 518 (and [Plut.] *Mor.* 849e, Athen. 13.590c–d) (Hyperides); 562 (Euctemon). One should add that Demosthenes appears to have had two houses, one, the more famous, in the Peiraeus, and the other in the *astu* (Dein. 1.69). See also Dem. 41.5–6, in which Polyeuctus's house is rented out and his inheriting daughters live in their husbands' houses.

have owned a house in the Peiraeus and land in Lesbos as well. Aeschines owned a house at Collytus, land at Halae, and land in Boeotia and Macedonia, probably gifts to him from Philip, who also rewarded Demades with land in Boeotia.[34] Although it is impossible to chronicle the number of times Athenians would visit their holdings outside Attica, some estates were merely rented out (Dem. 19.145–46), but at times Athenians did till their own land in these territories and resided there as well.[35] Carter has noted that the Athenians acknowledged the fact that foreign holdings were at some distance from their activities in Athens and that this fact was parodied in their comedies.[36] Any holding in Attica that was not the primary seat of residence for the *oikos* head was often rented out:[37] the lodgers in these houses could have a grave influence on the transmission of *oikos* wealth, as will be discussed more fully in the next chapter.

The second point to be stressed here is that, as Casson pointed out,[38] although landed wealth was the ideal, in many cases wealth was supplemented, if not supplanted by, nonlanded wealth. Again a cursory reading of Davies will suffice. In the fifth century, Themistocles, although landed, built up his fortune possibly through the use of the mines, but definitely through monetary contributions from powerful non-Athenian allies. Cimon, the Ceryces Callias II, Hipponicus II, and Callias III, and Nicias the general were all landed but received a great amount of their wealth from mines in Laurium or in Thrace. Cleon and Hyperbolus owned *ergastēria* from which the bulk of their wealth came. From the fifth century into the fourth, Plato the philosopher held two landed estates, but received large cash gifts from the Sicilian tyrant Dion. Isocrates was also landed, but received a great deal of his income from his flute workshop, his speechmaking, and gifts from foreign leaders. Besides his land, Ciron had a good deal of money out on loan; he had contracted a marriage for his daughter with Nausimenes of Cholargus, who seems to have held land, but whose wealth chiefly derived from his activities as a miller. The wealth of Demosthenes the orator was mostly nonlanded: he received his income from his *ergastēria*, his commercial ventures, and his speeches. Demades the orator, similarly, earned income

[34] Davies, *APF,* 215–16 (Themistocles); 310–11 (Cimon: Davies is uncertain just how much property, if any, the family owned in the Chersonese); 20–21 (Alcibiades; see also W. Ellis, *Alcibiades* [London and New York: Routledge, 1988], 93); 17 (Alcibiades of Phegous); 419 (Oionias); 408 (Nicides); 201, 508–9 (Nicophemus and Conon); 547 (Aeschines); 100 (Demades); see also L. Casson, "The Athenian Upper Class and New Comedy," *TAPA* 106 (1976): 33–34. To these I add Andocides' landed estate in Cyprus (And. 1.4): G. Herman, *Ritualised Friendship and the Greek City* (Cambridge: Cambridge University Press, 1987), 106, n. 116.

[35] Davies, *APF,* 469, 510; Pl. *Euthyphr.* 4 c–e.

[36] L. B. Carter, *The Quiet Athenian* (Oxford: Clarendon Press, 1986), 105.

[37] For examples of renting property, see Is. 6.19, 20; 8.35; 11.42; Lys. 7.4–10; 17.3; 32.15 (rent from the Chersonese); Dem. 41.5. See also the renting of a ward's property by his guardian, *misthōsis oikou:* Harrison, *Law,* 1:105–6, and discussion below, pp. 145–46. For a full discussion of leasing property in Greece, including Athens, see R. Osborne, "Social and Economic Implications of the Leasing of Land and Property in Classical and Hellenistic Greece," *Chiron* 18 (1988): 279–323.

[38] Casson, "Upper Class," 29–59.

from his speeches, while being active in shipping. Aeschines held land in and outside of Attica, but the commercial activities of several family members, including his father, raised his family from poverty, and Aeschines' own speech-making and political bribes vastly increased his fortune. Meidias, Demosthenes' enemy, owned some real property at Eleusis, but also received income from land that he owned in the mining area. Indeed, the list of landowners who worked the mines is impressive: many of these, although not all, owned land near their mines.[39]

This partial list will serve to show the complexity of the sources of wealth for the propertied families and leads to another, important point: the nature of *oikos* wealth could affect the composition of an *oikos*, an *oikia*, or *oikiai*. For instance, a shop or a factory could be an integral part of the *oikia* (Dem 21.16, 22), as in the Aeschines' passage above. One of the most famous cases was that of Demosthenes' family: in their house was lodged a sword factory and a couch factory (Dem. 27.24–25).[40] This appears to be the house in the Peiraeus in which Demosthenes lived as an adult and in which he also operated a school of oratory. His students frequently resided in the house (Aeschin. 1.175, 3.209; Hyp. *Dem.* 17; Dein. 1.69).[41] In Demosthenes 48.12, Comon had a factory in his *oikia*, but another factory apart from his residence.[42] In both cases, that is, the nuclear family under Demosthenes Senior residing with its workshop slaves, and the childless, perhaps unmarried man, Comon, living with his slave craftsmen, the slave could have a great deal of knowledge of the master's wealth and business activities.[43]

The bulk of Pasio the banker's estate consisted of his shield factory and his bank, the ownership of which was not necessarily lineally transmitted.[44] The bank's wealth and Pasio's residence allowed the easy transfer of the bank to the guardianship of Pasio's trusted slave manager, Phormio. Pasio's vault was in his city house in the Peiraeus, where he and Phormio conducted their daily transactions. Phormio was a fixture in Pasio's house, if not a permanent resident. In his will Pasio established Phormio as guardian of the estate, including the bank, and bequeathed his widow Archippe to Phormio as the latter's wife. Her dowry

---

[39] Davies, *APF,* 215 ff. (Themistocles); 236–37 and Plut. *Cim.* 14.1–2 (Cimon); 259 ff. (the Ceryces); 403 (Nicias); 318, 517 (Cleon and Hyperbolus); 335 (Plato); 246–47 (Isocrates); 314–15 (Ciron and Nausimenes); 128 ff. (Demosthenes); 99–100 (Demades); 547 (Aeschines); 385 (Meidias); 70, 139, 158, 164, 179, 182, 189, 341, 489, 525, 533 (landowners active in the mining district). R. K. Sinclair, *Democracy and Participation in Athens* (Cambridge: Cambridge University Press, 1988), 186, points out that opprobrium could accompany payment for speechmaking; nevertheless, Athenians frequently received money from this source.

[40] See also Davies, *APF,* 130.

[41] Demosthenes left from this house for his many visits outside Attica.

[42] Casson, "Upper Class," 36, n. 21; see also Davies's conjecture that Lysias's shield factory was either part of his house or close to it, *APF,* 588–89.

[43] See also, Xen. *Mem.* 2.7.2 ff.

[44] Davies, *APF,* 427–28.

included a *synoikia,* its furniture, its female slaves, and jewelry, over all of which Phormio then had managerial control and which he made use of ([Dem.] 45.28–30). The *synoikia* and the house containing the vault, if not identical, were probably located close to each other—the Demosthenic passage implies Phormio's residence in the *synoikia,* and because his activities were centered in the Peiraeus, his residence was there as well. On Archippe's death this wealth was then divided among all her children, including her sons by Phormio.[45]

Isaeus 6 shows this interplay between residence and acquisition of wealth. In the orations we are told that Euctemon owns several houses; in one house he resides with his second wife and their children, while his first wife and his children by her reside elsewhere. Euctemon also owns some land including a small farm to be inherited by a son of his second wife. However, he supplements his income through the activities of another two of his *synoikiai* which serve as brothels. In one of these Euctemon was known to have resided so frequently that the sons of his second wife were accused of being the offspring of one of the slave prostitutes (12–26).[46]

---

[45] Ibid., 431–36, and discussion below, p. 160, on absence from the *oikos* and in chapter 6, pp. 193–94, on the use of nonkinsmen. D. Whitehead, "Women and Naturalisation in Fourth-Century Athens: The Case of Archippe," *CQ* 36 (1986): 109–114, conjectures that the presence of the *synoikia* in Archippe's dowry is proof that Archippe's status was ambiguous—sometimes a citizen and sometimes a metic. Whitehead is followed by Sealey, *Women,* 18–19. Carey has recently responded by stating that Archippe was still a metic, despite Pasio's acquired citizenship, and as such did not own the lodging house. Carey conjectures, therefore, that the latter had been sold (C. Carey, "Apollodorus' Mother: The Wives of Enfranchised Aliens in Athens," *CQ* 41 [1991]: 84–89). Besides the fact that "ownership" by women is a vexed question, I would point out that if there was a sale of this property, the sense of [Dem.] 45.30 is that Archippe and Phormio still had use of it. In fact, to give an item in a dowry expressly so that a woman and her husband could not use it would have been quite unprecedented and would undercut the purpose of the dowry: to give the woman security, to add legitimacy to the union, and to bind both families. The use of the house by Phormio would have been less disruptive for the minor child. If Archippe could not own this property outright then perhaps, like so much of Pasio's property, it remained in his name or in that of Apollodorus and was leased to Phormio until the latter acquired citizenship. For comparison's sake, both Cleoboule and Diodotus's widow, though not willed their husband's house, were granted the use of it and were willed most of the effects within: Dem. 27.5, 46; Lys. 32.6. Finley (*SLC,* 255, n. 67) wondered whether the *synoikia* in question was not identical with that received by Apollodorus as *presbeia,* but Davies (*APF,* 431) assumes that they were different buildings. Because Dem. 52.8 states that Pasio in his later years lived in the *astu* and not in the Peiraeus, where the bank and a *synoikia* were located, residence in the *astu* may well suggest a second *synoikia.* Oikonomides conjectures that there was an "office" or "branch" of Pasio's bank in the Agora and therefore in the *astu:* A. N. Oikonomides, "An Epigraphical Mention of the Bank of Pasion and Phormion from the Athenian Agora," *AncW* 23 (1992): 107–8. For recent discussions of Pasio's wealth and bibliography on banking, see R. Bogaert, "La banque à Athenes au IVe siècle avant J.-C.: Etat de la question," *MusHelv* 43 (1986): 19–49; Millett, *Lending,* 197–217. See also V. Hunter, "Women's Authority in Classical Athens," *EMC* 33 (1989): 43, n. 22 on the bibliography of the question whether the house and furnishings given to Archippe were a bequest over and above the dowry proper.

[46] In his very informative article on supplementary income among the Athenian elite, Casson ("Upper Class") nowhere mentions this case in which revenue from prostitution supplements the landed income of an Athenian.

Sometimes estates consisted almost entirely of cash; when inherited, the cash could be converted to landed and real property (Dem. 38.7).[47] In one case there seems to have actually been no *oikia* associated with the cash *oikos:* the cash was then bitterly fought over by a series of rival claimants who had great difficulty proving their kinship with the deceased, since he had resided outside of Athens for many years (Is. 4, passim).[48] It is little wonder that large sums of cash, left in the hands of a "trusted" friend, were frequently embezzled, as we shall see.

Oikia composition could also be affected by insolvency. In Isaeus 10, the speaker argues that his mother, the only daughter of her father's *oikos*, was technically an heiress and should have been married to her father's closest agnate.[49] Because the estate seems to have been in debt, however, the daughter was married off to a nonkinsman: her brother, who had been adopted out of the *oikos* and therefore, strictly speaking, no longer belonged to it, paid off the estate's debts and had his sons posthumously adopted into his *oikos* of origin (Is. 10, passim).

The forms of wealth could influence the makeup of the *oikos*, to the point that the *oikos* could not be equated with the family nor could it, as household, necessarily be equated with one single residence. There were further complexities, however. The use of wealth and its transmission were inextricably bound up with the membership of the *oikos*; legally, this membership was defined in terms of kinship. Even here, however, the forms that kinship could assume in the *oikos* were not static.

THE DOMESTIC LIFE CYCLE AND ATHENIAN FAMILIES

As mapped out by social scientists, the life cycle of a family consists of three, sometimes overlapping, stages: (1) the first stage begins with the marriage of two people and ends when the procreation of the family has ended; then (2) fission occurs with the marriage of a child and (3) the older couple dies and is replaced by the family of their children.[50] Thus the elementary family, the conjugal family unit, is the nucleus and consists of two successive generations. Often a third generation is involved in the life cycle, and here are included collateral kinsmen who are linked closely to and therefore are living with the nuclear family.[51] Thus there can be various forms of the extended family under one roof: a relative of the older generation is an upward extension, a relative of the younger genera-

---

[47] Davies, *APF*, 416 f.; ibid., 508–10 for Timotheus.

[48] See Dem. 52.9, 22–24, for the estate of the metic Lycon, who was heirless. The entire cash estate was claimed by an Athenian, Callipus.

[49] On the laws concerning heiresses, see above, chapter 3, p. 95.

[50] Meyer Fortes, introduction to *The Developmental Cycle in Domestic Groups,* ed. J. Goody (Cambridge: Cambridge University Press, 1962), 4–5.

[51] Ibid., 8–9.

tion is an extension downwards, and a brother and sister of either spouse living with the conjugal family unit is a lateral extension.[52]

Such extensions are evident in the Athenian sources. Thomas Gallant has argued that based on three of the major orators, Isaeus, Demosthenes, and Lysias, as well as on Davies's listing of elite families, 60 to 67 percent of the wealthy households in Athens consisted on average of two to four free and related individuals. Only 29 percent of the elite families had households with four to six citizen members, and only in 4 percent were households larger than six members. These figures apply only to the wealthy, as it is next to impossible to determine mean household size for the poor. In any case, mean household size of four to five people presumably was common for all social groups in preindustrial societies in many parts of the world.[53] How, then, did household size change?

In classical Athens, the legal ideal stated that when the household head died, his estate was divided equally among his sons. Each son then established his own *oikos,* lived in a separate house, married, and together with his family lived off the wealth that he had inherited, and that which his wife had brought into the marriage.[54] The daughters of the original *oikos* were usually married off before their brothers, and usually resided in the husband's house.[55] The few examples of uxorilocal residence involve the man's marriage to an heiress or his guardianship of an (intended) wife's minor children.[56]

There were exceptions, however, to the ideal pattern of household fission. A brother and unmarried sister could live in the same *oikia* with their father, while their brothers lived elsewhere (Dem. 24.202–3). Or the household head could die before the marriage of his daughter, leading the daughter to live with her brother or brothers before marriages were arranged for all. This arrangement is evidenced

---

[52] P. Laslett, "Introduction: The History of the Family," in *Household and Family in Past Time,* ed. P. Laslett and R. Wall (Cambridge: Cambridge University Press, 1972), 28–29. Gallant, *Risk,* 27–30, recently has used this model for ancient Athens, computing a twenty-four-year cycle as a model for the Athenian household. He divides the household cycle into three triennia. In the second triennium the vertical and horizontal extensions are evidenced: in the third, both younger brother is married off and older widowed mother dies to leave a nuclear household, which in turn will undergo the various extensions. The following discussion adds to Gallant's model.

[53] Gallant, *Risk,* 23.

[54] For the practice of partibility in classical Athens, see above, chapter 4, p. 109.

[55] On the earlier marriage of daughters, see above, chapter 4, pp. 120–22. On virilocal residence, see, for example, Is. 2.4 ff., 35 ff.; 3.4 ff., 30 ff.; 5.11; 7.7; 8.7 ff., 19; 9.27 ff.; 11.41–42, 49; Dem. 30.11 ff., 40.4–15, 42.27; 44.9, 26–27; 48.4 ff.; 59.22, 50; Lys. 1.6, 14.28, 19.9 ff., 32.6–7; Ant. 1.12 ff.; [And.] 4.14; Lycurg. 1.22–23; Hyp. *Lyc.* fr. 4. For virilocality in the inscriptions, see the discussion in above, chapter 2, p. 42. For depressing descriptions of the negative aspect of virilocality, see R. Garland, *The Greek Way of Life* (Ithaca, N.Y.: Cornell University Press, 1990), 221–22; Golden, *Children,* 49.

[56] Dem. 41.1 ff.; the orations of Demosthenes on his estate: Dem. 27–30; Phormio's residence: [Dem.] 36.8, 45.28. Very rarely a house is given as a dowry; when it is given, the residence can be said to be uxorilocal (Is. 5.27). See S. C. Humphreys, "Family Quarrels," *JHS* 109 (1989): 182–83, n. 4, who conjectures that the house Plango lived in after her divorce from Mantias may have been the intended dowry. As Mantias had his own house, the dowry may not have been the intended residence for the married couple.

as early as the first decade of the fifth century with Cimon and his sister and down into the fourth century with Demosthenes the orator (Plut. *Cim.* 4.3–7; Dem. 27–30).[57] At times the widowed mother would stay with her grown children, or with her son and his family of marriage.[58] In some of these cases the widow could exert a great deal of influence in the household, making private loans from her dowry and even managing the financial affairs of the *oikos* as a whole.[59]

There are other variations. The estate might have been split up before the death of the father, with one unmarried brother living in a separate house, while the second brother shared the original *oikia* with his father and mother (Dem. 47.35 ff.). Widowed or divorced fathers might also reside with their children, who could be married. One of the most famous cases of conflict between father and son was that of Pericles and his son Xanthippus—the latter was married and living under his father's roof (see above, p. 85). In Antiphon 1.8 ff. some of the property (slaves) had been divided among two sets of half-brothers before their father's death. At other times, brothers could hold real property in common, but their residence was not always joint.[60] On the other hand, one brother could own Athenian property and reside in Athens, while another resided and owned or leased property outside of Attica.[61]

These are some of the variations that resulted from the interests of the members of the nuclear family in themselves. But not all household heads died when their children were grown, and not all men had children. These facts led many individuals to depend on the extended kin group to keep the *oikos* and its property intact, through three institutions that directly affected and added to the variability of the *oikos:* guardianship, adoption, and remarriage.

GUARDIANSHIP

On the death of the father of minor children, a guardian would be appointed to rear and care for them. The guardian would use the wealth from the testator's estate for this task, with the intention that the estate would be transmitted intact,

---

[57] See also Is. 2.3 ff.; Dem. 24.202, 44.9, 48.53 ff.

[58] For example, Aeschin. 1.171; Dem. 37.45, 41.3 ff., 42.27; 54.9, 20, 44; 55.23–24; Lys. 1.6–8, 7.41, 24.5–6. In one case a widow lived with her daughter and son-in-law, possibly in the latter's residence (Dem. 45.70). See also note 59 below.

[59] For a recent discussion of the widow's residence, either with her children or away from them, see Hunter, "Women's Authority," 47; "The Athenian Widow and Her Kin," *Journal of Family History* 14 (1989): 291–311, where she argues (297–98) that in most cases the widow of childbearing age was expected to remarry; for the elderly widow, 300–302, and for Hunter's conjecture that the widow of Polyeuctus in Dem. 41 lived with her married daughter, 309, n. 23. See also Golden, *Children,* 139.

[60] See above, chapter 4, p. 109, to which add: Lys. 18.14, 21 (and Davies, *APF* 405); Dem. 53.6, 10, 15; D. M. Lewis, "Attic Manumissions," *Hesperia* 28 (1959): 233, 237; Davies, *APF,* 571, 589.

[61] Davies, *APF,* 469: one brother leased temple property on Delos, whereas his brother owned property in the deme of origin.

if not increased, when the testator's sons reached their majority. Although the siblings of a child's parents were not always selected as guardians, and indeed there are cases in which nonkinsmen were chosen,[62] parents' siblings or the siblings' descendants played a dominant role. In many cases children were reared by their father's brother, their father's brother's son, or their father's sister's son, either with or without their mother residing with them.[63] In one case, an elder brother is the guardian of his younger brother (Lys. 10.4–5), and in another, a man is guardian of his wife's minor brothers (Lys. fr. 43 [Th]). Widowed or divorced women could return to their *oikos* of origin and their children be reared and cared for by the women's brothers (Is. 8.40–42; Lys. 3.6 ff., 19.33; Dem. 39.23 f., 28). Or the children could be reared by a mother's brother after the death of both parents.[64]

The complexity of *oikia* membership can be appreciated in the following instances. In Isaeus 1, minor brothers, after the death of their parents, are reared by their father's brother and after his death, by their mother's brother (10 ff.). In Lysias 19 the speaker cares for his widowed sister and her children in his house, presumably along with his own wife and children.[65] In Demosthenes 39 and 40, Plango, after being divorced by Mantias, lived with her two sons and her three adult brothers.[66] In Lysias 18.9, 21–22, the son of Diognetus seems to have been reared by Diognetus's brother who died shortly afterwards. Diognetus's son continued to live with his father's brother's sons, so that all three cousins lived in one *oikia*. In one of the most famous cases of guardianship, that of the great Alcibiades and his brother Cleinias undertaken by Pericles and his brother Ariphron, Pericles and Ariphron were first cousins (father's sister's sons) of Deinomache, the mother of Alcibiades and Cleinias.[67] Pericles had originally taken care of his

---

[62] Harrison, *Law,* 1:99–101; MacDowell, *Law,* 93.

[63] With the father's brother: Is. 1.9 ff., 7.5 ff., 10.5–6, 11.10 ff.; Lys. 17. 9–10, 21–22; 32.8 ff.; Dem. 38.23. Critias, one of the Thirty, was the guardian of his cousin Charmides, a father's brother's son (Pl. *Charm.* 155a, 156a; Davies, *APF,* 327–31), while Phrasicles was the guardian of Themistocles' youngest daughter, his father's brother's daughter (Plut. *Them.* 32.1–3 and discussion in the appendix, below, p. 218. With father's brother's son and father's sister's son: Dem. 27–30, passim.

[64] This was probably the case with Andocides' cousin, father's sister's son, who was reared by Andocides' father (Davies, *APF,* 30.).

[65] Ibid., 201–2, for the date of her marriage to Aristophanes, the marriage of her brother, and the date of Aristophanes' death; see also, Hunter "Athenian Widow," 297.

[66] Davies, *APF,* 365–66. There is the question of the birthdate of Plango's two sons by Mantias. Davies's reconstruction, following Rudhardt, posits that Plango gave birth to Boeotus, was divorced by Mantias, and gave birth to Mantias's second son some years later, after the death of Mantias's second wife. J. Rudhardt, "La reconnaissance de la paternité, sa nature et sa portée dans la société athénienne," *MusHelv* 19 (1962): 39–64; Humphreys, "Family Quarrels," 182–85, basically agrees with the sequence of births and marriages, although she would downdate Boeotus's birth from c. 382 to 378. If indeed Pamphilus was born after his brothers Boeotus and Mantitheus, then he would not have resided in Plango's household until the mid-370s (Davies, *APF,* 367; Humphreys, ad loc., 182–83).

[67] On the guardianship, see Davies, *APF,* 18, and sources therein; on Deinomache's relationship with Pericles, see ibid., 379, 455–57.

two wards in his house, but sent Cleinias away to be reared by Ariphron, apparently to thwart Alcibiades' influence on his younger brother (Pl. *Prot.* 320a). Another tradition states that Alcibiades, when he became the *eromenos* of a certain Athenian, Democrates, was almost ejected from his guardians' *oikos* until Pericles' leniency allowed Alcibiades to remain under the same roof with him.[68] Whatever the veracity of these stories, they do reflect the flexibility of residence arrangements.[69]

The variability of *oikia* membership was aggravated by the fusion of wealth from the testator's estate and that of the guardian. The job of guardian was a thankless one at many times, if the orations are an accurate indication. The many instances of a guardian, frequently an agnate, being charged with mismanagement attest to the precariousness of the position. The charge was easy to make because the use of the testator's property was left up to the individual guardian. If a guardian chose to lease out an orphan's estate, such charges of mismanagement were harder to bring. The leasing of an ophan's estate, known as *misthōsis oikou,* was initiated by a formal application in writing to the archon, who made no investigation of the lease but auctioned the estate for leasing at a regular court sitting. At that point interested parties could raise objections before the court, which made the final decision (Is. 6.37, 11.42; *P. Oxy.* 31.2357v 8–11).[70] Thus, if an orphan's estate was leased, the lessee had to be wealthy enough to put up part of his estate, equal in value to the orphans' estate, as security, although the *misthōsis* could be shared by guardians (Is. 2.9). At times, the security consisted of land in the orphans' deme; thus the guardian could also be a landed neighbor. The leasing of the estate ensured that the orphan received the estate. It would provide a steady income for the orphan's maintenance, and that the orphan would ultimately receive it as his father had left it. The procedure did have its drawbacks: when the estate was rented out, the orphan could be severed from the paternal residence and might have to live elsewhere with the guardian, unless the guardian himself was the lessee.[71]

Misthōsis oikou, although by no means obligatory,[72] nevertheless probably occurred frequently because of the high mortality rate of fathers with minor sons.[73] In one case, the guardian used his wards' largely cash estate to buy up land and *synoikiai* but did not let out the property as the wards' father's brother insisted. Only when a third party brought the guardians to court was the property

---

[68] Plut. *Alc.* 3.1 citing Antiphon; R. Littman, "The Loves of Alcibiades," *TAPA* 101 (1970): 264, doubts the actual flight of Alcibiades from his guardians' home but suggests that Democrates was indeed his lover.

[69] Also, Polystratus of Deiradiotae was brought up in the city by a guardian and returned on his majority to his family property in the country until the Decelean War: Lys. 20.11–12; Davies, *APF,* 467.

[70] Finley, *SLC,* 42–43; Harrison, *Law,* 1:105–8; Osborne, "Leasing," 305–10.

[71] Osborne, "Leasing," 313, 316.

[72] Finley *SLC,* and Harrison, *Law,* as cited above, note 70.

let out (Dem. 38.7, 23). Therefore, a guardian could become suspect if he did not let out his ward's estate, despite the absence of legal obligation to do so (Dem. 27.15, 40, 58–60; 28.15; Lys. 32.23). On the other hand, if the orphans' estate consisted largely of undeclared property, there was little incentive for leasing, although the guardian was more liable to charges of mismanagement.[74] Even if the guardianship proceeded smoothly, trouble could come from the lessees of the children's estate who could attempt to embezzle the property (*P. Oxy.* 31.2537v, 8–11) or from nonkinsmen who tried to claim it (Lys. fr. 32 [Th]).

Although some estates throve under *misthōsis oikou* (Dem. 27.58, 64), the burden of the charges in lawsuits against bad guardians was that they had used their wards' wealth for their own purposes. The lawsuit prosecuting the guardian was not a straightforward procedure, however, precisely because the ward's wealth had been absorbed into the guardian's estate. In Isaeus 7, the ward had to wait for his majority until he and his stepfather could sue his guardian (his father's brother) successfully for the ward's estate (7–8). In Isaeus 8 the child and his mother returned to the mother's *oikos* of origin: according to the speaker, her half-brother (matrilineal), as guardian, proceeded to encroach on the property of the orphaned boy (ibid., 41–42). In Isaeus 5 (10 ff.) the children are reared by their cousin, their mother's brother's adopted son, Dicaeogenes III. The children resided with Dicaeogenes III, but it is not known what happened to their mother. Furthermore, the original *oikia* of the wards, that of their father Theopompus, was physically destroyed by Dicaeogenes III, who converted the property into a garden. In fact, if the speaker can be believed, one of the children was contracted out as a servant to Dicaeogenes III's brother. There may well be exaggeration here, but the point is that the variability of *oikia* membership is underscored by the poverty of the *oikos,* its destruction, and the alleged use of the poorer relative by a wealthier one as a servant.[75]

In many of these instances *oikia* composition was in almost constant flux. Consider Lysias 32. Here Diogeiton's daughter was married to Diogeiton's brother, Diodotus. On the latter's death, the daughter with her children returned to her father's *oikia,* after he had remarried, but he changed their residence during the last stages of the Peloponnesian War. The shared residence in this case allowed the guardian to use the cash from his ward's estate and his daughter's dowry to pay for his own trierarchic expenses and, according to the speaker, to rear his children by his second marriage (9 ff.).

In Demosthenes 38, two wards, Nausimachus and Xenopeithes, charge that their guardian, Aristaechmus, whose relationship to the wards is not explicitly stated, had received one hundred staters from a Bosporan in payment for a loan from their father (11–12). Aristaechmus's son, the speaker, countered that nei-

---

[73] Osborne, "Leasing," 309–10.

[74] Ibid.

[75] The subjection of poorer kinsmen to wealthier was by no means uncommon in the nineteenth-century Baltic region. A. Carter, "Household Histories," in Netting, Wilk, and Arnould, *Households,* 50.

ther he nor his brothers nor their own guardian, who had never been away from Athens, had collected the money. Nausimachus and Xenopeithes then responded that their rivals' guardian, Demaretus, had sent an agent out to retrieve the money (ibid., 12 ff.).[76] The point here is not just the wards' love for litigation, though this is obvious, but the extended struggle to come to terms with *oikos* boundaries made even more indefinite by wealth accruing to it from outside Athens, which could be allegedly hidden and absorbed by a rival *oikos*.

The amalgamation of guardian's and ward's *oikoi* was further encouraged by the marriage of the guardian to the testator's widow, or in one case, the marriage of the guardian to his ward.[77] Apollodorus's complaint against Phormio was that his marriage to Apollodorus's mother encouraged Phormio's control over Pasio's property. Apollodorus even accused his own mother of colluding with Phormio (Dem. 36.10, 17–19, 60).

In the case of Demosthenes the orator, one of his guardians, Aphobus, had been assigned by Demosthenes' father to marry his widow, Cleoboule (Dem. 27.4–6). Aphobus had actually taken up residence in the house of Demosthenes' father and taken possession of Cleoboule's dowry (27.13–17, 46; 28.11, 15–16, 19; 29.33–34, 45), and perhaps some money left in the house (27.53 ff., 29.46 ff.). Indeed Cleoboule may have been unwilling to hand over control of her property after she had seen Aphobus's attempts at extortion.[78] Although these events are well known, my point here is that Aphobus lived with his wards and their mother, but his relationship with Cleoboule was not considered formal (27.17, 56).[79] Aphobus soon afterward went on a trierarchy, and on his return married the daughter of Philonides of Melite. Marital residence was in Aphobus' house (27.56; 29.27, 48; 30.7–8, 15), yet Aphobus retained Cleoboule's dowry for about ten years (27.69, 28.11). In the meantime Aphobus still held the guardianship of Demosthenes' estate, until Demosthenes successfully won his suit, thereby forcing Aphobus to return the wealth, or to compensate for the wealth he had embezzled from the estate of Demosthenes Senior.[80]

Guardianship did little, therefore, to delineate *oikos* boundaries because of the fluid use of property and wealth. Adoption did little to define boundaries, but

---

[76] On long-distance loans, see Millett, *Lending*, 8.

[77] There are three known instances in which the guardian married, or was intended to marry, his wards' mother: Callias III and Chrysilla, Aphobus and Demosthenes' mother Cleoboule, and Archippe and Phormio. The marriage of Callias will be discussed in the section on remarriage, p. 152, and that of Phormio will be discussed again in chapter 6, below, pp. 193–94. For the marriage of a guardian to his ward, see Is. 6.13. Harrison, *Law*, 1:24, n. 1, effectively answers the question of the legality of a marriage between a guardian and a ward's mother: either the tradition that a Solonian law forbade such marriages was erroneous, or the law so obsolete as to be ignored by all orators.

[78] Hunter, "Women's Authority," 40–44.

[79] The latter passage declares that Aphobus had not yet taken (λαβεῖν) Cleoboule as wife. The act of consummation is implied here.

[80] Davies, *APF*, 118–19.

this fluidity could be a benefit, for the adoptee who was saddled with some harsh legal restrictions regarding the *oikos* of his birth father.

ADOPTION

Besides guardianship, adoption was also designed to protect the *oikos* from extinction, but in the end the choice of heirs could be challenged and the adoptee viewed as a destroyer of the *oikos*. Adoption allowed the childless man, or the man without male heirs, to choose an heir for the sake of continuing his, the adopter's, line.[81] Although the law allowed a testator to adopt whomever he wished, he frequently adopted a kinsman, and particularly one through the female line (see above, p. 126). This preference can indicate the absence of agnates as possible heirs, but may also indicate mistrust among male agnates, who were the preferred heirs prescribed by law. At times the adoptee, if not descended from a male agnate, was a demesman or neighbor, so that proximity of holdings, residence and/or sphere of activities would have facilitated amalgamation of *oikoi* (see above, pp. 28–31).

A close reading of some of the cases of adoption, however, reveals the complexity of *oikia* composition. Let us consider first adoption *inter vivos*. Menecles, whose first wife had died, married the sister of the speaker in Isaeus 2, divorced her because of lack of children, but adopted her brother (7 ff.), thereby ignoring his agnates. In Isaeus 7 Apollodorus, rather than resorting to his patrilineal kinsmen, adopted his matrilineal half-sister by testament and then adopted her son *inter vivos*.[82] In Demosthenes 41 Polyeuctus, while his wife was living, adopted her brother and arranged a marriage between the brother and one of his, Polyeuctus's, daughters. The couple resided with Polyeuctus and his wife in their *oikia* (3 ff.). However, Polyeuctus and his adopted son quarreled, Polyeuctus initiated a divorce between his daughter and her husband, and the young woman was remarried to a certain Spudias, apparently a nonkinsman. Furthermore, she and Spudias seem to have resided in a separate house, as Polyeuctus's house, after his death, was rented out (ibid., 5).[83]

However, adoption did not always occur during the adopter's lifetime: besides

[81] On adoption, see Harrison, *Law,* 1:82–96; MacDowell, *Law,* 99–108, and chapter 4, above, pp. 125–28.

[82] Davies, *APF,* 44–45, following Wyse. Gernet, "La loi," 129, no. 10, conjectures that the adoption of the sister was by testament.

[83] Several other instances of adoption which are not clearly *inter vivos* involve that of a woman's son into her father's estate (Plut. *Them.* 32.1–2; Dem. 42.21, 58.31; [Plut.] *Mor.* 843a–b; Is. 10.4). The adoption of a woman's grandson into her brother's estate ([Dem.] 44.19, 46) may well have been *inter vivos,* but the instance in Is. 11.41, in which a girl is adopted by her mother's brother, is unclear. The adoption of Chariades by Nicostratus, if authentic, occurred *inter vivos* but outside Athens (Is. 4.3 ff.), while the adoption by Isocrates of his wife's son by her first marriage was *inter vivos* ([Plut.] *Mor.* 838a).

adoption *inter vivos,* there was testamentary adoption and the mysterious posthumous adoption. Testamentary adoption was a transaction by written will, in which the testator stated explicitly who would inherit his estate after his death; the will was written and sealed in front of witnesses and put in the care of a trusted kinsman or friend.[84] Posthumous adoption, in effect, allowed a kinsman, usually very close in line to the deceased, to assume control of the estate. In Pseudo-Demosthenes 43.12 the posthumous adoption of Sositheus's son into the estate of his wife's father apparently followed the explicit instructions of the testator before his death.[85]

The problems that testamentary adoption could cause a person claiming *oikos* membership after the testator's death are frequently described in the sources, the main concern being forgery.[86] In Isaeus 7.1–2, for instance, the speaker argues that through adoption *inter vivos* the adopter explicitly states his wishes, but through adoption by will the adopter makes his wishes unclear or secret, and for that reason many consider the will a forgery and consider challenging it. Furthermore, Isaeus 5.6 shows that some time could elapse between the actual drawing up of the will and the inheritance of the estate by the adoptee. In Isaeus 5, Dicaeogenes III's adoption by Dicaeogenes II seems to have been originally intended to keep the latter's whole estate intact, but because Dicaeogenes III was a minor, and the sisters of his adoptive father challenged the adoption, Dicaeogenes III lost two-thirds of his inheritance to the women. He eventually sued for and received the whole estate.[87] In Isaeus 11 and Pseudo-Demosthenes 43, Hagnias adopted his niece and then his homometric brother, but the adoptions were hotly contested after Hagnias's death by his kinsmen through the agnatic line. Although both niece and brother may have occupied Hagnias's house and estate for some time, the property was finally taken away from them and awarded to one of Hagnias's male agnates.[88]

Posthumous adoption could also be open to charges of fraud (Is. 6.36). The posthumous adoption of Cyronides' natural sons into the estate of his natural father, out of whose *oikos* he had been adopted, was strongly challenged by the son of Cyronides' sister (Is. 10.4 ff.). The complex machinations of the line through Archiades' sister, as described in Pseudo-Demosthenes 44, were finally challenged by descendants of Archiades' brother after three generations of adoptions, two of which were posthumous, into Archiades' estate.[89]

---

[84] Gernet, *Droit,* 129; for instance, Is. 1.9 ff., 3.55–56, 5.6, 6.5–7, 7.1 ff., 9.4–6, 11.8.

[85] For further instances of posthumous adoption, see Is. 10.6, 11.49; [Dem.] 44.19 ff.

[86] See Isaeus fr. 1 (Th) in which Aristogeiton and Archippus allegedly forged four wills. For a discussion of suspicions cast on the authenticity of wills, see W. E. Thompson, "Athenian Attitudes toward Wills," *Prudentia* 13 (1981): 13–23, who argues, however, that the Athenians were not prejudiced against bequests by will per se.

[87] Davies, *APF,* 146 following Wyse.

[88] The motivations behind the adoption and the events resulting from it are subjects of scholarly conjecture and debate. For more detailed discussion, see above, chapter 1, pp. 6–8.

[89] Davies, *APF,* 194–95.

The other side of the coin to this instability of *oikos* inheritance was the ability of the adoptee to influence two *oikoi,* the *oikos* of his or her origin, i.e., in the patriline, and that of his or her adoption. This influence could be so strong that one could argue that it was tantamount to membership. It is a well-known legal fact that in Athens the adoptee, at the time of his adoption, was legally severed from his *oikos* of origin, that is, he could not inherit from it.[90] Conversely, if he returned to his original *oikos* without leaving a natural son, he would forfeit his adoptive *oikos* ([Dem.] 44.19 ff.), although speakers were known to argue to the contrary (Dem. 58.30–31). One legal way in which the adoptee could return to his original *oikos* was that to make sure to leave a natural son in his place, thereby in effect consolidating the two estates.[91] Another way of circumventing the law, as outlined in chapter 1, was by marrying back into the patriline.

A third way of circumventing this law was through the mother. Naturally if an individual was actually adopted into the estate of a matrilineal kinsman, he could not inherit from his *oikos* of origin (Is. 9.2, 33; 10.3 ff.). However, regardless of the *oikos* into which the adoptee was adopted, the adoptee was never severed from his mother or from his maternal relatives. Thus, in Isaeus 7 Thrasybulus was adopted out of his father's *oikos,* but inherited half of the estate of his mother's brother (19 ff.).[92] The mother could also be a unifying link between her son's, the adoptee's, paternal *oikos* and the *oikos* of adoption. In Pseudo-Demosthenes 43.15, although Euboulides III, a minor, was adopted into his maternal grandfather's estate, and therefore no longer had his father as his *kyrios,* he nevertheless fell under the *kyrieia* of his elder brother. This control was possible because of the brothers' relationship to each other through their mother.[93]

In other instances of adoption one can legitimately question the force of the legally prescribed severance. In Isaeus 5, Dicaeogenes III, although adopted out of his patriline, the Gephyraei, nevertheless, reminded the court of his descent from them in order to gain some advantage over the speaker (45–47). The latter, however, criticized Dicaeogenes for this line of argument (ibid., 47). In Isaeus 11, besides owning his own estate, Stratocles manages the estate into which his daughter had been adopted (41 ff.). In the same oration, Theopompus, the speaker, includes in the listing of his property the estate of his wife's brother, into

---

[90] Harrison, *Law,* 1:93–94; MacDowell, *Law,* 100.

[91] R. Lane Fox, "Aspects of Inheritance in the Greek World," in *Crux: Essays in Greek History Presented to G. E. M. de Ste. Croix on his 75th Birthday,* ed. P. Cartledge and F. D. Harvey (Exeter: Academic Imprint, 1985), 225. Humphreys, *Family,* 65 followed by Garland, *Life,* 154, mentions briefly that the restriction was often circumvented but cites only two orations here (Is. 10; [Dem.] 44). In the latter oration the series of posthumous adoptions was quite legal, that is, the adoptee left a natural son in the house of adoption and returned to his natural *oikos.* My point here concerns practices that bent the law.

[92] Davies, *APF,* 45–47.

[93] Harrison *Law,* 1:94, n. 1.

which one of Theopompus's sons had been posthumously adopted (ibid., 47 ff.).[94] In Isaeus 2, the speaker's brother allows Menecles to adopt the speaker on the understanding that the speaker could manage the estate of his brother during the latter's frequent trips from Athens (12). The logical conclusion to this influence of the paternal *oikos* on an individual adopted out is seen in two instances. In Demosthenes 42.21, Phaenippus enjoys the wealth of two estates, that of his natural father and that of his maternal grandfather, into whose estate he has been adopted.[95] Indeed the speaker states (22) that Phaenippus had two fathers (οἱ δὲ σοὶ πατέρες), and challenged Phaenippus to an exchange of property (*antidōsis*), which included both properties. The nature of the challenge suggests that the wealth of both *oikoi* was amalgamated.[96]

Isaeus 10 sets out in detail how Cyronides actually achieved control of two estates. He was adopted into his maternal grandfather's estate, but when his natural father's estate became insolvent,[97] he married the daughter of his paternal uncle, who held guardianship over the estate. In fact, the daughter, Cyronides' first cousin, brought with her, as a type of dowry, title to the insolvent estate. Cyronides paid off the estate's debts, and his sons after his death were adopted into the original estate (10.4 ff., 15–16). Despite the law, therefore, it is clear from actual practice, that some individuals had either full membership in two *oikoi,* or at the very least were directly influential over the property of two *oikoi* for a considerable length of time.

There were, therefore, two conflicting sets of interests in the institution of adoption that added to the complexity of *oikos* boundaries: 1) the interest of the adopter to adopt someone trustworthy, the latter being frequently a kinsman through the female line; and 2) the interest of the adoptee to maintain ties with his or her patriline of origin. Severance from the patriline could be compensated for by endogamy into the patriline, but also by the adoptee's willingness and ability to bend, if not contravene, laws on adoption. Often overlapping the practices of guardianship and adoption was the strong Athenian propensity for remarriage, which also frequently challenged the male agnatic bias underlying property rights.

---

[94] Adoption of one of Aeschines' sons into his wife's brother's estate may very well lie behind the tradition that Aeschines inherited five talents from his brother-in-law. For the tradition, see Davies, *APF,* 544.

[95] Thompson argues that such enjoyment was possible only because Phaenippus probably sired a son and left him behind in the adoptive estate (Thompson, "Wills," 21, n. 27). However, at the time of the speech Phaenippus may have been around twenty years of age, quite young to have been married and sired a child, although one could argue that the urgent need to provide heirs for both *oikoi* prompted the early marriage. Davies, *APF,* 553, for Phaenippus's age; for the rarity of marriage of young men, see Humphreys, "Family Quarrels," 183, n. 8.

[96] V. Gabrielsen, "The *Antidosis* Procedure in Classical Athens," *ClMed* 38 (1987): 36.

[97] W. Wyse, *The Speeches of Isaeus* (Cambridge: Cambridge University Press, 1904; New York: Arno, 1979), 662.

REMARRIAGE

Besides guardianship and adoption, the practice of remarriage, the result of a high mortality rate, added to the complexity of *oikia* membership by allowing groups of half-siblings and affines to encroach on each other's property. Although many of the cases below have been mentioned in former chapters, they bear repeating here to underline the dynamics of *oikia* composition, which at times aggravated the tension between interests of the patriline and of the matriline. Themistocles' complex marital career will probably never be sorted out in every detail, precisely because the children of both marriages shared a residence, intermarried, and bonded together during political crisis (see appendix, pp. 217–18). Callias III's domestic arrangements, resulting from remarriage, made the rounds of gossip circuits at the end of the fifth century. His first wife, the daughter of Glaucon of Cerameis, bore him Hipponicus III, whom Callias attempted to marry to his second wife's daughter by that woman's first husband, Epilycus the son of Teisander. Callias's third wife was Chrysilla, the mother of his second wife; at one time the two women apparently shared Callias's *oikia* (And. 1.124–27). Although it is possible that Callias was fortune hunting in these marriages, Callias seems, nevertheless, to have been the legal guardian of Chrysilla's sons by her wealthy husband Ischomachus. The guardianship presupposes a good deal of trust, if not close kinship, between the two men. A marriage to Ischomachus's widow simply consolidated Callias's position as the estate's protector.[98]

Ciron in Isaeus 8 was at some point married to his first cousin (mother's sister's daughter) and sired a daughter. After the death of his first wife he married Diocles' matrilineal half-sister, who bore him two sons. Ciron's daughter lived in the same house in the meantime, and when she came of age was married, widowed, and remarried to the speaker's father (8–10, 35–38).[99]

In Isaeus 7.5 ff., Apollodorus, was reared by his mother's second husband Archedamus. When Apollodorus reached his majority he and his stepfather sued his paternal uncle, Eupolis, for a contested estate. In gratitude Apollodorus adopted his stepfather's daughter and then her son.[100] The temporary residence of Apollodorus and his half-sister in two *oikoi* and two *oikiai* served to unite the two families in their attempts to take property away from Apollodorus's agnates. Likewise, Aristogeiton and his brother seem to have lived

---

[98] C. A. Cox, "Incest Inheritance and the Political Forum in Fifth-Century Athens," *CJ* 85 (1989): 42–46, where I suggest that the marriage to Chrysilla may have been stipulated by Ischomachus. See also F. D. Harvey, "The Wicked Wife of Ischomachus," *EMC* 28 (1984): 68–70, who suggests that Xenophon's *Oeconomicus* was written after Andocides' attack and was meant to clear the reputation of Chrysilla.

[99] On Ciron's widow, see Hunter, "Athenian Widow," 297.

[100] Wyse, *Isaeus,* 557, points out that Apollodorus won *kyrieia* of his homometric sister by adopting her, and therefore had the power to marry her off.

with their homometric sister, since Aristogeiton gave her away in marriage ([Dem.] 25.55).[101]

Remarriage and adoption figure largely in the practices of other families.[102] Hagnias's mother was remarried to a fellow demesman of herself and her husband, probably while Hagnias was still a young child. He was brought up, therefore, with his two half-brothers, one of whom seems to have been Hagnias's preferred heir.[103]

Children of a mother's second marriage were liable to assert claims against their half-siblings. Pasio's son Apollodorus challenged his father's donation of some of his property to his mother's dowry for her second marriage to Phormio. The children from this second union lived in one of Pasio's residences with Apollodorus's younger brother Pasicles. Apollodorus, on the other hand, aged twenty-four at his father's death, resided at some distance on his farm in the northern plain.[104] Likewise, perhaps shared residence allowed Diocles in Isaeus 8 to be adopted into the estate of his mother's second husband, thereby preventing Diocles' younger half-sisters from inheriting from their father (40–41).[105]

Disputes resulted from the remarriage of the male household head precisely because there were likely to be more heirs among whom the property would have to be divided. In Lysias 32, after Diogeiton remarried, in his one household there were Diogeiton, his fraternal nephews who were also his grandsons, his second wife, and their children. When Diogeiton's wards reached their majority, it was understood that they would leave Diogeiton's house—with a substantially reduced inheritance, as it turned out (9), a reduction that their mother attributed to Diogeiton's concern for his second family (ibid., 17).[106] In Isaeus 6, it was precisely because Euctemon was guardian of a woman who resided with him and whom he later married that he stripped his only surviving son by his first

[101] Legally speaking it is difficult to know how Aristogeiton won *kyrieia* over the young woman: such rights went to patrilineal kinsmen or adoptive fathers. MacDowell, *Law,* 84, for the patrilineal rights. On the other hand, Aristogeiton's sister seems to have been given in marriage to a non-Athenian and sent outside of Attica, so that Athenian laws may not have applied in this case. On the similar case of Timocrates' sister, see below, chapter 6, pp. 206–7.

[102] In Isaeus 9.1 ff., Astyphilus shunned his agnates and was emotionally close to the son of his mother by her second husband. Isocrates adopted the son of his wife by her first marriage: Davies, *APF,* 247.

[103] See discussion in chapter 1, above, pp. 6–8; on Hagnias's age, see Davies, *APF,* 82–83.

[104] Ibid., 435, for Pasicles' minority and the birth of Archippe's sons. For Apollodorus's retreat to a rural estate, see [Dem.] 53.4.

[105] Davies, *APF,* 313, conjectures that if the two husbands of Diocles' mother were related, the adoption may have been legal, but this does not take account of Athenian law which stipulated that the adopted son should marry the adopter's daughter. The adoption was underhanded at best: see, above, chapter 4, p. 128.

[106] Although W. E. Thompson ("Athenian Marriage Patterns: Remarriage," *CSCA* 5 [1972]: 212) asserts that such "vehemence would be out of place if Diogeiton merely preferred his own children (by his second wife) to his grandchildren." Such vehemence, on the contrary, was quite common in the disputes between half-siblings, particularly patrilineal half-brothers; see above, chapter 4, pp. 112–13.

marriage of part of that son's inheritance (3 ff.). Mantias's children from his two marriages squabbled over his estate until two-thirds of it were finally awarded to his two sons from his first wife, Plango (Dem. 39.23–24, 28; 40.9). This division included the very *oikia* in which Mantitheus, the son of Mantias from his second wife, had been brought up (40.2, 13–14, 48, 50). After the judgment, therefore, in the one house of Mantias, which had been divided, Boeotus and his full brother Pamphilus lived in one part, while Mantitheus and his yet unmarried daughter lived in the other (ibid., 40.4–5).

Adoption, guardianship, remarriage—there is an extensive bibliography on two of these three, although few scholars have emphasized how the nature and membership of the wealthy *oikos* changed under their influence.[107] Let us view them in the context of the historical development of the family and domestic unit and in terms of the use of and interest in wealth. Although land was the ideal form of wealth, it was frequently supplemented, if not supplanted, by non-landed wealth, which in turn could modify the *oikia* by the addition of the workshop. At times there was no residence attached to the *oikos*. Even when an *oikos* was based on landed wealth, this often consisted of scattered holdings with several *oikiai*. Also, given the domestic life cycle of the propertied and elite family, the pure nuclear family is not seen frequently in the sources, nor is the male head of the household, as the father, a ubiquitous figure. Given the high mortality rate of both men and women, guardianship, adoption, and remarriage further complicated the life cycle and frequently undercut the power of agnates. Guardians, who were often agnates, were criticized for their management of a ward's estate, a criticism easily leveled because of shared *oikiai* and fluid *oikos* boundaries. So, too, adoption made use of kinsmen through the female (agnate) line or through the matriline, and remarriage, which fueled hostilities between patrilineal half-siblings, could encourage collusion between matrilineal half-siblings in wresting control of an *oikos* from the patriline. However, despite one's ambivalence toward one's patriline, one strove to retain one's place in it—hence the adoptee's attempts to retain membership in two *oikoi*.

Up until now the discussion has focused on the variabilities and complexities of *oikia* membership and *oikos* composition in Athens. But the Athenian elite was a very mobile group, traveling extensively outside Attica and even Greece. There were many reasons for the Athenian male to be absent from Athens and separated from his family and kinsmen. War was a common event in Athens, and the many political bouleversements were often either a consequence of war or an attempt to avoid it. Therefore, ostracism in the fifth century and exile throughout the classical era were persistent threats for the politically and militarily prominent. Furthermore, the elite were chosen as ambassadors in Athens' constant attempts to secure alliances or prepare for war. Outside of the realm of war, many

---

[107] Legal works have been especially informative on adoption and guardianship: Harrison, *Law,* 1:82–121; MacDowell, *Law,* 93–95, 99–101, and bibliography; for remarriage, see the classic study of Thompson, "Athenian Marriage Patterns," 211–25.

wealthy Athenians earned much of their income from overseas trade or traveled to visit foreign allies and friends. What becomes apparent in the sources is the profound effects that such severance from the *oikos* in Athens had on family life and on the use of *oikos* wealth, which again confused boundaries and definitions. If the typical Athenian of the elite constantly asserted his rights to or in an *oikos*, his mobility often rendered that membership illusory.

ABSENCE FROM THE *OIKOS*: WAR

Athens was at war more often than at peace.[108] Although it has been argued recently that campaigns tended to be border disputes arranged around the planting and harvesting seasons, and therefore would not disrupt agricultural production,[109] nevertheless, men did die or were captured as slaves. Also, because of the nature of the sources, we know most about the politically prominent and the propertied families: the sources indicate that for these people, war could be both costly and disruptive to family unity. A cursory reading of Davies's listing will show the extensive military activities over generations of some of the elite families. For instance, in Dicaeogenes' kin group, Dicaeogenes I, his son and grandson all died in battle. Military and trierarchical activities are recorded for Antimachus and his grandson, Critodemus and his son, Hagnon and his son Theramenes, Nicophemus and his son Aristophanes, Conon and his descendants, and Iphicrates and Lycomedes and their descendants, while Phocion—a unique case to be sure—was said to have been general no fewer than forty-five times.[110] *Stratēgoi* were too much away from Athens to be effective leaders by the end of the fifth century; hence, the severance of the political and military spheres.[111]

[108] For war as a natural state of affairs in the classical period, see J.-P. Vernant, introduction to *Problèmes de la guerre en Grèce ancienne* (Paris: Mouton, 1968), 10; J. de Romilly, "Guerre et paix entre cités," ibid., 207–20, who points out that war was much more lasting than peace. For the purpose of war and its effects on Athenian society and institutions, see M. I. Finley, *The Ancient Economy* (Berkeley, Calif.: University of California Press, 1973), 158 ff.; S. C. Humphreys, *Anthropology and the Greeks* (London: Routledge and Kegan Paul, 1978), 170–74; Sinclair, *Democracy*, 57.

[109] See R. Osborne, *Classical Landscape with Figures: The Ancient Greek City and Its Countryside* (London: George Philip, 1987), 13–14, 138–39, and Ellen Meiksins Wood, *Peasant-Citizen and Slave* (London: Verso, 1989), 59–60, who seem to argue against the view that long campaigns kept the soldier from home for extended periods of time, expressed in Humphreys, *Family*, 12; see also V. Hanson, "The Ideology of Hoplite Battle, Ancient and Modern," in *Hoplites: The Classical Greek Battle Experience*, ed. V. Hanson (London: Routledge, 1991), 6–7. Sinclair, *Democracy*, 57, 115, points out that overseas campaigns could stretch beyond the normal campaigning season.

[110] Davies, *APF*, 145–46 (Dicaeogenes' kin group); 37 (Antimachus); 61–62 (Critodemus and son); 228 (Hagnon and Theramenes); 201 (Nicophemus and Aristophanes); 507 ff. (Conon and his descendants); 249–50 (Iphicrates and son); 346 (Lycomedes and family); 559 (Phocion). Dem. 20.67 ff. shows that the ancients were quite aware of the mobility of their leaders.

[111] J. Ober, *Mass and Elite in Democratic Athens* (Princeton, N.J.: Princeton University Press, 1989), 92.

Trierarchical expenses were costly, approximately two thousand drachmae for a syntrierarchy and up to six thousand drachmae for a sole trierarchy.[112] Not all trierarchies mandated the active service of the trierarch—by the fourth century, although actual trierarchic expenses were paid for by the liturgist, the active duty of service and therefore the required absence from Athens could be contracted out.[113] Therefore not all trierarchies required absence; nevertheless, Athenians did leave Athens for military activity, but because the average Athenian was unwilling to participate in more distant wars, the equipping and manning of warships with mercenaries quickly became the private expense of propertied individuals.[114] Macartatus, a Bouselid affine, sold his property to purchase a trireme and sailed to Crete for a battle that cost him his life.[115] Most illustrative is the almost comic episode in Pseudo-Demosthenes 49 where Timotheus, the son of Conon, has hypothecated most of his property for debts to the state and for past and upcoming expeditions. When entertaining two foreign leaders in his empty house in the Peiraeus he is faced with the embarrassing situation of borrowing drinking vessels and linens from Pasio the banker (22 ff.).[116] The general Aristophanes was caught in an equally embarrassing situation when lodging envoys from Evagoras (Lys. 19.27).

Closely associated with military activity and expansion was the the colonial settlement. Colonization sometimes led families to split up, sending one member to a colony, while the remaining members stayed in Athens.[117] For example, Plato's father had been an oikist on Aegina, but Plato's residence and land were in Athens and the northern plain.[118] Nicias's associate Dionysius, while founding Thurii, left his son behind in Athens (see below, p. 198).

[112] Davies, introduction to *APF*, xxi–xxii. On the burden of the trierarchical service, see M. Christ, "Liturgy Avoidance and *Antidosis* in Classical Athens," *TAPA* 120 (1990): 148 ff., for the most recent discussion.

[113] Gabrielsen, "*Antidosis*," 31–32,

[114] Sinclair, *Democracy*, 59; on the increasing use of mercenaries: Gallant, *Risk*, 135–36; P. McKechnie, *Outsiders in the Greek Cities in the Fourth Century* B.C. (London: Routledge, 1989), 79–100; D. Whitehead, "Who Equipped Mercenary Troops in Classical Greece?" *Historia* 40 (1991): 105–13, for a recent defense of the traditional theory that mercenaries did, however, provide their own weapons.

[115] Davies, *APF*, 85.

[116] See also ibid., 509–10.

[117] Gallant, *Risk*, 136. For the close association of the colonial settlement with war, see F. Adcock and D. J. Mosley, *Diplomacy in Ancient Greece* (London: Thames and Hudson, 1975), 128–30; and most recently, T. J. Figueira, *Athens and Aigina in the Age of Imperial Colonization* (Baltimore: Johns Hopkins University Press, 1991), 172 ff., who argues for the static or passive defense of colonists. I leave to others the question of the differences in meaning among the terms *apoikia, epoikia* and *kleroukhia*. For a list of colonies in the fourth century, see ibid., 241 ff.; M. H. Hansen, "Demographic Reflections on the Number of Athenian Citizens 451–309 B.C.," *AJAH* 7 (1982): 182. Hansen conjectures that cleruchs may well have had to return to Athens to enrol their sons in their deme. On the precarious existence of cleruchies in wartime, see P. Gauthier, "A propos des clérouquies athéniennes du Vᵉ siècle," in Finley, *Problèmes*, 167.

[118] Davies, *APF*, 331, 334; Figueira, *Athens and Aigina*, 57–59. If the tradition that Plato was cap-

Moreover, the politically powerful and the affluent were often ambassadors to foreign parts.[119] Themistocles is the earliest example in the fifth century: he traveled extensively throughout the Aegean collecting tribute, and probably enriching himself thereby (Plut. *Them.* 21.1 ff.).[120] He along with Aristeides and Cimon, who were the foremost speakers in the debates in the early fifth century concerning Sparta, were sent there in 478. This tendency to send out as ambassador to a foreign state individuals who were trusted by that state or were prominent in debates concerning it is evidenced throughout the classical era.[121] Thrasybulus son of Thrason, Aristophanes and Carcinus among others combined trierarchic and strategic activity with their roles as ambassadors.[122] At other times, for instance, in the case of Callias II and his descendants, embassies were performed by several generations of a family,[123] even to the point that Hipponicus II's *nothos*, Hermogenes, was ambassador to Tiribazus in 392—an assignment that suggests that Hermogenes had acquired citizenship.[124] Callias's affine, Cimon, the famous *stratēgos* and ambassador to Sparta, had a son who was a *stratēgos* in the fifth century; in the late fourth century, Cimon IV was ambassador to Philip at least once in 346; and Cimon's son, Miltiades VII, was oikist in the Adriatic in 324.[125] Andocides the orator could boast that he and his grandfather had both been ambassadors to Sparta (And. 3.6 ff.). Demosthenes the orator was criticized by his enemies for rarely living in the *astu* or in the Peiraeus because his role as ambassador to Macedonia, the Peloponnese, and Thebes, as well as his commercial ventures, required long periods of travel (Hyp. *Dem.* 17; Aeschin. 3.209).[126]

Though the activities of the politically prominent may well give us some idea of their mobility in war or in efforts to avoid war, we must turn to the less politically elite to see the effects of war on the family. One has only to read Aristophanes' play *Lysistrata*, despite its comic exaggeration, to realize the disastrous effects of continuous warfare on family unity. The separation of men from their families was nowhere more dramatically displayed than in the burial of the war dead in the *dēmosion sēma:* fallen soldiers, recognized for their bravery, were buried in common graves apart from their parents, wives, and children (Thuc.

---

tured by pirates and almost sold into slavery on Aegina is reliable, then Plato's family seems not to have won many friends there. For the tradition of Plato's capture: McKechnie, *Outsiders*, 119.

[119] Adcock and Mosley, *Diplomacy*, 157–58.

[120] See also Davies, *APF*, 215.

[121] Adcock and Mosley, *Diplomacy*, 156–60.

[122] Davies, *APF*, 201–2 (Aristophanes); 239 (Thrasybulus); 283 (Carcinus).

[123] Adcock and Mosley, *Diplomacy*, 156–57.

[124] Davies, *APF*, 258 ff.; 269 for Hermogenes.

[125] For Cimon's son Lacedaemonius as *stratēgos*, see Davies, *APF*, 305–6; 309 for Cimon IV and Miltiades VII.

[126] Demosthenes in Dem. 18.10 seems to be defending himself against these charges. For Demosthenes' embassies, see Adcock and Mosley, *Diplomacy*, 156. For the frequent trips of the ambassador to and fro, see Y. Garlan, *War in the Ancient World*, trans. J. Lloyd (New York: Norton, 1975), 45.

2.34.6–8; Lys. 2.80–81).[127] In the fourth century, exactly when is uncertain, the *ephēbeia* was established: youths at eighteen were plucked from their *oikoi* and required to train for frontier guard duty. These young men lived on the Attic frontiers and were for the most part barred from testifying in court.[128]

Lysias 20 tells a poignant story of a wartime family. A father and his two eldest sons fought in the Peloponnesian War; the father was sent to Eretria, one son went to Sicily and the other to the Hellespont, while the youngest son remained behind in Athens (14, 24–25, 28–29; cf. Lys. 26.21–22). After the Sicilian catastrophe at the end of the fifth century, Athenians were said to have been either made prisoners of war or enslaved in Sicily; many of these are said to have been later freed and to have returned to Athens, but some stayed behind out of respect for their former masters (Thuc. 7.86.1; Plut. *Nic.* 29.1 ff.). In Demosthenes 57 the speaker explains that during the Decelean War his father was on military service, and was captured and sold as a slave in Leucas. In fact, he was absent from home so long that his wife had to hire herself out as a wet nurse—one of many women, the speaker informs us, who had to seek employment outside of their houses while their men were at war. Nevertheless, the speaker's father was lucky enough to have trustworthy uncles who kept his landed property intact until his return (18–19, 29–30, 41 ff.).[129] Even in less extreme circumstances, both military leader and common soldier might establish a temporary residence in a country within the war zone (Dem. 18.215–16; 50.32).

What effect did the individual's distance from Athens have on his property rights and membership in his *oikos* or that of a close family member? Isaeus 6.13 ff. states that Pistoxenus, an Athenian cleruch on Lemnos, left his daughter under the care of Euctemon in Athens during the Sicilian expedition. Some time afterward Pistoxenus died on military service, and the daughter married Euctemon and had two sons by him. These sons, however, had a great deal of trouble inheriting from Euctemon because of the jealousy of their half-brother, Philoctemon. In Isaeus 9.1 ff. the speaker states that he had every right to be adopted into the *oikos* of his matrilineal half-brother Astyphilus, but that while he was on military service, Astyphilus's agnatic kinsmen seized the estate. Hag-

---

[127] N. Loraux, *The Invention of Athens: The Funeral Oration in the Classical City,* trans. A. Sheridan (Cambridge, Mass.: Harvard University Press, 1986), 24; P. Vaughn, "The Identification and Retrieval of the Hoplite Battle-Dead," in Hanson, *Hoplites,* 42.

[128] Garlan, *War,* 175–76, on the marginality of the ephebe; for the archaic origins of the *ephēbeia,* see P. Vidal-Naquet, "The Black Hunter and the Origin of the Athenian *Ephebia,*" in *The Black Hunter: Forms of Thought and Forms of Society in the Greek World,* trans. A. Szegedy-Maszak (Baltimore: Johns Hopkins, 1986), 106–28. J. Ober, *Fortress Attica, Mnemosyne,* suppl. 84 (Leiden: Brill, 1985), 90 ff., argues for a date early in the fourth century for the establishment of the *ephēbeia;* see the bibliography ad loc. for the debate concerning the date.

[129] On the prisoner of war, see Y. Garlan, *Slavery in Ancient Greece,* trans. J. Lloyd (Ithaca, N.Y.: Cornell University Press, 1988), 47–48 and n. 35 for bibliography, to which add McKechnie, *Outsiders,* 118–21. For the woman as *kyria* of a household, see V. Hunter, *Policing Athens: Social Control in the Attic Lawsuits, 420–320 B.C.* (Princeton, N.J.: Princeton University Press, 1994), 15 ff.

nias II's embassy in the early fourth century led to his death; despite his detailed will, his estate was fought over for generations and finally devolved on a Bouselid not mentioned as an heir in his will (see above, p. 8). In Isaeus 10.20 the speaker is arguing, probably incorrectly, for his mother's right as an heiress to inherit her father's estate, no doubt with the hope of his subsequent adoption into it. In any case, his military service in the Corinthian War prevented him for some years from taking his case to court. In [Dem.] 40.36–37 Mantitheus the son of Mantias, while on military service with his father under Ameinias, spent some time collecting money from the *proxenos* and other Athenian allies at Mytilene for his mercenaries. His rival and half-brother, Boeotus, claimed that some of this money was really payment for one of Mantias's loans to leading Mytilineans. Boeotus was, therefore, claiming his share of this money as part of his father's estate. Mantitheus countered with a statement that would have been difficult for Boeotus to disprove, given the distance of the transaction from Athens, that Boeotus in fact confused two payments, one given for the mercenaries and one (presumably smaller) given to Mantias at the same time. The implication here seems to be that Mantias had already consumed this wealth.

In Pseudo-Demosthenes 48.24 ff. Olympiodorus, while on military service in Acarnania, lost all his effects to relatives who plundered his estate in Athens in the hope of receiving back wealth that had been adjudicated to Olympiodorus after the death of a kinsman. In Isaeus 4, in which the estate of a certain Nicostratus is at issue, the testator was a mercenary outside of Athens for a period of eleven years (8). On his death, his estate consisting of two talents cash (ibid.) was fought over by many contestants, the number increased by Nicostratus's long absence (21–22) and the resulting vague recollection of who he was and who his relatives were. In fact, his absence allowed two of the claimants to his estate to charge that he had been their freedman (7 ff.), and therefore as his former masters they were claiming his estate. Two of the contestants, whom the speaker represents, argue that precisely because they had remained in Athens all those years, they had a better claim to the wealth than their opponent, Chariades, the alleged adoptee of Nicostratus, a fellow mercenary and business associate in Asia. Chariades, furthermore, was a self-exile, which threatened his claim to the estate of an Athenian (ibid., 28–29).[130] Despite their hostility, the two claimants of the speech, however, must admit that they can neither prove nor disprove transactions that allegedly took place between Nicostratus and Chariades in Asia (ibid., 1).

In Hyperides' defence of Lycophron, it is stated that the defendant was serving as hipparch on Lemnos when his kinsmen informed him by letters that he was being charged by the relatives of the nameless testator in the oration with having had an affair with the man's wife before his death. The charges were meant to challenge the legitimacy of the widow's child left in the testator's estate. The

---

[130] See, McKechnie, *Outsiders,* 16, for this oration and suspicions cast on anyone who frequently traveled outside Athens.

relatives further charged that Lycophron encouraged the widow to continue the affair while her brother Dioxippus the wrestler was in Olympia and on the point of contracting a second marriage for her (Hyp. *Lyc.* 1.4b.3, 17–18; 2. fr. 13). Likewise one can only conjecture what wrangling there must have been when Xenocles, who had reportedly died as trierarch at Chios, and whose cash estate had been divided among his relatives, turned up alive and well, and returned to Athens (Is. frr. 15–16).[131]

One of the most famous lawsuits in the Demosthenic corpus resulted from the plaintiff's distance from Athens while serving on trierarchies. While Apollodorus, the son of Pasio the banker, was escorting ambassadors to Sicily and transporting grain in and around Sicily c. 368, his widowed mother Archippe married Pasio's ex-slave assistant, Phormio, who, Apollodorus contended, threatened Apollodorus's inheritance ([Dem.]45.3–4, 46.20–21). One may well suspect that Apollodorus feared as well the encroachment of his mother's children by Phormio on the estate's wealth. While away on a syntrierarchy in the northern Aegean c. 362–360, Apollodorus received news of his mother's illness, and of his estate and family in general, through letters from relatives. Apollodorus explicitly declares that while he was abroad he had no control over her assignment of her property to her children by Phormio. Apollodorus admits that he did not inherit from his mother as much as he wanted at a time when his land was suffering from his absence (Dem. 50.59–62).[132]

On the loftier political level, around 416, the famous Alcibiades was able to embezzle five or eight talents from his friend Teisias's estate. Alcibiades was given the money to purchase horses with which to win a victory for Teisias at Olympia, but while Teisias was away at the siege of Melos, however, Alcibiades claimed the horses, and the victory, as his own.[133]

More conjecturally, Thompson has suggested that the will in Isaeus 5 leaving Dicaeogenes II's full estate to his adopted son and thereby challenging the terms of an arrangement which left only a third of the estate to the son, might have come to light sooner, and by implication have prevented squabbling between Dicaeogenes II's sisters and their adoptive nephew, if the man who was executor of the will had not been abroad in the Ionian War.[134] In addition, Davies suggests that Menestheus, the son of Iphicrates by a Thracian wife, may have been forced by his father's enemies, while his father was in Amphipolis, to assume liturgies unusually early in life to offset charges of *xenias*.[135]

---

[131] Xenocles had initially handed his estate over to Eumathes, a metic, for safekeeping. V. Gabrielsen, "ΦΑΝΕΡΑ and ΑΦΑΝΗΣ ΟΥΣΙΑ in Classical Athens," *ClMed* 37 (1986): 103, is correct in noting that Eumathes was honest enough to hand over the estate to Xenocles' kinsmen and friends. My question here is how easily did Xenocles recover this dispersed wealth?

[132] On the date of the syntrierarchy, see Davies, *APF,* 440. For the younger sons and Archippe's bequest, see ibid., 435; Hunter, "Athenian Widow," 302.

[133] Davies, *APF,* 501–3.

[134] Thompson, "Wills," 18, n. 22.

[135] Davies, *APF,* 249–50.

There were other ways, too, in which *oikos* and *oikia* were vulnerable to the effects of war. At the time of the battle of Plataea, when the Persians threatened to invade Attica, the Athenians intended to send their women and children to reside for some time in Sparta, which had offered them refuge.[136] Likewise, Hyperides drafted a decree evacuating the women and children to the Peiraeus after Chaeronea (Lyc. 1.16; [Plut.] *Mor.* 848f–849a). It is unclear, however, whether any of these plans were implemented by the state, although wealthy individuals could take it upon themselves to send their families abroad in time of danger (Lys. 16.4, Lyc. 1.53). Furthermore, when the foundations of the democratic *polis* were being threatened during the *stasis* in the last decade of the fifth century, Athenian men sent to reinforce the Peiraeus left their wives and children behind in Attica: some of these women and children were taken into the households of relatives, severely straining their kinsmen's resources and considerably changing the composition of their kinsmen's *oikiai* (Xen. *Mem.* 2.7.2 ff.). Furthermore, the physical *oikia* could itself be destroyed: when the Spartans invaded Attica during the Peloponnesian War, Athenians were said to have taken the timbers of their houses away with them (Thuc. 2.4.1),[137] while the Boeotians disassembled Attic country houses during the Decelean War (*Hell. Oxy.*17.3 [McKechnie and Kern]).[138]

The sources, therefore, are unequivocal: war could have a destabilizing effect certainly on the *oikoi* of the propertied families, but also on the *oikoi* of many nameless and less influential Athenians. Closely associated with war was exile, which also demands a closer study in terms of its threat to family and *oikos* unity.

ABSENCE FROM THE *OIKOS:* EXILE AND OTHER CAUSES

Even a brief reading of the lives of famous Athenians can make one ponder about the nature of these men's *oikoi;* not only did their political successes compel them to be away from Athens, but so also did political disgrace. This study cannot begin to do justice to the lengthy controversies over any one political or military leader, let alone all of them. In his article on the treatment of the politically prominent by the Athenian *dēmos,* Ronald Knox has conveniently tabulated and cited the major primary sources that refer to many of the politically prominent individuals who were fined, ostracized, exiled, or otherwise threatened with execution.[139] In his survey, Knox has estimated that in the classical era approximately twenty men were exiled (including six known to have been ostracized in the fifth

---

[136] Plut. *Arist.* 10.2–3.

[137] Gallant, *Risk,* 92.

[138] Ober, *Fortress Attica,* 58, n. 18; see also 55 for a discussion of evacuations from the countryside.

[139] R. Knox, "'So Mischievous a Beaste'? The Athenian *Demos* and its Treatment of its Politicians," *GaR* 32 (1985): 134–61.

century). In the cases of exile, those involved either left Athens to escape prosecution, a heavy fine, or execution, or exile was an actual penalty imposed.[140] The fact that so many prominent individuals were threatened by the polis was not lost on the ancients themselves: Theopompus and Nepos the biographer, for instance, commented that because of Athenian jealousies and mistrust, prominent leaders spent a good deal of time away from Athens (Theopompus, *FGrHist* 115 F 105; Nep. *Chabrias* 3.3–4),[141] while Demosthenes states that the exile resides in a secure place in which he has committed no wrong (23.38 ff.). How did this absence affect the nuclear family?

To answer this question, the type of exile will not be important, but rather the response of kinsmen and family to that exile. In his *Crito,* Plato has Socrates state that if he, Socrates, were to go into exile, the only two possibilities left for his family—and here he is referring to his children—would be to go into exile with him or to remain separated from him in Athens and be cared for by his friends (Pl. *Crito* 54a). Other sources also reveal the trauma caused by exile. When Themistocles' ostracism resulted in his permanent exile (Thuc. 1.137.3 ff.; Plut. *Them.* 25.3 ff.; Nep. *Them.* 8.3 ff.),[142] his wife and family remained in Athens until Epicrates spirited them out of the city to join the famous politician; Epicrates was summarily executed for his action (Plut. *Them.* 24.6). Consequently, Themistocles' children settled temporarily in Asia and then returned to Athens after 459.[143] So, too, the famous Alcibiades, in the first stages of the Sicilian War, although he defused the threat of ostracism in 416, eventually fled to Asia to escape prosecution for profanation of the Eleusinian Mysteries. He was condemned to death and his property in Athens confiscated;[144] nevertheless he seems to have left his daughter and son in Athens (Isoc. 16.45–46), but later called his son to him in the Chersonese (Lys. 14.26 ff.).

At the end of the fifth century Gylon of Cerameis, permanently exiled because of treason, married, it seems, a non-Athenian from the Milesian colony of Cepi, but sent his two daughters back to Athens to marry Demosthenes the orator's father and Demochares of Leuconoeum.[145] Because of the distance be-

---

[140] Knox's table (ibid., 141–42), however, does not list all the victims he discusses in his narrative, nor is the latter complete; Knox does not mention Nicophemus and his son, for instance (see Davies, *APF,* 201–2). Other men, who were not politically active, nevertheless went into self-exile out of disapproval of one or other aspect of Athenian life; Plato, Aeschylus, and Euripides are among the most famous (*PA,* 11855, 442, 5953 respectively). See also M. H. Hansen, *Eisangelia* (Odense: Odense University Press, 1975), 35–36, for examples of men who fled to escape execution or whose death sentence was commuted to exile.

[141] See also, Knox, "Mischievous," 137; Casson, "Upper Class," 33–34, n. 12; E. M. Harris, "Iphicrates at the Court of Cotys," *AJP* 110 (1989): 264, 270.

[142] The bibliography on ostracism is extensive. For the ostracized victim's required distance from Athens, see T. J. Figueira, "Residential Restrictions on the Athenian Ostracized," *GRBS* 28 (1987): 281–305.

[143] Davies, *APF,* 218.

[144] Ellis, *Alcibiades,* 58 ff., for a recent summary of these events.

[145] Davies, *APF,* 121, 141–42.

tween the locale of Gylon's marriage and Athens, Demosthenes the orator had a difficult time disproving the charges that his mother's mother was a Scythian. (The line of Gylon's wife would be very difficult to trace.)[146] A similar difficulty seems to have been faced by the speaker in an oratorical fragment whose father, for commercial reasons this time, was resident as well in the Propontis region and married the daughter of one Antiphanes, whose citizenship was in doubt (*P. Oxy.* 2538 and commentary).

Nicophemus, exiled in Cyprus, had a non-Athenian wife and a daughter by her, while his son from a first marriage, Aristophanes, resided in Athens, married a woman from a prominent and wealthy Athenian family, but visited his father from time to time.[147] Conon was also exiled in Cyprus, married a non-Athenian, and sired a son; his elder son from a first marriage, the famous general Timotheus, resided in Athens and on Conon's death, converted the cash bequeathed to him by his father into real property.[148] The exiled Callistratus of Aphidna left his children behind in Athens, his son was active in Athenian affairs and his daughter was married to Timomachus of Acharnae, who visited Callistratus while the latter was in exile (Dem. 50.48 ff.). Timomachus was in turn exiled c. 360 (Aeschin. 1.56; Dem. 19.180, 36.53). While Callistratus was in Methone, furthermore, he resided near his exiled affine Callimedon living in Beroia.[149] Androtion and Aristogeiton endured the exile of their fathers who lived apart from their families.[150] Polyeuctus of Cydantidae visited his mother's second husband in exile in Megara, and the Greek implies that the woman was not with her husband (Dein. 1.58). When Demades the orator and his son left Athens, they were both killed in Macedonia, but Demades did leave another son behind in Athens (Plut. *Dem.* 31.4).[151] In other cases, whole families went into exile together.[152]

The exile or expatriate relied heavily on relatives and friends to safeguard his property in Athens, often turning over the ownership of the *oikos* and its property to the trusted associate. For instance, the purchasers of confiscated property in the *pōlētai* records of the Thirty and their adherents were frequently fellow demesmen or neighbors of the victims.[153] The earliest case of material aid given

---

[146] V. Hunter, "Gossip and the Politics of Reputation in Classical Athens," *Phoenix* 44 (1990): 318.

[147] Davies, *APF,* 201–2.

[148] Ibid., 508–10.

[149] Ibid., 279–80.

[150] Androtion's father was a public debtor (Dem. 22.34); Aristogeiton's father was condemned to death and fled (Dein. 2.8,18). For Aristogeiton and the obscure circumstances of his father's condemnation and exile, see R. Sealey, *Essays in Greek Politics* (New York: Manyland, 1967), 186–87.

[151] See also Davies, *APF,* 101–2.

[152] For example, Aeschines' parents: ibid., 544, and Aeschin. 2.148. See also Isoc. 4.168; Lys. 12.97; Diod. Sic. 18.8.4–7.

[153] M. B. Walbank, "The Confiscation and Sale by the Poletai in 402/1 B.C. of the Property of the Thirty Tyrants," *Hesperia* 51 (1982): 74–98; Osborne, *Demos,* 51–54; for the *pōlētai* records, see now *IG*³ 417–32.

by friends is that of Themistocles, in which his associates spirited his wealth to him in Asia, although about eighty or one hundred talents were confiscated (Thuc. 1.137.2; Plut. *Them.* 25.3). Alcibiades, after his first return from exile, was given his property back by vote of the people (Plut. *Alc* 33.3). Although the logistics of such restoration are far from clear, Lysias (fr. 1 [Th]) claims that property not sold off at the time of the victim's return to Athens would be given back to him. Otherwise, the possibility that some of the confiscated property was in the hands of friends and kinsmen would have facilitated its restoration. After Alcibiades' death in Asia, however, his son returned to Athens but was prevented by his father's enemies from receiving back the confiscated property restored to Alcibiades in 407.[154] After the execution of Aristophanes and his father Nicophemus, his wife's brother was accused of hiding from the state some of the precious metal that had been in Aristophanes' house, an accusation that the brother-in-law hotly denied (Lys. 19.27–28).[155]

Ergocles, one of the democrats in exile at Phyle during the rule of the Thirty, depended on his friend Philocrates to manage his property (Lys. 28.12–13; 29.1 ff.). Callimachus and Xenotimus kept money belonging to an exile in Peiraeus, and Callimachus himself, while in self-exile before the establishment of the Thirty, concealed his property (Isoc. 18.5–6, 48). Other sources reveal how such concealment was possible. When a certain Nicias was threatened by the Thirty, he hypothecated his house, sent his slaves outside of Attica, moved his furniture to the speaker's house, gave his fortune of three talents to his cousin Euthynus, and then retired to the country (Isoc. 21.2–3). Nicias was at the mercy of his associate however. When Nicias returned to the city and demanded his full three talents from Euthynus, he received only two (ibid., 2–3).[156] Other sources attest to the prosecution of individuals who cheated others of their claims to property that had been confiscated (Is. fr. 12 [Th]; *P. Oxy.* 3.415). Still others appear to have suffered permanent loss. Aeschines' father lost his property during the Peloponnesian War and under the Thirty retreated to Corinth with his wife. When he returned under the democratic restoration, he started life anew as a mercenary outside Athens and as a teacher within the city.[157]

---

[154] Davies, *APF,* 21. I must conjecture at this point that although the purchase of confiscated property by a fellow demesman could be a friendly takeover, the possibility of a local vendetta cannot be dismissed in one case. It might not have been purely coincidental that the one man who speedily returned to Athens after the disaster at Notium to denounce Alcibiades was Thrasybulus son of Thrason, whose sister may have married into the deme of Erchia around this time. This was the deme in which the elder Alcibiades owned three hundred plethra of land: Davies, *APF,* 20, for Alcibiades' estate; ibid., 239, for the conjectured marriage of Thrasybulus' sister.

[155] The speaker in the same oration (50–51) also argues that if the general Diotimus, whose estate had been overvalued, had died outside of Athens, his relatives would have been hard pressed to come up with an amount equal to the estimated value of the general's estate.

[156] Millett, *Lending,* 209.

[157] Davies, *APF,* 544. For the political events under the Thirty and on the refugees, see P. Krentz, *The Thirty at Athens* (Ithaca, N.Y.: Cornell University Press, 1982), and esp. 69 ff.

In the fourth century, if Davies is correct in his interpretation, Philon may have suffered exile, while his sons certainly did. Callipus and his brother Philostratus, sons of Philon of Aexone, resided with Dion the tyrant in Sicily to escape prosecution for their association with Callistratus. Their brother Philocrates, on the other hand, seems to have remained in Athens and kept the family property in the deme of origin, Aexone.[158] Leocrates had his sisters' husbands buy up his property during his self-exile in Megara, having fled Athens to escape military service in the campaign of Chaeronea. When Leocrates returned to Athens he recovered ownership of his original property.[159]

At the more private level of property disputes, Aphobus, Demosthenes' irresponsible guardian, depended on his brother-in-law and brother to take over and own his property outright to save it from being confiscated by Demosthenes. Aphobus then fled Athens to escape further prosecution.[160]

Besides war and exile, there were less traumatic reasons for being away from Athens and one's household; nevertheless, here as well one's claim to membership and wealth could be challenged, if not obstructed. In Isaeus 7.27–28, although the speaker had been adopted *inter vivos* into the estate of his mother's brother, and therefore resided with the uncle, the adoptee had not been offically enrolled in his uncle Apollodorus's deme. Unfortunately, Apollodorus died while the speaker was absent from Athens in order to celebrate the Pythia at Delphi, and the speaker's enrollment in his absence faced strong opposition from Apollodorus's agnates.[161] Likewise, Archiades chose a moment while his brother Meidylides was away from Athens as the time to adopt a son, thereby splitting up the brothers' joint estate. Archiades' share was transmitted to his adopted son and his descendants for two generations.[162] A similar situation is evidenced in Isaeus 9.4–5: the speaker, returning to Athens from abroad, found that an agnate of his matrilineal half-brother, Astyphilus, had claimed the estate as Astyphilus' adopted son. In Demosthenes 48, the speaker attempted to keep his half-brother from inheriting a share of a kinsman's estate while the half-brother was away from Athens (10).

Even distance from one's *oikos* while one was in Attica could affect an individual's influence in his or her *oikos* or claim on property from that *oikos*. In Isaeus 6 Euctemon's first wife and his daughters by her, who do not live with him, unsuccessfully attempt to lay claim to some furniture in one of his houses upon his death; one of his agnates, in complicity with his two (minor) sons who had been

---

[158] Davies, *APF*, 274–76, and above, chapter 2, pp. 45–46.

[159] See above, chapter 4; Millett, *Lending*, 138–39, states that the transactions between the sisters' husbands were formal because of the attenuated relationship between the two men. Closer kinsmen tended to contract less formally.

[160] See above, chapter 4, pp. 123–24. In Lysias 17 the speaker's father can prosecute only one of three brothers, who was in Athens; the other two were abroad (3–4).

[161] Wyse, *Isaeus*, 570–72.

[162] Davies, *APF*, 195, and above, chapter 4, pp. 110–11. See also the cryptic reference in Aeschin. 3.252 to a private man being condemned to death in his absence while he was sailing to Samos.

living with him, had secretly carried the furniture over to a neighbor's house before the women's arrival, and later sold it (40–43).

CONCLUSIONS

This chapter began by questioning Xenophon's unswerving equation of the *oikos* with the nuclear family. Although scholars have from time to time acknowledged that this strict equation is not appropriate to the complexities of *oikos* composition, they have nevertheless made the equation the foundation of discussions of the use and ownership of property, its transmission, and even of the relationship between *polis* and *oikos*. Recently some scholars have argued for a focus on the use of property rather than ownership to understand more fully the complexity of relationships within an *oikos*. With this focus as our starting point, we have explored how the nature of wealth and income affected the composition of an *oikos* and even the number of residences, as well as the complexities of the domestic life cycle, which frequently were responses to the high mortality rate. Guardianship could fuse two estates because of the shared residence of guardian and ward. Fusion could also be encouraged by adoption, but there was a further complexity here because of the very nature of adoption in classical Athens: often the adoptee was not adopted during the testator's lifetime. The adoptee therefore could face opposition from a kinsman of the testator, who in turn could win control of the estate temporarily only to find himself ousted by another opponent. Remarriage could further weaken *oikos* boundaries, resulting at times in the peaceful sharing of two estates by half-siblings and affines. At other times, however, the weakening of boundaries could precipitate disputes that lasted for generations.

Aggravating this ambiguity of the *oikos* was the tendency of and necessity for Athenian males to be away from Athens. War and exile forced the Athenian male to leave his *oikos* under the control and management of women, or of a trusted kinsman or friend.

The *oikos* therefore was certainly not a static unit and sometimes was not a stable one. Laws in themselves could not guarantee stability nor did they guarantee the rights of kinsmen to property. Given, therefore, the many facets of a family's life cycle and the frequent absence of an individual from his *oikos,* this domestic "unit"—and here English fails to translate the Greek adequately—was quite fluid. The implications of this fluidity are far-reaching, for if the *oikos* was the basis of the *polis,* and if the *oikos* often defied legal definitions or customary ideals,[163] then the interrelationship between *oikos* and *polis* was much more com-

---

[163] Wallace argues that the Athenians punished those who were thought to have harmed the *polis* and generally left private citizens alone: R. Wallace, "Private Lives and Public Enemies: Freedom of Thought in Classical Athens," in *Athenian Identity and Civic Ideology* ed. A. Boegehold and A. Scafuro (Baltimore: Johns Hopkins University Press, 1994), 146. Only when an individual's citizenship was

plex than the ancient sources would have us believe. Moreover, we have so far dealt mainly with the kinsman. The discussion of absence from the *oikos,* however, gave us from time to time a glimpse of another type of person who had an important role in the *oikos,* without even belonging to it: the friend. It is to the friend and the nonkinsman or nonkinswoman that we now turn, in order to reveal yet a further complexity in the dynamics of the *oikos.*

---

questioned by a rival did the *polis* step in to ensure that the proper safeguards of citizenship were in place: see A. Scafuro "Witnessing and False Witnessing: Proving Citizenship and Kin Identity in Fourth-Century Athens," ibid., 170.

CHAPTER 6

The Nonkinsman, the *Oikos,*
and the Household

THE FUSION and fission resulting from marriage, adoption and guardianship made the membership and the confines of the *oikos* much more complex than hitherto realized. However, kinship did not always lie at the heart of all households. Some households were defined rather by shared tasks of production and/or consumption, which often were not relegated to just one residence, so that several residences could constitute one household. In these instances the nonkinsman or nonkinswoman, whether a citizen or noncitizen, could be a member in an individual's *oikia,* and no matter how temporary such a person's residence there, he or she could have a permanent effect on that individual's *oikos* and property. On the other hand, for the citizen and his kinsmen household membership could at times be merely symbolic or illusory, that is, the citizen, or his family members, could be away from the household and not actively participate in household activities.[1] In such cases, mere sentiment would be the only criterion for an individual's membership in an *oikos.* The following discussion will focus on active membership in a citizen household, and hence on three types of nonkinsmen who affected the nature of the household and thereby undermined the Attic legal definition of the citizen *oikos:* the *hetaira,* the slave, and the friend or neighbor.

THE NATURE AND USE OF PROPERTY

The heading here may seem redundant, since the previous chapter discussed the types of wealth in individuals' *oikoi* and how the nature of wealth or property could affect the nature and composition of *oikia* membership. For the sake of that discussion and its focus on the complexity of life within the *oikos* and away from it, however, it was assumed that the value of an individual's estate was a fixed and completely known and identifiable quantity; and this was, very often not the case. In his discussion on secured property E. M. Harris has argued that the claim to ownership of such property was a matter of convenience for debtor and creditor; that is, if it suited the debtor to continue claiming ownership on a

---

[1] See A. Carter, "Household Histories," in *Households: Comparative and Historical Studies of the Domestic Group* ed. R. McC. Netting, R. R. Wilk, and E. Arnould (Berkeley: University of California Press, 1984), 45.

piece of property which he had hypothecated he did so, but his creditor could also claim ownership. The ownership of secured property, argues Harris, remained in a "legal limbo" with the parties involved being guided by self-interest.[2]

In a series of articles on the use and nature of property, Vincent Gabrielsen has studied further the "grey area" of ownership. Gabrielsen has argued that there was no *polis*-wide mechanism for estimating or recording the wealth of individuals—that such estimates were left up to the individual himself, and that therefore his estate was valued upon what he chose to declare, his *phanera ousia;* there were, however, possessions that he often chose not to declare, *aphanēs ousia.* Significantly, any type of property could be *aphanēs,* undeclared or unacknowledged. Although money and movables were much more easily concealed than realty, even the latter could be concealed if it was not rented out or if it was converted to cash. The insidious ramification to this was that *aphanēs ousia* could be entrusted to someone else—a holder who was not the owner, but who could nevertheless argue that the wealth was his because proof to the contrary, particularly as regards cash, was very difficult to offer.[3] Note has already been made of the exile's dependence on the good faith of kinsmen and friends to protect his wealth.

Nowhere are the fluid boundaries of *oikoi* more apparent than in the procedure for compulsory exchange of property known as *antidosis.* Certainly this procedure brings into new perspective any notions of the Athenian's absolute attachment to his *oikos.* In *antidosis* an individual who felt unfairly burdened by state services or liturgies would find someone with a larger estate who was willing to exchange property—or more often challenge him to do so by legal action—so that the encumbered man could finance his state service from his new estate. In this way, the burdened individual would then fulfill his obligation to the state by assuming control of another person's property.[4] Although actual *antidosis* seems to have occurred rarely—the challenged individual usually just assumed the liturgy instead of handing over his property—[5] in theory the exchange involved all property, including dotal items brought into the *oikos* (Dem. 42.5 ff.; 27). Furthermore, men of wealth did expect to be embroiled in challenges on a fairly regular basis.[6] The procedure depended upon the burdened man's ability to find a replacement who was willing to undergo the exchange.

[2] E. M. Harris, "When is a Sale not a Sale? The Riddle of Athenian Terminology for Real Security Revisited," *CQ* 38 (1988): 351–81, esp. 366–70; see also P. Millett, *Lending and Borrowing in Ancient Athens* (Cambridge: Cambridge University Press, 1991), 224.

[3] V. Gabrielsen, "ΦΑΝΕΡΑ and ΑΦΑΝΗΣ ΟΥΣΙΑ in Classical Athens," *ClMed* 32 (1986): 99–114.

[4] D. M. MacDowell, *The Law in Classical Athens* (Ithaca, N.Y.: Cornell University Press, 1978), 162–63.

[5] Dem. 21.78–79, 154; 28.17; Isocr. 15.4–5; [Plut.] *Mor.* 837 f.; Davies, *APF,* 247 (Isocrates), 385 (Thrasylochus's challenge of Demosthenes).

[6] M. Christ, "Liturgy Avoidance and *Antidosis* in Classical Athens," *TAPA* 120 (1990): 163 and n. 78 for a full list of ancient references.

The absolute cooperation which was fundamental to the exchange is never seen in our sources—the challenged individual could be brought to court and forced into the exchange, if the challenger was successful in convincing the jury that the exchange was justified. At no time, however, did the challenger or challengee necessarily have precise or complete information on his rival's wealth—estimates were based on declared property, *phanera ousia*.[7] To be stressed here is the extent to which property, its ownership, its use, and its nature, vacillate. As Gabrielsen cogently states: "To the extent that individuals other than the owner himself were granted the right of disposition of the property, we are justified to assert that the question of ownership had already transcended the boundaries of its unambiguous juridical definition and moved into a 'grey' area. And we may go so far as to define ownership subjected to such restrictions as *conditional* or even *limited*."[8]

Conditional or limited use could well define the interest of the nonkinsman or nonkinswoman in property. To what extent, then, did he or she aggravate the indefinite and ambiguous quality of property and ownership?

THE *HETAIRA* AND THE CONCUBINE

The following pages will use the term *hetaira* to mean both "prostitute," its strict sense, and also "concubine" (strictly *pallakē*), unless the facts of a particular case require the distinction to be made: as Wolff argued in his classic study on marriage law, *hetairai* were generally the sort of women who became *pallakai*.[9] Furthermore, my interest here is not so much in how "permanent" these relationships between men and women were,[10] for after all there were times when marriages were not terribly permanent either, but on how these women were able to encroach on the *oikos* despite the laws of the *polis* limiting such en-

[7] V. Gabrielsen, "The *Antidosis* Procedure in Classical Athens," *ClMed* 38 (1987): 7–38; "ΦΑΝ-ΕΡΑ," 100–101.

[8] Gabrielsen, "*Antidosis*," 19.

[9] H. J. Wolff, "Marriage Law and Family Organization in Ancient Athens," *Traditio* 2 (1944): 73–74; W. Wyse, *The Speeches of Isaeus* (Cambridge: Cambridge University Press, 1904; New York: Arno, 1979), 318.

[10] Wolff, "Marriage Law," 73–74, insists that *pallakia* was a permanent situation, while Sealey maintains that the relationship was even contractual: R. Sealey, "On Lawful Concubinage in Athens," *ClAnt* 3 (1984): 116. C. Patterson, "Response to Claude Mossé," *Symposion* (1990): 281–87, argues that most *pallakai* were slaves. It is quite clear, from the instances discussed further below, that *pallakai* were often shared by men, as were *hetairai*. This is paralleled in other societies, where concubinage was not terribly permanent and the women were shared: P. Ebrey, "Concubines in Sung China," *Journal of Family History* 11 (1986): 7–8. Ebrey argues that the young woman's training for her role was not unlike that of the courtesan. In fact, concubines were called upon by their lovers to entertain guests. D. Herlihy, "Households in Early Middle Ages: Symmetry and Sainthood," in Netting, Wilk and Arnould, *Households,* 392–93, where it is argued that both men and women were sexually active inside and outside of marriage.

croachment. Nor will I define closely the various types of bastardy in Athens. Cynthia Patterson has recently argued, for instance, that *nothos* was a quasi-juridical term defining an illegitimate child whose paternity was acknowledged by his father.[11] The focus of the following discussion will be on the legal marginality of all offspring born outside of a formal union, or marriage, that is, the giving of the bride by *engyē*.

From early on in its democracy Athens framed its laws on both the *hetaira* and the concubine to emphasize male domination and inheritance through the male line. Prostitution was institutionalized by the state fairly early in the sixth century to service the needs of citizen males. By keeping citizen women separated from citizen men and therefore keeping women in the private sphere, it was seen as fundamental to the ideal of democracy.[12] One might argue that institutionalized prostitution was a means of social control. J. Rossiaud in his work on legalized prostitution in the Middle Ages has pointed out that the late age of marriage for men and early age of marriage for women resulted in bands of youths wandering the streets of villages and cities displaying sexual aggression and frequently raping women, usually from the least affluent levels of society. Prostitution therefore tempered such aggression.[13] Although Rossiaud's thesis has been criticized by medievalists who point rather to the decline in the female population after the Black Death as a cause of institutionalized prostitution,[14] it is not without validity for Athenian society. Athenian daughters ideally were kept indoors and discouraged from venturing too far from the house;[15] therefore, these future brides were inaccessible to Athenian youths. Instead, these youths had access to the female *hetaira* or the male lover (sometimes also a prostitute).[16]

Very much as in medieval society, the Athenian sources refer from time to time to bands of youths, *hetairiai* and the like, and although these "clubs" are seen more often in the assembly and lawcourts, there were street gangs of male youths de-

---

[11] C. Patterson, "Those Athenian Bastards," *ClAnt* 9 (1990): 54–65.

[12] D. M. Halperin, *One Hundred Years of Homosexuality* (London: Routledge, 1990), 100–101; E. Keuls, *The Reign of the Phallus: Sexual Politics in Ancient Athens,* 2d ed. (Berkeley: University of California Press, 1993), 206.

[13] J. Rossiaud, *Medieval Prostitution,* trans. L. G. Cochrane (Oxford: Blackwell, 1988), 15 ff., 48.

[14] L. Otis, *Prostitution in Medieval Society: The History of an Urban Institution in Languedoc* (Chicago: University of Chicago Press, 1987), 100–105.

[15] S. Cole, "Greek Sanctions against Sexual Assault," *CP* 79 (1984): 97; D. Cohen, "Sexuality, Violence, and the Athenian Law of *Hubris,*" *GaR* 38 (1991): 183, and *Law, Violence and Community in Classical Athens* (Cambridge: Cambridge University Press, 1995), 15, who points out that the young Athenian male was not afforded the same protection from sexual aggression. In an earlier article Cohen, however, has questioned the strict rigidity of female seclusion: "Seclusion, Separation, and the Status of Women in Classical Athens," *GaR* 36 (1989): 3–15; and "The Social Context of Adultery in Athens," in *Nomos: Essays in Athenian Law, Politics and Society,* ed. P. Cartledge, P. Millett, and S. Todd (Cambridge: Cambridge University Press, 1990), 147–65. See also *Law, Sexuality, and Society* (Cambridge: Cambridge University Press, 1991), 149–54. Though women were not necessarily secluded, they were protected and separated from men, as Cohen himself admits.

[16] For the male lover see the discussion below.

voted to irreligious acts and to pursuing and fighting over *hetairai*. At times such gangs were distinguished by a name, sometimes obscene, but membership may well have been fluid and seems not to have been displayed by any type of insignia or "colors," to use modern American parlance.[17] In any case, prostitution certainly diverted their aggression away from citizen women.

To return to the legal position, the law distinguished the concubine kept for the purpose of having free children from slave concubines, whose children would also have been considered slaves.[18] By the classical era, however, in terms of property inheritance, the distinction between the two types of concubines was confused. All *nothoi* recognized by their fathers or bastards of other types of slave or free noncitizen mothers were restricted from inheriting; neither the bastard nor his mother legally belonged to the father's *oikos*.[19] The father was not legally responsible for the actions of the *nothos* (Dem. 54.26), even though the *nothos* was given a *notheia* from his father's estate. The sum, either five hundred or one thousand drachmae, was a fraction of a wealthy man's estate.[20] The *nothos* was legally entitled to nothing more and could rely only on gifts from his kinsmen to alleviate the very real poverty he could face.[21]

There has been considerable debate as to whether the *nothos* from an informal union between two Athenians would be considered an Athenian citizen. Patterson, in her recent article on *nothoi,* has extensively outlined the debate that began with Buermann's thesis that there was legal concubinage in ancient Athens in which the offspring of such a union would also be a *gnēsios*. This thesis was then modified to suggest that given the nature of citizenship laws, only the offspring of two Athenians from an informal union could be citizens and, therefore, inherit.[22] However, I would argue that a fragment of Metagenes the comic poet at the very least reveals what Athenians thought of such children: in the fragment (fr. 14 [Kassel-Austin]) the *nothos* of Callias, that is, the son of Callias born from Chrysilla in an irregular union, according to gossip, was equated with a *xenos,* a Mysian.[23] Although *nothoi* were legitimized at the end of the

---

[17] The classic oration on street activity is Demosthenes 54. For brief commentaries on this oration, see G. Calhoun, *Athenian Clubs in Politics and Litigation* (Reprint ed., New York: Burt Franklin, 1970), 31–36; J. Ober, *Mass and Elite in Democratic Athens* (Princeton, N.J.: Princeton University Press, 1989), 257–58. For street activity see also Millett, *Lending,* 150. On brawls over *hetairai,* see Lys. 3.43; 4, passim; and perhaps Dem. 47.18–19. For a *hetaira* who was protected by a thesmothete during an assault, see Dem. 21.36.

[18] D. M. MacDowell *The Law in Classical Athens* (Ithaca, N.Y.: Cornell University Press, 1978), pp. 89–90.

[19] Dem. 59, passim and especially 122; Is. 3, passim; A. R. W. Harrison, *The Law of Athens,* vol. 1 (Oxford: Clarendon Press, 1968), 15; S. C. Humphreys, "The Nothoi of Kynosarges," *JHS* 94 (1974): 89, n. 5.

[20] Ar. *Av.* 1655 and schol.; Harp. s.v. notheia; Suda, *epiklēros*.

[21] Humphreys, "Nothoi," 93.

[22] Patterson, "Bastards," 41 ff.

[23] C. A. Cox, "Incest, Inheritance, and the Political Forum in Fifth-Century Athens," *CJ* 85 (1989): 43; Patterson, "Bastards," 69, n. 81.

Peloponnesian War, from that time onward throughout the fourth century there were increasingly harsher laws regarding marriages between citizens and noncitizens, which by implication excluded illegitimate children of all types from the *oikos*.[24]

Added to these legal restrictions on the concubine and *hetaira* was the fact that these women were generally foreigners, or if citizens, were from lower strata in society (Athen. 13.583e; Xen. *Oec.* 3.11.1 ff.; Is. 3.8 ff., 37, 39; Dem. 39, 40) There were differences among *hetairai;*[25] some could become the concubine of a single man or of several men, but could be threatened at any time with dismissal from the man's *oikos*.[26] In Antiphon 1, Philoneus threatened his *pallakē* with dismissal and wanted to put her into a brothel (14–15).[27] In Pseudo-Demosthenes 25.56–57 Aristogeiton turned out of his house his *pallakē*, Zobia, a metic, and according to the speaker, dragged her off to the *pōlētai;* Zobia was saved from being sold into slavery because she could prove she had paid the *metoikion*, the metic tax.[28]

Hetairai could also be specially trained as entertainers, such as flute players, and as such they were regular fixtures at symposia. Vase paintings reveal how these women were passed around among the male guests, activities substantiated by

[24] For the legitimization, see schol. Aeschin. 1.39; *PA*, 10967–68 for Nicomenes; Is. 6.47, 8.43; [Dem.] 43.51, 57.30. For the fourth century, see [Dem.] 59.16, 62 f.; and see Patterson, "Bastards," 62 for the most recent discussion. The legitimization may be the basis of the late tradition that a so-called "bigamy decree" was promulgated in Athens which allowed a man to have legitimate children by his wife and another woman (Athen. 13.555d–556b; Suda s.v. *leipandrein*). Scholars have interpreted this statement in various ways. Some argue that the decree allowed full bigamy: J. P. Vernant, "Le mariage en Grèce antique," *PP* 28 (1973): 55, 62, with qualifications, however, and R. D. Cromey, "Sokrates' Myrto," *GB* 9 (1980): 62; while others have argued that the law allowed the citizen woman to become a concubine to a citizen man already married: for instance, MacDowell, *Law*, 89–90; C. Patterson, *Pericles' Citizenship Law of 451–0* (New York: Arno, 1981), 142–43. Still others feel that the decree allowed for legitimization of all bastards: S. Pomeroy, *Goddesses, Whores, Wives, and Slaves* (New York: Schocken, 1975), 66–67; W. E. Thompson, *De Hagniae Hereditate: An Athenian Inheritance Case, Mnemosyne,* suppl. 44 (Leiden: Brill, 1976), 90–91. On the alleged bigamy of Socrates and Euripides see the skepticism of L. Woodbury, "Socrates and Aristides' Daughter," *Phoenix* 27 (1973): 7–25, and further bibliography, 24–25.

[25] The poverty and foreign status of prostitutes in the medieval ages have been noted in Otis, *Prostitution,* 64–65; for the various types of prostitution in medieval society, see Rossiaud, *Medieval Prostitution,* 5–7.

[26] The classic examples here are Menander's *Samia* and Antiphon 1.

[27] There has been some debate as to the status of this woman. E. W. Bushala challenged the traditional opinion that she was a slave: "The *pallake* of Philoneus," *AJP* 90 (1969): 65–72, pointing out that although the woman was tortured after the alleged homicide, free noncitizens could also be tortured in such cases. However, as C. Carey correctly notes ("A Note on Torture in Athenian Homicide Cases," *Historia* 37 [1988]: 244), Bushala nowhere considers the case of Lysias 4 in which the slave *pallakē* is freed by her master and therefore cannot be tortured in a case of assault. Carey further argues that free noncitizens had legal recourses and could summon citizen help, although he could have strengthened his argument by citing [Dem.] 25, to be discussed directly below.

[28] On the punishment of slavery for metics who failed to pay the *metoikion*, see MacDowell, *Law*, 76–77, 256.

the orations ([Dem.] 59.33 ff.; Is. 3.13–17).[29] Some *hetairai* could be the intellectual equals of the men with whom they associated, but the great majority were simply *pornai,* prostitutes relegated to brothels, many of which were located in the Peiraeus or the Cerameicus.

One such brothel has been excavated in the Cerameicus close to the Sacred Gate; in fact, one scholar suggests that this might be one of Euctemon's brothels known to us from Isaeus 6. The use of physical space here is noteworthy: the building known as "Bau Z" in the reports dates to a little before the mid-fifth century B.C. and appears originally to have been a lodging house or "hotel." This original building was destroyed and another built on a similar floor plan with the *hetairai* introduced toward the end of the fifth century. The floor plan, it should be noted, was not unlike that of the typical Athenian house: several rooms around a central courtyard.[30]

The slave *hetaira* was at times a war captive;[31] others could be foreigners, either free or freed. For example, the most famous concubine, Aspasia, came from Miletus, Neaera was a freedwoman from Corinth, and Phryne a freedwoman from Thespiae.[32] Some of these foreign *hetairai* were transients, traveling frequently from festival to festival to ply their trade and staying at an Athenian's house as a guest ([Dem.] 59.23–24); or they might accompany Athenian soldiers on campaigns.[33] Other *hetairai* remained permanently in Athens, plying their trade in a brothel which would have to be a house or building owned by an Athenian, as metics could not own real property (Isaeus 6.19 ff.).[34]

Most Athenian *hetairai* lived much the same kind of life. That the *hetaira* was originally from a poor background is a stock theme in Attic comedy: in a frag-

---

[29] On the various types of prostitutes and for the concubine, see Halperin, *One Hundred Years,* 109–12, who also discusses the indistinct line between *pallakē* and *hetaira.*

[30] For a recent discussion of *hetairai* and the brothel found in the Cerameicus, see C. Reinsberg, *Ehe, Hetärentum und Knabenliebe im antiken Griechenland* (Munich: Beck, 1989), 82–89 (the various types of *hetairai*); 140–42 (the brothel in the Cerameicus). Reinsberg's emphasis is on how these women were represented in the vases (91 ff.). For the possible identification of "Bau Z" with one of Euctemon's brothels, see H. Lind, "Ein Hetärenhaus am Heiligen Tor?" *MusHelv* 45 (1988): 158–69. For comparison's sake, a similar stratification can be seen in medieval society where the majority of prostitutes were poor, but some were rich and even owned real property, and traveled in the highest circles serving as confidantes to both the wealthy and powerful: Rossiaud, *Medieval Prostitution,* 31; Otis, *Prostitution,* 65. Rossiaud (5–7) also states that one kind of brothel was a building with a courtyard, bedrooms, and kitchens.

[31] Dem. 19.309; Dein. 1.23; Athen. 13.588c for Lais from Hyccara; for Alcibiades' slave concubine from Melos, see [And.] 4.22; Plut. *Alc.* 16.5; for other examples of slaves used for sexual purposes, see Lys. 1.12, 4.12 ff.

[32] On Neaera: [Dem.] 59.23 ff.; on Aspasia: Plut. *Per.* 24.2; schol. Plat. *Menex.* 235e; Suda s.v. *Aspasia, dēmopoiētos;* Athen. 12. 533 c–d erroneously states that Aspasia was from Megara; for Phryne, see Athen. 13.590 f., 591c; [Plut.] *Mor.* 849e.

[33] Y. Garlan, *War in the Ancient World,* trans. J. Lloyd (New York: Norton, 1975), 135 for Pericles and the Samian campaign. See also Athen. 12.532c for Chares the general who brought a group of *hetairai* with him on his campaigns.

[34] See also K. Schneider, "Hetairai," *RE* 8.2:1340.

ment of Antiphanes an Athenian *hetaira* living in the house of an Athenian man was poor and at times without guardian or kinsman (Athen. 13.572a).[35] The Athenian *hetaira* Euphrosyne was apparently a fuller's daughter (Athen. 13.583e). Although the tradition is late, the association of Euphrosyne with wool and the certain archaeolgical evidence of the Cerameicus brothel linking *hetairai* with wool spinning suggests that it may have a kernel of truth.[36] The *hetaira* Theodote, made famous by her appearance in Xenophon's *Oeconomicus,* although living luxuriously, owned neither land nor shop and admitted to being totally dependent on payments from her lovers.[37] This impression of poverty and low status is reinforced by the biases in the orations. In Isaeus 3, where the speaker wishes to portray Phile's mother as a *hetaira* and a mere concubine to Phile's father Pyrrhus, the speaker states that the woman's brother gave her to men as a prostitute and did not provide her with a dowry when she entered Pyrrhus's house. Furthermore, the citizenship status of her family of origin was not above suspicion (Is. 3.8 ff., 37, 39). In the popular mind a *hetaira* could be a citizen though her low status was underscored by calling that citizenship into question. The oration further states that when men are giving their kinswomen in concubinage they see to it that the women receive benefits from their lovers (ibid., 37) In Demosthenes 39 and 40 the link between poverty and concubinage is explicit.[38] Although Plango was married to Mantias, and her father was a prestigious general, Mantias divorced Plango and then entered into a liaison with her only after it was clear that she had lost any chance of receiving a dowry from her father's financially encumbered estate ([Dem.] 40.22).[39]

Both the low status of the *hetaira* and her constant exposure to the public eye were manifested by the social custom of nicknaming her.[40] Frequently these names were given to the *hetairai* by others, as the use of the aorist passive ἐκλήθη, "she was called or named," suggests Such names were coined most of the time to describe either a physical attribute, an activity commonly associated with the woman, or more rarely, the type of prostitute she was. For instance, one woman was called "Louse Gate" (Phtheiropule) because she picked lice off her-

---

[35] See also J. Rudhardt, "La reconnaissance de la paternité, sa nature et sa portée dans la société athénienne," *MusHelv* 19 (1962): 44.

[36] Reinsberg, *Ehe,* 142, for the evidence of wool spinning.

[37] 3.11.1 ff.; Theodote's citizenship status is implied by Socrates' questions as to whether she owned property, the right of the citizen only. Athen. 12.535c gives her citizenship as Athenian.

[38] R. Sealey, *Women and Law in Classical Greece* (Chapel Hill: University of North Carolina Press, 1990), 31–32; Patterson, "Bastards," 60, n. 80, argues that the giving of poor women as concubines was not a common practice. I would add that [Dem.] 59.112–13 would indicate that there was certainly strong disapproval of such a practice, and in fact, many poor women were given dowries by the state (probably at the expense of a wealthy private individual), for which see Dem. 45.54, Millett, *Lending,* 62–63.

[39] See also Davies, *APF,* 365.

[40] Otis, *Prostitution,* 63, states that prostitutes in medieval Languedoc were often called by nicknames, often referring to a physical abnormality.

self while standing at her door (Athen. 13.586a). Some women were called "Anchovy" because of their light skin color (586b), while Oia was nicknamed "Hellebore" (Anticyra) for her participation in wild men's drinking parties or because of her association with a physician (586f). Nannion was nicknamed "Proscenium" because she looked better with her clothes on than off (587b). Metiche was known as Clepsydra, or "Water Clock," because she timed her sessions with customers by that device (567c). Phryne was called Sieve because she was said to have sifted and stripped her clients so thoroughly (591c). One aging *hetaira* in her youth was known as Sinope, a prosperous town, but in her later years was named Abydus, a town in a state of decay (585f–586a); another was referred to as Tethe, "Grandmother" (Athen. 13.587b–c).[41] Yet other *hetairai* were given animal names: Callistion was called "Sow" (583a), an obvious reference to the female genitalia;[42] her mother was Corone ("Crow") (583a, e) and another woman was "She-goat" (Aix) (582e–f, 587b). Likewise, the original name of the famous Phryne ("Toad") was Mnesarete (591e–f).[43] Whatever humor there is in such names, the narrator in Athenaeus, the chief source for them, explicitly states that they were associated with *hetairai*, with immoral women (587c–d).

Pseudo-Demosthenes 59 bears out this association of the nickname with the woman of immoral reputation. In the oration, Stephanus had apparently tried to argue that a young woman whom he had given in marriage to an Athenian was not Neaera's daughter but his own by a citizen wife (119). In his refutation of that argument, Apollodorus, the speaker, stresses the point that not only was the young woman Neaera's daughter, and therefore foreign and illegitimate, but her original name was Strybele, which had been changed to Phano "brightness" (50, 121)—contemporaneously with Stephanus's and Neaera's alleged attempts both to sell the younger woman's services and to marry her off to respectable Athenians. In fact, this line of argument seems to have been used against Phryne in her prosecution for impiety by Aristogeiton—it was in this connection that Aristogeiton mentioned that her name had been changed from Mnesarete (Athen. 13.591 f.). In only one other case do we know of a man who changed his *hetaira*'s name: the lover of the Athenian *hetaira* Melitta called her instead Mania (Athen. 13.578b–d). This aspect of name changing is significant: Athenians were reluctant even to mention the name of a citizen woman in public, nor is there any evidence to suggest that a citizen woman's original name could be

---

[41] The Greek is unclear as to whether the name was given because she was a prostitute for three generations or because she inherited her practice from two former generations.

[42] For the most recent discussion of the use of the word "pig" for the female genitalia: M. Golden, "Male Chauvinists and Pigs," *EMC* 32 (1988): 1–12, who argues that the word connotes both hostility toward and fear of female sexuality.

[43] A. Raubitschek, "Phryne," *RE* 20.1:894–95. *Hetairai* and the politicians with whom they associated were also referred to by names of fish (for instance, Athen. 8.338e ff., 359a ff.). This has been discussed by Craig Cooper, "Hyperides and the Case of the Tainted Tuna: Fishy Politics in Athens" (paper presented at the annual meeting of the Classical Association of Canada, Ottawa, Ontario, May 1993). The names of fish could also be given to known pederasts (Athen. 8.342d).

changed by anyone in her family of marriage: Demosthenes explicitly states that children do not have the right to give themselves a name—only the parents have the right to give one and to renounce it (39.39). In Isaeus 3 the speaker makes a great deal of the fact that the name of Pyrrhus's daughter, allegedly by a *hetaira,* was given as Phile by her husband but as Cleitarete by Pyrrhus's maternal uncles; the implication here is that if a woman's name changed, her status was suspect and her claim to an inheritance was to be viewed as fraudulent (Is. 3.30–31).[44]

The restrictions on the *hetaira* and the concubine in classical Athens are in keeping with the practices of other European, Asian, and African societies. In traditional Sung China, although among the imperial families the concubine could enjoy high status as second consort, this was not necessarily the case in less exalted families. Here the concubine's relationship with her lover was not permanent: she could be shared with or passed on to another man or men.[45] In European societies concubinage was associated with the practice of monogamy and with high sociopolitical status of the lover in a hierarchical society. Concubines in both European and African societies were often taken from the poorest people and those discriminated against on ethnic grounds.[46] In Anglo-Saxon soci-

---

[44] Wyse, *Isaeus,* 310, misses the point when he states that such name changing was not incredible, and to prove this he cites the case of Neaera's daughter—the daughter of a *hetaira*—the only type of person with whom such name changing occurred! For Athenian reluctance to mention the name of a respectable woman in public, see R. Just, *Women in Athenian Law and Life* (London: Routledge, 1989), 27–28, with bibliography. Given this bias, therefore, the force of Demosthenes' slur against Aeschines' mother, who had been nicknamed Empousa, can now be appreciated (18.130). Demosthenes used the nickname in the course of asserting that she participated in some mystery cult and that she came from low origins. Plut. *Per.* 24.7; *Artax.* 3.5; Athen. 13.576d; Ael. *VH* 12.1 for Cyrus's renaming of his concubine Milto as Aspasia. The reliability of the tradition is unknown: W. Judeich, "Aspasia," *RE* 3.2:1721–22.

[45] P. Ebrey, "Concubines in Sung China," *Journal of Family History* 11 (1986): 1–24 and esp. 15–18 on renaming. Ebrey also suggests that the concubine saved money for a dowry with a view to a future marriage, although it was likely that a woman once given as a concubine would be given again to other men as a concubine, and not as a wife. In South China concubinage and sexual slavery existed until the 1920s. The *mooi-jai,* young girls sold to a go-between for the purposes of concubinage and prostitution, were always from poverty-stricken families. Although the concubine, as a favorite of the household head, could enjoy a good deal of influence in the household, she was constantly the target of the family members' jealousy and gossip, and her child remained an outsider: M. Jaschok, *Concubines and Bondservants* (London: Zed Books, 1988).

[46] M. C. Ross, "Concubinage in Anglo-Saxon England," *PastPres* 108 (1985): 3–34; Flandrin, *Parenté,* 177; D. Herlihy, "Households in the Early Middle Ages," in Netting, Wilk, and Arnould, *Households,* 393; P. E. Lovejoy, "Concubinage and the Status of Women Slaves in Early Colonial Northern Nigeria," *Journal of African History* 29 (1988): 245–66, points out that concubines in the Caliphate were always slaves used for the sexual enjoyment of the masters of wealthy families. The female slaves usually came from non-Muslim ethnic groups. Lovejoy conjectures that most female slaves were concubines at one point in their lives. In medieval Ghent, on the other hand, although concubines could be aristocratic women as well as farm and domestic servants, neither the women nor their children enjoyed legal rights equivalent to those of the wife and legitimate children: D. Nicholas, *The Domestic Life of a Medieval City: Women, Children, and the Family in Fourteenth-Century Ghent* (Lincoln: University of Nebraska Press, 1985), 67–68, 154–55.

ety, much like in ancient Athens, but unlike many other societies in which illegitimate children suffered few legal disadvantages, the sexual services of the concubine were not rewarded by a defined legal status and by rights automatically devolving upon her and her children.[47] In Viking society, as well, free concubinage was closely associated with slavery, and neither the free nor the slave concubine were respected. Children of concubines inherited only if their fathers permitted it.[48]

Despite the severe legal restrictions on the *hetaira* and her children in ancient Athens, these women and their children were a threat to the *oikos* for several reasons. First, the *hetaira* could have a *kyrios* who contracted a liaison for her and made sure either that some property went with her or that she would be well treated while she lived with her partner (Is. 3.39; Lys. fr. 82 [Th]; [Dem.] 59.38 ff.).[49] On dissolution of the relationship the property could be returned to the concubine ([Dem.] 59.45–46) in much the same way that a dowry was returned to the wife's family of origin on the termination of her marriage.

Secondly, though marriage defined the rights of children and their membership in a certain *oikos,* in classical Athens the very nature of marriage itself could be quite vague or even illusory at times.[50] Robin Osborne in his work on the Attic deme has touched upon this vagueness:

> The tension between the formation of marriage links as a a matter of kinship and the role of the new household as part of the local community is brought out by the equivocation about what marriage actually is. In lawcourt speeches the stress is sometimes laid on the legal connection formed at marriage through the ritual of *enguē*. This ritual was a distinctly *family act*. . . . it is the act of giving away by the father . . . which creates the legal bond. At other times the emphasis in the orators is rather different: it is the *public recognition* by the local community of the offspring as legitimate that makes a marriage.[51]

There were no marriage certificates in classical Athens. Marriage was based upon betrothal, *engyē,* an oral contract in which the household head, father or brother in most cases, handed the woman over to the groom, usually in front of

[47] Ross, "Concubinage," 6; Ross notes (14, n. 36) that "the Athenian situation seems remarkably like the Anglo-Saxon in many respects." In the other societies referred to in the note above, illegitimate children suffered few, if any, legal repercussions in terms of inheritance.

[48] R. M. Karras, "Concubinage and Slavery in the Viking Age," *Scandinavian Studies* 62 (1990): 141–62.

[49] Stephanus as Neaera's *prostatēs* protected her against recriminations from former lovers; for the pact between Stephanus and Phrynion whereby both men share Neaera, see [Dem.] 59.45 ff.

[50] Wolff, "Marriage Law," 75: "At any rate . . . the boundary between respectable and disrespectable associations was fluid." See also D. Konstan, "Between Courtesan and Wife: Menander's *Perikeiromene,*" *Phoenix* 41 (1987): 127–28, who states that Polemon's relationship with his concubine, Glycera, is viewed as marriage.

[51] *Demos: The Discovery of Classical Attika* (Cambridge: Cambridge University Press, 1985), 137–38 (my emphasis).

witnesses. This ritual was then followed by consummation which constituted the actual marriage (see above, pp. 92–93).

Certainly the tension between the private act of marriage and public recognition is evident in political slander. The earliest instance of such slander in the political forum was Pericles' insult to Cimon's sons, calling them the sons of a woman of Arcadian Cleitor. The insult was twofold: there were both the ethnic "Cleitor," which referred to the female genitalia, and also the allegation that Cimon's sons were born of a non-Athenian mother and were therefore of mixed parentage. In fact, Cimon's sons were probably born of an Athenian woman who was a distant relative of Pericles himself.[52] Aeschines' insults to Demosthenes' parentage were means to undermine Demosthenes' power; so too were Demosthenes' innuendos concerning the behavior of Aeschines' mother.[53] The speaker in Demosthenes 57 had to defend and prove the Athenian citizenship of both his parents which his enemies disputed.[54] Demosthenes, again, slandered his enemy Meidias by accusing him of being a supposititious child (21.149–50),[55] while Aristogeiton's matrilineal half-sister was accused of being of foreign citizenship (25.55).

In many of these cases the slander was ineffective: the targeted individual often continued to be active in the political sphere. A look at the orations concerning private disputes, however, will reveal how the nature of the marriage act made slander not only possible, but also in some cases so effective that the formality of a union and the legitimacy of the children from that union are still being debated by scholars today.[56] The importance of the testimony of living relatives is evidenced in Isaeus 6, where the claimant, Philoctemon's adopted son Chaerestratus, attempts to prove the illegitimacy of Philoctemon's half-brothers by declaring that no kinsman knew of the marriage of Philoctemon's father to Philoctemon's stepmother (10–11, 14–15). In fact, the speaker claims that Philoctemon's half-brothers were uncertain of the identity of their mother (ibid., 12–13), an indication not so much of the informality of the union but perhaps of the early death of the mother.[57]

[52] Davies, *APF,* 304–5, and bibliography in appendix.

[53] On this point, see for instance, G. Kennedy, *The Art of Persuasion in Greece* (Princeton, N.J.: Princeton University Press, 1963), 229 ff.; P. Harding, "Rhetoric and Politics in Fourth-Century Athens," *Phoenix* 41 (1987): 25–39; Cox, "Incest," 37; V. Hunter, "Gossip and the Politics of Reputation in Classical Athens," *Phoenix* 44 (1990): 318.

[54] W. K. Lacey, "The Family of Euxitheus (Demosthenes LVII)," *CQ* 30 (1980): 57–61, suggests that the speaker's father had been taken prisoner during the Decelean War, had been prisoner more than fifteen years, and hence had acquired a non-Athenian accent; the accent was the target of attack by the speaker's opponent, Euboulides.

[55] For Demosthenes' tendency to lie in this and other orations, see E. M. Harris, "Demosthenes' speech against Meidias," *HSCP* 92 (1989): 12–24.

[56] On gossip stemming from the private nature of marriage, see R. Garner, *Law and Society in Classical Athens* (New York: St. Martin's Press, 1987), 85; Hunter, "Gossip," 316–21.

[57] Davies, *APF,* 563.

In Pseudo-Demosthenes 43, although the speaker assembles a host of kinsmen to declare that Phylomache I was the full sister of the Bouselid Polemon, his witnesses' testimony depended on hearsay for the most part, on the statements made by their parents and grandparents (35–37, 42–46). Phylomache's legitimacy or paternity was suspect enough for the court to award the estate of Polemon's son, Hagnias II, to Theopompus, whose legitimacy and Bouselid descent through the male line could not be seriously challenged.[58]

Even when witnesses were alive they could simply be called liars. In Isaeus 3, although Pyrrhus's maternal uncles witnessed his marriage to Nicodemus's sister and the tenth-day ceremony following Phile's birth, their testimony was challenged by Pyrrhus's nephew (sister's son) who was intent on inheriting Pyrrhus's estate (13–14, 26–34, 63 ff.). The speaker further emphasized that Nicodemus's sister did not bring a dowry with her when she entered Pyrrhus's house, and that her daughter Phile had been given away in marriage by Pyrrhus's adopted son as the daughter of a *hetaira,* the proof being that he gave her a small dowry of one thousand drachmae (ibid., 44–53).

All these instances have one element in common, that the alleged bastard lived in the same residence as the members of the legitimate family, although not necessarily contemporaneously. Shared residence could, therefore, confound the definition of marriage and rights to kinship. The living arrangements in the elder Demosthenes' household, outlined 5 above (p. 147), demonstrated how Aphobus and Cleoboule shared the testator's residence without being formally married. Aphobus's own marriage to Onetor's sister also underlines the dichotomy between private and public. The machinations of Aphobus and his brother-in-law Onetor are well known. When Onetor initiated a divorce between his sister and her first husband Timocrates, Timocrates did not hand over the woman's dowry to Aphobus, the woman's second husband. Rather, Aphobus secured his house and land as collateral for the nonexistent dowry. When Demosthenes won his lawsuit against Aphobus and claimed his property, Onetor, Aphobus's brother-in-law, immediately declared that his sister was now divorced from Aphobus and seized the hypothecated farm and house (Dem. 30.7–8, 15, 17–18). More to the point, although Onetor's sister publicly declared her intention to divorce before the archon, Demosthenes emphasizes that the woman's public act was insincere: both Aphobus and the woman continued to cohabit as husband and wife (the verb συνοικέω is used here) (ibid., 25 ff., 31.10 ff.). Given the Athenian emphasis on proper female behavior, a woman's continued cohabitation with a man from whom she had publicly declared herself divorced might have injured her reputation. An enemy of either Onetor or Aphobus could easily confuse the chronology of the public divorce, the cohabitation, and the birth of Aphobus's daughter by Onetor's sister (Dem. 29.52).[59] The chronological

---

[58] For this latter point, see Thompson, *De Hagniae Hereditate,* 106–7. For further discussion of the dispute, see above, chapter 1, pp. 6–8.

[59] This daughter is not mentioned by Davies, *APF,* 119–20, 423.

confusion could lead to the questioning of the daughter's legitimacy, though whether this slandering ever occurred is unknown.

Other sources attest to the difficulty of determining when concubinage ended and marriage began between a man and a woman who shared an *oikia*. The case of Mantias and Plango in Demosthenes 39 and 40 is again instructive. According to the speaker, Mantias refused to acknowledge his paternity of Plango's sons, and only through a ruse did she force him to enrol the sons in his phratry (39.3–4; 40.2–3, 10–11). Furthermore, the speaker insisted that Plango brought no dowry, to which his opponent asserted that the speaker's mother brought no dowry ([Dem.] 40.14–15, 20–24). Such charges were easily made because in neither of Mantias's two marriages was there a written contract accompanying the dowry: this was typical of Athenian practice.[60] Plango did indeed marry Mantias and bore their elder son, Boeotus. When Plango's dowry was not forthcoming, however, Mantias divorced her in order to avoid footing the bill for her father's financial ruin, and married the speaker's, Mantitheus's, mother. During this time Mantias continued his relationship with Plango, perhaps maintaining her in a second residence, and after the death of his second wife, sired his youngest son, Boeotus's full brother, Pamphilus. Mantias acknowledged both sons as legitimate (Dem. 39.4; 40.8–12, 27–28).[61] The deliberate confusion of the chronology in the two orations, and the deliberate obfuscation of the details surrounding Mantias's first union with Plango and the vagueness of his second union with her, only underscore the very private nature of marriage.[62] It is uncertain whether the second union simply presumed the formality of the first, or whether there was a second act of *engyē* deliberately left unmentioned by the speaker.[63] Nevertheless, by enrolling his sons in his phratry, Mantias allowed both of them to inherit his estate, and Pamphilus's son certainly was politically active in the early third century.[64]

Andocides' account of Callias's marital career contains similar elements, rejection of the woman only to have her return to the man's *oikos* and a final (forced) acceptance of the son she bears.[65] According to Andocides, Callias was married to the daughter of Ischomachus but also lived with her mother, Ischomachus's widow Chrysilla. The daughter ran away from the situation and some time after Callias dismissed Chrysilla. When informed that Chrysilla was

---

[60] Finley, *SLC,* 21.

[61] The speaker at first denied that his father had continued his relationship with Plango: Dem. 39.26. For a reconstruction of the events in the orations, see Rudhardt, "La reconnaissance," particularly 46 ff.

[62] Rudhardt terms this second union "quasi-conjugal," and Davies, following him, describes it as an "expensive liaison": Rudhardt, "La reconnaissance," 48; Davies, *APF,* 367. Humphreys, "Family Quarrels," *JHS* 109 (1989): 183, n. 4, conjectures that Plango may never have lived under Mantias's roof.

[63] Rudhardt, "La reconnaissance," 49–50.

[64] Davies, *APF,* 367.

[65] Cox, "Incest," 42, n. 27; Patterson, "Bastards," 60–61.

pregnant and had given birth, Callias disowned the son, but after the woman's kinsmen intervened, Callias received Chrysilla back into his *oikos* and entered his son into his *genos,* the Ceryces, thereby formalizing his union with Chrysilla (1.124–27).[66] Given the private nature of marriage and the fact that the remarriage of a widow still in her childbearing years was often a very hasty transaction, the ease with which Andocides was able to confuse informality with formality is not surprising.[67] This ability to confuse was founded, furthermore, on the composition of Callias's *oikos:* both his unions, or on the most skeptical view of Andocides, both of Callias's marriages, seem to have taken place within one house, Callias's own.[68]

The Greek language did little to clarify the definition of marriage; in fact Aristotle declared that there was no term for the union of man and woman (*Pol.* 1253b9).[69] Verbs such as χράομαι and πλησιάζω were commonly associated with a man's relationship with a *hetaira* or even a male prostitute.[70] The term *engyē,* on the other hand, was always associated with the act of betrothal, signifying in turn a formal marriage. Several verbs, however, could be used to define either marriage or a less formal union, and an orator could take advantage of the double-meaning in such words. The most common ambiguous verbs are ἔχω, to have, συνοικέω, to live with, and λαμβάνω, to take. A few choice examples will suffice. Isaeus seems to be quite exact in the use of the three verbs in his orations on Pyrrhus and Euctemon: the three verbs connote marriage or the intention to marry.[71] So, too, in the case of Plango and Mantias: the speaker uses the verbs συνοικέω and ἔχω to define Mantias's second marriage, but the verb πλησιάζω to describe Mantias's relationship with Plango.[72] On the other hand, the verb ἔχω describes Plango's influence on Mantias (40.51). More revealing, in Andocides' attack on Callias III, which resulted from Callias's attempts to charge Andocides with profanation, Andocides uses all three verbs to confuse the nature of Callias's relationships with Ischomachus's daughter and widow, Chrysilla. Andocides states that Callias married (γαμεῖ) Ischomachus's daughter but after living with her (συνοικήσας) for less than a year, took (ἔλαβε) her

---

[66] Davies, *APF,* 268 for a skeptical discussion of Andocides.

[67] On the remarriage of the young widow, see V. Hunter, "The Athenian Widow and Her Kin," *Journal of Family History* 14 (1989): 296–98; also Cox, "Incest," 43–45.

[68] Hunter, "Athenian Widow," 307–8, n. 11.

[69] On this point, see Patterson, "Marriage and the Married Woman in Athenian Law," in *Women's History and Ancient History,* ed. S. Pomeroy (Chapel Hill: University of North Carolina Press, 1991), 49.

[70] For the use of χράομαι, see, for instance, Is. 3.10; Dem. 24.197, 25.56; Aeschin. 1.68. For πλησιάζω, see Is. 3.10 and below, note 72.

[71] See W. A. Goligher and S. W. Maguiness, *Index to the Speeches of Isaeus* (Cambridge: Heffer, 1961), under each verb; on the meaning of *synoikeō:* M. Golden, *Children and Childhood in Classical Athens* (Baltimore: Johns Hopkins University Press, 1990), 142 and the discussion in Just, *Women,* 43–44, 62–63, for bibliography. Just feels, however, that the term was fairly specific by the fourth century, meaning "to live with a wedded wife." See also Patterson, "Marriage," 58–59.

[72] συνοικέω: Dem. 40.7; εἶχε: 40.8; πλησιάζω: 40.8, 27.

mother and then lived with (συνῴκει) both women, he took (εἶχε) both women in the same house (οἰκία).[73] Although Andocides in the same oration uses the verb ἔχω (106) to describe the marriage of his ancestors, the verb here defines Callias's less than proper living arrangements. To confuse the issue even more, both λαμβάνω and συνοικέω in a later section (128) describe Callias's alleged unions with three women, Ischomachus's widow, daughter, and granddaughter. In this passage there is the implication of bigamy, but finally Andocides concedes that all alliances or intended alliances would have been *gamai.*

Other orators play on the ambiguity of the word ἔχω. In the corpus of orations ascribed to Lysias, on the one hand the word is used to describe the younger Alcibiades' maintenance of a *hetaira* before he reached his majority (Lys. 14.25), but on the other it can also refer to actual marriage (19.18). In Aeschines, Timarchus allegedly possessed (ἔχῃ) flute girls and the most expensive *hetairai* (1.75). In Pseudo-Demosthenes 59 Apollodorus puns on both verbs ἔχω and συνοικέω to describe his opponent Stephanus's attempts to pass off Neaera, a foreigner and *hetaira,* as his wife by claiming her children as his own (118, 126).[74] As alrealdy stated, Stephanus tried to argue that the children were his by a former marriage to a kinswoman (ibid., 119), but the ease with which Apollodorus was able to question the assertion only demonstrates the difficulty of proof.[75]

An additional way in which the *hetaira* could pose a threat to a man's *oikos* arose from the fact that she often belonged to it, and could bear him children. Even a cursory reading of the orations will show the Athenian obsession with inheritance, and therefore, with having heirs for one's *oikos.* Certainly this obsession with heirs prompted lawmakers to emphasize the fidelity not only of the wife but even of the concubine who was kept for the purpose of producing free children: there was an ancient law, traditionally ascribed to Solon, which insisted that a man whose *pallakē* had intercourse with another man could kill his rival with impunity. This legal ideal allowed the *nothos* to use his patronymic.[76] Al-

---

[73] The verb λαμβάνω could refer to sexual intercourse both inside and outside marriage: Lys. fr. 18 (Th) and above, chapter 5, n. 79, on Aphobus. The verb is also associated with the act of adultery: Is. 8.44.

[74] Wolff, "Marriage Law," 65–68, on the use of the word as a technical term and its ambiguity here.

[75] The absence of written records and the resulting confusion were not unique to classical Athens. In medieval Ghent records were so poorly kept that even some members of the local aristocracy were uncertain whether they were legally married to each other. There was inevitably confusion about the legal standing of the children from such unions. Nicholas, *Domestic Life,* 159.

[76] For the law, see Lys. 1.31–32; Dem. 23.53; Pomeroy, *Goddesses,* 81–83, 86–87; Sealey, *Women,* 28–29; D. Cohen, "The Athenian Law of Adultery," *RIDA* 31 (1984): 147–65, argues that laws on adultery pertained only to the wife and the concubine, and not, as the common consensus would have it, to the widowed mother, sister, daughter, or niece. On this point I must part company with Cohen, however, who discusses legal concubinage for the fourth century (154–55, n. 15). The law on adultery probably dates to a preclassical time when concubines could bear children who could be heirs in the absence of legitimate children. See Patterson, "Bastards," 50–51. *Nothoi* who used the patronymic: Hermogenes the son of Hipponicus II: Pl. *Cra.* 384c, e; 391 b–c; Xen. *Mem.* 2.10; Antisthenes: Diog. Laert. 6.1–3; see also Humphreys, "Nothoi," 93.

though these strict ideals of fidelity were abandoned by the fourth century, so strong was the desire for children and heirs that young males, as they grew older, certainly were expected to give up the homosexual lifestyle that meant so much to them in favor of heterosexual relations.[77] In any case, the ability of the *hetaira* to bear children certainly inspired fear in a society in which a man did not always get along with his kinsmen—nuclear family members and extended kin alike—and instead might prefer to rely on the *hetaira*.

The earliest and most famous instance in classical Athens of a *hetaira*'s encroaching on an *oikos* is that of Aspasia. In her case, reports to this effect combined with rumors about her influence in public matters. Because of her association with the most powerful politician of the day, Pericles, she was feared and therefore slandered.[78] Although the veracity of such stories has been questioned,[79] they do indicate the potential of the marginal figure for having some control over powerful people in extrapolitical contexts.[80] Aspasia was attacked in the lawcourts on the charge of impiety, but her association with Pericles also allowed Lysicles, with whom she engaged in a relationship after Pericles' death, to rise out of political obscurity (Plut. *Per.* 24.4).[81] Furthermore, the Socratics did a great deal toward legitimizing her by depicting her as an authority on the *oikos* and the *polis* (Xen. *Oec.* 3.13; Plut. *Per.* 24.2–3).[82] Aspasia's intellectual acumen and her influence were not entirely unique: as stated above, there were *hetairai* who were associated with various philosophical circles;[83] Aspasia, in fact, was compared to the famous Thargelia, an Ionian *hetaira* who associated with prominent Greeks and Persians of Asia Minor (Plut. *Per.* 24.2–3).

There are other cases as well in which a *hetaira* was attacked in the courts by the political rival of the man with whom she was associated. One of the most famous cases was the prosecution of Neaera, the *hetaira* of Stephanus, by Apollodorus the son of Pasio; Stephanus had before the trial succeeded in procuring

[77] On this point see for instance, K. J. Dover, *Greek Homosexuality*, 2d ed. (Cambridge, Mass.: Harvard University Press, 1989), 171; the point is elaborated by D. Cohen, "Law, Society and Homosexuality in Classical Athens," *PastPres* 117 (1987): 3–21; and *Law, Sexuality*, 171–202; R. Garland, *The Greek Way of Life* (Ithaca, N.Y.: Cornell University Press, 1990), 207–10.

[78] Aspasia was said to have influenced Pericles in promulgating the Megarian Decree and in allying with Miletus during the Samian affair: Ar. *Ach.* 527; Plut. *Per.* 24–25.1; Athen. 13.569f–570b; Harp. s.v. *Aspasia*.

[79] Davies, *APF,* 458.

[80] S. C. Humphreys, *The Family, Women and Death* (London: Routledge and Kegan Paul, 1983) 24.

[81] Some sources state that she was actually married to Lysicles: schol. Pl. *Menex.* 235e; schol. Ar. *Eq.* 132; Davies, *APF,* 459. Lysicles was a prominent figure by 428: he was *stratēgos* in the campaign to exact tribute from Caria in 428 and died in battle. Thuc. 3.19; Plut. *Per.* 24.4; Harp. s.v. *Aspasia;* schol. Pl. *Menex.* 235e = *FGrHist* 372 F 40 and commentary. Kirchner, *PA,* 9417 conjectured that he was the proposer of the decree on *nauklēroi* in *IG* I² 128 = *IG* I³ 130: decree on Delian (?) Apollo.

[82] See also Pomeroy, *Goddesses*, 90.

[83] Reinsberg, *Ehe*, 82–85.

a fine of one talent against Apollodorus ([Dem.] 59.1–13).[84] In another instance, Hyperides and Aristogeiton had clashed over a decree Hyperides had proposed after Chaeronea that urged the grant of citizenship to resident aliens and manumission of slaves. It is not purely coincidental that Phryne, one of Hyperides' *hetairai*, was prosecuted by Aristogeiton on the charge of impiety ([Plut.] *Mor.* 848f–849a, 849e; Athen. 13.590c–d, 591e).

Equally significant was Aspasia's ability to encroach on the rights of the formal wife, rights which lay at the heart of the citizen *oikos*. The laws as described in the orations insist that the woman given in marriage by *engyē* has to be given away by her father, or homopatric brother, or paternal grandfather (Dem. 44.9, 46.18). in other words, they affirmed the right of male agnates over their female kinfolk. In Pericles' case, he not only divorced his wife, a kinswoman, at about the same time that he began his relationship with Aspasia, but when his two sons by his wife died, the assembly granted that Pericles enrol his bastard son by Aspasia in his phratry, thus making the young man legitimate (Eupolis frr. 112–14 [Kock]; Plut. *Per.* 37.2–5; Suda s.v. *dēmopoiētos*). In this way the *polis* allowed Pericles' son by a foreign woman to be considered a citizen.[85] Significantly, Pericles did not adopt any kinsman. The paradox in his action is that although he refused to observe the laws of the *polis* which protected the kin group, the descent of the *oikos*, and the rights of the household head,[86] Pericles defined even more sharply his right as the head of the household to choose the heir he wished. By so doing, however, he undermined the law's definition of the wife.[87]

Was Aspasia's influence on the *oikos* entirely unique? Certainly there are many examples of prominent politicians and figures in Athenian society who had concubines and *hetairai*. Themistocles was said to have had a *hetaira*, adding a further complexity to his already complex household.[88] Hipponicus II, the father of Callias III, apparently sired a *nothos*, while Antisthenes the Socratic was said to have been the product of an Athenian father and a non-Athenian mother.[89] Aristophon, the orator and proposer of the reinstatement of the citizenship law

[84] Because Demosthenes the orator appears as a witness for Apollodorus in 59.123, Gernet has inferred that the speech is a product of rivalry between two political factions: the one consisting of Stephanus and Callistratus and the other of Apollodorus and Demosthenes. See L. Gernet, *Demosthène: Plaidoyers civils,* 4 vols. (Paris: Les Belles Lettres, 1954–60), 4:65 ff.

[85] Vernant, "Le mariage en Grèce antique," *PP* 28 (1973): 55.

[86] See J. K. Davies, "Athenian Citizenship: The Descent Group and the Alternatives," *CJ* 73 (1978): 106, 111 for the kinship group as both citizen and interest group.

[87] Later traditions in fact tended to call Aspasia Pericles' *gametē*: schol. Ar. *Ach.* 527 states that there were two Aspasias, one Pericles' concubine and the other his wife. Schol. Pl. *Menex.* 236e claims that she was *gunē Perikleous.*

[88] Reinsberg, *Ehe,* 120.

[89] For Hipponicus's *nothos,* see Davies, *APF,* 269; on Antisthenes, Diog. Laert. 6.1.4 implies that his mother was not free, or freed after his birth; no formal union is mentioned. Humphreys, however, conjectures a marriage before 450, the date of the promulgation of Pericles' citizenship law: Humphreys, "Nothoi," 93–94 and n. 15.

in 403/2, had children by the *hetaira* Choregis (Athen. 13.577b–c). Demosthenes was said to have had children by a *hetaira* (ibid., 592d), and the very late tradition in Sophocles' *Vita* claims that Sophocles, besides his legitimate sons, had a son by a certain Theoris.[90]

As for the actual domicile of these women, at times the *oikia* established with the *hetaira* was the only *oikia* the man possessed.[91] In some cases the men had relationships with *hetairai* and concubines in the same *oikia* as their family of marriage ([And.] 4.13–14; Plut. *Alc.* 8.3–4),[92] and produced in the meantime a parallel family to the legitimate one. In other cases men had a separate *oikia* (Plut. *Cim.* 4.8; Dem. 36.45–46; [Dem.] 59.22; Is. 6.19 ff.).[93] Pericles lived with his sons after his divorce (Plut. *Per.* 16.4–5, 26.1 ff.), but Antisthenes the Socratic, according to a late source, claimed that Aspasia resided in her own house (Athen. 13.589f). On the other hand, the famous Alcibiades did keep his *hetairai* and concubines in the same house with his wife Hipparete, the ostensible reason for his wife's attempts to divorce him ([And.] 4.13–14; Plut. *Alc.* 8.3–4).[94] Although the attempted divorce was contemporaneous with the growing instability of the Callias III–Alcibiades alliance (see appendix, pp. 225–27). Hipparete may also have felt that some of her wealth was being spent on these women because her enormous dowry would have been part of Alcibiades' *oikos*.[95] Because one of the women, a Melian war captive, seems to have produced a son, Hipparete's fears were partially justified.[96]

Besides Pericles and Alcibiades, we do know that Demosthenes sired two illegitimate children and was married to a citizen woman from Samos, upon whom he sired a daughter. The sources do not state whether the informal relationship was contemporaneous with the marriage.[97] For other men, relation-

---

[90] 129.53 (Westermann); see also schol. Ar. *Ran.* 78; Suda s.v. *Sophoklēs, Iophōn.*

[91] Lyc. 1; Lys. 4.2, 5 ff.; 14.25, 41; Dem. 59.30 ff., 24.197; 25.56–57, 79–80; 48.53; Is. 3.10; Ant. 1.14 ff.

[92] The passages cited disagree as to the citizenship of the *hetairai* of Alcibiades. Plutarch claims that they were foreign and citizen, while [And.] 4 claims that they were slave and free. There has been a long history of scholarship for and against the reliability and authenticity of [And.] 4. The most recent defense of the oration as a contemporary piece written by Andocidesis W. D. Furley, "Andokides IV ('Against Alcibiades'): Fact or Fiction," *Hermes* 117 (1989): 138–56.

[93] Of less certainty are Ar. *Plut.* 179, 303.

[94] It may well have been one of these *hetairai* resident in Alcibiades' *oikos* who accompanied him to Agathon's house, the scene of Plato's *Symposium*: Reinsberg, *Ehe,* 120.

[95] See below, note 99.

[96] On this son, see Davies, *APF,* 19. It would be very tempting to add as proof here the recent translation by Oikonomides of a large sherd found in the Agora ("Graffitti-Inscriptions from the Excavations of the Athenian Agora at Kerameikos," *Horos* 4 [1986]: 57–58). The translation, which suggests that the sherd was a letter from an Athenian woman complaining about her husband's concubine, is fraught with difficulty. The inscription was first catalogued by Mabel Lang, *The Athenian Agora: Graffiti and Dipinti,* vol. 21 (Princeton, N.J.: American School of Classical Studies at Athens, 1976), no. B10.

[97] Davies, *APF,* 138–39.

ships with *hetairai* and concubines began after the termination of their marriages by either death or divorce. These men maintained the women in their own houses and frequently produced a second family. Hyperides and Stephanus both began their relationships with *hetairai* after the termination of their marriages and while the children by their first marriages still lived with them.[98] The case of Hyperides, in fact, is quite instructive: he had three residences, one in Athens, one in Peiraeus, and one at his estate in Eleusis—in all three of which he kept a *hetaira;* in fact, Phila became a type of *tamias* or *oikouros* of the Eleusinian estate ([Plut.] *Mor.* 849e; Athen. 13.590 c–d). Isocrates, who did not marry until late in life and adopted the son of his wife by her first marriage, at a very advanced age took up with Lagisca and was said to have had a daughter by her (Athen. 13.592d).

Men such as Euctemon in Isaeus 6 and Mantias in Demosthenes 39 and 40 reared their children and kept their concubines in separate *oikiai*. Euctemon was said to have had relations with a prostitute during his first marriage, after his divorce from his first wife, and during his second marriage (18 ff.). Mantias continued his relationship with Plango throughout his second marriage and after the death of his second wife ([Dem.] 40.8–9). Although Lysias the orator was a noncitizen, and his *oikos* therefore not a citizen one, his actions are illustrative. Lysias lived with his mother and wife, who was also his sister's daughter. He also had a *hetaira,* but out of respect for his wife, and perhaps so that any wealth she brought into the marriage would not go toward the upkeep of another woman, Lysias kept his *hetaira* in the *oikia* of a friend ([Dem.] 59.22).[99] On the fictional level, in Old Comedy the *hetaira* is depicted as greedy and the vehicle for political corruption. With New Comedy, in Menander's *Samia,* Demeas urges his Samian *hetaira* to abandon her child by him, but there is the overt remark that she could have influenced him to let her keep the baby (ibid., 69–94). Later in the play Demeas believes that the child has really been fathered by his son while he, Demeas, was away on an extended business venture (ibid., 220–60). In general, the *hetaira* is an ambivalent figure in New Comedy; on the one hand, she is a threat to the *oikos,* but on the other she acts as a mediatrix in family quarrels and therefore can unify domestic relationships.[100] The historical sources are not too different.

---

[98] For Stephanus, see [Dem.] 59.119–20, or at least Stephanus claimed that the children were from his first wife; for Hyperides, Athen. 13.590 c–d; [Plut.] *Mor.* 849d. Both sources on Hyperides state, however, that he threw his son out of the house before he brought in one of his *hetairai,* Myrrhine.

[99] See Hyp. 3 *Against Athenogenes* for the relationship between a metic and his *hetaira.* Both colluded, even after the relationship was long over, to extort money from a citizen. For a fictional account of a concubine's residence, see Menander *Epit.* 1–17, which depicts the hero Charisius living with a *hetaira* in a separate house from that of his wife. There is the suggestion (540 ff.) that the two houses will be maintained with substantial assistance from the wife's dowry (704–19).

[100] M. M. Henry, *Menander's Courtesans and the Greek Comic Tradition,* Studien zur klassischen Philologie 20 (Frankfurt am Main: Verlag Peter Lang, 1985) 28–31, 42–48, 112–15.

In any type of semipermanent relationship, the *hetaira/concubine* had access to the wealth of her male partner. In fact, a common topos in criticisms of youths is the destruction of their *oikoi* through their associations with *hetairai;*[101] the fact that flute-girls could be hired out at a higher price than that set by law is one way in which a young man could be defrauded (Hyp. *Euxen.* 3). Among historical individuals Phocion's son, for instance, was said to have spent a good deal of his wealth on freeing a slave *hetaira,* while in comedy Chaerephilus's sons were time and again associated with Harpalus's *hetaira* Pythionice,[102] and one of the Athenian ambassadors to Philip allegedly used much of the money given to him by Philip on prostitutes (Dem. 19.229). Besides his many relationships with male lovers, according to Aeschines, Timarchus also dissipated his patrimony and wealth on *hetairai* (1.75, 115). Chares the general expended large amounts of money on having *hetairai* accompany him on his campaigns (Athen. 12.522c). Alce, a prostitute in Isaeus 6 living in a brothel owned by Euctemon, was said to have influenced Euctemon to sell a good deal of his property to support her and her illegitimate sons (18 ff.). The speaker in Demosthenes 39 and 40 states that Plango, whom the speaker insists was not married to his father, wasted a good deal of his father's wealth (40.51), while Olympiodorus is castigated by his sister's husband for spending too much of his wealth on his *hetaira* to buy her freedom and not enough on his sister: this *hetaira,* according to the speaker, influenced Olympiodorus to deprive the speaker and speaker's wife, Olympiodorus's sister, of their rightful share of an inheritance (Dem. 48.53). Indeed the speaker in Isaeus 3 claims that young men were known to have ruined their lives over a prostitute by marrying her (17–18). The expenditures of the father of Onetor, Demosthenes' enemy, on a *hetaira* were well known in Athens (Ar. *Plut.* 179, 303), while Apollodorus the son of Pasio not only spent money on his *hetairai,* but also acted as the *kyrios* for one of them, giving her away in marriage (Dem. 36.45–46). It is likely that Phrynion took up with the infamous Neaera after his father's death.[103] Neaera not only used the wealth given to her by Phrynion, but also took much of it, in the form of clothing, jewelry, and slaves, with her when she terminated her relationship with him. It was this wealth that she took to Stephanus's *oikia* ([Dem.] 59.39 ff.). In a speech of Hyperides, Antigone the *hetaira* was said to have ruined the *oikos* of a citizen of Cholleidae and then colluded with Athenogenes, an Egyptian metic, to defraud the young speaker during Athenogenes' attempts to sell three slaves and a perfumery to him (*Athen.* 3.5 ff.).

One of the most informative orations on the concubine, Lysias 4, reveals her importance as a member of the *oikos*. Lysias 4 is evidence for an actual exchange

---

101 Golden, *Children,* 57.

102 For Phocion's son, see Plut. *Phocion* 38.2; on Chaerephilus's sons, Davies, *APF,* 566–67, and the sources cited therein.

103 Davies, *APF,* 143–44.

in *antidosis*. The speaker and his opponent had shared the sexual services of a slave woman. Eventually, both the speaker and his opponent put down money to buy her freedom (7–12). Meanwhile the speaker had challenged his opponent to an *antidosis:* in the exchange the speaker handed over his oxen, slaves, household goods, and the concubine. On the advice of friends, however, the speaker rescinded the challenge, and his opponent returned all the property— except the woman (ibid., 1–2). The speaker then insisted he be given back his share of the woman's manumission fee; in this way, he claimed, the woman's freedom would not yet have been purchased, she would in fact be still a slave, and could be tortured so as to give evidence that she had been shared by the speaker and his opponent. At this point the speaker's opponent simply declared that he had in fact freed the woman and she therefore could not be tortured (ibid., 14–20).

Some sources allude to the attempts of men to pass off their children by concubines as citizens (Dem. 22.61; Dein. 1.71). In Isaeus 4 one of the many disputants over Nicostratus's estate was a certain Chariades who attempted to lay claim to the cash estate for himself and his son by his *hetaira* (10). The case of Demosthenes 39 and 40 has already been discussed: Plango's residence with Mantias, even after her divorce, allowed her to encroach on his wealth. Whether truthfully or not, the speaker in Isaeus 6.19 ff. describes his fear that his father, Euctemon, influenced by a *hetaira* living in his *synoikia,* will pass her children off as his own legitimate offspring, by bequeathing to them part of his landed property. According to Apollodorus, shared residence allowed Stephanus to pass Neaera's daughter off as his own and to give her in marriage to two citizens. One of the husbands, Phrastor of Aegilia, a poor man, later learned of the identity of Neaera's daughter and divorced her. However, he soon became ill and fearing he would die without heirs, refused to adopt any close kin because of a family feud. Instead he attempted to enlist his son by his ex-wife in his *genos* and phratry, a situation not too dissimilar to that of Pericles. Phrastor, unlike Pericles, was unsuccessful in his attempts ([Dem.] 59.50–60).[104]

To sum up, the basic dichotomy between law and practice was frequently underscored by the *pallakē* and *hetaira*. Though a legally marginal figure and not considered a family member in the man's *oikos*, the *hetaira*, nevertheless, could be a member of his household, enjoying its wealth. In turn, a man's dependence on a *hetaira* was perceived as a threat to the inheritance rights of both family and kin, rights defined and ideally enforced by law. This partial absorption of the nonkinsman or nonkinswoman could extend also to the slave, and to the male friend or associate.

---

[104] Note that in Isaeus 12.2 the speaker asserts that the individuals who attempt to pass off supposititious children as their own either are those who have no legitimate children or are poor and are therefore receiving a bribe from aliens. See also Dem. 57.25, 52.

THE SLAVE

There are countless detailed discussions on the institution of slavery in classical antiquity;[105] the focus here, however, is on the position of the slave in the *oikos* so far as it gave him or her the opportunity to influence the *oikos* and intrude into the family as a member. This discussion, however, will not be an apology for the institution of slavery; Garlan's definition of slavery in Greece, and particularly Athens for which we have the most information, sums up the horrors of the institution. The Athenian slave was a possession and as such was transferable. The slave in Athens enjoyed no legal rights to property; he or she was allowed a family, but that family could be split up at any time by the master. To underscore the marginality of the slave, he or she was frequently a non-Greek plucked from Thrace, Scythia, Caria, and other countries of Asia Minor. Slaves were used for a variety of duties: at the bottom were the slaves at Laurium; in the middle were the artisans and domestic slaves; and at the top were the public slaves.[106] The following discussion will focus on the domestic slave, or the slave living under the roof of his or her master.

The domestic slave was a more or less permanent member of a great many households. Indeed, it seems difficult at times to tell who were the slaves and who the free individuals in an *oikia:* young children were known to have been mistaken for slaves (Dem. 47.61, 53.16).[107] In some households there was only the male head of the *oikos* and his slaves (Xen. *Mem.* 2.7.2 ff.; Lyc. 1.17; Dem. 48.5 ff.). Furthermore, the words *oikeas* and *oiketēs,* derived from the word *oikos,* suggest this membership.[108] Therefore, although the slave was a nonperson, his master could seek redress for damages done to his slave or could be held to account for any damage done by his slave. These were rights ascribed by family

[105] See, for instance, the series of essays and the bibliography in M. I. Finley, ed., *Slavery in Classical Antiquity* (Cambridge: Heffer, 1960), and *Ancient Slavery and Modern Ideology* (Harmondsworth: Penguin, 1986); Y. Garlan, *Slavery in Ancient Greece,* trans. J. Lloyd (Ithaca, N.Y.: Cornell University Press, 1988); P. Cartledge, "Rebels and Sambos in Classical Greece: a Comparative View," in *Crux: Essays Presented to G. E. M. de Ste Croix on His 75th Birthday,* ed. P. Cartledge and F. D. Harvey (Exeter: Academic Imprint, 1985), 16–46; Golden, *Children,* 145–63 and V. Hunter, *Policing Athens: Social Control in the Attic Lawsuits, 420–320 B.C.* (Princeton, N.J.: Princeton University Press, 1994), 70–95; 154–84 on domestic slaves. Golden and Hunter emphasize the trust between family members and slaves. For a good synthesis and starting point for cross-cultural discussions of slavery, see P. Kolchin, "Some Recent Works on Slavery Outside the United States: An American Perspective," *Comparative Studies in Society and History* 28 (1986): 767–77.

[106] Garlan, *Slavery,* 40–41, for the definition of slavery; 46–47 for the origins of slaves; 145–46 for the hierarchy of slaves.

[107] See also Lys. 22.1 ff. on how a slave allegedly passed as a free Plataean.

[108] M. I. Finley, *Economy and Society in Ancient Greece,* ed. and introd. B. Shaw and R. Saller (Harmondsworth: Penguin, 1981), 98, and Hunter, *Policing Athens,* appendix 2, 93–94, for the words for slaves. Finley (100) points out that the Athenian agricultural festival, the Kronia, was unique in that it insisted that master and slave eat at the same table. For further terms used for "slave", see Garlan, *Slavery,* 20–22.

law. Also, the slave was ritually bound to his master's *oikos;* the new slave was welcomed to the household with a showering of fruits and nuts and received a new name.[109] The parallel is clear between this situation and that of the *hetaira,* also a legally marginal figure, who frequently was given a name or nickname by others. In the case of prostitutes and slaves, having one's name changed is a mark of social inferiority.

The equation of slave with household needs qualifying, however: there were slaves who were the property of particular *oikoi* but resided and worked in a small business apart from the master's residence and paid a rental fee to him.[110] In other cases, slaves born or raised in the house were rented out (Dem. 53.19–20).

Although not considered a kinsman within the *oikos,* the slave nevertheless worked the fields or in the business associated with the *oikos,* prepared food, made articles of clothing, and even had a say in the use and storage of money, as Xenophon describes (see above, pp. 130–31). A skilled slave therefore could anticipate managerial status,[111] and for these skills could win the trust and affection of the family members or household head. Furthermore, because the wealthy Athenian household, which might have up to fourteen or sixteen slaves, usually lacked privacy, they would be aware of everything from the financial activities of the master to the domestic relationships within the *oikia.*[112]

Besides her household duties, the female slave could act as a nurse for the children or—as was discussed above—as a sexual partner for one of the men in the household.[113] But the life of the female slave was not confined to performance of domestic and sexual services alone. Although Lysias the orator may never have been granted Athenian citizenship, and therefore his *oikos* was not an Athenian one, his behavior toward his slaves may not have been too far different from that of the wealthy and influential Athenians with whom he consorted. On his return to Athens after the downfall of the Thirty, Lysias was intent on obtaining

[109] See [Dem.] 45.74, for instance. For discussions, see Garlan, *Slavery,* 41; Cartledge, "Rebels," 27. This practice is similar to the greeting of a new bride in the husband's household. For the welcoming of the new bride, the *katakhysmata,* see J. Oakely and R. Sinos, *The Wedding in Ancient Athens* (Madison: University of Wisconsin Press, 1993), 34.

[110] M. I. Finley, *Economy and Society,* 110; A. H. M. Jones, "Slavery in the Ancient World," in Finley, *Slavery in Classical Antiquity,* 188–89; W. L. Westermann, "Slavery and the Element of Freedom in Ancient Greece," ibid., 20–25; Garlan, *Slavery,* 70–71. In some cases the slave living apart did reside near the master: *IG* II² 1576 for a slave living in Collytus, whose master's deme was Melite. On this fragment and others belonging to a stele recording manumitted slaves, see D. M. Lewis, "Attic Manumissions," *Hesperia* 28 (1959): 208–38. For the living arrangements for slaves in the household, see Hunter, *Policing Athens,* 75 ff.

[111] Finley, *Economy and Society,* 110; Garlan, *Slavery,* 61–62, for the domestic slave's role in the family economy; 146 for the respect that a domestic slave could earn. Garlan also notes, however, that the domestic slave, being under the same roof as the master or mistress, could be immediately affected by the owner's bad temper. On this point, see O. Patterson, *Slavery and Social Death* (Cambridge, Mass.: Harvard University Press, 1982), 175.

[112] Hunter, *Policing Athens,* 75 ff.

[113] Garlan, *Slavery,* 146, on concubines as domestic slaves.

the property that he had owned and used prior to his persecution by the oligarchs. In his attempt to purchase back the confiscated property which had been sold by the Thirty to one Hippotherses, Lysias had a *therapaina,* a female servant, probably a slave, act as his agent to evict Hippotherses and his associates (*P. Oxy.* 13.1606 with commentary; Lys. fr. 1 [Gernet]). In his turn, Hippotherses sued the servant.

As for the role of the female slave as nurse, in Demosthenes 47.55 ff. an old woman had been the slave nurse of the speaker when he was a child.[114] When she was freed by the speaker's father, she married, left the *oikos,* and lived in a separate residence with her husband until his death. Because she had no one to care for her in her old age, the speaker, out of a sense of duty and affection, took her into his *oikos* once again; she ate meals with the family and resided with them away from the slave quarters. Furthermore, she kept the speaker's wife company during his frequent trips from Athens. Although sociologists have argued that the use of female slaves as nurses does not promote humanity in slaveholding societies, but may very well foster arrogance in the children of the master class,[115] my point here is that this exceptional case shows the flexibility of the boundaries of the *oikos* and the attempts of some individuals to offer social inferiors a partial place in the family structure.[116]

Although the older or debilitated male slave was frequently a *paidagōgos* in the household, looking after the education and upbringing of the boys.[117] the young and healthy male slave was often associated with the owner's agricultural or business activities. According to Plutarch, Pericles had an *oikētēs,* Euangelus, who managed Pericles' *oikos* including, it would seem, his land and financial affairs, some of which entailed keeping the expenses of Pericles' sons under control (Plut. *Per.* 16.4–5).[118] The owner's business was often housed in the *oikia* itself: the most famous cases are those of Demosthenes the Elder, Comon, and Pasio. As business manager, the slave in these households could have a good deal of knowledge of both business and household finances. Milyas was the chief slave in Demosthenes the Elder's workshop; he was an expert craftsman and accountant, and was finally freed by the orator's father (Dem. 29.25 ff.). Comon's slave knew his master's finances in detail and was entrusted with money kept in Comon's house (Dem. 48.12 ff.).[119] As for the prominent field slave, Demos-

---

[114] For the slave nurse, see Golden, *Children,* 149 ff., citing philosophers who were fearful of the nurse's influence on the child.

[115] Patterson, *Slavery,* 88, who further points out (220) that the possibility of manumission was an effective means to encourage all slaves to accept their fate and perform their duties well.

[116] Another oratorical fragment, *P. Hamb.* 133, depicts a freedwoman's suit against a certain Zoilos for killing her child. Her lawsuit was later undertaken by her former master.

[117] Golden, *Children,* 147–49.

[118] See also R. Osborne, *Classical Landscape with Figures: The Ancient Greek City and Its Countryside* (London: Georg Philip, 1987), 23; Garlan, *Slavery,* 69–70.

[119] On the trusted slave in business see M. I. Finley, *The Ancient Economy* (Berkeley: University of California Press, 1973), 74; L. Casson, "The Athenian Upper Class and New Comedy," *TAPA* 106 (1976): 36 and n. 21 on Demosthenes and Comon.

thenes 55.31 reveals that a slave was responsible for his master's farm for so long that neighbors attempted to sue him personally for the alleged misuse of the land by his master.

The most famous cases of male slaves, of course, were the banker Pasio and his assistant Phormio, although Pasio is known to have been quite dependent on another less famous slave, Cittus (Isoc. 17, passim). Although real property descended to family members, professional competency was more important than family rights in determining the inheritance of the bank.[120] The banking business was a world apart, dominated by metics and ex-slaves.[121] Pasio was a trusted slave of two bankers, Antisthenes and Archestratus, and, when freed, inherited the business, displacing Archestratus's son as its head. In turn, Phormio was a devoted slave to Pasio, and was not only freed by Pasio, but also became guardian of Pasio's estate, which at first included full managerial control of both Pasio's bank and his sword factory. In addition, Phormio married Pasio's widow Archippe. These maneuvers were no doubt aided by the proximity of the bank to Pasio's residence. Phormio not only managed the wealth placed in the bank by other people, but also Pasio's personal fortune stored in the vault.[122] Furthermore, Archippe brought Pasio's residence, its furnishings and slaves, into her marriage with Phormio, and intended that her children by Phormio inherit some of this property (Dem. 45.28).[123] Although one could argue that banking families, who held sway over other people's money, were a special case, the fact that Pasio and Phormio acquired citizenship warrants the inclusion of this household in a discussion on *oikoi*. It provides an example of a fortunate slave who was absorbed into the kinship structure: here the widow's marriage to the chief slave protected the bank's assets.[124] Nor was this fact lost on Apollodorus, a cantankerous and litigious individual even by Athenian standards. Apollodorus's slandering of his brother Pasicles and of his mother Archippe ([Dem.] 45.83–84) demonstrates the confusion in status within an *oikos* where slaves were so promi-

[120] For this view and the history of Pasio's and Phormio's careers, see Davies, *APF,* 428–37. E. E. Cohen, *Athenian Economy and Society: A Banking Perspective* (Princeton, N.J.: Princeton University Press, 1992), 73 ff., on how bankers were dependent on slave labor and how slaves frequently succeeded their masters in the operation of the banks. See also Cohen, "Banking as a 'Family Business': Legal Adaptations Affecting Wives and Slaves," *Symposion* (1990): 239–63; J. Ober, "Response to Edward Cohen," ibid., 270.

[121] Millett, *Lending,* 206 ff., who downplays the importance of the bank for many Athenian citizens. Millett argues that the bank was the last resort for citizens who needed loans; it functioned, rather, for the *xenoi,* merchants and shipowners, staying temporarily in Athens.

[122] R. Bogaert, *Banques et banquiers dans les cités grecques* (Leiden: Sijthoff, 1968), 376–88; Cohen, *Athenian Economy,* 68–69; J. Trevett, *Apollodorus the Son of Pasion* (Oxford: Clarendon Press, 1992), 18–19, n. 3, conjectures that Pasio leased the bank initially from his masters and then purchased it.

[123] See also Davies, *APF,* 435, following Gernet's commentary on the threat posed by the second group of children; and Hunter, "Athenian Widow," 301. The ownership of the *synoikia* in Archippe's dowry is a vexed question centering on Archippe's status as *xenē* or *astē*. On the debate between Whitehead and Carey over this, see above, chapter 5, note 45. See Cohen, "Banking" 253–56.

[124] Cohen, *Athenian Economy,* 80 ff.

nent, which was compounded by the fact that Archippe and Pasio had resided together for some time but had not been married.[125] Fear of encroachment by the ex-slave was again apparent when Apollodorus declared, wrongly, that Phormio's sons stood a good chance of marrying one of his, Apollodorus's, inheriting daughters, as the sons were closest in line.[126]

Besides being the manager of an estate, the male slave could be the lover of one of the male members in an *oikos*.[127] In Hyperides 3, *Against Athenogenes,* the father of the speaker may well reside with the speaker, but both are actively involved in purchasing a male slave as a lover for the speaker; the slave will then reside with the speaker. Included in the purchase of the slave are the slave's father and brother, also slaves; all three work in a perfumery whose debts the speaker has been forced to assume.[128] Timarchus, according to Aeschines, had a public slave as his lover, but resided in the slave's house, not in his own (Aeschin. 1.54 ff.).

This affection toward and trust in the slave or ex-slave was no doubt fairly exceptional, and in fact in Athens there was no institutionalized relationship, established by law, to be maintained between master and ex-slave.[129] Yet the nurse of Demosthenes 47 and the cases of Pasio and Phormio display the ex-slave's partial, if not full, absorption into a family and lineage,[130] and the resulting blurring of the boundaries of the *oikos*.

THE FRIEND AND NEIGHBOR

The role of the neighbor and fellow demesman in an Athenian's life has been considered in several studies to date.[131] The stress here will be on how the friend and neighbor could influence *oikos* decisions over wealth and the marriage alliances that defined that *oikos*. After all, it was acknowledged that neighbors knew each other's business even when they attempted to keep it secret (Lys. 7.8, 18; [Dem.] 43.70; Is. 3.13–14, 9.18; Dem. 54.20, 55.1 ff.). and it could be a sign of

[125] Davies, *APF,* 429, nicely states: "Apollodorus' aspersions on his [Pasicles'] legitimacy . . . tell us more about Apollodorus than about Pasikles." Cohen, *Athenian Economy,* 76, notes that it was the residence of Phormio in the household of Pasio that led to Apollodorus's charges.

[126] Actually, Pasicles as Apollodorus's full brother stood a far better chance, but the fact that Apollodorus gave his daughter in marriage to his wife's brother was an indication of the deep antagonism between Apollodorus and Pasicles: for a discussion of the dispute, see chapter 4, p. 110, above. Furthermore, Apollodorus, being well aware of his background, may have wanted to give his daughter to a "true Athenian" on both sides.

[127] Patterson, *Slavery,* 231, conjectures that many male slaves were manumitted on the basis of such male concubinage.

[128] Finley, *Ancient Economy,* 74, for a brief discussion.

[129] Patterson, *Slavery,* 253.

[130] See Patterson's insistence that such absorption into the family of the ex-master would be at an inferior status: ibid., 241.

[131] See bibliography in chapter 1, nn. 64, 78–79.

one's mean status or unassuming nature if the neighbors were not interested in one's affairs (Plut. *Phoc.* 30.3; Dem. 19.244). The role of the neighbor in marital alliances has already been discussed in detail: unions with neighbors, who were not always fellow demesmen (Lys. 20.11–12).[132] were frequently reinforced through a complex web of marriages within and without the kin, and through the practice of adoption. These marital ties were a presupposition for the mutual support that neighbors offered each other: the neighbor occupied an intermediate position between the immediate *oikos* and the wider community of the *polis*. The neighbor was economically important: he could take care of a man's property while that man was out of Athens, and in compensation could receive some of his fortune ([Dem.] 53.4–5). Or an individual could protect his neighbor's family from recriminations in settling a debt, appear as a witness in court, or indeed loan money to pay off a debt.[133] A landed neighbor could be the lessee of an orphan's estate,[134] or the fellow demesman, who was often a neighbor, could be chosen as guardian to a testator's estate.[135] Mention has already been made of Philoctemon's adoption of his sister's son into his nonexistent estate; the sister's son was a fellow demesman of Philoctemon. In turn, in order to protect the property of Philoctemon's father, Euctemon, from Euctemon's ex-wife and daughters, Euctemon's kinsman (relationship uncertain) had a neighbor, who was leasing the house next door, hide the bulk of Euctemon's household effects, which were later sold (Is. 6.39 ff.). In Isaeus 5, Dicaeogenes III lived next door to the marital residence of his adoptive sister, paid off the debts of her husband Theopompus on Theopompus's death, demolished the house, and incorporated the property into his own. Dicaeogenes then assumed the guardianship of the children (10–11). Of course, neighbor could either help or harm neighbor, at times working the land with him and at other times trying to appropriate his land or movables (Dem. 53.4 ff.; 55.1, 32; Lys. 7.18–19; Is. fr. 4 [Th]).[136]

Closely associated with the concept of the neighbor is that of the friend. The Greek term *philia,* or friendship, is a complex one defining both affective ties inside the family, but also ties of obligation, duty, and reciprocity outside it. In fact,

[132] The speaker emphasizes that two demesmen never resided close to each other. See D. Whitehead's list (*The Demes of Attica 508/7–ca. 250 B.C.* (Princeton, N.J.: Princeton University Press, 1986), 231–34), based largely on comedy and philosophy, of demesmen who were *philoi.*

[133] For the demesman, see for instance, Dem. 35.6–10, 40.52, 43.35; for his testimony in court, see Whitehead, *Demes,* 227, n. 18; Dem. 52.28 states that a demesman would not state anything against a fellow demesman unless the statement were true. See also Dem. 45.8 for the demesman as arbitrator. For the neighbor, see, for instance, Dem. 22.53, 47.60 ff.; 49.17 ff. (Pasio and Timotheus lived in the Peiraeus), 53.8 ff.; Is. 5.10–11. See also Millett, *Lending,* 2–3, 139–48.

[134] See the discussion above on guardianship in chapter 5, p. 145.

[135] As in the case of Demosthenes, where the fellow demesman was not a kinsman: Dem. 27.4, 12–49; 28.12–16; 29.6, 33, 43, 45; [Plut.] *Mor.* 844c–d.

[136] See also Osborne, *Demos,* 145–46; Gabrielsen, "ΦΑΝΕΡΑ," 112; T. W. Gallant, *Risk and Survival in Ancient Greece* (Stanford, Calif.: Stanford University Press, 1991), 157–58.

the relationship based on expectations of reciprocity was the most prominent type of *philia:* help is given and is expected to be returned, and the advantages of the relationship are carefully considered by both parties.[137] Not all friendships were long-lasting, nor did they necessarily involve equals.[138] We are concerned here both with associates on a more or less equal socioeconomic and political level and also with those on different levels, where one is less than equal, that is, the hireling and the tenant.

Much has been written in the past on the political friend, how clubs of political associates, or *hetairia,* could sit together in the assembly, for instance, and influence voting. Political friends could also show favors to one another, such as prosecuting the political or social rival of an associate.[139] Little, however, has been said about the role of the friend in the use of *oikos* wealth. Isaeus fr. 1 (Th) states that Hagnotheus was prompted by members of his *hetairia* to sue an uncle for property. Outside of the *hetairia,* Melas, an Egyptian and perhaps a metic,[140] was a good friend of Dicaeogenes III and allegedly influenced the latter to keep intact all of the property of Dicaeogenes II, the adoptive father of Dicaeogenes III. As a consequence, Dicaeogenes II's sisters and their children were excluded from the estate (Is. 5.7–11). The speaker and his rival in Lysias 4 were reconciled by friends and handed back each other's property (1–2). Thrasylochus and his brother Meidias, by challenging Demosthenes to *antidosis,* temporarily aided their friend Aphobus in avoiding Demosthenes' lawsuit. If the exchange of property had been conducted, Thrasylochus, as temporary owner of Demosthenes' estate, would have dropped the lawsuit. The chance of this forced Demosthenes to accept the liturgy, thereby delaying his lawsuit against Aphobus (Dem. 21.76–79, 28.17).[141] Timocrates aided Androtion in the latter's attempts to retain nine and a half talents which Androtion had plundered from a ship off Naucratis (Dem. 24.9 ff.).

Demosthenes 37 is notorious for its complicated loans and the thin lines it constructs between leasing, use of wealth, and ownership. Noteworthy here is how friends' actions and use of wealth are intermingled. In the complex transactions, although the speaker was away from Athens on a commercial venture (10, 25–26, 53–54), he and his associate Evergus were charged with trying to deprive Pantaenetus, the lessee/holder of a mine and workshop, of his right to use the premises. Pantaenetus had apparently defaulted on a payment of interest to Evergus and had secured the mine, which had already been secured to the speaker

---

[137] Millett, *Lending,* 113–23; Gallant, *Risk,* 146–47, 150–57; Cohen, *Law, Sexuality,* 84–85, on friendship breaking down the barriers of privacy. See ibid., 84–91, for his discussion of friends and neighbors in general.

[138] Millett, *Lending,* 195–96, on temporary friendships.

[139] R. K. Sinclair, *Democracy and Participation in Athens* (Cambridge: Cambridge University Press, 1988), 142–44, for ancient references and the literature of the subject.

[140] Wyse, *Isaeus,* 415.

[141] Gabrielsen, "*Antidosis,*" 34.

and Evergus, to another set of creditors.[142] The oration is useful as a source not only on the disadvantages of travel from Athens, but also on the batting back and forth of charges implicating the friend and business partner—just as Pantaenetus accused Evergus and the speaker of collusion (22 ff.), so too the speaker accused Pantaenetus of being influenced by his friends, who may have included his creditors, to undercut the original deal made with the speaker and Evergus (ibid., 39).[143]

Although the role of residence in these cases is not clear, other sources show the frequency with which the *oikia* composition included the friend, either citizen or metic, of more or less equal equal standing (for instance, Lys. 1.18, 23; frr. 29, 34 [Th]): one could argue that a rival's associate was not a true friend because he was neither the rival's kinsman nor his *oikeios,* a member of his household (Dem. 24.195). Lysias the orator was said to have been a frequent guest at the Athenian Epicrates' house, while he lodged his *hetaira* at the house of Philostratus of Colonus ([Dem.] 59.20–22).[144] At times frequent visits to a house could lead to allegations of treachery or illegal or immoral collusion (Dem. 18.137; Lys. 14.25; And. 1.12).

In Demosthenes 39 and 40, Boeotus and Pamphilus were greatly encouraged by their friends to sue Mantitheus, their homopatric half-brother, for two-thirds of their father's estate (40.32). The subsequent lawsuits resulted in a division of the estate and *oikia:* two-thirds of the house went to Boeotus and Pamphilus, while the remaining third went to Mantitheus. These seem to have been separate living quarters, with Boeotus and Pamphilus living in their part of the house, and Mantitheus and his young unmarried daughter living in the remaining third (56–57 ff.). Furthermore, Boeotus and Pamphilus lodged their influential friends frequently in their part of the house (ibid., 57). Mantitheus, ostensibly worried about the influence of these men on his daughter, was considering selling, or perhaps, securing his third, and only his third of the house to another party, Crito, presumably a nonkinsman (ibid., 58–59).[145]

---

[142] E. M. Harris, "When Is a Sale not a Sale? The Riddle of Athenian Terminology for Real Security Revisited," *CQ* 38 (1988): 370 ff., for discussion of the bibliography on this difficult case.

[143] Millett, *Lending,* 193–96, for the argument that the relationship between Evergus and the speaker, Nicobulus, was on an ad hoc basis and not a close affective one. See also E. M. Harris, "The Liability of Business Partners in Athenian Law: The Dispute between Lycon and Megacleides ([Dem.] 52.20–21)," *CQ* 39 (1989): 339–43, who argues that there was no sense of the corporate partnership in Athens. The case of Pantaenetus reveals that he did not bring a suit against the two partners as one body, but rather against each individual separately.

[144] For Lysias's frequent visits to Epicrates' house, see Pl. *Phaedr.* 227a–b; Epicrates' house had originally been owned by one Morychus, the frequent butt of comic jokes (*PA,* 10421, for some of the ancient references). [Plut.] *Mor.* 839 f. states that Isaeus resided in Demosthenes' house for four years; although the tradition may indeed be a victim of exaggeration, the fluidity of residence is the issue here.

[145] Humphreys, "Family Quarrels," 185, n. 16, states that this is a case of *prasis epi lysei,* but quickly adds that one cannot dismiss the possibility that Crito actually resided in the *synoikia.* For the concept of selling in hypothecation as revealed by the orations, see Harris, "When Is a Sale," 363 ff.

In this context, it should be restated that Euctemon was the guardian of, and housed, the daughter of a friend from Lemnos (Is. 6.13). Close residence in this case led to the marriage of Euctemon with the young woman, and their sons then contended for Euctemon's estate with their half-brother, Philoctemon, a son by Euctemon's first marriage. In the early postclassical era, Dinarchus, after his exile and return to Athens, was housed by a friend Proxenus, who then proceeded to steal the wealth Dinarchus had brought with him from Chalcis (Dein. fr.14 [Burtt]).

Thus both the equal and the slave, individuals from opposite ends of the social scale, could be influential residents in an Athenian's *oikos*. There lies somewhere between these two the not so equal figure who could also be a resident of the *oikos:* there were those who performed services on a fairly regular basis for more powerful Athenians. It is common knowledge that the famous political figures of the fifth century housed philosophers, tutors, and artists.[146] Besides these cases, Nicias the general had a public spokesman, Hiero, who relayed Nicias's political and military questions and decisions to clients and seers. Hiero, who claimed to be the son of the poet and rhetorician Dionysius, the Athenian oikist in Italy, was apparently raised in Nicias' house (*oikia*) (Plut. *Nic.* 1 ff.).[147] Aeschines' father was said to have been employed as a teacher by another teacher, Elpias, in the latter's house (Dem. 18.129). Aristion, a Plataean, once lived for a long time in Demosthenes' house, perhaps in a homosexual relationship; in any case, the friendship facilitated Demosthenes' attempts to communicate with Alexander of Macedon (Aeschin. 3.162).[148] On his frequent trips from Athens Timotheus the general was said to have depended on many Athenian citizens and metics to look after his affairs; two of these Athenians were his *tamias* Antimachus and the latter's *grammateus* ([Dem.] 49.7–8). In fact these two men were so intimately connected with Timotheus and his estate that when Timotheus was brought to trial in the 370s and threatened with execution, Antimachus's property was confiscated and he was executed, although Timotheus himself escaped capital punishment (ibid., 9–10). Philondas, a Megarian metic in Athens, and a hireling of Timotheus, aided the general by procuring a loan for a shipment of timber given to Timotheus by Amyntas; Philondas moved the wood to Timotheus's house in the Peiraeus ([Dem.] 49.26).[149]

---

[146] For example, on Pericles' tutor, see L. B. Carter, *The Quiet Athenian* (Oxford: Clarendon Press, 1986), 142; on an artist's (forced) residency in Alcibiades' house: Dem. 21.147; [And.] 4.17; Plut. *Alc.* 16.4.

[147] On Dionysius the oikist, see *PA,* 4084.

[148] Aristion appears to have been designated a Samian by later sources: Davies, *APF,* 138, for Aristion of Samos mentioned by Hesychius s.v. *Aristion* as being Demosthenes' agent. There may be some confusion here with the fact that Demosthenes' wife came from Samos, perhaps as a cleruch (*APF,* 138). Davies, ad loc., nowhere mentions the passage in Aeschines; see also Golden, *Children,* 145.

[149] On the gifts of foreign leaders to Athenians, see below, pp. 202–4.

Archedamus the orator was poor but was hired by the Socratic Crito to fend off prosecutors in the lawcourts. In this function Archedamus often resided in Crito's house, considering it a haven of refuge, and was frequently paid in kind from the produce of Crito's farm (Xen. *Mem.* 8.3 ff.). Though the place of residence is less clear, Hermogenes, Callias III's bastard brother, whose destitution indicated that he was denied inheritance from his father's estate, was the subordinate, *hyperētēs,* or servant, of one Diodorus (Xen. *Mem.* 2.10.1 ff.).

In some instances the conflation of *oikoi* was not a result of shared residence, for there may have been none associated with the *oikos,* but rather an amalgamation of property. Eumathes, a metic, safeguarded Xenocles' cash estate while Xenocles was off on military duty in Chios. For Eumathes' loyal service, Xenocles financed Eumathes' banking operation and testified in court to his freed status (Is. frr. 15–16). So too when Ergocles the general was condemned to death and his estate confiscated, his *tamias* Philocrates was said to have hidden thirty talents of his fortune, and as a consequence Philocrates was threatened with confiscation. Lysias tells us a little about this Philocrates: he was a common soldier in the infantry who won the trust of Ergocles and was assigned as manager of Ergocles' estate. Philocrates seems to have made a small fortune of his own by assuming a trierarchy with Ergocles' help and encouragement (Lys. 29.3 ff.).

Besides the hireling, the tenant or lodger could either share the same *oikia* or rent a house and property of a man's *oikos.* This discussion will focus on the leasing of private property only; the fact that individuals could lease public property for ten years or longer adds another dimension to the definition of *oikos,* but the evidence for this kind of leasing is inscriptional and therefore gives us little information about the use, or abuse, of the property over time.[150] Outside of *misthōsis oikou,* private leases, on the other hand, were frequently of short duration, perhaps on average for a year. Thus in Lysias 7 there are five lessees of a piece of property and two purchasers (4, 9–11).[151] Osborne has argued that the lessee of private land, excluding orphans' estates, would be a poor individual, making "the best of a bad job"; lessees of buildings were marginal figures, either poor or metic,[152] though there were exceptions. In Isaeus 6, Alce, a prostitute, rented a *synoikia* from Euctemon and was accused of passing her sons off as Euctemon's (18 ff.). In Demosthenes 48 the speaker argues that his former friend and current rival, Olympiodorus, is now reneging on their deal to share an estate inherited by Olympiodorus. Rather, Olympiodorus now claims that the speaker was merely renting one of the inherited houses and borrowed some of the money. The speaker neither vacated the house nor made good on the loan (44–45).

---

[150] R. Osborne, "Social and Economic Implications of the Leasing of Land and Property in Classical and Hellenistic Greece," *Chiron* 18 (1988): 281–82.

[151] Ibid., 307 and n. 47, lists ancient sources on private leasing.

[152] Ibid., 317–19.

In Isaeus 5, Dicaeogenes III, in order to prevent the estate of his adoption from being claimed by the speaker, hypothecated or sold much of the property, and the speaker is now reluctant to eject the new holders (22–24).[153] In one such attempt, when the speaker had tried to eject a certain Micion from a bathhouse formerly owned by Dicaeogenes III, both Dicaeogenes and Micion cooperated in court to block the speaker's challenge (22–24).

Less certainly, in Lysias 17, although the speaker successfully confiscated his opponent's landed property at Sphettus, he may be suggesting that land and a house at Cicynna were rented out and that the holders (τοῖς ἔχουσι) refused to vacate (5).

There was another facet to male friendships and associations. Residence under the same roof could lead to allegations of homosexual liaisons between two men. It is a truism that for Athens friendship between males could be based on or reinforced by homosexual activity. There has been a great deal written on homosexuality in Greece in the recent past, most of which emphasizes that the *idealized* homosexual relationship was that between the older *erastēs* and the younger *erōmenos,* which constituted a type of patron-client relationship with the older man introducing the younger to his associates and generally facilitating the younger man's entrée to Athenian society. The younger man, in turn, when older, could assume the role of *erastēs.* It has been argued that the whole homosexual phase, in idealized form, was preparatory to marriage and was approved of only if it was moderate and not overpassionate.[154] In keeping with the general thesis of the present discussion on indistinct boundaries, two points should be stressed. First, homosexuality cannot be seen as a polar opposite to heterosexuality. This bisexuality is quite evident in the fact that homosexual activity, which often took place in the *andron* of the house, also took place in the presence of *hetairai.*[155] Men such as Themistocles, Alcibiades, Demosthenes, and even Plato had homosexual affairs and associated as well with *hetairai.* With the exception of Plato these men married as well.[156] In Lysias 4, the speaker, who

[153] Harris, "When Is a Sale," 365–66, discusses how the speaker confuses the property which was actually sold with that which had been merely hypothecated or held as security.

[154] Major works in the recent past are here cited: Dover, *Greek Homosexuality;* M. Golden, "Slavery and Homosexuality at Athens," *Phoenix* 38 (1984): 308–24; and *Children,* 58 ff.; Cohen, "Law," 3–21; and *Law, Sexuality,* 171–202; Halperin, *One Hundred Years;* J. Winkler, "Laying Down the Law: The Oversight of Men's Sexual Behavior in Classical Athens," in *The Constraints of Desire* (London: Routledge, 1990), 45–70; for an excellent overview and critique of recent work on the subject, see M. Golden, "Thirteen Years of Homosexuality (and Other Recent Work on Sex, Gender and the Body in Ancient Greece)," *EMC* 35 (1991): 327–40.

[155] Garland, *Life,* 207–10.

[156] On Themistocles' homosexuality, see Plut. *Them.* 3.2, *Arist.* 2.3; for Alcibiades' affairs, see R. Littman, "The Loves of Alcibiades," *TAPA* 101 (1970): 263–76; on Demosthenes' illegitimate children, Athen. 13.592e, and for his homosexuality discussion below. References for Plato's homosexuality need not be cited, but for the overlooked tradition concerning his *hetaira,* Archeanassa of Colophon, see Athen. 13.589c–d; Diog. Laert. 3.31.

shared a slave concubine with his rival, admits to having gone out one night to search for boys and flute-girls (7–8). What needs to be stressed in the sexual activity of citizen males is the notion of hierarchy built into the sex act with either homosexual lover or *hetaira:* frequently, though not always, the older, or citizen male, is seen in the dominant position, and both boys and women are viewed as sexually passive.[157] The second point is that homosexual attraction and activity were not necessarily separated from the kinship structure; at times the *erastēs* was a kinsman to the *erōmenos.* For example, Axiochus the uncle of Alcibiades appears to have been attracted to the latter as well as sharing in his relationships with women.[158] Lysias fr. 75 (Th) states that a certain Pytheas, the guardian of Teisias, assigned to Teisias by his father, and therefore possibly related to Teisias, was attracted to his young ward.

Besides revealing to the modern reader the bisexuality of men in classical Athens, the sources also reveal to what extent the individual resided with his male lover and to what extent he shared and used his companion's wealth. One has only to read Plato's *Phaedrus* to realize that it was accepted that male lovers shared their wealth and property; just as in the physical and emotional sense sexual activity can become immoderate, so too in the material sense men could waste their wealth on their male lovers (232b–c, 239c–40a, 252a). However much one may mistrust philosophical tracts as reflections of societal concerns and whatever the exaggeration may be in the sentiments in the *Phaedrus,* the underlying fear of the use of private wealth and the potential for misuse are expressed by other sources. These sources reveal the nature of such expenses: one of Socrates' friends was said to have purchased a war captive, Phaedon of Elis, for sexual purposes. Alcibiades was known to have loaned money to his lover Democrates, a metic, and to have shared his wealth with Socrates, while at the same time using, if not appropriating, the precious metal objects in Anytus's household.[159] One could of course exaggerate one's expenditures: the speaker in Lysias 3 scoffs at Simon's assertion that he, Simon, had paid 300 drachmae for a young boy's services when in fact at an earlier time Simon had claimed that his property was worth only 250 drachmae (22–24).

The orations are the most informative on the use of wealth by and the *oikos* membership of the *erastēs.* Although laden with exaggeration and diatribe, Aeschines' description of Timarchus's and Demosthenes' homosexual liaisons

---

[157] See, for instance, Halperin, *One Hundred Years,* 34–35, 47, although Halperin qualifies this absolute in his addendum (225), where he now admits that some vases do show the *erōmenos* in a position normally associated with the *erastēs.* Reinsberg argues that the increased depiction of men in the dominant position in the sex act with *hetairai* correlates with the advance of democracy in the fifth century: *Ehe,* 118–19.

[158] Littman, "Loves," 265.

[159] On Pheidon, see Gellius 2.18.1–4, and Reinsberg, *Ehe,* 202–3; on Democrates, see Plut. *Alc.* 3.1; on Socrates, Pl. *Sym.* 218c–d; Dover, *Homosexuality,* 157–58; Littman, "Loves," 271–75; on Anytus, Plut. *Alc.* 4.5.

may well have a kernel of truth: Demosthenes, Timarchus's defender, as part of his argument exonerating Timarchus's behavior, apparently cited the great and noble pederastic relationships in Greek literature and Athenian history (Aeschin. 1.132 ff.). According to Aeschines, homosexual relationships were often short-lived, taking place in one of the men's houses. At times a man resided with his lover and the latter's marital or original family. In Lysias 3.5–6 the speaker lives with his widowed sister and her children and a male lover, a young boy from Plataea. Eventually, however, the speaker smuggles the boy out of Athens to protect him from the attentions of a rival.[160] Timarchus was said specifically to have left his father's *oikia* and after a series of homosexual affairs, to have lived with Hegesandrus while the latter was married to an heiress (Aeschin. 1.95). Hegesandrus, defended by his brother, denied the charge, a denial difficult to prove, no doubt (1.69 ff.). Demosthenes was said to be the lover of Aristarchus son of Moschus, and not only resided from time to time in Aristarchus's house, which was under the *kyrieia* of Aristarchus's widowed mother, but was also given managerial control of three talents from the estate to aid Aristarchus in his exile (Aeschin. 1.171–72, 2.166; Din. 1.30–31). Furthermore, the orator reportedly lodged a young boy, Cnosion, but whether this latter was Athenian or not is uncertain. The slander that Demosthenes' wife also slept with the boy suggests that the relationship with the *erōmenos* was contemporary with Demosthenes' marriage, which did yield one daughter.[161] In turn, Aeschines engaged in homosexual activities at the age of forty-five while married and with children (Aeschin. 1.49, 136; 2.151).

XENOI

Besides the friend, both citizen and noncitizen resident in Athens, the foreign friend whose residence was not predominantly in Athens could also have a significant influence on household composition and the use of *oikos* wealth, at least among wealthy and prominent people who spent time away from Athens. The previous chapter has stressed the frequency with which the prominent Athenian traveled for purposes of war, or of avoiding war, or for commercial ventures. In his work on ritualized friendships, Gabriel Herman has demonstrated how *xe-*

---

[160] The status of this boy is a matter of debate. E. W. Bushala, "Torture of Non-Citizens in Homicide Investigations," *GRBS* 9 (1968): 61–68, contends that the boy was a free noncitizen, even though there was the possibility that he could be tortured for testimony concerning an assault case. Dover, *Greek Homosexuality,* 32–33, also assumes his free status, although he could not have been one of the Plataeans granted Athenian citizenship after the Spartan capture of Plataea, as Athenian citizens could not be tortured for evidence. C. Carey, "A note on Torture in Athenian Homicide Cases," *Historia* 37 (1988): 242–43, suggests that the boy could have been a slave, based again on Lysias 4 in which a slave concubine is freed by her master so she cannot be tortured for testimony in a case of assault.

[161] Hyp. *Ag. Dem* col. 13; Aeschin. 2.149, who also slandered Demosthenes' wife: Athen. 13.592f–593a. For Demosthenes' daughter, see Davies, *APF,* 138.

niai for the prominent Athenian were the means by which he could go abroad introducing himself to prominent foreigners, even foreign leaders. These alliances could also increase the Athenian's wealth. There are frequent attestations to Athenians receiving landed estates from foreign potentates; so too this reciprocity of favors could also take the form of military assistance, cash gifts, food, and timber. In the end *xeniai* proved so essential that they produced conflicts between the Athenian's loyalty to foreigners or foreign powers and his loyalty to Athens.[162]

Our concern here is with the importance of residence and lodging in *xeniai;* a *xenos*'s close proximity to the Athenian could change the kinship structure of the *oikos,* affect its wealth, or benefit the political career of the Athenian. For instance, Callias III, the *proxenos* of the Lacedaemonians, was said to have frequently lodged prominent Spartans in his house (Xen. *Mem.* 8.39). Xenophon sums up the need for the friend, both Athenian and foreign, succinctly, in an exchange between Socrates and the Athenian Chaerecrates in the *Memorabilia.*

> *Socrates.* And suppose you wanted to encourage one of your friends to look after
> your affairs during your absence from home, what would you do?
> *Chaerecrates.* Of course, I would first look after his affairs while he was away.
> *Socrates.* And if you wanted a *xenos* to entertain you when you visited his city, what
> would you do?
> *Chaerecrates.* I would first entertain him whenever he came to Athens, certainly
> (*Mem.* 2.3.12–13).[163]

Timotheus the general lodged two very powerful foreigners, Alcetas, the king of the Molossi, and Jason, tyrant of Pherae, who were both responsible for pressuring the Athenians to acquit Timotheus when he was brought to trial in the 370s (Dem. 49.10, 22 ff.). Dion the tyrant of Sicily proved a beneficial ally to Callipus and his brother Philostratus. Dion frequently resided with Callipus in Athens, and when the two brothers fled Athens in anticipation of repercussions of their association with the exiled Callistratus, they were housed by Dion.[164] Plato as well was a close associate of Dion, being housed by the tyrant during his frequent absences, if not periods of self-exile, from Athens; Plato appears to have received a substantial amount of money from Dion, and at one point, Dionysius was said to have considered giving Plato the proceeds of Dion's estate.[165] Satyrus

---

[162] G. Herman, *Ritualised Friendship and the Greek City* (Cambridge: Cambridge University Press, 1987), 109–10, for his table of those receiving land; 82 ff. discusses the reciprocity of favors; for the tension resulting from an individual's friendships in Athens and elsewhere, see 142 ff. On this latter point see also F. Adcock and D. J. Mosley, *Diplomacy in Ancient Greece* (London: Thames and Hudson, 1975), 158–59.

[163] Gallant, *Risk,* 146–47, who also quotes this passage.

[164] Davies, *APF,* 274–75.

[165] For a complete listing of the ancient sources on Plato's relationships with the Sicilian tyrants, see *PA,* 11855. See Davies, *APF,* 335, who also notes that Dion's beneficence was a gesture to gain Athenian goodwill.

the comic actor, an Olynthian, was a frequent visitor in Demosthenes' house: through this association Satyrus was able to save the family of a friend of his which had been residing in Olynthus, when the latter town was invaded and destroyed by Philip.[166] Nowhere is the foreigner's effect on *oikia* composition and the privacy of the household more blatantly revealed than in a fragment of Lysias, quoted by Herman in his study. An Athenian, residing in Athens, was returning a favor to a Theban exile and his family; the exile's father had housed the speaker when the speaker himself had been exiled from Athens: "Thinking that I owed them [the exile and his family] a very great favour, I received them in my house in such a way that none of those entering the house, unless he knew beforehand, knew which one of us owned the house" (Lys. fr. 78 [Th]).[167]

How did the sharing of the same *oikia* affect the use of its wealth or its kinship structure? As was stated, influential Athenians frequently received money from foreign leaders and prominent *xenoi*. For instance, in the early fifth century Themistocles increased his wealth by collecting tribute from Aegean allies.[168] Cimon was offered money by a Persian exile so that the Persian could be one of Cimon's associates in Athens (Plut. *Cim.* 10.8–9). In the fourth century, according to Pseudo-Demosthenes 59, Epaenetus of Andros was such a frequent guest in Stephanus's household that he was said to have been responsible for its financial upkeep. Not only did Epaenetus give a great deal of money for his use of Neaera and her daughter, he even contributed to the daughter's dowry (64 ff.). Regardless of any exaggeration, if the young woman was indeed Stephanus's daughter by a marriage to an Athenian and kinswoman, as Stephanus reportedly claimed, then this close association leading to a contribution to a dowry fits standard *xenia* practice in other sources.[169]

As for kinship structures, Herman has noted that *xeniai* also encouraged fictive kinship, an institution that could directly affect *oikia* membership in Athens and outside of it. Iphicrates the general had established *xeniai* in both Thrace and Macedonia; the Macedonian king Amyntas adopted Iphicrates and gave timber to Iphicrates' son-in-law, ([Dem.] 49.26).[170] and one can suspect that there were many more grants that our texts do not record. In any case, because of this *xenia,* after Amyntas's death, his wife and their two sons found refuge with Iphicrates at the time he was sent out to Amphipolis (Aeschin. 2.28; Nep. *Iph.* 3.1–2).[171] The general Phocion, besides rearing in Athens Ctesippus the son of the Athen-

---

[166] Dem. 19.193; Aeschin. 2.156; Diod. Sic. 16.55.3; Plut. *Dem.* 7.1; Athen. 13.591e for Satyrus's *hetaira; PA,* 12604. [Plut.] *Mor.* 845 a–b claims that the actor Andronicus frequently resided with Demosthenes, allegedly training the orator in elocution.

[167] See also Herman, *Ritualised,* 28.

[168] Davies, *APF,* 215.

[169] Herman, *Ritualised,* 26, 121.

[170] See also ibid., 82.

[171] See also ibid., 23.

ian general Chabrias after the latter's death, also took care of the daughter of the notorious Harpalus by the *hetaira* Pythionice after Harpalus's death (Plut. *Phoc.* 22.3–4).

Herman maintains that *xeniai* could be more effective than marriage as a bond with non-Athenians because in many Greek cities—and Athens was certainly no exception—there were restrictions on marriage to foreigners. For Herman such restrictions were particularly directed at the wealthy and elite.[172] Even so from time to time Athenians did contract marriage alliances with prominent foreigners. The earliest known example in the fifth century is the marriage of Themistocles' daughter to a Chian, an alliance no doubt founded on Themistocles' associations with the Aegean islands.[173] This is not the first foreign marriage recorded for Themistocles' family: Themistocles' father Neocles had also married a non-Athenian.[174] According to Ion of Chios, Themistocles' daughter lived with her husband on Chios and was considered a *xenē*.[175] This marriage occurred before Pericles' citizenship law and was, therefore, quite legal. However, even after the promulgation of that law, the tendency for elite Athenians to contract marriages to non-Athenians did not stop altogether—especially in the case of Athenians who lived frequently or permanently outside of Athens. At the end of the fifth century, Gylon of Cerameis was charged with treason for betraying Nymphaeum in the Crimea to the Bosporan Spartacids; Gylon fled to the Bosporus where he married a non-Athenian at Cepi, a Milesian colony. Although it does not appear that Gylon ever returned to Athens, his daughters did, no doubt because of the legitimization of *nothoi* at the end of the Peloponnesian War, and married prominent Athenians, Demosthenes the Elder and Demochares of Leuconoeum.[176] It appears as well that Demosthenes had ties of *xenia* with the Bosporan tyrants, perhaps as a result of his maternal grandfather's activities. In the fourth century Demosthenes set up statues to the tyrants in

---

[172] Ibid., 36; Herman, "Patterns of Name Diffusion within the Greek World and Beyond," *CQ* 40 (1990): 349–63. The historicity of citizenship laws at Athens is undisputed, but for skepticism about the pervasiveness of citizenship restrictions in marriage laws in other Greek states, see J.-M. Hannick, "Droit de cité et mariages mixtes dans la Grèce classique," *AntCl* 45 (1976): 133–48.

[173] Davies, *APF,* 217.

[174] Ibid., 212–13.

[175] *FGrHist* 392 F11 and commentary; F. Jacoby, "Some Remarks on Ion of Chios," *CQ* 41 (1947): 12 and n. 8; A. Podlecki, *The Life of Themistocles* (Montreal: McGill–Queen's University Press, 1975), 55–56; R. Lenardon, *The Saga of Themistocles* (London: Thames and Hudson, 1978), 225, n. 29; F. J. Frost, *Plutarch's Themistocles* (Princeton, N.J.: Princeton University Press, 1980), 232; see also Suda s.v. *Athenaias.*

[176] Davies, *APF,* 121–22, who argues that because Cepi was a Milesian colony, Gylon's wife could have been Greek, even Athenian. If she were Greek, the marriage would still have violated law, and it is far from certain that she was Athenian; in fact, as Davies remarks, Demosthenes' silence on the issue may indicate that Aeschines' charge that she was an alien—a Scythian to be exact—had a kernel of truth. For further discussion on Cleoboule, see V. Hunter, "Women's Authority in Classical Athens," *EMC* 33 (1989): 39–48.

Athens and in return received a thousand medimni of wheat a year.[177] A fragment of an oration preserved in *P. Oxy.* 31.2538 tells how the speaker's father married a woman in Selymbria: the father, a trader, met Antiphanes before 403/2 and married Antiphanes' daughter at that time. The legitimization of *nothoi* in 403/2 allowed the speaker to be a citizen in Athens.[178] Iphicrates' *xenia* with the Thracians, and his frequent residency in Thrace, resulted in his marriage to a kinswoman, either a sister or daughter, of Cotys of Thrace. In fact, Davies argues that the marriage may well have taken place shortly before Cotys received Athenian citizenship (Nep. *Iph.* 3.4).[179] Ergocles advised Thrasybulus to occupy Byzantium and marry Seuthes' daughter precisely so as to gain power and squelch the slanderers in Athens (Lys. 28.5 ff.).

Cyprus was a harbor for Greek exiles, and according to Isocrates, under Evagoras the Cypriots were encouraged to marry Greek women (9.49–50). Among the exiles were three prominent Athenians: Andocides, Conon, and Nicophemus. Nicophemus, although remaining a citizen, had a wife and daughter on Cyprus and held considerable property there. Conon also had a wife and son on Cyprus; because he appointed his nephew, a brother's son, as guardian of his estate there and left to his nephew one talent and four thousand drachmae, we can infer that certainly some of this wealth was intended for the care of his family on Cyprus. Conon bequeathed a further three talents to his brother; some of this wealth may have been intended for his second family as well (Lys. 19.35–41).[180] The facts that Aristophanes son of Nicophemus visited his father frequently in Cyprus and that Conon left large bequests to his nephew, brother, and particularly his son Timotheus, who inherited seventeen talents and used this wealth in Athens, suggest that Nicophemus and Conon retained interests in their native state as well.[181]

Nor were such marital alliances restricted to those domiciled outside Athens. In Demosthenes 24.202–4 the Athenian politician Timocrates had a friend, a Corcyraean influential in Corcyraean politics, who was lodged by Timocrates on his frequent visits to Athens. As a result, the Corcyraean met Timocrates' sister also residing in the same house and later married her. The woman then resided permanently in Corcyra. There may even have been some sort of contribution by the Corcyraean to the woman's dowry: the orator expresses shock that Timocrates exported his sister (ἐπ' ἐξ ἀγωγῇ φησὶ μὲν ἐκδοῦναι,

---

[177] S. Burstein, "*I.G.* II² 653, Demosthenes and Athenian Relations with Bosporus in the Fourth Century B.C.," *Historia* 27 (1978): 432; Herman, *Ritualised,* 82.

[178] P. McKechnie, *Outsiders in the Greek Cities in the Fourth Century B.C.* (London: Routledge, 1989), 180. See also *P. Oxy.* 31.2537, 34 ff., for a speaker's *apologia* concerning his being charged with *xenia.* The speaker may be arguing, however, that the charges were false, trumped up by his enemies.

[179] See also Davies, *APF,* 250.

[180] See also ibid., 201–2, for Nicophemus; 508 for Conon's will.

[181] On Aristophanes' visits to Cyprus see ibid., 201–2; on Timotheus' inheritance, ibid., 508.

πέπρακε δὲ τῷ ἔργῳ), implying perhaps that Timocrates received some payment for the transaction. On the other hand, the orator may be deliberately misdescribing gifts given to the Athenian by the Corcyraean, such as were typical of *xeniai*. Whether there were legal repercussions to such a marriage is uncertain. The law by the mid-fourth century strictly forbade the marriage of an Athenian man to a non-Athenian woman, but the evidence does not indicate whether a marriage between an Athenian woman and non-Athenian man was also explicitly forbidden.[182] Timocrates apparently referred to the union as a marriage (ibid., 203); the orator's shock stems from the cash transaction between the groom and the bride's *kyrios,* not from the concept of marriage to a foreigner as such.[183]

Nor is this case unique in the Demosthenic corpus. Pseudo-Demosthenes 25.55 also refers to a marriage, described in similar language, contracted by an Athenian man between his matrilineal half-sister and a foreigner. The details are unclear, and in fact the woman's citizenship was questioned, although such slandering of a rival's kinswomen is common in the orations.[184] Both cases appear to undercut the spirit of Athens's citizenship laws, and certainly in the case of Pseudo-Demosthenes 24, shared residence helped to forge a marriage alliance with a prominent foreigner. But marriages to foreigners were possible precisely because the families of marriage resided outside Athens. Conon's will clearly separates the wealth left to his son in Cyprus and that bequeathed to Timotheus. Athenian women were sent out to reside in foreign cities; or a legitimization of *nothoi* allowed an Athenian man's children by a non-Athenian to reside in Athens; or the granting of citizenship to a powerful foreigner then allowed his descendants through an Athenian affine to be active and own property in Athens. Whatever legal obstacles existed to discourage or outlaw mixed marriages, it was precisely the elite, wealthy, and mobile Athenian who from time to time circumvented or broke the law by contracting marriages with powerful non-Athenians.

The basic dichotomy in the activities of the wealthy and prominent Athenian, therefore, was that between law and practice. Because the law did not always meet the needs of or ran counter to the interests of the elite individual, there were frequent attempts, at times unsuccessful, either to circumvent or to disobey the law. During the life cycle of the domestic unit, as an individual's interests changed and conflicted with those of family members and kinsmen, the nonkinsman domiciled in the *oikos* was relied upon to provide heirs and/or protect the *oikos*'s wealth. Exacerbating this fluidity of interests and *oikos* boundaries was the often illusive nature of property, ownership, and use. Within this variability the

---

[182] Harrison, *Law,* 1:27 and n. 1; Sealey, *Women,* 16–17.

[183] Davies, *APF,* 514, wrongly states that the woman was Timocrates' daughter. Herman nowhere mentions this case.

[184] Hunter, *Policing Athens,* 111 ff.

hetaira, the slave, the friend, and the *xenos* challenged static or legal ideals defining the *oikos* as an entity structured in terms of the legally prescribed selection of marriage partners and the transmission of property. To the extent that the Athenian *polis* was based on an aggregate of *oikoi,* the variability of the elite *oikos* was an important element in the life cycle of the *polis.*

To PARAPHRASE Pierre Bourdieu, between the responsible man who obeys the rules and the irresponsible man who defies them there is also the well-meaning lawbreaker. The latter recognizes rules that he cannot always respect but which he cannot deny either. This behavior contributes to the entirely official survival of the rules.[1] One rule in classical Athens, certainly for elite individuals, was their commitment to kin and family; this rule was reinforced by the laws of the *polis*, particularly the succession laws. These laws decreed that an individual should define himself through male lines, that ideally property was to pass on from the father to his sons in equal shares, and that only in the absence of sons could daughters inherit. When a man died intestate, again agnation dominated; the deceased's brothers and their descendants acquired his property, and only in the absence of brothers could sisters and their descendants inherit. If siblings from the same father did not exist, only then did the property devolve on kinsmen through the matriline. Succession law, therefore, was strongly agnatic, and under the rubric "agnatic," male agnates were to be preferred, though female agnates could be resorted to in the absence of males.

To what extent, however, did elite individuals pay heed to the law? The answer can best be summed up by stating that they did so whenever the law fulfilled their needs in the course of their conflicts over property. The emphasis on the patriline is evident in kinship endogamy: although it was not practiced by all Athenians, those who did practice it tended to seek a spouse through the male agnatic line. The choice of a marital partner through the matriline could leave the offspring of such a union legally disadvantaged and liable to be preyed upon by agnates who were legally protected. Marriage through the matriline usually involved a man's marriage to an heiress, who was often a mother's brother's daughter. Their son would be the heir to the *oikos* of the heiress's father; this right of descent was protected by law, though, again, the efficacy of the law was dependent upon individual interests. The commitment to the patriline was also quite apparent when an individual was adopted out; in order to compensate for the absence of the adopted individual, either members of his patriline married amongst themselves, or the individual himself or a direct descendant married back into the patriline. Thus, for instance Themistocles' son and daughter from two different wives married each other, and another daughter married her father's brother's son, after Themistocles' son was adopted out (appendix, pp. 217–18). After Sositheus's son was adopted out, his daughter married his

---

[1] Pierre Bourdieu, *Outline of a Theory of Practice*, trans. R. Nice (Cambridge: Cambridge University Press), 40.

brother's son. Cyronides married into his patriline after being adopted out, while Dicaeogenes III's son's son married into the Gephyraei after Dicaeogenes had been adopted out of this clan. This reinforcement of the patriline could also include women and their descendants: a daughter or sister could be sent out in marriage, and her descendant then brought back, also through marriage. Thus Dicaeogenes II's sister was married out of her deme but her daughters married back into it. Deinias sent his sister and daughter out of his deme and patriline, but the daughter's daughter was brought back to the patriline by marriage to Deinias's son. Implicit in these patterns is the attempt to maintain one's ties with the kin group of origin, but in many cases the consolidation of property and its preservation were at issue as well.

Although the texts make precision impossible, it seems that the occurrences of kinship endogamy were not numerous. Nevertheless, because the agnatic bias in succession law could actually precipitate disputes among agnates, the low rate of endogamy is not surprising. That it occurred at all is surprising. The reasons for endogamy may have been different for each family. For instance, in the family of Isaeus 10, Cyronides married his father's brother's daughter who brought with her as a dowry the insolvent estate of Cyronides' father. Kinship endogamy, therefore, secured the future of an insolvent *oikos*. Thus endogamy and law could work together to enforce the patriline's claims to an estate in that line. In the case of the Bouselidae, there were marriages through the patriline, but Sositheus's endogamous union solidified relationships through women, whose agnatic ties were not always clear. These marriages justified, perhaps, false claims to an estate. The male agnate, Theopompus, long separated from his patriline, finally was awarded the contested estate, because he had the clearest legal rights through the male line.

In general, the agnatic bias was displayed publicly through group burials, which included kinsmen through the male line far more frequently than kinsmen through the matriline. On the other hand, the agnatic bias in succession law produced friction between the male transmitter of property and his male heirs. Although symbolic unity could be quite strong—in fact, it was a matter of honor to display unity in public—nevertheless, the sources make it clear that behind this unity was conflict and, sometimes, tragedy. The emphasis of the sources is on downward transmission of property, in which husband and wife strive to keep their family together and have their sons inherit. Fathers and sons were expected to be united in their public attempts to undermine a political enemy or social rival. Thus fathers defended their sons in the lawcourts and together with their sons protected their property rights in court. This public unity extended to the adoptive father: the adopted son had to display close affective ties with his adoptive father to justify the adoption. The unity between father and son was symbolized in terms of inheritance: a son inherited his father's virtues and faults as well as his friends and enemies. Yet when it came time for the son to inherit property or even to gain some control of the estate before actual inheritance, transmission could be fraught with jealousy and resentment. The sources attest to the reticence of fathers to hand over management of their estates to their sons, and to the resentment of sons at not receiving the expected amounts. In Isaeus 6 and Demosthenes 39 and 40 sons contended with fathers over property transmission. In Isaeus 6 Euctemon quarreled with his son Philoctemon because he wished to hand over some of his estate to sons by another marriage. In Demosthenes 39 and 40 Mantias rejected his son Boeotus by his first wife because the wife had not brought a dowry into the marriage. Boeotus was heavily criticized by his half-brother for his quarrels with his father. As there was friction between father and son so there was conflict between brothers. The role of death is important in these conflicts, a topic that needs more attention and further study. Conflicts between brothers, for instance, or among their descendants, could be kept under control until a central and powerful figure of the older generation died. Usually this figure was male, a father for instance, but at times a woman could prevent a conflict from being aired publicly in the courts. Therefore, although the law stressed the importance of the male, the woman's informal influence as mediatrix and ally was a balance to the sometimes bitter disputes that could erupt among male siblings or between fathers and sons. Thus, there are two words that must be reexamined in these dynamic struggles within the nuclear family—"woman" and "power."

Women were not just women, but daughters, sisters, wives, and mothers. Outside the family, but not necessarily outside the *oikos,* were the concubine and prostitute. Within the nuclear family women maintained the honor of their family members through their chaste behavior. The daughter's relationship with her father could be ambivalent as she too stood to inherit some wealth, though never wealth equal to that of her brothers. Laws protecting her agnatic rights as an heiress could prove ineffective. The wife's influence could be situational, often dependent upon the grown male relatives who were accessible and who could defend her claim to property either in the informal sphere of private arbitration or in the public sphere of the lawcourts. As a mother, the woman stood at times as mediatrix between father and son, but as a widow she could prove to be a key figure in arguments over property from her family of marriage and/or her family of origin. A twice-married woman could be a link between three *oikoi,* her family of origin and the families of her marriages. For instance in Isaeus 7 and 9 sets of homometric siblings shared each other's property. The woman as sister was fairly consistently the ally of a brother; the sister could protect her brother in court or in the political sphere. Both were concerned in her dowry and in the property in general of her family of origin. The closeness between a woman's brother and her children is almost a cliché in the sources and serves to show that informal genealogy, that which is downplayed by inheritance law, could prove to be important to an individual in his disputes with those male agnates who posed a threat to him. Emotions and interests frequently led the individual to try to appropriate the wealth of an agnate—this is a common complaint against guardians.

This mistrust then led to adoption practices that often sought potential heirs through females, thus using testamentary adoption law to undercut the letter of succession law. This threat to legal restrictions was further encouraged by remarriage, particularly the remarriage of widows. Half-siblings through the mother could at times cooperate closely against the acquisitiveness of an individual's patrilineal kin. Women, therefore, could prove to be important sources of support and of potential, though not legally guaranteed, wealth. Why was there so much defiance of *polis* law and the patriline it protected?

Despite the friction so often produced by legal biases, the law itself was only partially relevant to Athenian society. First, the law defined succession in terms of the nuclear family, and specifically the heirs in the family. According to many sources, the nuclear family was the unit referred to as the *oikos,* and it is a model upon which much historical theorizing has been based. The model in turn explained the intent of the law: to define the *oikos* as family and property and to ensure that those by blood and preferably those in a direct line of descent inherited. There was, therefore, some circularity in this reasoning. Ideals, both social and legal, both written and unwritten, must now be compared to actual practice. For instance, the high death rate in Athens necessitated three institutions to carry on the *oikos* and its line, adoption, guardianship, and remarriage. Although all three institutions were subject to strict laws, they led to variabilities of *oikos* composition, and composition again differed from *oikos* to *oikos.* Boundaries between units of property became fluid as, for instance, guardians shared in their wards' wealth. In the case of remarriage, between the nuclear family and the extended family stood the family in which there were two spouses and perhaps their children from other marriages. And then there was the guardian with his orphaned wards or the adoptee and his widowed or single adoptive father.

The historical construct of the nuclear family must now be modified so far as classical Athens is concerned. In addition to the effects of adoption, guardianship, and remarriage, the almost continuous warfare left many households destitute of their adult male members for at least some time. In general, the mobility of elite male Athenians frequently rendered them only quasi-members of their households, with little control over the daily transactions concerning property use and transmission within their *oikoi.* The whole concept of absence and its effects on Athenian society needs more investigation. Indeed, in the discussions of anthropologists and historians on the effects of time, this dimension of distance needs now to be considered, especially given the tendency for many anthropological treatises to depict the societies observed as self-contained units with little movement to and fro. The *polis* was not a self-contained unit for the elite Athenian who traveled extensively outside Athens, and even Greece, for commerce, war, or inspection of his possessions, or as a result of exile. Thus, many Athenians were dependent upon the trustworthy kinsman or friend to conceal or protect property, movables and cash. At times, war or political disgrace could leave an *oikos* without an *oikia,* or residence, further complicating conflicts over property inheritance. At other times, several residences made up an *oikos,* so that a particular residence was not always occupied by family members and kin, nor were the activities sustaining the livelihood of the residences necessarily dependent upon or performed by family and kin.

As the interests in and use of property were affected by distance, so too the interests in and use of wealth affected domestic relationships within the *oikos.* The ideal source of wealth was landed wealth, but practice did wander from this ideal. In many cases landed wealth was supplemented, even supplanted, by nonlanded wealth; and different forms of wealth could in turn affect the composition of the *oikos.* Nonlanded income from workshop activities often led to the workshop's incorporation into the *oikos,* and the influence of workshop slaves could then affect the use of wealth. The cases of Demosthenes, Comon, and Pasio all show that the slave could have extensive knowledge of the master's wealth and even be incorporated into the kinship structure of the master's family. To this fundamental reliance on nonlanded wealth and on the workshop slave must be added the fluctuating, or even illusory value of estate wealth and property: no state records preserved accurate knowledge of an individual's wealth, and, therefore, an indvidual could declare himself as poor or as wealthy as the situation demanded.

Just as the ideal of accurate estimates of wealth must now be adjusted, so too must we adjust our notion that the law automatically protected families and kinsmen's use of *oikos* wealth. As indicated by our sources, the transmission of property through the will was only a single event, resulting from many interests that led up to and followed it. The wrangling over estates and the overturning of wills signify only too clearly that the testator's wishes, which could defy the law, were only part of the ongoing interests of the *oikos.* These interests from time to time included those of the marginal figure who attempted, at least, to undercut the very letter of laws guarding the rights of family members and kin in inheritance. Because there were no records of marriages, it was perhaps inevitable that legally marginal figures such as the prostitute and concubine could control a great deal of wealth in a man's *oikos,* and that their children could become the preferred heirs when a man's natural sons died or when he had a dispute with kinsmen. This control contrasted with the public denigration of the prostitute and concubine whose inferior status was underscored by the custom of nicknaming. On the other hand, although the absence of proof for marriage could be temporarily beneficial to the lawbreaker, over time the absence of proof could well work in favor of agnates: in the case of the Bouselidae, Phylomache's inability to prove her legitimate parentage resulted in the court's awarding the estate to a true agnate, whose agnatic links to the testator, Hagnias II, were clear. Even despite Hagnias II's wish to bequeath his property to cognates and homometric kin, the court's award upheld the right of agnates to an individual's estate. This agnatic right, however, was not always guaranteed or protected by the courts.

Also, the state could ignore the law in an individual's interest if that individual was perceived as especially beneficial. Thus inheritance law was laid aside to some extent for Pasio's *oikos:* both Apollodorus's insistence on the rights of natural sons and his horror that a slave had been incorporated into the kinship structure reveal how earnestly he wished to be treated as a citizen.[2] The fact that the courts let custom overrule law, that indeed Phormio won guardianship of Pasio's estate and married his widow, may attest to the *polis's* appreciation of Pasio's abilities, but may also reveal a certain bias in its supervision of an *oikos* that had emerged from legal marginality: the law was overlooked because Pasio's *oikos* was not one founded by a man who had been originally a free citizen.

Just as dependence on the slave and concubine could lead to defiance of the law, so too decisions on the use of wealth were often influenced by neighbors, friends, and social inferiors in the employ of a wealthier and more influential man. Dependence on the neighbor as potential affine is attested at times in the literary sources and frequently in the inscriptions. In a family's attempts to expand its ties and/or property and wealth, it could marry outside of and then within the kin group. In this balancing act the neighbor could be selected as a trustworthy affine, a trust reinforced at times through both marriage and adoption. Although in recent years the neighbor has been defined as the fellow demesman, this definition may have to be extended to include the propertied neighbor who was not always a demesman in the rural setting, or the urban neighbor who could come from a distant deme. In general, however, rural families tended to select affines from their own deme or from proximate demes, while heterogamy, the marriage of spouses from disparate demes, occurred at a higher rate in the city demes. Thus the urban setting encouraged to a higher degree the association of individuals from far-flung parts of Attica. If alliances were forged through marriage to families from disparate demes in the country, such alliances were usually reinforced by sending women out in marriage. Thus, although the mobility of men is frequently attested in our literary sources, the inscriptions in particular give us important information on the mobility of women within Attica.

The *oikoi* of elite Athenians could be the residences of slaves and *hetairai* as well as of family members. Also in these households resided social inferiors who were Athenians but who performed services for the wealthier *oikos* members. However, elite Athenians did not associate only with fellow citizens. Dependence on *philoi* in general, who could be *xenoi,* was reinforced and facilitated by residence. Although there is no evidence that dependence on social inferiors could result in a marriage, the sources indicate that several Athenians either considered contracting, or indeed contracted, marriages with powerful and prominent *xenoi,* despite citizenship laws and social opinion that discouraged such alliances.

---

[2] J. Davies, "Athenian Citizenship: The Descent Group and the Alternatives," *CJ* 73 (1978): 113 talks of Apollodorus being extremely status-conscious; see, most recently, J. Trevett, *Apollodorus The Son of Pasion* (Oxford: Clarendon Press, 1992), 167–79.

Despite claims by some historians that the Athenian male's identity was caught up more with the *polis* than with the *oikos*,[3] there is a good deal to indicate that the prestige of an individual, both male and female, relied heavily upon the *oikos*. Much of this prestige depended on concerns regarding the use, acquisition, and transmission of wealth. These concerns then consumed a great deal of the ancient Athenian's time in the informal structures of the *polis*, the *oikos*, the family, and the community. Though historians have asked how effective or relevant the *oikos* was to political or formal institutions,[4] and have answered the question in the negative, now we must ask to what extent the reverse is the case: how relevant were the formal institutions of the *polis* and its laws to the *oikos*, particularly when for most of the individuals in the orations, concerns regarding *oikos* wealth often discouraged an individual from observing the letter of the law. Despite the confidence of the ancients such as Xenophon and Aristotle, and despite the confidence of modern scholars, in their definition of the word *oikos*, it is now time that we, as students of ancient Athens, ask ourselves this: When we use the term *oikos*, what do we mean?

[3] S. C. Humphreys, *Anthropology and the Greeks* (London: Routledge and Kegan Paul, 1978), 200–201.

[4] Ibid.

The Political Families

ANY DISCUSSION of marriage strategies in classical Athens should consider how the political elite of the fifth century contracted their marriages, what marriage patterns emerge, and to what extent these are indicative of the desire not just for political reinforcement, but also for kinship and even property consolidation. Unfortunately, to reconstruct these patterns one must depend for the most part upon scattered information throughout every source: the Greek historians and the historical fragments, ostraka, comedy, and comic fragments, as well as Plutarch and Nepos, who were far removed in time and place from the events they were discussing. Despite these drawbacks, this information, and the scholarly reconstructions based upon it, yield marriage patterns that, as we have seen, were practiced throughout the classical era by families in the orations and the inscriptions—both those who were wealthy and prominent and those who were relatively obscure. For this discussion of the political families, of particular interest will be why and when kinship endogamy occurred and what role a particular deme played in a family's marital transactions as that family positioned itself for power, or regrouped after political disgrace, or tried to guard itself against severe losses in wealth and property. The political biographies will be the main source for the following discussions. It will be obvious that any examination of the marriages of the political families depends on the political biases of the sources. Unlike in the orations, there is little sense of material considerations. The following pages will focus on three groups, for which alone there is substantial information on marriage patterns: Themistocles' family, two lines of the Alcmaeonids and Salaminii, and the Ceryx house of Callias II, which maritally allied with Cimon in the early fifth century and with Alcibiades in the latter part of the century.

THEMISTOCLES' FAMILY

This study could not possibly do justice to the scholarly work done on Themistocles' political career and the various debates on who his rivals and allies were.[1]

[1] The literature on Themistocles' political career and background is voluminous. I cite only certain works here since the publication of Davies's listing to give an idea of the extent of the scholarship: A. Podlecki, *The Life of Themistocles* (Montreal: McGill-Queens University Press, 1975); R. J. Lenardon, *The Saga of Themistocles* (London: Thames and Hudson, 1978); F. J. Frost, *Plutarch's Themis-*

The concern here is merely with how the marriages of Themistocles and his children reflect both political and material concerns. The traditions consistently state that Themistocles increased his three-talent inheritance to the vast sum of one hundred talents: this increase was due partly to the political payments that he received from allies, but given that he came from Phrearrhii in south Attica, and given that he more than anyone else saw the potential of the silver mines as a basis for building the Athenian navy during the Persian Wars, Themistocles' wealth was probably based to some extent on this mineral source as well.[2] Although Themistocles' deme was in south Attica, his residence in the city (Melite) and his marriage to a woman from the city deme of Alopece[3] form a pattern that recurs throughout the classical era among the residents of the southern portion of Attica: migration of individuals from this area could result in marriage with people from city demes or who resided in the city. At the same time, however, these people from south Attica did not always sever themselves from their native deme or region, or from family members who still resided there.

Themistocles' first wife was Archippe, the daughter of Lysander of Alopece.[4] Alopece was a deme in which several prominent families were domiciled, including branches of the Alcmaeonidae, the family of Aristeides, and the family of Callias II.[5] Although our major source for Themistocles' family, Plutarch, is vague on the matter of how many times Themistocles married and which children were born of which union, it appears that Themistocles had five sons by Archippe, his first wife: Neocles, who died in childhood; Diocles, who was adopted by his maternal grandfather; Archeptolis, Polyeuctus and Cleophantus

---

tocles (Princeton, N.J.: Princeton University Press, 1980); Peter J. Bicknell, "Themistokles' Father and Mother," *Historia* 1 (1982): 161–67; E. M. Carawan, "Eisangelia and Euthyna: The Trials of Miltiades, Themistocles and Cimon," *GRBS* 28 (1989): 167–208; and "Thucydides and Stesimbrotus on the Exile of Themistocles," *Historia* 38 (1989): 144–61. For the political trials of the early fifth century, see R. A. Bauman, *Political Trials in Ancient Greece* (London and New York: Routledge, 1990), 22 ff.

[2] Davies, *APF,* 214–17, for Themistocles' wealth.

[3] Ibid., 217.

[4] P. J. Bicknell, "Athenian Politics and Genealogy: some Pendants," *Historia* 23 (1974): 158–60, connects Lysander's family agnatically to the family of the famous Aristeides. Bicknell conjectures that Lysander was the brother of Lysimachus the father of Aristeides the statesman, and a brother of Xenophilus, the father of an Aristeides who was in turn the father of the general Archippus (425/4). The name Archippus is the masculine form of the name Archippe, the name of Lysander's daughter. Bicknell further conjectures that the name of Lysander's father-in-law would have been Archippus. The link with Aristeides is attractive, and would show how marriage with a member of a politician's kin does not necessarily mean alliance with the politician himself. This will be the central thesis in the discussion of the Callias/Alcibiades alliance below. Bicknell's stemma, however, runs into the problem that the name Archippe was popular and is traceable in many families throughout Attica. Furthermore, the demotic for the general Archippus is not known and may not certainly be Alopece: for Davies's caveat, see *APF,* 53.

[5] For a branch of the Alcmaeonidae, see Davies, *APF,* 379 ff.; for Aristeides, 48 ff.; for Callias II, 254 ff.

(Plut. *Them.* 32.1–3).[6] The adoption of Diocles by Lysander indicates that at some time in Archippe's marriage, if not before, she became sole heir to her father's estate.[7] The adoption of Diocles into a house not belonging to his patriline was then followed by the marriage of two of his siblings to kinsmen. The chronology is again vague, but perhaps after Themistocles' fall from power in the late 470s,[8] Archeptolis married Mnesiptolema, a daughter of Themistocles from his second wife. Only marriage between homopatric (and not homometric) half-siblings was permitted in Athens.[9] The family, including Themistocles' second wife, followed him into exile and resided in Magnesia on the coast of Asia Minor (Plut. *Them.* 24.4, 30.1 ff.).[10] After Themistocles' death, his nephew Phrasicles, possibly his brother's son,[11] sailed to Magnesia, married Themistocles' daughter Nicomache, and assumed the guardianship of Themistocles' youngest child, a daughter, Asia. It seems that the family was allowed to return to Athens and to own property there (Plut. *Them.* 32.1–2).[12] Of interest in terms of kinship links forged within a certain deme is the fact that a descendant of Themistocles in the fourth century seems to have contracted a marriage alliance once again with a family in Alopece.[13]

Themistocles' exile and its significance for the nature of the *oikos* have been discussed above (p. 162) chapter 5. Of importance here is the fact that Themis-

---

[6] Ibid., 217, assigns all the boys to Themistocles' first marriage to Archippe and three of Themistocles' daughters, Mnesiptolema, Nicomache, and Asia to the second wife. I follow his reconstruction here, although, due to the nature of the sources, Davies is silent on the maternity of two other daughters, Italia and Sybaris. Frost, *Plutarch's,* 230, suggests there may have been a third wife, as does R. Littman ("Kinship in Athens," *AncSoc* 10 [1979]: 23–24), but, as Frost admits, the sources are silent on this question.

[7] A daughter who was sole heir to her father's estate could be given in marriage to a nonkinsman before her father's death. Although an agnate could claim a married heiress, only if she was unmarried at her father's death did the law insist on her marriage to a close agnate of her father. See the discussion above on the inheriting daughter, chapter 3, pp. 95–96.

[8] For the date of his fall, see Podlecki, *Themistocles,* 38 ff.; Frost, *Plutarch's,* 186 ff. Davies (*APF,* 217) suggests that, given her name, Mnesiptolema was born around 480; if so, she would have been of marriageable age around 465 and, therefore, after Themistocles' fall.

[9] For instance, A. R. W. Harrison, *The Law of Athens,* vol. 1 (Oxford: Clarendon Press, 1968), 22–23; see also Dem. 57.20–21.

[10] His wife and children were forbidden to join him, but were spirited out of Athens through the help of Epicrates of Acharnae, who was then condemned to death for his act: Plut. *Them.* 24.6; Stesimbrotus *FGrHist* 107 F3. There is an Epicrates, son of Diocles of Acharnae recorded as *epistatēs proedrōn* in *PA,* 4887. It would be tempting to see him as a descendant of the Epicrates who aided Themistocles' family; the name of his father, Diocles, might suggest some kinship or marital link between the families, but the name Diocles was very popular.

[11] Davies, *APF,* 217, 598 no. 6669, II, where Davies conjectures that the Menon son of Neocles on an ostrakon was the brother of Themistocles and the father of Phrasicles.

[12] Ibid., 218.

[13] Ibid., 219. Davies also mentions that Diocles, adopted into Alopece, also had a later namesake, but this might be coincidence. The coincidence is well worth mentioning, however, given the "coincidence" again of the name in Acharnae, the deme of Epicrates, who helped Themistocles' family to join the famous politician in exile. See above, note 10.

tocles' marriage out to Lysander's daughter was then followed by two endogamous unions of his children, which may well have been reactions to the adoption of Diocles into Lysander's *oikos* and to the isolation that seems to have resulted from political disgrace.[14] In fact, because it was not unknown to adopt a child out of an insolvent estate into a more secure one (Is. 10.17), it is worth hazarding a guess that Diocles' adoption, if contemporary with Themistocles' disgrace, was a means to protect Diocles from the estate's confiscation. In other words, because the choices of Themistocles' children for spouses were limited, they contracted two marriages within the patriline, and the guardianship of his youngest child was assumed by a patrilineal kinsman.

ALCMAEONIDS AND SALAMINII

Based on the scholia on Aristophanes' *Clouds* and on Isocrates, Shear's classic reconstruction of the family tree of the sixth- and early fifth-century Alcmaeonids posits a first-cousin marriage between the daughter of the famous Cleisthenes and the latter's brother's son, Megacles (IV), the son of Hippocrates (see figure 3).[15] If the construction is correct, the marriage seems to have taken place around the time of the elder Megacles' ostracism in 487/6,[16] so that the endogamous union again may reflect a family's attempts at pulling together during political crisis. On the other hand, Megacles' daughter Deinomache married out, in the late 450s, to Cleinias II, a member of the Salaminii of Scambonidae, and became the mother of the famous Alcibiades.[17]

On the other hand, Megacles' sister, Agariste, was married to Xanthippus, the father of Pericles, whose background, oddly enough, is shadowy. There is a case,

[14] S. C. Humphreys, *The Family, Women and Death* (London: Routledge and Kegan Paul, 1983), 25.

[15] T. Leslie Shear Jr., "Koisyra: Three Women of Athens," *Phoenix* 17 (1963): 99–112; schol. Ar. *Nub.* 46, 48, 64, 800; *Ach.* 614; Isoc. 16.25–27; Lys. 14.39; [And.] 4.34. As Shear points out, in Isoc. 16.25–27 Cleisthenes is stated to be the maternal great-grandfather (ὁ δὲ πρὸς μητρὸς ὢν πρόπαππος) of Alcibiades. If the statement is accurate, the mother of Deinomache and Megacles V would have to be the daughter of Cleisthenes. Therefore, since Alcibiades' paternal great-grandfather was Hippocrates, the brother of Cleisthenes, Hippocrates' son, Megacles IV, and Cleisthenes' daughter, first cousins, were married and became the parents of Megacles V and Deinomache, the mother of the famous Alcibiades. The stemma has been accepted by, among others, W. E. Thompson, "The Marriage of First Cousins in Athenian Society," *Phoenix* 21 (1967): 27; and P. J. Bicknell, *Studies in Athenian Politics and Genealogy, Historia Einzelschriften* 19 (Wiesbaden: F. Steiner, 1972), 68–69; but not by Davies, *APF,* 380–81. See most recently Brian Lavelle, "Koisyra and Megakles, the Son of Hippokrates," *GRBS* 30 (1989): 503–13, who conjectures, based on ostraka, that Coisyra I was an Eretrian wife of Peisistratus; her daughter Coisyra II was the wife of Hippocrates and mother of Megacles (IV), son of Hippocrates.

[16] For the date of the ostracism, see Davies, *APF,* 379. For the onslaught of ostracisms against this family, see ibid., 381.

[17] Ibid., 16, 379.

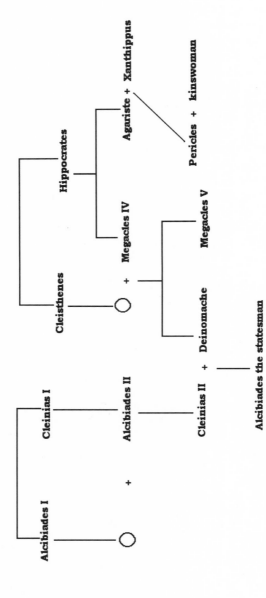

Figure 3. Alcmaeonids and Salaminii

however, for suggesting that Agariste's marriage into Xanthippus's *oikos* followed a marriage of an ascendant from the latter kin group into the Alcmaeonidae.[18] In other words, Xanthippus's kin group sent out a woman and then brought her descendant back; this use of a fairly common practice of the classical era suggests an attempt at regaining some of the wealth taken out of the family by the first woman. Whatever links of kinship there were between Xanthippus and Agariste, their son Pericles married a kinswoman.[19]

The tendency to marry outside and then within the kinship group marks the marriage practices of the early Salaminii. Based on the historians, the ostraka, and Isocrates, scholars have conjectured that Alcibiades II, the paternal grandfather of the famous Alcibiades, may have married a cousin, a father's brother's daughter, the daughter of Alcibiades I.[20] If so, Alcibiades II's son Cleinias was marrying out when he wed the Alcmaeonid Deinomache. Cleinias obviously found his wife's kinship with the powerful Pericles quite beneficial and publicly displayed his link with the statesman: he appointed Pericles and his brother, Ariphron, his wife's father's sister's sons, as guardians of his own sons, the states-

---

[18] Ibid., 455, 600 no. 11811, I, suggests that a marriage between the Alcmaeonidae and the line of Xanthippus and his father Ariphron had occurred prior to the marriage of Agariste. The reconstruction is based on one ostrakon bearing the name of Xanthippus, son of Hippocrates, whose patronymic suggests he may be a brother of Megacles IV and Agariste, children of Hippocrates (I), or their first cousin once removed, that is, their father's father's brother's son, Hippocrates II, son of Alcmaeonides. For Hippocrates II's place in the Alcmaeonid stemma, see ibid., 371–73.

[19] Ibid., *APF,* 457.

[20] This particular reconstruction has a long history: Kirchner (*PA,* 597) first suggested that the Alcibiades who expelled the Peisistratids was the victim of ostracism in the 480s and was to be identified as the father of Cleinias, who in turn was the father of the famous statesman Alcibiades. Dittenberger, who pointed out that the stemma entailed very long careers for the men concerned, added another generation, thereby positing two Alcibiades: a father, who expelled Peisistratus, and a son who was ostracized. Dittenberger was quickly followed by Kirchner: W. Dittenberger, "Die Familie des Alkibiades," *Hermes* 37 (1902): 1–13; Kirchner, *PA,* 2:442. Vanderpool, however, pointed out that according to the ostraka of the second quarter of the fifth century, the father of the ostracized Alcibiades (II) was called Cleinias, and so revised the stemma accordingly, placing Cleinias (I) as the son of Alcibiades (I) and father of Alcibiades (II). E. Vanderpool, "The Ostracism of the Elder Alcibiades," *Hesperia* 21 (1952): 4–6. Raubitschek soon countered that according to Isocrates an Alcibiades was a great-grandfather of the famous statesman; the only way in which the statement can be accurate is if Alcibiades I was the father-in-law of Alcibiades II: A. Raubitschek, "Zur attischen Genealogie," *RhM* 98 (1955): 260, n. 4. Vanderpool then countered that it would be a strange coincidence if the relatively rare name of Alcibiades appeared in two distinct families unless Alcibiades II and his wife were cousins. E. Vanderpool, "Alcibiades," *Hesperia* 37 (1968): 398. Raubitschek's stemma has been accepted by among others, W. E. Thompson, "The Kinship of Pericles and Alcibiades," *GRBS* 11 (1970): 28–29; and M. B. Wallace, "Early Greek Proxenoi," *Phoenix* 24 (1970): 197–98, n. 12, who, however, erroneously assumes some kinship connection between Isocrates and Alcibiades. Davies, *APF,* 10, remains skeptical of Isocrates' authority on Alcibiades' ancestry. See most recently, W. Ellis, *Alcibiades* (London: Routledge, 1989), 8, who dismisses the stemma of first-cousin marriages in Alcibiades' maternal and paternal ancestry for being "cluttered" and "incestuous." However, the foregoing pages have shown just how "cluttered" and "incestuous" ancient Athenian genealogies were.

man Alcibiades and Cleinias (IV). Significantly, the elder Cleinias did not choose any of his patrilineal kinsmen or even his wife's brother.[21] As Socrates remarked in one of Plato's dialogues, Alcibiades' power rested on that of his mother's and his father's families, but he valued the power of Pericles above all these (Pl. *Alc.* 1.104c–d).

Unfortunately, in all of this one can only witness the jostling for political power, not the concern for property; the sources are mute in this regard. For the role of wealth acquisition and consolidation, we must turn to the powerful descendants of Cimon and Callias II the Ceryx.

CIMON, CALLIAS II, AND THEIR DESCENDANTS

The marriage of Elpinice, Cimon's sister, in the 480s, to the very wealthy Ceryx, Callias II (see figure 4), *dadoukhos* of the Eleusinian rites, followed by Cimon's marriage to Isodice, an Alcmaeonid who was possibly domiciled in Sunium, was a coalition of three families that had experienced the threat of ostracism on a charge of Medism or alliance with tyrants.[22] Ostraka of the 480s and 470s show the names of Callias, the son of Hipponicus, and Cimon, while those actually ostracized included Megacles, the son of Hippocrates, an Alcmaeonid, Xanthippus, the son of Ariphron and husband of the Alcmaeonid Agarista, and Aristeides, a cousin of Callias.[23] It might also be conjectured that Cimon's marriage to a woman whose family seems to have been residing in south Attica c. 480 may well have been related to the increased exploitation of the mines at that time and to Cimon's alliance with Callias II, whose vast wealth, estimated to be around two hundred talents, was to a large extent based on the mines. These alliances coincided also with the interests of both Cimon and his father Miltiades the Younger in the mineral wealth in Thrace.[24]

[21] Davies, *APF,* 18 where a Cleinias III is a nephew (brother's son) of Cleinias II. This balancing of kinship endogamy with exogamy is in some societies the mark of elite families whose power is sustained by the practice: J. Goody, *The Development of the Family and Marriage in Europe* (Cambridge: Cambridge University Press, 1993), 31–33, 186–87; J. Tucker, "Marriage and Family in Nablus 1720–1856: Toward a History of Arab Marriage," *Journal of Family History* 13 (1988): 174. With two exceptions, classicists have ignored this marriage pattern: it has been briefly discussed by Broadbent in her study of the Bouselidae (see above, chapter 1, pp. 3–8, and n. 11) and is briefly alluded to by R. D. Cromey, "On Deinomache," *Historia* 32 (1984): 392; and "The Mysterious Woman of Kleitor: Some Corrections to a Manuscript Once in Plutarch's Possession," *AJP* 112 (1991): 90.

[22] Davies, *APF,* 302–5, for the marriages; 378–79 for Isodice's domicile; for the political cohesion of the marriage in threatening times, see Humphreys, *Family,* 25–26.

[23] Podlecki, *Themistocles,* 9–11; Lenardon, *Saga,* 46–48; A. Raubitschek, "The Case Against Alcibiades," *TAPA* 79 (1948): 204; D. M. Lewis, "The Kerameikos Ostraka," *ZPE* 14 (1974): 2–3, dating the ostraka for Callias to the 470s; G. M. E. Williams, "The Kerameikos Ostraka," *ZPE* 31 (1978): 108–9, dating the ostraka to the 480s.

[24] Miltiades the Younger, Cimon's father, had married Hegesipyle, the daughter of King Olorus of Thrace (Davies, *APF,* 302). Cimon had been sent out in the 460s to secure the mines on Thasos,

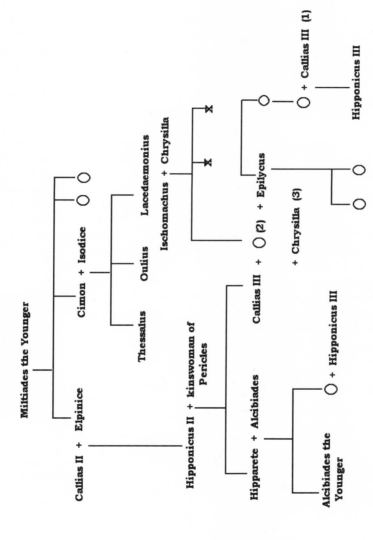

Figure 4. The Kin Group and Affines of Callias III

Cimon followed his alliance with Callias II, from Alopece, with the marriage of another sister to Thucydides, the son of Melesias, also of Alopece, who seems to have been a frequent Periclean adversary. In other words, the first marriage to Callias II was a stepping-stone to the second alliance, with Thucydides.[25] This pattern of sending two kinswomen out to the same deme is repeated in other families of the classical era and is typical for other European agrarian societies in which one sibling will follow another into the village of marriage.[26] Besides the obvious political maneuvering in the marriage pattern, the practice does theoretically allow kinswomen to reside close together.

Besides expanding his influence in Alopece by sending two kinswomen into that deme, Cimon may have contracted a marriage for another sister with the anonymous father of Olorus of Halimous. Although Olorus's family is obscure, it may have been connected with an old cult of Demeter Thesmophorus;[27] the common denominator here is Cimon's alliances with two priestly families of Demeter cults. Furthermore, Olorus, the son of this union, may have married the daughter of Thucydides, the son of Melesias, who may have been his first cousin (mother's sister's daughter). The offspring of this union was Thucydides the historian.[28] If the reconstruction has any validity, then again, the marriage out of two sisters (one of whom followed her older sister, Elpinice, into Alopece) was then followed by the consolidation of these ties by the endogamous union of the two sisters' children. The endogamous union then allowed Cimon's niece to be married into Halimous, following her mother's sister there.

Of interest for both political and social history are the unions contracted by the descent group emanating from Elpinice and Callias II. Their son, Hipponicus, seems also to have married out by marrying Pericles' kinswoman who may have been also Pericles' ex-wife.[29] Callias II and his son, Hipponicus II, both ap-

---

which would have included the mines at Scaptesyle on the mainland; these latter were inherited by Thucydides the historian: Thuc. 1.101.3, 4.104.5; Plut. *Cim.* 14.1 ff.; Davies, *APF,* 233 ff.

[25] C. A. Cox, "Sisters, Daughters and the Deme of Marriage: A Note," *JHS* 108 (1988):186. Davies, *APF,* 234–35, maintains that Olorus, who was siring children by 460, was probably born c. 490–480 and was therefore of an age to be Cimon's brother-in-law.

[26] Cox, "Sisters," 186.

[27] Davies, *APF,* 234–35. Herman is skeptical of the marriage connection between Olorus's father and Cimon's sister. The stemma, generally accepted by scholars, is based on homonymity: the Athenian Olorus was somehow related to Miltiades, father of Cimon, whose wife, Hegesipyle, was the daughter of the Thracian king, Olorus. Herman feels that ties of *xenia,* rather than of marriage, are more likely the reason behind the homonymity. Yet, as Herman himself admits, there were two other cases that, like the marriage of Miltiades to Hegesipyle, were archaic in date, and in which a foreign name was transmitted to offspring or descendants: G. Herman, "Patterns of Name Diffusion within the Greek World and Beyond," *CQ* 40 (1990): 349–52.

[28] H. T. Wade-Gery, "Thucydides the son of Melesias," *JHS* 52 (1932): 210–11, where the union is inferred from Marcellinus (*Thuc.* 2). Marcellinus states that the historian's mother was named Hegesipyle, the name of Cimon's mother, the Thracian princess. Davies, *APF,* 233–36, is more skeptical.

[29] The identity of this woman is not certain: see C. A. Cox, "Incest, Inheritance and the Political Forum in Fifth-Century Athens," *CJ* 85 (1989): 35, n. 3, for the debate. See also the following note.

pear to have married out, but the marriage of Hipponicus's daughter Hipparete to Alcibiades was significant in several ways. Hipparete and Alcibiades, through their mothers, appear to have been related to Pericles.[30] These distant links of kinship were concentrated in the next generation by a marriage between first cousins: the daughter of Hipparete and Alcibiades was married to the son (Hipponicus III) of Hipparete's brother, Callias III, c. 399.[31] However, despite these marriage alliances the unity between Callias's house and Alcibiades' house was not strong, an instability to be traced back to the early fifth century.

The enmity between Cimon and Pericles, Alcibiades' guardian, is well known: Pericles' father Xanthippus had prosecuted Cimon's father, Miltiades, in 489 for the ruinous Parian expedition (Hdt. 6.38–41, 136), while Pericles himself had been one of the prosecutors who charged Cimon for bribery. According to Plutarch, however, Pericles' leniency was prompted by Elpinice's intervention (*Cim.* 14.2 ff.; *Per.* 10.4–5; Athen. 13.589e–f). Even so, despite the alliance of her son to Pericles' kinswoman, Elpinice was stated to have been a vociferous critic of Pericles and a supporter of her brother (Plut. *Per.* 28.4–5) at a time when Cimon's affine, Thucydides, the son of Melesias, may have been challenging Periclean policy and been behind the prosecution of Pericles' associates.[32] On the other hand, Pericles was not above slandering the maternity of Cimon's sons.[33]

Furthermore, even though Hipponicus, Elpinice's son, gave his daughter in marriage to Alcibiades with the enormous dowry of twenty talents,[34] Hipparete

---

[30] Davies, *APF,* 262–63, whose stemma we follow, assumes that Hipparete's mother was Pericles' kinswoman. Because Hipparete married Alcibiades in the late 420s, her mother would have had to have been married after 450. On the other hand, Plutarch (*Per.* 24.8) claims that Hipparete's mother married Hipponicus first and then Pericles. However, Pericles' son, before his death in 430, was married. If we follow Plutarch's sequence, a birthdate for Pericles' son around 440 would leave him under marriageable age at his death. In order to solve this chronological crux, some scholars have reversed Plutarch's order (Davies, *APF,* 262, following Beloch), while others follow Plutarch, but maintain that Hipponicus II married twice. In this view, Pericles' kinswoman was Hipponicus' first wife and the mother of Callias III; Hipponicus then divorced her and married Hipparete's mother, who would by implication, therefore, not necessarily be related to Pericles. See Cox, "Incest," 36, n. 6, for bibliography, to which add R. D. Cromey, "On Deinomache," *Historia* 32 (1984): 385–401, for his ambitious conjecture that Pericles' wife and, therefore, Hipponicus's wife, was Deinomache the wife of Cleinias and the mother of Alcibiades. Ellis, *Alcibiades,* 9 is skeptical of such an assignment, which is ultimately based upon Nepos.

[31] Davies, *APF,* 19.

[32] See P. Krentz, "The Ostracism of Thoukydides, son of Melesias," *Historia* 33 (1984): 499–504, for the debate as to whether Cimon's affine or Cleon spearheaded the attacks against Pheidias, Aspasia, and Anaxagoras. R. A. Bauman, *Political Trials in Ancient Greece* (London: Routledge, 1990), 49 ff., assumes that Cleon used the judicial system to further his career.

[33] Stesimbrotus *FGrHist* 107 F61. See Cox, "Incest," 36–37, nn. 6–7, for bibliography on this subject. Cromey, "Kleitor," 87–101, most recently conjectures that Pericles' supposed slander referring to Cimon's wife as an Arcadian woman of Cleitor is actually based on a misreading of *aleitērios,* or "accursed," as *Kleitorias.* The epithet *aleitērios* would refer to the Alcmaeonid ancestry of Cimon's wife, Isodice.

[34] Davies, *APF,* 19, on the dowry.

attempted to divorce her husband. Although she was not successful, after her death Alcibiades was charged with profaning the Eleusinian Mysteries, the very rites which Callias III as a Ceryx and *dadoukhos* would have overseen. One of the denouncers in the *boulē* was none other than Thessalus, the son of Cimon, Callias III's kinsmen through his father's mother, who had been one of Cimon's sons slandered by Pericles.[35]

The point here is that despite the conjecture of historians that the Cimon/Callias alliance failed,[36] the sources suggest the reverse, that the alliance between Callias's house and that of Alcibiades was unstable. Moreover, Callias's association with Cimon may have been advertised in the deme of Alcibiades, Scambonidae, as late as the end of the first half of the fourth century. According to two gravestones, *IG* II² 7404 and 7410, Callias of Scambonidae, archon for 412/11, commemorated on 7404 at the beginning of the fourth century, was the father, it seems, of the anonymous son of Callias who was commemorated on 7410 along with the latter's kinswoman, Elpinice. Although the name Callias was extremely popular and any attempt to associate this man with the Ceryx house may seem foolhardy, the association of his name with the name Elpinice, not a popular one, should give us pause. Also, Callias's son and Elpinice appear on the gravestone with a Hierocleides of Scambonidae and the latter's son Hierocles. The name Hierocleides is a common religious name and, therefore, naturally enough, associated with priests of the Eleusinian Mysteries.[37] We know from the historical fragments of Androtion and Philochorus that the *dadoukhia* by 350/49 had been handed over to a Hierocleides (demotic unstated).[38] The appearance of the names Callias and Elpinice, in association with the priestly name Hierocleides, in a deme famous for being the domicile of an important branch of the Salaminii, the affines of the Ceryces, probably goes beyond the realm of coincidence. Because Callias of Scambonidae was archon in 412/11, and therefore born in or before 442, it is possible that the Callias/Hipponicus group sent out a kinswoman to Scambonidae some time around the mid-fifth century. If so, her association with the Cimonids, by way of her descendant's name, Elpinice, was being publicly declared even by the second quarter of the

---

[35] Cox, "Incest," 38–39.

[36] Davies, *APF,* 259, in particular.

[37] *PA,* 7470, hierophant of the mid-fourth century. See also the Hierocleides of Alopece (the deme of the Ceryces) who proposed a decree with reference to Eleusis or an Eleusinian in 349/8: *IG* II² 209. See further the next note.

[38] *FGrHist* 324 F 30 (Androtion); *FGrHist* 328 F 155 (Philochorus). The Hierocleides recorded on 7410, however, may not be the *dadoukhos* of 350/49, as the letters of the inscription are dated to some time before the mid-fourth century. Unless the inscription was prospective (for which, see R. Garland, "A First Catalogue of Athenian Peribolos Tombs," *ABSA* 77 (1982): 130), the Hieroclei-des in the historical fragments may have been a relative of the homonymous man in our inscription. Jacoby, in his commentary on the Philochorus fragment, suggested that Hierocleides the *dadoukhos* was related to Thrasyphon, son of Hierocleides, of Xypete who in 274 B.C. moved honorific decrees for Eleusinian cult officials: *IG* II² 682, 1235.

fourth century, the date of 7410. If this reconstruction is correct, Hipparete, Hipponicus II's daughter, was following her ascendant when she married into the deme of Scambonidae.

Given the instability of the Callias/Alcibiades alliance, what would have been gained by the marriage of Callias III's son, Hipponicus III, to Alcibiades' daughter by Hipparete? First, Alcibiades' disgrace at the end of the fifth century would have left him politically isolated: his property was confiscated in 415 and although he was given property equal in value on his return in 407, by the turn of the century his son Alcibiades IV was prevented by his political enemies from claiming the property.[39] Second, Callias III was experiencing a similar decline in his fortunes: by the 420s his estates had been secured to creditors, while the disastrous effects of the Peloponnesian War on the Laurium mines in 413 would have caused him further losses, since his wealth came mainly from the mines.[40] The chief sources on the losses of Alcibiades and Callias are the orations. Granted that the orators tend to exaggerate, and the complaint of poverty, is a stock motif even from the mouths of very wealthy men,[41] nevertheless, if the consistent tradition in the sources indicates a reduction in wealth caused by political disgrace for Alcibiades and the loss of the mines for Callias, the marriage of Callias's son to Callias's sister's daughter united the kin group during these setbacks. Also, for Callias, the marriage may have been intended to bring back some of Hipparete's enormous dowry to her family of origin. From the orations, we know that a mother's dowry could be transmitted, in part at least, to her daughter; therefore, the pattern in which a woman was sent out of her patriline and her female descendant was then brought back into it would be one means of circulating wealth.[42] Nevertheless, the alliance was again unsuccessful: Hipponicus III divorced his wife, his father's sister's daughter, c. 395 (Lys. 14.28).[43]

[39] Davies, APF, 21, based on Isoc. 16.46–47; see also Lys. 14.31.

[40] Davies, APF, 261, based on Lys. 19.48; see also And. 1.131; Ar. Eccl. 810; Athen. 12.537c on Callias's extravagance. See recently D. Rankin, "The Mining Lobby at Athens," AncSoc 19 (1989): 196, 198. For the loss of the Laurium mines, see J. Ober, Fortress Attica, Mnemosyne, suppl. 84 (Leiden: Brill, 1985), 14, who states that to judge from the dates of the mine leases, the Laurium mines were not operating near fifth-century levels until the mid-fourth century.

[41] The most obvious is Apollodorus the son of Pasio in [Dem.] 59. Davies, APF, 246–47, argues that Isocrates consistently undervalued his wealth. For further bibliography on this "poor-mouthing" see J. Ober, Mass and Elite in Democratic Athens (Princeton, N.J.: Princeton University Press, 1989), 221, 254–58, who points out that a litigant could gain an advantage if he portrayed himself as modest and poor. See also R. K. Sinclair, Democracy and Participation in Athens (Cambridge: Cambridge University Press, 1988), 121.

[42] For the dowry of Demosthenes' mother, who seems to have inherited wealth brought by her mother into the latter's marriage with Cleoboule's father, Gylon, see Dem. 27.4, 13; Aeschin. 3.172; see also [Dem.] 40.4–5, 61, in which Mantitheus, who had no sister, wished to use his mother's dowry for his daughter.

[43] See also Davies, APF, 269. Hipponicus III charged his wife with incest. A similar charge had been hurled against Hipponicus III's ancestors, Callias II and Elpinice, for which see Cox, "Incest," 40, n. 21. Not until Nepos do we see an apology for Callias II; according to the biographer, Callias

The use of kinsmen from both the patriline and matriline may be seen in a prominent kin group of the fifth century. Perictione, the mother of Plato the philosopher, was married first to Ariston of Collytus, who seems to have claimed the same background in terms of his *genos* as his wife, although actual kinship is impossible to determine. Her brother, on the other hand, was under the guardianship of their father's brother's son, Critias IV.[44] On Ariston's death, Perictione was given in marriage to her mother's brother, Pyrilampes, a prominent ambassador of the mid-fifth century and a Periclean associate.[45] In other words, Pyrilampes' sister, Perictione's mother, was sent out but her daughter came back.

The complexities in the marriage practices of the Athenian elite of the fifth century can be almost dazzling. In the case of Themistocles and his family the patriline was able to consolidate to mitigate the effects of political crisis, a crisis that followed the adoption out of Themistocles' son into the house of his maternal grandfather. For the Cimonids, sister followed sister into Alopece as Cimon was expanding his political base with influential families from that deme. Cimon contracted alliances for his three sisters to nonkinsmen but in the next generation the marital families of two sisters allied by the marrriage of the son of one sister to the daughter of the other. For the Alcmaeonids, a first cousin marriage may have been contracted for Cleisthenes' daughter to her father's brother's son, Megacles IV. The union occurred at the time of the ostracism of Megacles IV; hence this powerful family was consolidating at a time of political crisis. The marriage was followed by the exogamous union of Megacles' daughter, while Megacles' sister may have followed an ascendant into her family of marriage.

Among the early Salaminii the endogamous union of Alcibiades II was followed by the marriage out of his son Cleinias to an Alcmaeonid. Among the Ceryces, Callias II and his son Hipponicus II both married out but Hipponicus II's daughter, Hipparete, and her husband, Alcibiades, were both related to Pericles through their mothers; in fact Hipparete may have followed an ascendant into Alcibiades' deme. In the next generation distant kinship links were consolidated by the marriage of Hipparete's daughter to her brother's son, Hipponicus III the son of Callias III. Despite this union with Alcibiades' house the alliance between Callias and Alcibiades was unstable. Although the endogamous union occurred at the time of Alcibiades' disgrace and would ideally have brought some of Hipparete's vast dowry back to her family of origin, the marriage did not last.

---

and Elpinice were homopatric half-siblings and, therefore, properly married. Nepos's apology makes any tradition of marriage between the two siblings suspect; if the marriage is historical, it can be added to the list of marriages through the patriline in chapter 1, note 96 above. L. Piccirilli, "Il filiolaconismo, l'incesto e l'ostracismo di Cimone," *Quaderni di storia* 10 (1984): 171–77, argues that the charge of incest against Callias II was a taunt against his Spartan sympathies: the Spartans permitted marriage between homometric siblings.

[44] See Davies, *APF,* 326–31, for the family stemma.

[45] See ibid., 329, for the tradition that he was also an ally of Thucydides the son of Melesias.

For the Alcmaeonids, Cimonids, and Ceryces political and material consolidation were attempted through the alternation of kinship exogamy with kinship in-marriage: this balancing act is a common marriage strategy for the ruling families of other societies in the course of their attempts to maintain power, and can be seen in the orations as a strategy for material consolidation. At times, the strategies for both the political elite and the families in the orations involved sending siblings out to the same deme. In other cases, one woman was sent out and her descendant brought back.

In short, therefore, the sources seem to indicate that the same strategy could be used for different reasons by a family in an oration and a fifth-century political family, though any discussion of interests and concerns is at the mercy of different kinds of primary sources. The political elite families of the fifth century are known to us primarily through the biographies, which emphasize political rather than material concerns. The families of the orations, who included the politically powerful, quarreled over property, so that, naturally enough, material considerations emerge more clearly. Whatever the motivation, marriage patterns reflect the aims of the kin group, and although such aims, whether in expansion or consolidation, may not always be achieved, or are only temporarily achieved, the same strategies can, nevertheless, be repeated for generations.

References

Adock, F., and D. J. Mosley. *Diplomacy in Ancient Greece*. London: Thames and Hudson, 1975.

Bauman, R. A. *Political Trials in Ancient Greece*. London: Routledge, 1990.

Beauchet, L. *Histoire du droit privé dans la république athénienne*. 4 vols. Paris: Chevalier Marescq, 1897.

Behar, R., and Frye, D. "Property, Progeny and Emotion: Family History in a Leonese Village." *Journal of Family History* 13 (1988):13–32.

Berkner, L. "Inheritance, Land Tenure and Peasant Family Structure: A German Regional Comparison." In *Family and Inheritance: Rural Society in Western Europe 1200–1800*. Ed. J. Goody, J. Thirsk, and E. P. Thompson. Cambridge: Cambridge University Press, 1976. 71–95.

Bicknell, P. J. *Studies in Athenian Politics and Genealogy. Historia Einzelschriften 19*. Wiesbaden: F. Steiner, 1972.

———. "Athenian Politics and Genealogy: Some Pendants." *Historia* 23 (1974): 146–63.

———. "Themistokles' Father and Mother." *Historia* 31 (1982): 161–67.

Boegehold, A., and A. Scafuro, eds. *Athenian Identity and Civic Ideology*. Baltimore: Johns Hopkins University Press, 1994.

Bogaert, R. *Banques et banquiers dans les cités grecques*. Leiden: Sijthoff, 1968.

———. "La banque à Athènes au IVᵉ siècle avant J.-C.: Etat de la question." *MusHelv* 43 (1986):19–49.

Bonfield, L. "Normative Rules and Property Transmission: Reflections on the Link between Marriage and Inheritance in Early Modern England." In *The World We Have Gained: Histories of Population and Social Structure*. Ed. L. Bonfield, R. M. Smith, and K. Wrightson. Oxford: Blackwell, 1986. 155–76.

Boose, L. E. "The Father's House and the Daughter In It: The Structures of Western Culture's Daughter-Father Relationship." In *Daughters and Fathers*. Ed. L. E. Boose and B. S. Flowers. Baltimore: Johns Hopkins University Press, 1989. 19–74.

Bourdieu, P. "Marriage Strategies as Strategies of Social Reproduction." In *Family and Society*. Ed. R. Forster and O. Ranum, trans. E. Forster and P. Ranum. Baltimore: Johns Hopkins University Press, 1976. 117–44.

———. *Outline of a Theory of Practice*. Trans. R. Nice. Cambridge: Cambridge University Press, 1977.

Bourriot, F. "La famille et le milieu sociale de Cléon." *Historia* 31 (1982): 404–35.

Bradeen, D. W. *The Athenian Agora: Inscriptions. The Funerary Monuments*. Vol. 17. Princeton, N.J.: American School of Classical Studies at Athens, 1974.

Bradley, K. *Discovering the Roman Family*. Oxford: Oxford University Press, 1991.

Bremmer, J. "The Importance of the Maternal Uncle and Grandfather in Archaic and Classical Greece and Early Byzantium." *ZPE* 50 (1983): 173–86.

Broadbent, M. *Studies in Greek Genealogy*. Leiden: Brill, 1968.

Brock, R. "The Labours of Women in Classical Athens." *CQ* 44 (1994): 336–46.

Buermann, H. "Drei Studien auf dem Gebiet des attischen Rechts." *Jahrbücher für classische Philologie,* suppl. 9 (1877–78): 569–91, 619–46.

Burstein, S. "*IG* II² 653, Demosthenes and Athenian Relations with Bosporus in the Fourth Century B.C." *Historia* 27 (1978): 428–36.

Bushala, E. W. "Torture of Non-Citizens in Homicide Investigations." *GRBS* 9 (1968): 61–68.

———. "The *pallake* of Philoneus." *AJP* 90 (1969): 65–72.

Cairns, D. L. *Aidōs: The Psychology and Ethics of Honour and Shame in Greek Literature.* Oxford: Clarendon, 1993.

Calhoun, G. M. *Athenian Clubs in Politics and Litigation.* New York: Burt Franklin, 1970, reprint.

Campbell, J. K. *Honour, Family and Patronage.* Oxford: Oxford University Press, 1964.

Carawan, E. M. "Eisangelia and Euthyna: The Trials of Miltiades, Themistocles and Cimon." *GRBS* 28 (1989): 167–208.

———. "Thucydides and Stesimbrotus on the Exile of Themistocles." *Historia* 38 (1989): 144–61.

Carey, C. "A Note on Torture in Athenian Homicide Cases." *Historia* 37 (1988): 241–45.

———. "Apollodorus' Mother: The Wives of Enfranchised Aliens in Athens." *CQ* 41 (1991): 84–89.

Carter, A. T. "Household Histories." In *Households: Comparative and Historical Studies of the Domestic Group.* Ed. R. McC. Netting, R. R. Wilk, and E. J. Arnould. Berkeley: University of California Press, 1984. 44–83.

Carter, L. B. *The Quiet Athenian.* Oxford: Clarendon Press, 1986.

Cartledge, P. "Rebels and Sambos in Classical Greece: A Comparative View." In Cartledge and Harvey, *Crux.* 16–46.

———. *The Greeks.* Oxford: Oxford University Press, 1993.

Cartledge, P., and F. D. Harvey, eds. *Crux: Essays in Greek History presented to G. E. M. de Ste Croix on His 75th Birthday.* Exeter: Academic Imprint, 1985.

Cartledge, P., P. Millett, and S. Todd, eds. *Nomos: Essays in Athenian Law, Politics and Society.* Cambridge: Cambridge University Press, 1990.

Casson, L. "The Athenian Upper Class and New Comedy." *TAPA* 106 (1976): 29–59 = *Ancient Trade and Society.* Detroit: Wayne State University Press, 1984. 35–69.

Cath, S. H., A. Gurwitt, A. and L. Gunsberg, eds. *Fathers and Their Families.* Hillsdale, N.J.: The Analytic Press, 1989.

Catling, H. W. "Archaeology in Greece," in "Archaeological Reports for 1988–89." *JHS* 109 (1989): 3–116.

Chojnacki, S. "Kinship Ties and Young Patricians in Fifteenth-Century Venice." *Renaissance Quarterly* 38 (1985): 240–70.

———. "The Power of Love: Wives and Husbands in Late Medieval Venice." In *Women and Power in the Middle Ages.* Ed. M. Erler and M. Kowaleski. Athens, Ga.: University of Georgia Press, 1988, 126–48.

Christ, M. "Liturgy Avoidance and *Antidosis* in Classical Athens." *TAPA* 120 (1990): 147–69.

Cohen, D. "The Athenian Law of Adultery." *RIDA* 31 (1984): 147–65.

———. "Law, Society and Homosexuality in Classical Athens." *PastPres* 117 (1987): 3–21.

———. "Seclusion, Separation, and the Status of Women in Classical Athens." *GaR* 36 (1989): 3–15.

———. "The Social Context of Adultery at Athens." In *Nomos: Essays in Athenian Law, Politics and Society.* Ed. P. Cartledge, P. Millett, and S. Todd. Cambridge: Cambridge University Press, 1990. 147–65.

————. *Law, Sexuality and Society*. Cambridge: Cambridge University Press, 1991.

————. "Sexuality, Violence and the Athenian Law of *Hubris*." *GaR* 38 (1991): 171–88.

————. *Law, Violence and Community in Classical Athens*. Cambridge: Cambridge University Press, 1995.

Cohen, E. "Banking as a 'Family Business': Legal Adaptations Affecting Wives and Slaves." *Symposion* (1990): 239–63.

————. *Athenian Economy and Society*. Princeton, N.J.: Princeton University Press, 1992.

Cole, S. "Greek Sanctions Against Sexual Assault." *CP* 79 (1984): 97–113.

Collomp, A. "Tensions, Dissensions, and Ruptures inside the Family in Seventeenth- and Eighteenth-Century Haute-Provence." In *Interest and Emotion*. Ed. H. Medick and D. Sabean. Cambridge: Cambridge University Press, 1988. 145–70.

Connor, W. R. *The New Politicians of Fifth-Century Athens*. Princeton, N.J.: Princeton University Press, 1970.

Cooper, J. P. "Patterns of Inheritance and Settlement by Great Landowners from the Fifteenth to the Eighteenth Centuries." In *Family and Inheritance: Rural Society in Western Europe 1200–1800*. Ed. J. Goody, J. Thirsk, and E. P. Thompson Cambridge: Cambridge University Press, 1976. 215–21.

Cox, C. A. "Sisters, Daughters and the Deme of Marriage: A Note." *JHS* 108 (1988): 185–88.

————. "Incest, Inheritance and the Political Forum in Fifth-Century Athens." *CJ* 85 (1989): 34–46.

————. "The Names of Adoptees: Some Prosopographical Afterthoughts." *ZPE* 107 (1995): 249–254.

Cromey, R. D. "Sokrates' Myrto." *GB* 9 (1980): 57–67.

————. "On Deinomache." *Historia* 32 (1984): 385–401.

————. "The Mysterious Woman of Kleitor: Some Corrections to a Manuscript Once in Plutarch's Possession." *AJP* 112 (1991): 87–101.

Damsgaard-Madsen, A. "Attic Funeral Inscriptions: Their Use as Historical Sources and some Preliminary Results." In *Studies in Ancient History and Numismatics Presented to Rudi Thomsen*. Ed. A. Damsgaard-Madsen, E. Christiansen, and E. Hallager. Aarhus: Aarhus University Press, 1988. 55–68.

Davies, J. K. *Athenian Propertied Families 600–300 B.C.* Oxford: Clarendon Press, 1971.

————. "Athenian Citizenship: The Descent Group and the Alternatives." *CJ* 73 (1978): 105–21.

Davis, J. *People of the Mediterranean*. London: Routledge and Kegan Paul, 1977.

De Romilly, J. "Guerre et paix entre cités." In *Problèmes de la guerre en Grèce ancienne*. Ed. J.-P. Vernant. Paris: Mouton, 1967. 207–20.

De Ste Croix, G. E. M. "Some Observations on the Property Rights of Women." *CR* 20 (1970): 273–78.

Dittenberger, W. "Die Familie des Alkibiades." *Hermes* 37 (1902): 1–13.

Dixon, S. "The Marriage Alliance in the Roman Elite." *Journal of Family History* 10 (1985): 353–78.

————. *The Roman Family*. Baltimore: Johns Hopkins University Press, 1992.

Dover, K. J. *Greek Popular Morality in the Time of Plato and Aristotle*. Berkeley: University of California Press, 1974.

————. *Greek Homosexuality*. 2d ed. Cambridge, Mass.: Harvard University Press, 1989.

Dubisch, J., ed. *Gender and Power in Rural Greece*. Princeton, N.J.: Princeton University Press, 1986.

Du Boulay, J. *Portrait of a Greek Mountain Village*. Oxford: Clarendon Press, 1974.

Ebrey, P. "Concubines in Sung China." *Journal of Family History* 11 (1986): 1–24.

Eickelman, D. *The Middle East*. 2d ed. Englewood Cliffs, N.J.: Prentice Hall, 1989.

Eliot, C. W. J. *The Coastal Demes of Attica: A Study of the Policy of Cleisthenes*. Toronto: University of Toronto Press, 1962.

Ellis, W. *Alcibiades*. London: Routledge, 1989.

Erdmann, W. *Die Ehe im alten Griechenland*. Munich: C. H. Beck, 1979.

Erler, M., and Kowaleski, M., eds. *Women and Power in the Middle Ages*. Athens, Ga.: University of Georgia Press, 1988.

Etienne, R. "Collection Dolly Goulandris, II.: Stèle funéraire attique." *BCH* 99 (1975): 379–84.

Ferguson, W. S. "The Salaminii of Heptaphylai and Sounion." *Hesperia* 7 (1938): 1–74.

Figueira, T. J. "Residential Restrictions on the Athenian Ostracized." *GRBS* 28 (1987): 281–305.

————. *Athens and Aigina in the Age of Imperial Colonization*. Baltimore: Johns Hopkins University Press, 1991.

Finley, M. I. "Marriage Sale and Gift in the Homeric World." *RIDA* 2 (1955): 167–94.

————. *The Ancient Economy*. Berkeley: University of California Press, 1973.

————. *The World of Odysseus*. 2d ed. London: Chatto and Windus, 1977.

————. *Economy and Society in Ancient Greece*. Ed. and introd. B. Shaw and R. Saller. Harmondsworth: Penguin, 1981.

————. *Studies in Land and Credit in Ancient Athens, 500–200 B.C.* Rev. ed., introd. P. Millett. New Brunswick: Transaction Books, 1985.

————. *Ancient Slavery and Modern Ideology*. Harmondsworth: Penguin, 1986.

————. *The Use and Abuse of History*. New York: Penguin, 1987.

Finley, M. I., ed. *Slavery in Classical Antiquity*. Cambridge: Heffer, 1960.

————, ed. *Problèmes de la terre en Grèce ancienne*. Paris: Mouton, 1973.

Flandrin, J.-L. *Familles: Parenté, maison, sexualité dans l'ancienne société*. Paris: Hachette, 1976.

Forster, R., and O. Ranum, eds. *Family and Society*. Baltimore: Johns Hopkins University Press, 1976.

Fortes, Meyer. Introduction to *The Developmental Cycle in Domestic Groups*. Ed. J. Goody. Cambridge: Cambridge University Press, 1962. 1–14.

Fox, R. *Kinship and Marriage: An Anthropological Perspective*. Harmondsworth: Penguin, 1967.

Fox, R. Lane. "Aspects of Inheritance in the Greek World." In *Crux: Essays in Greek History presented to G. E. M. de Ste Croix on His 75th Birthday*. Ed. P. Cartledge and F. D. Harvey. Exeter: Academic Imprint, 1985. 208–32.

Foxhall, L. "Household, Gender and Property in Classical Athens." *CQ* 39 (1989): 22–44.

Friedl, E. *Vasilika: A Village in Modern Greece*. New York: Holt, Rinehart and Winston, 1962.

————. "The Position of Women: Appearance and Reality." In *Gender and Power in Rural Greece*. Ed. J. Dubisch. Princeton, N.J.: Princeton University Press, 1986. 42–52.

Frost, F. J. *Plutarch's Themistocles*. Princeton, N.J.: Princeton University Press, 1980.

Furley, W. D. "Andokides IV ('Against Alkibiades'): Fact or Fiction?" *Hermes* 117 (1989): 138–56.

Gabrielsen, V. "ΦΑΝΕΡΑ and ΑΦΑΝΗΣ ΟΥΣΙΑ in Classical Athens." *ClMed* 37 (1986): 99–114.

———. "The *Antidosis* Procedure in Classical Athens." *ClMed* 38 (1987): 7–38.

Gallant, T. W. *Risk and Survival in Ancient Greece.* Stanford, Calif.: Stanford University Press, 1991.

Garlan, Y. *War in the Ancient World.* Trans. J. Lloyd. New York: Norton, 1975.

———. *Slavery in Ancient Greece.* Trans. J. Lloyd. Ithaca, N.Y.: Cornell University Press, 1988.

Garland, R. "A First Catlogue of Attic Peribolos Tombs." *ABSA* 77 (1982): 125–76.

———. *The Peiraeus.* Ithaca, N.Y.: Cornell University Press, 1987.

———. *The Greek Way of Life.* Ithaca, N.Y.: Cornell University Press, 1990.

Garner, R. *Law and Society in Classical Athens.* New York: St. Martin's Press, 1987.

Gaulin, S., and Boster, J. "Dowry as Female Competition." *American Anthropologist* 92 (1990): 994–1005.

Gauthier, P. "A propos des clérouquies athéniennes du Ve siècle." In *Problèmes de la terre en Grèce ancienne.* Ed. M. I. Finley. Paris: Mouton, 1973. 163–78.

Gernet, L. "La création du testament." *REG* 33 (1920): 123–68, 249–90.

———. "Sur l'epiclérat." *REG* 34 (1921): 337–79.

———. *Demosthène: Plaidoyers civils.* 4 vols. Paris: Les Belles Lettres, 1954–60.

———. *Droit et société dans la Grèce ancienne.* Paris: Sirey, 1955.

———. *The Anthropology of Ancient Greece.* Trans. J. Hamilton and B. Nagy. Baltimore: Johns Hopkins University Press, 1981.

Golden, M. "Slavery and Homosexuality at Athens." *Phoenix* 38 (1984): 308–24.

———. "Male Chauvinists and Pigs." *EMC* 32 (1988): 1–12.

———. *Children and Childhood in Classical Athens.* Baltimore: Johns Hopkins University Press, 1990.

———. "Thirteen Years of Homosexuality (and Other Recent Work on Sex, Gender and the Body in Ancient Greece)." *EMC* 35 (1991): 327–40.

Goligher, W. A., and Maguinness, W. S. *Index to the Speeches of Isaeus.* Cambridge: Heffer, 1961.

Gomme, A. W., et al. *A Historical Commentary on Thucydides.* Vols. 1–5. Oxford: Clarendon Press, 1945–81.

Goody, J. *The Development of the Family and Marriage in Europe.* Cambridge: Cambridge University Press, 1983.

Goody, J., ed., *The Developmental Cycle in Domestic Groups.* Cambridge: Cambridge University Press, 1962.

Goody, J., J. Thirsk, and E. P. Thompson, eds. *Family and Inheritance: Rural Society in Western Europe 1200–1800.* Cambridge: Cambridge University Press, 1976.

Gould, J. "Law, Custom and Myth: Aspects of the Social Position of Women in Classical Athens." *JHS* 100 (1980): 38–59.

Halperin, D. M. "The Democratic Body: Prostitution and Citizenship in Classical Athens." In *One Hundred Years of Homosexuality.* London and New York: Routledge, 1990. 88–112, 180–90.

Hannick, J.-M. "Droit de cité et mariages mixtes dans la Grèce classique." *AntCl* 45 (1976): 133–48.

Hansen, M. H. *Eisangelia.* Odense University Classical Studies, vol. 6. Odense: Odense University Press, 1975.

———. "ATIMIA in Consequence of Private Debts?" *Symposion* (1977): 113–20.

———. "Demographic Reflections on the Number of Athenian Citizens 451–309 B.C." *AJAH* 7 (1982): 172–89.

Hansen, M. H., et al. "The Demography of the Attic Demes: The Evidence of the Sepulchral Inscriptions." *AnalRom* 19 (1990): 25–44.

Hanson, V. "The Ideology of Hoplite Battle, Ancient and Modern." In *Hoplites: The Classical Greek Battle Experience*. Ed. V. Hanson. London: Routledge, 1991. 3–11.

Harding, P. "Rhetoric and Politics in Fourth-Century Athens." *Phoenix* 41 (1987): 25–39.

Harris, E. M. "When is a Sale not a Sale? The Riddle of Athenian Terminology for Real Security Revisited." *CQ* 38 (1988): 351–81.

———. "Iphicrates at the Court of Cotys." *AJP* 110 (1989): 264–71.

———. "Demosthenes' Speech Against Meidias." *HSCP* 92 (1989): 12–24.

———. "The Liability of Business Partners in Athenian Law: The Dispute between Lycon and Megacleides ([Dem.] 52.20–21)." *CQ* 39 (1989): 339–43.

———. "Did the Athenians Regard Seduction as a Worse Crime than Rape?" *CQ* 40 (1990): 370–77.

———. "APOTIMEMA: Athenian Terminology for Real Security in Leases and Dowry Agreements." *CQ* 43 (1993): 73–95.

Harrison, A. R. W. *The Law of Athens*. Vol. 1. Oxford: Clarendon Press, 1968.

Harvey, F. D. "The Wicked Wife of Ischomachus." *EMC* 28 (1984): 68–70.

Hatzfeld, J. *Alcibiade*. 2d ed. Paris: Presses universitaires de France, 1951.

Hedrick, C. W., Jr. *The Decrees of the Demotionidae*. Atlanta, Ga.: Scholars Press, 1990.

Henry, M. M. *Menander's Courtesans and the Greek Comic Tradition*. Studien zur klassischen Philologie 20. Frankfurt am Main: Verlag Peter Lang, 1985.

Herlihy, D. "Households in the Early Middle Ages: Symmetry and Sainthood." In *Households. Comparative and Historical Studies of the Domestic Group*. Ed. R. McC. Netting, R. R. Wilk, and E. J. Arnould. Berkeley: University of California Press, 1984. 383–406.

Herman, G. *Ritualised Friendship and the Greek City*. Cambridge: Cambridge University Press, 1987.

———. "Patterns of Name Diffusion within the Greek World and Beyond." *CQ* 40 (1990): 349–63.

———. "Tribal and Civic Code of Behaviour in Lysias I." *CQ* 43 (1993) 406–19.

———. "Honour, Revenge and the State in Fourth-Century Athens." In *Die athenische Demokratie im 4. Jahrhundert v. Chr.* Ed. W. Eder. Stuttgart: Franz Steiner, 1995. 43–60.

Herzfeld, M. "Dowry in Greece: Terminological Usage and Historical Reconstruction." *Ethnohistory* 27 (1980): 225–41.

———. "Social Tension and Inheritance by Lot in Three Greek Villages." *Anthroplogical Quarterly* 53 (1980): 91–100.

———. *The Poetics of Manhood*. Princeton, N.J.: Princeton University Press, 1985.

Hodkinson, S. "Inheritance, Marriage and Demography: Perspectives upon the Success and Decline of Classical Sparta." In *Classical Sparta: Techniques behind Her Success*. Ed. A. Powell. Norman: University of Oklahoma Press, 1988. 79–121.

Holladay, J. "Medism in Athens 504–480 B.C." *GaR* 25 (1978): 174–91.

Holy, L. *Kinship, Honour and Solidarity*. Manchester: Manchester University Press, 1989.

Humphreys, S. C. "The Nothoi of Kynosarges." *JHS* 94 (1974): 88–95.

———. *Anthropology and the Greeks*. London: Routledge and Kegan Paul, 1978.

———. *The Family, Women and Death*. London: Routledge and Kegan Paul, 1983.

———. "The Date of Hagnias' Death." *CP* 78 (1983): 219–25.

———. "Social Relations on Stage: Witnesses in Classical Athens." *History and Anthropology* 1 (1985): 313–69.

————. "Kinship Patterns in the Athenian Courts." *GRBS* 27 (1986): 57–91.

————. "Family Quarrels." *JHS* 109 (1989): 182–85.

————. "Phrateres in Alopeke, and the Salaminioi." *ZPE* 83 (1990): 243–48.

Hunter, V. "The Athenian Widow and Her Kin." *Journal of Family History* 14 (1989): 291–311.

————. "Women's Authority in Classical Athens." *EMC* 33 (1989): 39–48.

————. "Gossip and the Politics of Reputation in Classical Athens." *Phoenix* 44 (1990): 299–325.

————. "Agnatic Kinship in Athenian Law and Athenian Family Practice: Its Implications for Women." In *Law, Politics and Society in the Ancient Mediterranean World*. Ed. B. Halpern and D. Hobson. Sheffield Academic Press, 1993. 100–121.

————. *Policing Athens: Social Control in the Attic Lawsuits, 420–320 B.C.* Princeton, N.J.: Princeton University Press, 1994.

Isager, S. "The Marriage Pattern in Classical Athens: Men and Women in Isaios." *ClMed* 33 (1981–82): 81–96.

Jacoby, F. "Some Remarks on Ion of Chios." *CQ* 41 (1947): 1–17.

Jameson, M. "Domestic Space in the Greek City-State." In *Domestic Architecture and the Use of Space*. Ed. S. Kent. Cambridge:Cambridge University Press, 1990. 92–113.

Jaschok, M. *Concubines and Bondservants*. London: Zed Books, 1988.

Joint Association of Classical Teachers. *The World of Athens*. Cambridge: Cambridge University Press, 1984.

Jones, A. H. M. "Slavery in the Ancient World." In *Slavery in Classical Antiquity*. Ed. M. I. Finley. Cambridge: Heffer, 1960. 1–15.

Jones, J. E. "Town and Country Houses of Attica in Classical Athens." In *Thorikos and the Laurion in Archaic and Classical Times, Miscellanea Graeca* 1 (1975): 63–140.

Jones, J. E., L. H. Sackett, and A. J. Graham. "The Dema House in Attica." *ABSA* 57 (1962): 75–114.

Judeich, W. "Aspasia." In *RE* 2.2, 1716–22.

Just, R. *Women in Athenian Law and Life*. London: Routledge, 1989.

Karabélias, E. "La succession *ab intestat* en droit attique." *Symposion* (1982): 41–63.

Karnezis, J. *The Epikleros*. Athens: n.p., 1972.

Karras, R. M. "Concubinage and Slavery in the Viking Age." *Scandinavian Studies* 62 (1990): 141–62.

Kassel, R., and C. Austin, eds. *Poetae Comici Graeci*. Vol. 7. Berlin: de Gruyter, 1989.

Kennedy, G. *The Art of Persuasion in Greece*. Princeton, N.J.: Princeton University Press, 1963.

Kertzer, D. "Anthropology and Family History." *Journal of Family History* 9 (1984): 201–16.

Kertzer, D., and C. Brettell. "Advances in Italian and Iberian Family History." *Journal of Family History* 12 (1987): 87–120.

Keuls, E. *The Reign of the Phallus: Sexual Politics in Ancient Athens*. 2d ed. Berkeley: University of Californian Press, 1993.

Kirchner, J. *Prosopographia Attica*. 2 vols. Berlin: G. Reimer, 1901–3; Chicago: Ares, 1981.

Klapisch-Zuber, C. *Women, Family, and Ritual in Renaissance Italy*. Trans. L. Cochrane. Chicago: University of Chicago Press, 1985.

Klat, M., and Khudr, A. "Religious Endogamy and Consanguinity in Marriage Patterns in Beirut." *Social Biology* 33 (1986): 138–45.

Kluckhohn, C. *Anthropology and the Classics*. Providence, R.I.: Brown University Press, 1961.

Knox, R. "'So Mischievous a Beaste'? The Athenian *Demos* and its Treatment of its Politicians." *GaR* 32 (1985): 134–61.

Kokula, G. *Marmorlutrophoren*. *AM Beiheft* 10. Berlin: Gebr. Mann, 1984.

Kolchin, P. "Some Recent Works on Slavery outside the United States: An American Perspective." *Comparative Studies in Society and History* 28 (1986): 767–77.

Konstan, D. "Between Courtesan and Wife: Menander's *Perikeiromene*." *Phoenix* 41 (1987): 122–39.

Krentz, P. "The Ostracism of Thoukydides, son of Melesias." *Historia* 33 (1984): 499–504.

Lacey, W. K. *The Family in Classical Greece*. Ithaca, N.Y.: Cornell University Press, 1968.

———. "The Family of Euxitheus (Demosthenes LVII)." *CQ* 30 (1980): 57–61.

Lalonde, G., et al. *Inscriptions: Horoi. Poletai Records. Leases of Public Lands. The Athenian Agora*, vol. 19. Princeton, N.J.: American School of Classical Studies at Athens, 1991.

Lamb, M. *The Father's Role: Cross-Cultural Perspectives*. Hillsdale, N.J.: Lawrence Erlbaum Associates, 1987.

Lambert, S. D. *The Phratries of Attica*. Ann Arbor: University of Michigan Press, 1993.

Lang, M. *Graffitti and Dipinti. The Athenian Agora*, vol 21. Princeton, N.J.: American School of Classical Studies at Athens, 1976.

Langdon, M. K. "The Topography of Coastal Erechtheis." *Chiron* 18 (1988): 43–54.

Laslett, P. "Introduction: The History of the Family." In *Household and Family*. Ed. P. Laslett and R. Wall. Cambridge: Cambridge University Press. 1–89.

Laslett, P., and R. Wall, eds. *Household and Family in Past Time*. Cambridge: Cambridge University Press, 1972.

Lavelle, B. M. "The Nature of Hipparchos' Insult to Harmodios." *AJP* 107 (1986): 323–28.

———. "Koisyra and Megakles, the Son of Hippokrates." *GRBS* 30 (1989): 503–13.

Ledl, A. "Das attische Bürgerrecht und die Frauen." *WS* 29 (1907):173–227; 30 (1908): 1–46, 173–230.

Lenardon, R. J. *The Saga of Themistocles*. London: Thames and Hudson, 1978.

LeRoy Ladurie, E. "Family Structures and Inheritance Customs in Sixteenth-Century France." In *Family and Inheritance: Rural Society in Western Europe 1200–1800*. Ed. J. Goody, J. Thirsk, and E. P. Thompson. Cambridge: Cambridge University Press, 1976. 37–70.

Levy, H. "Inheritance and Dowry in Classical Athens." In *Mediterranean Society: Essays in the Social Anthropology of the Mediterranean*. Ed. J. Pitt-Rivers. Paris: Mouton, 1963. 137–43.

Lewis, D. M. "Attic Manumissions." *Hesperia* 28 (1959): 208–38.

———. "The Kerameikos Ostraka." *ZPE* 14 (1974): 1–4.

Lewis, I. M. "Problems in the Comparative Study of Unilineal Descent." In *The Relevance of Models for Social Anthropology*. Ed. M. Banton. London: Tavistock, 1965. 87–112.

Lind, H. "Ein Hetärenhaus am Heiligen Tor?" *MusHelv* 45 (1988): 158–69.

Lipsius, J. H. *Das attische Recht und Rechtsverfahren*. 3 vols. Leipzig: O. R. Reisland, 1905–15.

Littman, R. "The Loves of Alcibiades." *TAPA* 101 (1970): 263–76.

———. "Kinship in Athens." *AncSoc* 10 (1979): 5–31.

Loizos, P. "Changes in Property Transfer among Greek Cypriot Villagers." *Man* 10 (1975): 503–23.

Loraux, N. *The Invention of Athens: The Funeral Oration in the Classical City*. Trans. A. Sheridan. Cambridge, Mass.: Harvard University Press, 1986.

Lovejoy, P. E. "Concubinage and the Status of Women Slaves in Early Colonial Northern Nigeria." *Journal of African History* 29 (1988): 245–66.

MacDowell, D. M. *Andokides on the Mysteries*. Oxford: Clarendon Press, 1962.

———. "Bastards as Athenian Citizens." *CQ* 26 (1976): 88–91.

———. *The Law in Classical Athens*. Ithaca, N.Y.: Cornell University Press, 1978.

———. "The *Oikos* in Athenian Law." *CQ* 39 (1989): 10–21.

MacFarlane, A. *Marriage and Love in England: Modes of Reproduction, 1300–1840*. Oxford: Basil Blackwell, 1986.

McKechnie, P. *Outsiders in the Greek Cities in the Fourth Century* B.C. London: Routledge, 1989.

Martin, J. F. "Genealogical Structures and Consanguineous Marriage." *Current Anthropology* 22 (1981): 401–6.

Matthaiou, A. P. "Ἡρίον Λυκούργου Λυκόφρονος Βουτάδου." *Horos* 5 (1987): 31–44.

Medick, H., and D. Sabean. Introduction to *Interest and Emotion*. Ed. H. Medick and D. Sabean. Cambridge: Cambridge University Press. 1–8.

———. "Interest and Emotion in Family and Kinship Studies: A Critique of Social History and Anthropology." In Medick and Sabean, *Interest and Emotion*. 9–27.

Medick, H., and D. Sabean, eds. *Interest and Emotion*. Cambridge: Cambridge University Press, 1988.

Meritt, B. D. "Athenian Archons 347/6–48/7 B.C." *Historia* 26 (1977): 161–91.

Meritt, B., and Traill, J. S. *Inscriptions: The Athenian Councillors. The Athenian Agora*, vol. 15. Princeton, N.J.: American School of Classical Studies at Athens, 1974.

Miller, S. "Mortgage Horoi from the Athenian Agora." *Hesperia* 41 (1972): 274–81.

Millett, P. Introduction to M. I. Finley, *Studies in Land and Credit in Ancient Athens, 500–200 B.C.* 2d ed. New Brunswick: Transaction Books, 1985. vii–xxxvii.

———. *Lending and Borrowing in Ancient Athens*. Cambridge: Cambridge University Press, 1991.

Morgan, G. "Euphiletus' House: Lysias 1." *TAPA* 112 (1982): 115–23.

Mossé, C. "The 'World of the Emporium' in the Private Speeches of Demosthenes." In *Trade in the Ancient Economy*. Ed. P. Garnsey, K. Hopkins, and C. R. Whittaker. Berkeley: University of California Press, 1983. 53–63.

Müller, O. "Untersuchungen zur Geschichte des attischen Bürger- und Eherechts." *Jahrbücher für classische Philologie* 25 (1899): 661–866.

Netting, R. McC., R. R. Wilk, and E. Arnould eds. *Households. Comparative and Historical Studies of the Domestic Group*. Berkeley: University of California Press, 1984.

Neuberg, M. "How Like a Woman: Antigone's Inconsistency." *CQ* 40 (1990): 54–76.

Nicholas, D. *The Domestic Life of a Medieval City: Women, Children, and the Family in Fourteenth-Century Ghent*. Lincoln: University of Nebraska Press, 1985.

Nielsen, T. H., et al. "Athenian Grave Monuments and Social Class." *GRBS* 30 (1989): 411–20.

Nikolaides, A. G. "Plutarch's Contradictions." *ClMed* 42 (1991): 153–86.

Oakley, J., and Sinos, R. *The Wedding in Ancient Athens*. Madison: University of Wisconsin Press, 1993.

Ober, J. *Fortress Attica. Mnemosyne*, suppl. 84. Leiden: Brill, 1985.

Ober, J. *Mass and Elite in Democratic Athens*. Princeton, N.J.: Princeton University Press, 1989.

———. "Response to Edward Cohen." *Symposion* (1990): 265–71.

Ober, J., and B. Strauss, "Drama, Political Rhetoric, and the Discourse of Athenian Democracy." In *Nothing to Do With Dionysos? Athenian Drama in Its Social Context*. Ed. J. Winkler and F. Zeitlin. Princeton, N.J.: Princeton University Press, 1990. 237–70.

Oikonomides, A. "Graffitti-Inscriptions from the Excavations of the Athenian Agora." *Horos* 4 (1986): 43–64.

———. "An Epigraphical Mention of the Bank of Pasion and Phormion from the Athenian Agora." *AncW* 23 (1992): 107–8.

Osborne, M. J. "Attic Epitaphs—A Supplement." *AncSoc* 19 (1988): 5–60.

Osborne, R. "Buildings and Residence in Classical and Hellenistic Greece." *ABSA* 80 (1985): 119–28.

———. *Demos: The Discovery of Classical Attika*. Cambridge: Cambridge University Press, 1985.

———. "Law in Action in Classical Athens." *JHS* 105 (1985): 40–58.

———. *Classical Landscape with Figures: The Ancient Greek City and Its Countryside*. London: George Philip, 1987.

———. "Social and Economic Implications of the Leasing of Land and Property in Classical and Hellenistic Greece." *Chiron* 18 (1988): 279–323.

Osswald, H. "Dowry, Norms and Household Formations: A Case Study from North Portugal." *Journal of Family History* 15 (1990): 201–24.

Otis, L. *Prostitution in Medieval Society: The History of an Urban Institution in Languedoc*. Chicago: University of Chicago Press, 1987.

Ottenheimer, M. "Complementarity and the Structures of Parallel-Cousin Marriage." *American Anthropologist* 88 (1986): 934–39.

Patterson, C. *Pericles' Citizenship Law of 451–0*. New York: Arno, 1981.

———. "Those Athenian Bastards." *ClAnt* 9 (1990): 40–73.

———. "Response to Claude Mossé." *Symposion* (1990) 281–287.

———. "Marriage and the Married Woman in Athenian Law." In *Women's History and Ancient History*. Ed. S. Pomeroy. Chapel Hill: University of North Carolina Press, 1991. 48–72.

Patterson, O. *Slavery and Social Death*. Cambridge, Mass.: Harvard University Press, 1982.

Pečirka, J. "Homestead Farms in Classical and Hellenistic Hellas." In *Problèmes de la terre en Grèce ancienne*. Ed. M. I. Finley. Paris: Mouton, 1973. 119–78.

Peek, W. "Attische Inschriften." *AM* 67 (1942) 1–217.

———. *Attische Grabinschriften* II. Berlin: Akademie-Verlag, 1957.

Peristiany, J. G. "Honour and Shame in a Cypriot Highland Village." In *Honour and Shame: The Values of Mediterranean Society*. Ed. J. G. Peristiany. Chicago: University of Chicago Press, 1966. 171–90.

Peristiany, J. G., ed. *Contributions to Mediterranean Sociology*. Paris: Mouton, 1968.

Peristiany, J. G., ed. *Mediterranean Family Structures*. Cambridge: Cambridge University Press, 1976.

Peters, E. L. "Aspects of Affinity in a Lebanese Maronite Village." In *Mediterranean Family Structures*. Ed. J. G. Peristiany. Cambridge: Cambridge University Press, 1976. 27–79.

Piccirilli, L. "Il filiolaconismo, l'incesto e l'ostracismo di Cimone." *Quaderni di storia* 10 (1984): 171–77.

Plakans, A. *Kinship in the Past: An Anthropology of European Family Life 1500–1900.* Oxford: Blackwell, 1984.

Podlecki, A. *The Life of Themistocles.* Montreal: McGill-Queen's University Press, 1975.

Pomeroy, S. *Goddesses, Whores, Wives, and Slaves.* New York: Schocken, 1975.

———. "Mark Golden, *Children and Childhood in Classical Athens.*" *EMC* 36 (1992): 73–76.

———. *Xenophon's Oeconomicus: A Social and Historical Commentary.* Oxford: Clarendon Press, 1994.

Pritchett, W. K. "The Attic Stelai II." *Hesperia* 25 (1956): 178–328.

Rankin, D. "The Mining Lobby at Athens." *AncSoc* 19 (1989): 189–205.

Raubitschek, A. "Phryne." *RE* 20.1:893–907.

———. "The Case Against Alcibiades." *TAPA* 79 (1948): 191–210.

———. "Zur attischen Genealogie." *RhM* 98 (1955): 258–62.

Reinsberg, C. *Ehe, Hetärentum und Knabenliebe im antiken Griechenland.* Munich: Beck, 1989.

Rhodes, P. J. "Bastards as Athenian Citizens." *CQ* 28 (1978): 89–92.

Rosenfeld, H. "The Contradiction Between Property, Kinship and Power as Reflected in the Marriage System of an Arab Village." In *Contributions to Mediterranean Sociology.* Ed. J. G. Peristiany. Paris: Mouton, 1968. 247–60.

———. "Social and Economic Factors in Explanation of the Increased Rate of Endogamy in the Arab Village in Israel." In *Mediterranean Family Structures.* Ed. J. G. Peristiany. Cambridge: Cambridge University Press, 1976. 115–36.

Ross, M. C. "Concubinage in Anglo-Saxon England." *PastPres* 108 (1985): 3–34.

Rossiaud, J. *Medieval Prostitution.* Trans. L. G. Cochrane. Oxford: Blackwell, 1988.

Rubinstein, L. *Adoption in IV. Century Athens.* Copenhagen: Museum Tusculanum Press, 1993.

Rudhardt, J. "La reconnaissance de la paternité, sa nature et sa portée dans la société athénienne." *MusHelv* 19 (1962): 39–64.

Ruschenbusch, E. *Solonos Nomoi. Historia Einzelschriften* 9. Wiesbaden: F. Steiner, 1966.

Russell, D. A. *Plutarch.* London: Duckworth, 1973.

Sabean, D. W. "Aspects of Kinship Behaviour and Property in Rural Western Europe before 1800." In *Family and Inheritance: Rural Society in Western Europe 1200–1800.* Ed. J. Goody, J. Thirsk, and E. P. Thompson. Cambridge: Cambridge University Press, 1976. 96–111.

———. "Young Bees in an Empty Hive: Relations between Brothers-in-Law in a South German Village Around 1800." In *Interest and Emotion.* Ed. H. Medick and D. W. Sabean. Cambridge: Cambridge University Press, 1988. 171–86.

Salamone, S. D., and Stanton, J. B. "Introducing the *Nikokyra:* Ideality and Reality in Social Process." In *Gender and Power in Rural Greece.* Ed. J. Dubisch. Princeton, N.J.: Princeton University Press, 1986. 97–120.

Saller, R. "Men's Age at Marriage and Its Consequences in the Roman Family." *CP* 82 (1987): 21–34.

———. *Patriarchy, Property and Death in the Roman Family.* Cambridge: Cambridge University Press, 1994.

Sant Cassia, P. "Property in Greek Cypriot Marriage Strategies." *Man* 17 (1982): 643–63.

Sant Cassia, P., and C. Bada. *The Making of the Modern Greek Family.* Cambridge: Cambridge University Press, 1992.

Savage, C. A. *The Athenian Family: A Sociological and Legal Study Based Chiefly on the Works of the Attic Orators.* Baltimore: Lord Baltimore Press, 1907.

Scafuro, A. "Witnessing and False Witnessing: Proving Citizenship and Kin Identity in Fourth-Century Athens." In *Athenian Identity and Civic Ideology.* Ed. A. Boegehold and A. Scafuro. Baltimore: Johns Hopkins University Press, 1994. 156–98.

Schaps, D. M. "The Woman Least Mentioned: Etiquette and Women's Names." *CQ* 27 (1977): 323–30.

———. *Economic Rights of Women in Ancient Greece.* Edinburgh: University of Edinburgh Press, 1979.

Scheidel, W. "The Most Silent Women of Greece and Rome: Rural Labour and Women's Life in the Ancient World (I)." *GaR* 42 (1995): 202–17.

Schmidtbauer, P. "The Changing Household: Austrian Household Structure from the Seventeenth to the Early Twentieth Century." In *Family Forms in Historic Europe.* Ed. R. Wall, J. Robin, and P. Laslett. Cambridge: Cambridge University Press, 1983. 347–78.

Schneider, K. "Hetairai." *RE* 8.2:1332–72.

Sealey, R. *Essays in Greek Politics.* New York: Manyland, 1967.

———. "On Lawful Concubinage in Athens." *ClAnt* 3 (1984): 111–33.

———. *Women and Law in Classical Greece.* Chapel Hill: University of North Carolina Press, 1990.

Segalen, M. *Historical Anthropology of the Family.* Trans. J. C. Whitehouse and S. Matthews. Cambridge: Cambridge University Press, 1986.

Shear, T. L. "The Campaign of 1936." *Hesperia* 6 (1937): 333–81.

Shear, T. L., Jr. "Koisyra: Three Women of Athens." *Phoenix* 17 (1963): 99–112.

Siewert, P. *Die Trittyen Attikas und die Heeresreform des Kleisthenes. Vestigia* 23. Munich: Beck, 1982.

Sinclair, R. K. *Democracy and Participation in Athens.* Cambridge: Cambridge University Press, 1988.

Smith, R. M. "Families and Their Land in an Area of Partible Inheritance: Redgrave, Suffolk 1260–1320." In *Land, Kinship and Life Cycle.* Ed. R. M. Smith. New York: Cambridge University Press, 1984. 135–95.

———. "Marriage Process in the English Past: Some Continuities." In *The World We Have Gained: Histories of Populations and Social Structure.* Ed. L. Bonfield, R. M. Smith, and K. Wrightson. Oxford: Blackwell, 1986. 43–99.

Stamiris, G. "Attische Grabinschriften." *AM* 67 (1942): 218–29.

Strauss, B. *"Oikos/Polis:* Towards a Theory of Athenian Paternal Ideology 450–399 B.C." In *Aspects of Athenian Democracy. ClMed Dissertationes* 11. Ed. W. R. Connor et al. Copenhagen: Museum Tusculanum Press, 1990. 101–127.

———. *Fathers and Sons in Athens.* Princeton, N.J.: Princeton University Press, 1993.

Thompson, W. E. "The Marriage of First Cousins in Athenian Society." *Phoenix* 21 (1967): 273–82.

———. "The Kinship of Pericles and Alcibiades." *GRBS* 11 (1970): 27–33.

———. "Athenian Marriage Patterns: Remarriage." *CSCA* 5 (1972): 211–26.

———. *De Hagniae Hereditate: An Athenian Inheritance Case. Mnemosyne,* suppl. 44. Leiden: Brill, 1976.

———. "Athenian Attitudes toward Wills." *Prudentia* 13 (1981): 13–23.

Tilly, C. "Family History, Social History, and Social Change." In *Family History at the Cross-*

roads. Ed. T. Hareven and A. Plakans. Princeton, N.J.: Princeton University Press, 1987. 319–30.

Todd, S. "The Purpose of Evidence in Athenian Courts." In *Nomos: Essays in Athenian Law, Politics and Society.* Ed. P. Cartledge, P. Millett, and S. Todd. Cambridge: Cambridge University Press, 1990. 19–39.

Todd, S., and P. Millett. "Law, Society and Athens." In *Nomos.* 1–18.

Traill, J. S. *The Political Organization of Attica. Hesperia,* suppl. 14. Princeton, N.J.: American School of Classical Studies at Athens, 1975.

———. *Demos and Trittys.* Toronto: Athenians, Victoria College, 1986.

Trevett, J. *Apollodorus the Son of Pasion.* Oxford: Clarendon Press, 1992.

Tucker, J. "Marriage and Family in Nablus 1720–1856: Toward a History of Arab Marriage." *Journal of Family History* 13 (1988): 165–79.

Tuplin, C. "Some Emendations to the Family-Tree of Isocrates." *CQ* 30 (1980): 288–305.

Vanderpool, E. "The Ostracism of the Elder Alcibiades." *Hesperia* 21 (1952): 4–6.

———. "Alcibiades." *Hesperia* 37 (1968): 398.

Vaughn, P. "The Identification and Retrieval of the Hoplite Battle-Dead." In *Hoplites: The Classical Greek Battle Experience.* Ed. V. Hanson. London: Routledge, 1991. 38–62.

Vernant, J.-P. "Le mariage en Grèce antique." *PP* 28 (1973): 51–74.

Vernant, J.-P., ed. *Problèmes de la guerre en Grèce ancienne.* Paris: Mouton, 1968.

Vidal-Naquet, P. "The Black Hunter and the Origin of the Athenian *Ephebia.*" In *The Black Hunter: Forms of Thought and Forms of Society in the Greek World.* Trans. A. Szegedy-Maszak. Baltimore: Johns Hopkins University Press, 1986. 106–28.

Wade-Gery, H. T. "Thucydides the Son of Melesias." *JHS* 52 (1932): 205–27.

Walbank, M. B. "The Confiscation and Sale by the Poletai in 402/1 B. C. of the Property of the Thirty Tyrants." *Hesperia* 51 (1982): 74–98.

———. "Leases of Sacred Properties in Attica." *Hesperia* 52 (1983): 100–35, 177–231.

Walcot, P. "Romantic Love and True Love." *AncSoc* 18 (1987): 5–33.

Wall, R., Robin, J., and P. Laslett, eds. *Family Forms in Historic Europe.* Cambridge: Cambridge University Press, 1983.

Wallace, M. B. "Early Greek Proxenoi." *Phoenix* 24 (1970): 189–208.

Wallace, R. "Private Lives and Public Enemies: Freedom of Thought in Classical Athens." In *Athenian Identity and Civic Ideology.* Ed. A. Boegehold and A. Scafuro. Baltimore: Johns Hopkins University Press, 1994. 127–55.

Westermann, W. L. "Slavery and the Elements of Freedom in Ancient Greece." In *Slavery in Classical Antiquity.* Ed. M. I. Finley. Cambridge: Heffer, 1960. 17–32.

Wevers, R. F. *Isaeus: Chronology, Prosopography and Social History.* Paris: Mouton, 1969.

Wheaton, R. "Affinity and Descent in Seventeenth-Century Bordeaux." In *Family and Sexuality in French History.* Ed. R. Wheaton and T. Hareven. Philadelphia: University of Pennsylvania Press, 1980. 111–134.

Whitehead, D. *The Demes of Attica 508/7–ca. 250 B.C.* Princeton, N.J.: Princeton University Press, 1986.

———. "Women and Naturalisation in Fourth-Century Athens: The Case of Archippe." *CQ* 36 (1986): 109–14.

———. "Who Equipped Mercenary Troops in Classical Athens?" *Historia* 40 (1991): 105–13.

Williams, G. M. E. "The Kerameikos Ostraka." *ZPE* 31 (1978): 103–13.

Winkler, J. "Laying Down the Law: The Oversight of Men's Sexual Behavior in Classical Athens." In *The Constraints of Desire*. New York and London: Routledge, 1990. 45–70.

Wolff, H. J. "Marriage Law and Family Organization in Ancient Athens." *Traditio* 2 (1944): 43–95.

———. "Προίξ." *RE* 23:134–170.

Woodbury, L. "Socrates and Aristides' Daughter." *Phoenix* 27 (1973): 7–25.

Wood, Ellen Meiksins. *Peasant-Citizen and Slave*. London: Verso, 1989.

Wycherley, R. E. *The Stones of Athens*. Princeton, N.J.: Princeton University Press, 1978.

Wyse, W. *The Speeches of Isaeus*. Cambridge: Cambridge University Press, 1904; New York: Arno, 1979.

Young, J. H. "Studies in South Attica, Country Estates at Sounion." *Hesperia* 25 (1956): 122–46.

Young, R. S. "An Industrial District of Ancient Athens." *Hesperia* 20 (1951): 135–288.

Index

The following abbreviations are used (with examples given):

n. = note   7*n*.11
f. = figure   220*f.*
t. = table   45*t.*

Orators and orations are indexed when needed to identify an event or family, to indicate the speakers' own involvement in events, or when the orator's opinions are cited, but not as sources.

Authors are cited where they are mentioned in the text, but as a rule, not when cited in footnotes.

ABOUT THE AUTHOR

Cheryl Anne Cox is Assistant Professor of Classics
in the Department of Foreign Languages and Literatures
at the University of Memphis.